Asia Pacific Economic Cooperation (APEC)

Asia Pacific Economic Cooperation (APEC) leaders and ministerial meetings have grown in significance as intergovernmental forums in Asia and the Pacific over the last ten years. This book provides the most up-to-date and comprehensive account of this important regional organisation and examines the challenges APEC now faces at the beginning of the new century. Subjects covered include:

- the history of APEC
- APEC and the new WTO round
- case studies of countries in the region including China, Japan, Malaysia, Korea and Taiwan
- APEC's approach to competition and deregulation policy
- assessment of APEC's standing as an international institution

Featuring contributions from distinguished groups of international academic experts, this book is essential reading for all those interested in political and economic developments in the Asia Pacific.

Ippei Yamazawa is Emeritus Professor at Hitotsubashi University, Japan and has published widely on the Asia Pacific economies.

Asia Pacific Economic Cooperation (APEC)

Challenges and tasks for the twenty-first century

Edited by Ippei Yamazawa

London and New York

First published 2000
by Routledge
2 Park Square, Milton Park, Abingdon, Oxon, OX14 4RN

Simultaneously published in the USA and Canada
by Routledge
270 Madison Ave, New York NY 10016

Routledge is an imprint of the Taylor & Francis Group

Transferred to Digital Printing 2005

©2000 Pacific Trade and Development Conference for selection and editorial
material; and the contributors for individual chapters

Typeset in Garamond by the Australia–Japan Research Centre, ANU,
Canberra, Australia

British Library Cataloging in Publication Data
A catalogue record for this book is available from the British Library

Library of Congress Cataloging in Publication Data
A catalogue record for this book has been requested

ISBN 0-415-24805-1 (hbk)
ISBN 0-415-24806-X (pbk)

Publisher's note
This book has been prepared from camera-ready copy provided by the editor

Printed and bound by Antony Rowe Ltd, Eastbourne

Contents

Figures

Tables

Contributors

Vinod K. Aggarwal, Professor, Department of Political Science and Director, Berkeley APEC Studies Center, University of California, Berkeley.

Kanemi Ban, Professor of Economics, Osaka University.

Peter Drysdale, Professor of Economics, Director of Australia–Japan Research Centre.

Andrew Elek, Research Associate, Australia–Japan Research Centre, Asia Pacific School of Economics and Management, Australian National University.

Tsu-Tan Fu, Research Fellow and Deputy Director, Institute of Economics, Academia Sinica, Taipei.

Ross Garnaut, Professor of Economics and Director, Asia Pacific School of Economics and Management, Australian National University.

Loke Wai Heng, University of Malaya, Kuala Lumpur.

Ralph W. Huenemann, Professor of Economic Relations with China, Centre for Asia-Pacific Initiatives and Faculty of Business, University of Victoria.

Akira Kohsaka, Professor of Economics, Osaka School of International Public Policy, Osaka University.

Peter Lloyd, Ritchie Professor of Economics and Director, Asian Business Centre, University of Melbourne.

Charles E. Morrison, President, East West Centre.

Peter A. Petri, Dean and Carl J. Shapiro Professor of International Finance, Graduate School of International Economics and Finance, Brandeis University.

Sieh Lee Mei Ling, Professor and Deputy Director, Institute of Economics, Academia Sinica.

Hadi Soesastro, Executive Director, Centre for Strategic and International Studies, Jakarta.

Shujiro Urata, Professor, School of Social Sciences, Waseda University.

Kerrin M. Vautier, Consultant Research Economist.

Ippei Yamazawa, Emeritus Professor, Hitotsubashi University and President, JETRO-Institute of Developing Economies.

Mahani Zainal-Abidin, Associate Professor, Faculty of Economics and Administration, University of Malaya.

Preface

Ten years have now passed since APEC was initiated as an annual meeting of foreign and trade ministers to sustain the momentum of market opening and economic cooperation which are of such vital importance to the growth and prosperity of the Asia Pacific region. In these ten years APEC has undergone remarkable development, deepening and broadening its agenda and membership. Although APEC was unprepared to deal with the late 1990s financial crisis, it has remained an effective bulwark in sustaining commitment to the strategy of promoting outward-looking economic development.

The 25th PAFTAD conference was held in Osaka on 16–18 June 1999, focusing on APEC, the challenges it faces and its tasks in the twenty-first century. This formed our contribution to the Eleventh APEC Leaders' meeting in Auckland, New Zealand, in September 1999.

PAFTAD started in Tokyo in January 1968 as a policy-oriented economists' meeting to discuss economic cooperation in the Asia Pacific region. The topic of its first meeting was the Pacific Free Trade Area proposed by Professor Kiyoshi Kojima, a founding father of PAFTAD. Although the proposal was premature thirty years ago, it was realised partly in the form of the Pacific Economic Cooperation Council (PECC) in 1980 and was fully actualised in the form of APEC in 1989.

It is therefore fitting for PAFTAD to select APEC as the main theme of its silver jubilee conference. Over eighty economists, political scientists, and government officials in charge of APEC from nineteen APEC member economies participated in the conference. This volume contains edited versions of the twelve papers presented at the conference as well as the Summary and Recommendations contributed to APEC in New Zealand. The authors have monitored APEC's development closely since its inception and their analyses and suggestions will enhance the understanding of this unique form of regional cooperation. It will assist leaders, ministers, and government officials to implement APEC activities effectively in the new millennium.

The first two chapters provide a broad overview of APEC. Garnaut examines APEC's ideas through its history and prospects, while Kohsaka analyses macroeconomic interdependence among APEC member economies with reference to APEC's role in preventing another financial crisis. Chapters 3–5 focus on the APEC's agenda for liberalisation and facilitation. Yamazawa and Urata measure APEC's progress toward the Bogor target and suggest ways to strengthen it, Petri examines APEC's function in promoting liberalisation in cooperation with the WTO regime, while Mahani investigates an alternative channel for the promotion of liberalisation through sub-regional trading arrangements. The following three chapters deal with case studies of liberalisation efforts. Huenemann focuses on the automobile industry in China, Ling and Heng on telecommunication services in Malaysia, and Fu on the rice sector in Japan, Korea and Taiwan. Chapters 9–11 deal with economic cooperation, another major track of APEC. Elek and Soesastro overview Ecotech activities and suggest ways to strengthen capacity building in the Asia Pacific. Vautier and Lloyd examine competition and deregulation policies to improve the market mechanism in member economies. Ban takes up the environmental protection policies of APEC members and suggests the application of CEG modelling to it. To conclude our conference, we invited two political scientists, Aggarwal and Morrison, to examine APEC as an international organisation and provide advice on how to strengthen its organisational structure to enhance its potential.

Particular thanks are in order for the support of those responsible for financing, undertaking the detailed planning, making the international and local arrangements, and for managing the publication of this volume. The major source of financial support for PAFTAD 25 came from the Japan Foundation Center for Global Partnership, Tokyo. We wish particularly to thank Yoshihisa Akiyama, the chair of Kansai Economic Research Center (KERC), Osaka, who hosted PAFTAD 25 and delivered the welcoming address. We also wish to thank Kiyoshi Kojima and Hugh Patrick, current chair of PAFTAD, for their continued support and encouragement. The conference and this volume received substantial support from the PAFTAD Secretariat, located at the Australian National University in Canberra. We also wish to acknowledge the Foundation support which makes it possible for the secretariat to maintain PAFTAD's activities. This includes contributions from The Ford Foundation (USA), the Institute for Southeast Asian Studies (Singapore), the University of Toronto, the University of Victoria, the Australian National University, the Taiwan Institute for Economic Research, Korea Member Committee PBEC, National Centre for Development Administration (Thailand), Centre for Strategic and International Studies (Indonesia), the Foundation for Advanced Information Research (Japan), the Japan Federation of Economic Organisations (Keidanren), the Rockefeller Brothers Fund (USA), the Korea

Development Institute, the Ministry of Foreign Affairs (Japan), the Asia Foundation (USA) and the Chinese Taipei PECC Secretariat. Peter Drysdale and the staff of the PAFTAD secretariat also deserve special mention, with particular appreciation to Pamela Hewitt for copy-editing the volume. Finally, we owe much to Katsutoshi Kojima, Kyoko Arai and other staff at KERC for their most efficient logistical arrangements. I also wish to acknowledge support from other members of the host organising committee, Shujiro Urata, Akira Kohsaka and Shigeyuki Abe.

Ippei Yamazawa
July 2000

Abbreviations

ABAC	APEC Business Advisory Council
ADB	Asian Development Bank
AFTA	ASEAN Free Trade Area
AIP	(China) Automotive Industry Policy
AMC	American Motors Corporation
AMS	aggregate measurement of support
ANZCERTA	Australia–New Zealand Closer Economic Relations Trade Arrangement (see also CER)
APEC	Asia Pacific Economic Cooperation
ASEAN	Association of South East Asian Nations
ASEM	Asia–Europe Meeting
BAW	Beijing Automobile Works
BIFB	Bangkok International Banking Facility
BIS	Bank of International Settlements
BJC	Beijing Jeep Corporation
BKPM	Investment Coordination Agency
CAP	collective action plan
CEPT	Common Effective Preferential Tariff
CER	Australia–New Zealand Closer Economic Relations (see also ANZCERTA)
CIA	covered interest rate arbitrage
cif	cost insurance freight
CHT	Southern China, Chinese Taipei and Hong Kong, China
CKD	completely knocked down assembly
CPI	consumer price index
CSIS	Centre for Strategic and International Studies, Jakarta
CTI	(APEC) Committee for Trade and Investment
CUL	concerted unilateral liberalisation
DMEG	Dispute Mediation Expert Group
DMS	(APEC) Dispute Mediation Service
DPR	(Indonesian) House of Representatives
DPRK	Democratic People's Republic of Korea

DSM	dispute settlement mechanism
EAEC	East Asian Economic Caucus
EAEG	East Asian Economic Group
EAI	Enterprise of the Americas Initiative
Ecotech	economic and technical cooperation
EDI	Electronic Data Interchange
EPG	Eminent persons group
EU	European Union
EV	equivalent variation
EVSL	early voluntary sectoral liberalisation
FAGC	First Automobile Group Corporation (formerly No. 1 Automobile Works)
FDI	foreign direct investment
fob	free on board
FTAA	Free Trade Agreement of the Americas
GATS	General Agreement on Trade in Services
GATT	General Agreement on Tariffs and Trade
GDP	gross domestic product
GNP	gross national product
GPT	General Preferential Tariff
HS	Harmonised System
ICMI	Indonesian Association of Moslem Intellectuals
IAP	individual action plan
IMF	International Monetary Fund
IMS-GT	Indonesia, Malaysia and Singapore growth triangle
IMT-GT	Indonesia, Malaysia and Thailand growth triangle
IPR	intellectual property rights
ITA	Information Technology Agreement
ITU	International Telecommunication Union
JANCPEC	Japan National Committee for Pacific Economic Cooperation
JIT	just in time
KERC	Kansai Economic Research Center
MAFF	Ministry of Agriculture, Forestry and Fisheries
MAI	Multilateral Agreement on Investment
MAPA	Manila Action Plan for APEC
MERCOSUR	The Southern Common Market
MFA	Multi-fibre Arrangement
MFG	Manila Framework Group
MFN	most-favoured nation
MITI	Ministry of International Trade and Industry (Japan)
MMA	minimum market access
MPR	(Indonesian) People's Consultative Assembly
MSF	(Korean) Grain Management Special Fund
NACF	(Korean) National Agricultural Cooperative Federation

NAFTA	North American Free Trade Agreement
NIE	newly industrialising economy
NTB	non-tariff barrier
NTM	non-tariff measure
NZAFTA	New Zealand–Australia Free Trade Agreement
OAA	Osaka Action Agenda
OECD	Organisation for Economic Cooperation and Development
PAFTAD	Pacific Trade and Development
PBEC	Pacific Basin Economic Council
PECC	Pacific Economic Cooperation Council
PEG	Partnership for Equitable Growth
PPF	Partners for Progress project (Japan)
PPP	purchasing power parity
PSE	producer subsidy equivalent
PTA	Preferential Trading Arrangement
QR	quantitative restrictions
RMB	renminbi (Chinese currency)
RTA	regional trade arrangements
S&C	Standards and Conformance
SAIGC	Shanghai Automotive Industry Group Corporation
SCCP	(APEC) Subcommittee on Customs Procedures
SEZ	Special Economic Zone
SIJORI	Indonesia–Malaysia–Singapore Growth Triangle
SME	small and medium enterprises
SOM	Senior Officials' Meeting
SRTA	sub-regional trading arrangement
TEP	Transatlantic Economic Partnership
TILF	trade and investment liberalisation facilitation
TMB	Telekom Malaysia Berhad
TRIMS	Trade-Related Investment Measures
TRIPS	Trade-Related Intellectual Property Rights
TPF	Trade Policy Forum (PECC)
UIA	uncovered interest rate arbitrage
UIP	uncovered interest rate parity
UNCTAD	United Nations Conference on Trade and Development
UR	Uruguay Round
VER	voluntary export restraints
WCO	World Commerce Organisation
WTO	World Trade Organisation

1 Introduction – APEC ideas and reality

History and prospects

Ross Garnaut

INTRODUCTION

The need for Asia Pacific Economic Cooperation (APEC) emerged from the reality of deepening economic integration of the East Asian, North American and Southwest Pacific economies during the period of sustained, rapid internationally oriented economic growth in East Asia. The increasing scale of Asia Pacific economic transactions and their expanding relative importance to all economies in the region generated awareness that national policy decisions taken in ignorance of their regional implications could damage a beneficent process of market integration. The success of economic integration in the Asia Pacific also generated awareness of the opportunity for further gains through the provision of a more certain and open environment for market exchange (Drysdale and Garnaut 1989, 1993; Yamazawa 1992; Garnaut 1996; Drysdale, Elek and Soesastro 1998).

More particularly, as the scale of the Japanese and later other East Asian economies and external transactions expanded, there was recognition of a need for an international framework to contain the inevitable trans-Pacific tensions from rapid structural change. A need was recognised for providing a secure regional trade environment within which large, new entrants to the international economy, particularly Indonesia and China, could confidently commit themselves to internationally oriented development strategies. There was also a need to provide a more open alternative to inward-looking sub-regional arrangements, which were given greater legitimacy through the 1980s. Within the Southwest Pacific, the interest in Asia Pacific Economic Cooperation derived partly from recognition that the alternatives to an open international economic framework in the Asia Pacific included the danger of exclusion from or invidious choice between inward-looking blocs in North America and East Asia.

Thus the motive for Asia Pacific Economic Cooperation was essentially conservative: to preserve and extend a process of market integration amongst rapidly growing economies and their major regional partners. Asia Pacific Economic Cooperation in its first decade has had some success from this perspective. Along the way to realisation of these conservative aims, APEC became more ambitious, even radical, with the Leaders' commitment at Bogor in 1994 to free and open trade and investment in the Asia Pacific region by 2010 and 2020. The elevation of ambitions increased interest in and the energy levels of APEC activities. It has contributed significantly to trade liberalisation in a number of APEC member economies over the past half decade. It has also introduced tensions into Asia Pacific Economic Cooperation, and a risk of disillusionment and reaction against APEC and trade liberalisation. Doubts about whether APEC has the right membership, constitution and institutional structure to realise the radical ambitions have contributed to a sense of crisis in APEC in the two years following the onset of financial crisis in East Asia. The manner of resolution of the tensions in the radical APEC agenda will determine whether APEC continues to play a major role in regional affairs.

The APEC story is about the evolution of ideas to fit an Asia Pacific reality that was different from that which shaped regional economic cooperation in Western Europe and later North America. It is the story of institutions being developed to fit the ideas that have emerged in response to the different reality. The evolution of APEC has faced a special challenge from the strength in North America of ideas and political perceptions formed in a North Atlantic reality. The contemporary tensions in APEC have their origins partly in this challenge. The resolution of the tensions and therefore the future of APEC depends significantly on the ideas which have shaped APEC expanding their influence in the North American intellectual and political heartland.

The influence of the APEC ideas in North America is closely dependent on Western Pacific economies demonstrating that the unusual Asia Pacific approach to regional economic cooperation can deliver substantial trade and investment liberalisation. This has become more difficult in the aftermath of financial crisis in some East Asian economies, and in the current circumstances of economic stagnation and policy incoherence in Japan.

This chapter introduces the realities and the ideas that have shaped Asia Pacific Economic Cooperation, and evaluates their influence on economic policy and contribution to regional economic integration. Have the results justified the intellectual and political investment in APEC? Is it possible to build on APEC successes, and to correct APEC approaches productively in response to some undoubted failures? Or will the weaknesses in APEC lead to disillusionment, and eventually to failure in APEC's most fundamental purposes? The chapter argues that much is at stake, because the successes of APEC have been considerable, and failure would signal the emergence of sub-regional economic cooperation in forms that would impose large costs on APEC members and the global economic system.

APEC boundaries and membership

APEC's origin in regional integration through market processes defined membership naturally, according to the extent of countries' integration into the Asia Pacific economy. The initial natural selection was embodied in the participation in the first Pacific Economic Community meeting (later Pacific Economic Cooperation Council – PECC) in Canberra in 1980, and also in the first APEC meeting in Canberra in 1989. It included the then market economies of East Asia (Korea, Japan, the member states of ASEAN) which had sovereign political status, Australia and New Zealand in the Southwest Pacific, and the United States and Canada in North America. These were economies that were committed to internationally oriented growth and which conducted a high proportion of their trade with other Asia Pacific economies.

On these criteria, China (in the years of central planning until the new strategy of 1978 took hold and began to transform the economy and its international relations through the 1980s), Vietnam (until the collapse of COMECON in 1991), and the Democratic People's Republic of Korea (DPRK) (still today) were initially excluded by the weakness of commitment to integration into the international economy.

While Hong Kong and Taiwan both qualified from the beginning on the economic criteria, there was an obvious difficulty until China was a member, given the international recognition of Chinese sovereignty. These issues were resolved with Chinese membership of APEC in 1991, importantly in a way that allowed full participation of China, Taiwan and Hong Kong.

The South Asian economies and the Soviet Union and its successors were not committed to deep integration into the international economy until the early 1990s, and have never yet conducted the major part of their external trade with Asia Pacific economies.

The small island economies of the Southwest Pacific were strongly internationally oriented in economic structure and conducted the large majority of their foreign economic relations with other Asia Pacific economies. But in their case, size and its implications for political and administrative capacity were an issue. At the first PECC meeting in 1980 the island economies were represented by the South Pacific Forum, and subsequently Papua New Guinea (by far the most populous, with around five million people) alone was admitted to APEC membership.

The boundaries were difficult to draw in Pacific Latin America, where international orientation was sometimes equivocal and where Asia Pacific orientation was overwhelming with a single APEC member, the United States. The formation of the North American Free Trade Agreement (NAFTA) settled the issue for Mexico. Chile was straightforward on the original criteria; Peru less so.

The recent admission of Russia adds new complexity. It raises special complications because of the embryonic nature of market reforms and the fact that Russian external economic relations remain strongly weighted towards Europe.

APEC has now placed a moratorium on membership.

The original membership of APEC, while gaining coherence from commitment to internationally oriented growth and Asia Pacific concentration of foreign economic relations, was highly diverse in scale, levels of development, political culture and institutions, domestic economic structure, and openness to the international economy. This diversity carried large implications for regional economic cooperation. Amongst other things, it required a framework of international pluralism that allowed differences in domestic political and economic structure to sit comfortably alongside far-reaching economic integration.

The expansion of membership to China was necessary for APEC to achieve its fundamental objectives. An inevitable consequence of Chinese participation was to reinforce the original conception that APEC could not be a vehicle for formal regional cooperation on strategic and defence matters.

THE ASIA PACIFIC REALITY

Sustained, rapid internationally oriented growth in East Asia created the beginnings of an Asia Pacific community, and prompted the early discussion of Asia Pacific economic cooperation. The phenomenon emerged first in Japan, Hong Kong and Taiwan in the early 1950s. Openness to foreign trade and payments, at first partial and halting except in Hong Kong, allowed large and rapid gains from specialisation in production of labour-intensive goods for export. This was facilitated by the openness of the United States economy, reinforced then by the US strategic commitment to the success of non-communist Northeast Asia. Maintenance of reasonably stable macroeconomic conditions encouraged high rates of savings and investment once growth momentum was established. Strong societal commitment to the primacy of the growth objective overcame the inevitable resistance to the structural effects of sustained, internationally oriented growth. High levels of public investment in education, health and infrastructure – more effectively in Northeast Asia than later in Southeast Asia – removed bottlenecks to growth, and helped to maintain political support for growth by dispersing its benefits widely.

Economic success in Japan, Hong Kong and Taiwan provided models and opportunities for others. By the early 1960s, coinciding with reforms in Taiwan and Korea to increase international orientation and growth, labour scarcity and rising costs in Japan were corroding competitiveness in simple labour-intensive exports and strengthening comparative advantage in more capital-intensive industry. Hong Kong, Taiwan and Korea took over part of Japan's share in labour-intensive imports into North America and Europe. Japanese direct investment began to strengthen growth in labour-intensive manufacturing industries in developing Northeast Asia.

Singapore's separation from Malaysia in 1965 marked the first unequivocal commitment of a Southeast Asian economy to export-oriented growth. Singapore was joined by Malaysia and Thailand from the early 1970s, with exports and direct foreign investment then being enhanced by rising costs and structural change in Taiwan and Korea as well as Japan. Continued structural change in Japan towards more technologically sophisticated production created new opportunities for investment in and exports from standard technology capital-intensive manufacturing industries in Taiwan and Korea.

The Philippines made its first attempts at trade and payments liberalisation to support an internationally oriented growth strategy in the early 1970s, but political economy constraints prevented clear success until the 1990s.

Indonesia had abolished exchange controls as part of its macroeconomic stabilisation program in the late 1960s but, unlike any of the Northeast Asian economies, and more strongly than Malaysia, its comparative advantage in the early years of opening to the international economy was in natural resource-based products, especially oil. In the oil boom from late 1973 to the early 1980s, it responded to 'Dutch Disease' effects on the competitiveness of manufacturing industry by increasing protection. It was not until the large falls in the oil price in the mid-1980s, supported by trade liberalisation and regulatory reform, that Indonesia joined the East Asian pattern of growth supported initially by rapid expansion of labour-intensive manufactured exports.

China's engagement in internationally oriented growth was initiated in December 1978, when the Communist Party's Central Committee adopted Deng Xiaoping's approach to reform and opening to the international economy. The reflection of strategy in detailed policy, institutional development and regulatory reform was slow, with important landmarks in 1984 (industrial economy and trade reform), in 1987 (the commitment to a 'planned socialist market economy'), in 1988 (the 'coastal economic strategy') and in 1997 (radical reform of the public sector and state-owned enterprises). China's economy responded quickly to reform, with export specialisation in line with comparative advantage being reflected in rapid expansion of labour-intensive manufactured exports from the mid-1980s. At first, international orientation and rapid growth were concentrated in the coastal provinces, but regulatory reform and investment in transport and communications infrastructure supported the gradual extension inland in the second half of the 1990s.

Vietnam's entry into the Asia Pacific economy was held back by central planning and membership of COMECON until the collapse of the Soviet Union. Since then, there has been rapid growth in output and foreign trade, but market reforms have been tentative and state-owned enterprises continue to dominate external transactions. Vietnam's foreign trade and investment is overwhelmingly with APEC members, but equivocation on reform, reinforced by the East Asian financial crisis since mid-1997, limits its scale.

For the past quarter-century, the preponderance of the increase in East Asian external trade and investment transactions was with other East Asian economies and North America. From the mid-1980s until the eve of the financial crisis, the majority of export growth was to other East Asian economies. Access to the United States market had underwritten the beginnings of export-oriented growth, and the absolute size of the North American market remained substantial. From 1997, the United States temporarily resumed its role as the prime destination for export growth.

The United States was always closely linked to East Asian growth, as a market and as a source of financial services, direct foreign investment and ideas and institutional models for economic and business management. As East Asian production and trade expanded through the 1980s and 1990s, the United States became linked to the region's fortunes in other ways, with trans-Pacific exceeding trans-Atlantic trade in the mid-1980s and continuing to grow more rapidly.

The Southwest Pacific was closely integrated into East Asian trade expansion from the beginning, as a result of proximity and exceptional complementarity in resource endowments. The East Asian trade and investment opportunity was an encouragement to trade liberalisation in Australia, which became more oriented towards East Asia in its export patterns than any economy in East Asia itself.

The deepening integration of Asia Pacific economies required as a starting point reasonably open trade and payments, and liberalisation was important to the initiation of internationally oriented growth in each new entrant. In China, the hangover of political constraints and uncertainties from the civil war and Cold War limited trade and investment with Hong Kong prior to the Sino–British Agreement in 1984, and with Taiwan and Korea until the late 1980s.

Deepening economic integration, the demonstration effect of successful trade liberalisation, and competition for direct foreign investment encouraged unilateral trade and investment liberalisation. This was important throughout the Western Pacific region in the decade from the mid-1980s, when there were major unilateral reductions in trade barriers in Japan, Korea and Taiwan (each mainly in relation to manufacturing), China, Indonesia, Malaysia, the Philippines, Thailand, Vietnam, Australia and New Zealand. Trade liberalisation in the major higher-income East Asian economies, Japan, Taiwan and Korea, encouraged the transfer of manufacturing capacity in labour-intensive activities into China and Southeast Asia.

Unilateral trade and payments liberalisation for reasons of development strategy provided the opportunity, and market forces delivered the deepening integration. Market processes generated progressively lower transaction costs, expanding trade as surely as reductions in protection. This was especially important to the explosion of trade and investment ties between mainland China and its neighbours, and across the Chinese business communities of East Asia.

There has been debate through the 1990s about the extent to which liberalisation in the Western Pacific was unilateral, as an instrument of development strategy, rather than in response to conditions from aid donors, pressures from trading partners or negotiated outcomes of multilateral negotiations. Multiple causes reinforced each other. Generally the East Asian macro-economies were strong, allowing governments to implement development strategies independently of conditions from bilateral donors and international agencies. But aid-linked external pressures were important in the early 1960s in Taiwan and Korea, in the stabilisation period of the late 1960s in Indonesia, in Papua New Guinea through the 1990s, and in Indonesia, Thailand and Korea after the onset of financial crisis. US political pressures connected to bilateral trade imbalances played some role in the liberalisation of the mid- and late-1980s in Japan, Taiwan and Korea. While most APEC countries were members of GATT (General Agreement on Tariffs and Trade), participation in multilateral negotiations prior to the Uruguay Round was important to liberalisation decisions only for Japan. Amongst Western Pacific economies, Uruguay Round commitments went beyond the momentum of unilateral liberalisation only in Japan and Korea, and in each of these mainly in hard corners of agriculture and services. As we will see, APEC participation added to the momentum of unilateral liberalisation in the 1990s. The wider international community, particularly the multilateral institutions, influenced trade liberalisation, mainly through encouragement and provision of technical assistance in support of internationally oriented economic strategy.

Thus, for several decades, and most powerfully from 1985 until the financial crisis, there was a virtuous circle linking rapid economic growth, trade and payments liberalisation, increased direct foreign investment, trade expansion and reduction of private transaction costs through East Asia. Growth was supported by the rapid expansion of intra-regional trade, which accounted for a majority of the export growth in East Asia in the decade from 1985.

This was the reality from which ideas emerged about more formal processes of Asia Pacific economic cooperation.

APEC IDEAS

It is common for new entrants to any discussion of Asia Pacific economic cooperation to think in terms of conventional free trade areas, and to judge progress by the conventional criteria of such institutions. This was true of Japanese and Australian contributions to the first Pacific Trade and Development Conference in Tokyo three decades ago (Kojima 1966; Drysdale 1968). It was true of participants from mainstream American policy discussion when they focused seriously for the first time in the 1990s on Asia Pacific regional economic arrangements (Bergsten 1994).

Mature consideration has always taken discussion down a different path, focusing on private transaction costs as well as official barriers, emphasising the positive sum nature of trade liberalisation rather than adversarial negotiation, and stressing the roles of information, trust in international partners and their policies, and arrangements that are voluntary rather than enforced by supra-national authority (Crawford and Seow 1980; Elek 1992; Findlay and Intal 1998; PECC 1999).

This different path reflects strengths as well as weaknesses in the Asia Pacific environment for deeper economic integration. The Asia Pacific reality has limited the scope for progress through formal, negotiated, enforceable agreements. But the powerful momentum of unilateral liberalisation and deepening integration through market processes provided exceptional scope for gains through consultation, peer encouragement and voluntary cooperation.

The distinctive features of Asia Pacific economic cooperation emerged from academic discussion from the late 1960s in the Pacific Trade and Development conference series, business discussion from the mid-1960s in the Pacific Basin Economic Council and, from 1980, tripartite (business, academic and official) exchange within the Pacific Economic Cooperation Council.

Closer cooperative association and communication amongst government officials, business and a wider intellectual community caused all parties to recognise their shared interests in open trade and investment more closely. They reduced perceived and real risks that commitment to international orientation would leave economies vulnerable to the adoption of protectionist or disruptive policies in Asia Pacific partner countries. They led directly to reductions in transaction costs in intra-regional exchange. The potential for such gains from cooperative association and communication caused two experienced participants in the Asia Pacific discussion to recommend in a paper to the United States Congress the formation of an OECD-type institution, an Organisation for Pacific Trade, Aid and Development (Drysdale and Patrick 1979). Australian Prime Minister Bob Hawke reached for an OECD analogy in his call for the establishment of APEC in Seoul in early 1989 (Hawke 1989).

If deeper Asia Pacific economic integration has been emerging from unilateral liberalisation and the actions of market forces, why is any inter-governmental process like APEC required? The conceptual answer, emphasised before the formation of APEC, is that some of the communication and cooperation services that reduce transaction costs and deepen integration have characteristics of public goods and are under-supplied in the absence of leadership and explicit effort to internalise external costs and benefits. Now, ten years after the formation of APEC, we can apply an empirical test: has APEC raised the gains from regional economic integration? We will come back to this question later in the chapter.

The task of APEC was to expand gains from deeper regional economic cooperation. Four aspects of this cooperation came to be identified in the APEC discussion. All four emerged from the general objective, and were closely related to each other: an information-sharing and confidence-building role (the 'OECD function'), trade and investment facilitation, trade and investment liberalisation, and economic and technical cooperation.

In the early years of APEC, there was considerable focus on the 'OECD function' and trade facilitation. These tended to be seen by outsiders to the process and some insiders as soft areas of cooperation. Trade and investment liberalisation tended to be seen as the hard areas, by which APEC would be judged.

President Clinton's elevation of APEC annual meetings from Ministerial to Leaders level in 1993 was partly a reflection of growing recognition of the importance of the regional organisation. But for some, it was also a reflection of disappointment that APEC had not achieved more – of a desire to raise APEC's aspirations. The elevation certainly raised aspirations, notably with the 1994 commitment under President Soeharto's leadership to a radical program of deepening regional integration, including through free and open trade and investment in the Asia Pacific region by 2010 (developed economies) and 2020 (developing).

Early APEC discussion of trade and investment liberalisation concentrated on the role that APEC could play within the multilateral system. This built on and extended the Western Pacific senior trade-official meetings of the mid-1980s, which had encouraged Western Pacific support for what became the Uruguay Round, including a comprehensive agenda covering agriculture and textiles, and for full participation by East Asian developing economies. It also assigned an important role to convergence of perspectives on the advantages of internationally oriented economic strategies, supporting more confident expectation that such strategies would not suddenly be undermined by protectionism in important Asia Pacific trading partners.

Support for the GATT/WTO (World Trade Organisation) and for unilateral trade liberalisation within internationally oriented strategies sat easily alongside established APEC approaches to regional cooperation. In principle, the Bogor commitment to free and open trade in the Asia Pacific was also fully consistent with APEC-style cooperation. But the mention of regional free trade in the Bogor declaration brought traditional North Atlantic perceptions of discriminatory free trade areas into play, especially but not only in North America, despite the fact that formal trading blocs had been explicitly rejected whenever the possibility had arisen in informed Asia Pacific discussion.

The Eminent Persons Group's two reports (1993; 1994) contained two contradictory models of regional trade liberalisation. The dominant one was the preferential or discriminatory free trade area – never explicitly defined, but implicit in much of the detailed discussion of the way forward. At the same time, there was more than genuflection to the established APEC commitment to open or non-discriminatory liberalisation. The contradiction was neither addressed nor resolved, and the irresolution introduced elements of uncertainty into the development of APEC for several years.

Given APEC's strong support for the multilateral trade institutions, a free trade area was feasible only under Article XXIV of the GATT, which requires formal agreement on comprehensive liberalisation over a defined period (by the early 1990s, said to be ten years). On any reasonable assessment, this was simply not feasible.

So, was the Bogor Declaration mere puff, the only possible consequence of which was disillusionment with APEC as an effective regional organisation?

A paper delivered to a CSIS Conference in Jakarta on the eve of the Bogor meeting argued that there were ways in which the trade liberalisation component of the emerging Bogor Declaration could be given substantial content without trade discrimination (Garnaut 1994). The key was to use an agreed goal of free and open trade by 2010 and 2020 to reinforce the on-going momentum of unilateral liberalisation in the Western Pacific. If all liberalisation were to be on a most-favoured nation basis, the established momentum could be reinforced by sectoral agreements on free trade on a most-favoured nation basis amongst sub-sets of APEC members. APEC, including Leaders' meetings, could review progress towards the Bogor free trade objective, building confidence in each country that it was not acting alone. Ultimately the sanctions were peer disapproval and recognition that some economies' slow progress could reduce the chances of success in a process that was valuable to each participant.

It was unlikely that the United States would initially be an enthusiastic participant, given its longstanding political commitment to reciprocity in trade agreements. But the United States was already a reasonably open market. It was not essential that the United States be a leading participant in new market opening from the beginning. The ultimate realisation of the Bogor objectives would depend on the US polity being informed through the APEC discussions, and especially the Leaders' meetings, that internationalisation of historic importance was occurring in the Western Pacific, and accepting that this diffuse reciprocity was a basis for substantive American response. At this point, APEC could take the Bogor objectives into a new round of multilateral trade negotiations, with the goal of global free trade by 2020. The most difficult elements of protectionism in the Asia Pacific region ultimately would be addressed in global negotiations within the WTO.

The APEC process gradually developed an approach to the Bogor objective. The Osaka meeting in 1995 made it clear that APEC liberalisation would be comprehensive, non-discriminatory and voluntary. Manila in 1996 saw the tabling of individual country plans on liberalisation towards the Bogor objective, and approaches to measurement and peer review. Manila was the venue for agreement on sectoral liberalisation in information technology, which was taken up by the WTO at and beyond the 1996 Singapore ministerial meeting. Continuing frustration at apparent slow progress on liberalisation, especially in the United States, saw the initiation of more formal negotiations for Early Voluntary Sectoral Liberalisation (EVSL) in fifteen sectors in Vancouver in 1997. The realisation of failure of that initiative at Kuala Lumpur in 1998, marked by Japanese unwillingness to participate in liberalisation of forestry and fisheries, and realisation of US incapacity to enter commitments except in the WTO, triggered disillusionment.

Economic and technical cooperation ('Ecotech') has always been important to ASEAN participation in APEC, but has not been high in the priorities of developed members. Increasingly, Ecotech within APEC has been defined in terms of technical assistance related to human resource development in support of internationally oriented development strategies. This is more acceptable in developed and developing members alike than development assistance in the form of financial flows. Ecotech's success in this form is important to the future effectiveness of APEC as a regional organisation (Soesastro 1998).

While I have defined 'OECD-type', 'trade facilitation', 'trade liberalisation' and 'economic and technical cooperation' components of Asia Pacific Economic Cooperation, the APEC discussion has not drawn tight boundaries between them. The sharing of perspectives on economic trends, strategies and policies is an important element in trade facilitation, trade liberalisation and technical cooperation. Economic and technical cooperation in its APEC context strengthens the base for trade facilitation and trade liberalisation. Trade expansion and accelerated economic growth deriving from trade facilitation and liberalisation underpin commitments to all aspect of the APEC process.

Reflecting ASEAN preferences, there has been little development of executive capacity within APEC. APEC has neither supra-national authority, nor the means for executive action if it had that authority. APEC members can agree on objectives and desirable courses of action. Members must then rely on decisions by member governments to implement agreed actions, with these decisions being taken either unilaterally, or through agreement between member governments.

EVALUATION OF APEC

What difference has APEC made? Such an evaluation is complex, since Asia Pacific economic integration had been proceeding prior to the formation of APEC and would have delivered gains in any event.

There has been a significant APEC contribution on the *OECD functions* of sharing information and perspectives on economic performance, strategy and policy. There is increased awareness amongst business, official and intellectual communities in every APEC member of developments in other APEC economies.

One would presume without having hard evidence that the reduction in transaction costs associated with the considerable increase in interpersonal contact and information exchange contributed to the acceleration of expansion of intra-regional trade and investment flows that occurred through the 1990s.

The financial crisis of 1997–9 provided a shock to regional trade expansion that might have led to major fractures in the regional trading system, and therefore might have contributed to cumulative decline into protection and trade contraction. It provided in an extreme form the type of shock that might have generated retreat into the inward-looking policies against which the conservative original conception of APEC was meant to provide protection. Again, we cannot be certain of causation, but we do know that, unlike the developed world in the Great Depression and most economies in postwar recessions, there was no significant retreat into protection in the crisis of the late 1990s – neither in the countries in deep recession, nor in their Asia Pacific trading partners (notably the United States, China and Australia) where continued strong economic growth and East Asian currency depreciation and output contraction generated historically large deficits (or in China's case, declines in the surplus) in current payments. The story is not yet over in the United States, where the intensification of anti-dumping actions may yet accumulate into a problem of macroeconomic significance. But Asia Pacific governments' trade policy responses generally did not gratuitously magnify the trade-contracting effects of the crisis. APEC's contribution came through increased awareness of the regional effects of individual economies' responses.

APEC in 1997 was not geared to respond to financial crisis, and its initial actions were clumsy. The Leaders' response at Vancouver in 1997, when crisis was evident only in parts of Southeast Asia, was banal. The Asia Pacific lost an opportunity to mitigate the contagion when APEC failed to sculpt a constructive regional response to the Japanese Ministry of Finance's proposal for an Asia Fund for this purpose, pushing a major part of the Japanese financial response into bilateral channels. Subsequently, APEC showed that it could play a useful role in response to financial crisis through the establishment of the Manila Framework, within which a number of senior Finance and Central Bank officials came together formally to discuss policy responses and institutional reform within the financial sector. The Kuala Lumpur Leaders' meeting provided an effective setting for some regionalisation of Japanese bilateral financial support, through US participation in activities complementary to the Miyazawa Plan.

At the same time, there were some obvious failures in cooperative policy development within APEC. Chinese membership of the WTO is an essential element in an effective regional and global trading system. In addition to being important in itself, it is a condition of Taiwan membership. In 1994 and 1999, China made major reform efforts designed to attract support for WTO membership, and each time the United States failed to respond creatively. Contact within APEC was not unhelpful, but in the end was ineffective. The failure in 1994 greatly complicated Chinese integration into the global food economy, and the failure in the first half of 1999 was potentially a setback for the Millennium Round of global trade negotiations.

In *trade facilitation*, APEC was unambiguously if modestly successful in contributing to reduction in transaction costs. For this success to be brought fully to account, a major research effort is required to quantify benefits.

In *trade liberalisation*, current perceptions are unreasonably dominated by the failure of EVSL in 1998. On the credit side, APEC's continued and unequivocal support for the multilateral trading system helped to bring the

Uruguay Round to a successful conclusion, and in 1996 played a major role in the WTO's first liberalisation success, the information technology agreement.

The first eight years of APEC's life saw a considerable acceleration of unilateral liberalisation in many economies of the Western Pacific, and especially in economies which had once applied high protection to manufacturing (Australia and New Zealand) or all industries producing tradables (China, Indonesia, the Philippines and Vietnam).

In Australia, the final and largest step in a process of dismantling high protection was taken in March 1991, and was strongly influenced by the discussion of Australia's expanding relations with the Asia Pacific region. New Zealand followed Australia, and its decision to take the final step to complete free trade by a date early in the next century became part of its APEC Individual Action Plan (IAP). While Australian liberalisation preceded the 1994 Bogor Declaration, Australia's participation in the Bogor understandings was of large and direct importance in preventing backsliding in the recession of the early 1990s.

Like Australia and New Zealand, developing economies of East Asia were on a path of unilateral liberalisation prior to the formation of APEC, and the new regional association provided a context for the acceleration of reductions in protection in the 1990s. China announced major packages of trade liberalisation measures in APEC ministerial meetings in 1995 (Osaka) and 1996 (Manila), preferring voluntary action in APEC to the appearance of responding to bilateral pressures, in the absence of participation in WTO multilateral negotiations.

In Indonesia and the Philippines, major steps in trade liberalisation were directly related to the hosting of APEC Leaders' meetings and to the Bogor commitment to free and open trade and investment by 2020. There was some shift in the direction of liberalisation in the complex political economy of trade policy in Indonesia following President Soeharto's close association with the Bogor declaration, and this was influential in the liberalisation packages announced in 1995 and 1996. In the Philippines, the linkage was immediate. After several decades in which Presidents had failed to implement much-discussed liberalisation strategies, in 1996 the Philippines Congress supported the Ramos program of radical reductions in protection in the lead-up to, and to provide the President with a platform of leadership for, the Manila Leaders' meeting. In the Philippines, as in Indonesia and China, the APEC framework of voluntary commitments was more acceptable politically than response to pressure in bilateral or multilateral negotiations.

Elsewhere in East Asia, the links with APEC were more distant. Malaysia's down-beat pronouncements on APEC suggest that that country's large reductions in tariffs, announced annually with the budget, had other origins.

Liberalisation in Western Pacific economies – unilaterally as a matter of domestic strategy and through participation in APEC, and in multilateral negotiations – proceeded after 1994 at a rate that, if maintained, would achieve the Bogor objectives (Yamazawa 1998). This was revealed in the Individual Action Plans defined in Osaka, presented in Manila, and subsequently updated annually. Did the Manila Action Plan and the IAP process assist this outcome? At least, it was part of the wider process of assuring individual APEC members that their own liberalisation was supported by continued expansion of opportunities in major regional trading partners.

When we focus on the APEC objective of free trade by 2010 (Australia, New Zealand, Korea and Taiwan) or 2020 (developing East Asia and Papua New Guinea), the protection that remains may be harder to eliminate than that which has so far been removed or promised away. The voluntary processes and peer influence that have been influential so far will need to be supplemented by formal negotiations within the WTO before member economies get to the end of the road.

APEC influence on trade liberalisation is not so clear in the Eastern Pacific, especially in the United States. The test there will be whether the US polity eventually recognises the importance of helping to sustain the historic opening of the Western Pacific economies through its own commitment to free trade by 2010.

APEC seems to have influenced the shape of trade liberalisation within the region's three discriminatory trade blocks: the ASEAN Free Trade Agreement (AFTA), Australia–New Zealand Closer Economic Relations (CER) and NAFTA. Reductions in protection on a most-favoured nation basis are in the process of removing most (Australian) or virtually all (New Zealand) discrimination against third country imports. In New Zealand the choice of end points was influenced by Bogor commitments. Similarly, AFTA members have mostly been implementing their commitments to intra-regional free trade by 2003 through most-favoured nation liberalisation – in the Philippines explicitly in recognition of Bogor commitments, and in Indonesia and Thailand with APEC considerations being influential. APEC has been less important to NAFTA, but, at least at the margins, the APEC commitments and process have heightened official awareness of the external costs of trade diversion.

The APEC process constrained proliferation of discriminatory sub-regional trading agreements. It made United States overtures on free trade agreements to some individual Western Pacific economies less compelling than they otherwise would have been. The presence of APEC inhibited enthusiasm for the emergence of an East Asian trading bloc, once briefly favoured by Malaysia. APEC was used explicitly by the Indonesian and Japanese governments in opposition to proposals for discriminatory free trade in East Asia. The ground may be slipping with perception of diminished success in APEC following failure in the EVSL in 1998, most importantly with MITI's promotion of discussion of a Northeast Asian or Korea–Japan free trade area without clear definition of whether it would be preferential in character.

Economic and technical cooperation attracted the least enthusiastic response from the developed members. Yet its success is crucial to ASEAN participation, and important to APEC's realising its full value for all members. Amongst modest achievements, technical assistance in the financial sector delivered through APEC Finance Ministers and the Manila Framework has had value in the recovery from financial crisis, and has contributed to the strengthening of financial institutions and therefore to the view that open capital accounts can be consistent with domestic economic stability. The most important development in relation to Ecotech has been the clarification of its role within APEC over the past several years. (Soesastro 1998). Gains will follow as these intellectual clarifications are absorbed into policy.

THE FUTURE

The growth in interdependence among East Asian economies and between East Asia and the Southwest Pacific and North America placed more formal cooperative arrangements on the regional agenda. If APEC did not exist, there would be efforts to build something like it. If the something like it were an East Asian bloc, it would be much less helpful to realisation of gains from cooperation, and it would be damaging to the global trading system.

The unusual *modus operandi* of APEC, the distinctive commitment to support of the multilateral system and to non-discrimination, and the emphasis on voluntary association, are all inevitable consequences of APEC's history and membership. Three decades of regional discussions culminating in the APEC process have achieved a great deal in defining a new approach to regional economic cooperation, fully supportive of and complementary to the multilateral system, within the special constraints of a politically and economically diverse region.

APEC does not have the membership that everyone would choose. Papua New Guinea's political and administrative weakness raises questions that are best answered by a concerted effort through economic and technical cooperation within APEC. Papua New Guinea has committed itself to the Bogor objectives, and has taken major policy steps to achieve them. In the Christian idiom favoured in that country, the spirit is willing but the flesh is weak. International technical assistance can strengthen the flesh. Russia's weak economic connections to the Asia Pacific raise many questions, most of which must be answered within Russia. It is as important for Russia as it is for APEC that its initial Individual Action Plans reveal commitment to progress towards free and open trade and investment. If they do, it is important that APEC members respond with encouragement, including through economic and technical cooperation. If they do not, it will be time for Russia and its APEC partners seriously to consider whether Russian membership can add value for either Russia or the regional institution.

APEC has important achievements to its credit, but the contemporary mood in mid-1999 is one of disillusionment. The causes of this disappointment must be addressed urgently, or the process and commitments that have delivered positive results will disintegrate.

The central causes of disillusionment are the apparent irrelevance of APEC to the financial crisis, and the apparent ineffectiveness of APEC in contributing to expansion of trade and investment within the Asia Pacific.

APEC was not geared to play a major role in the financial crisis. Its traditions were oriented towards support of the multilateral organisations – in the case of financial crisis, the International Monetary Fund and the World Bank. In the end, APEC played this role, but with false starts, and with too little adding of value. It could have played a larger role in providing advice to the international organisations on recovery policy and strategy. The meetings of APEC Finance Ministers and the Manila Framework provide a suitable mechanism for APEC members now to do more that is of value through technical assistance in the financial sector. It would be helpful if the Finance Ministers' meetings were integrated more tightly into other APEC processes.

While the urgent requirements when the crisis struck were for actions that lay outside APEC's comparative advantage, the established agenda of APEC is highly relevant to recovery from crisis. APEC has an important role to play, especially in Leaders' meetings, in building support for the maintenance of open trade policies in the economies now experiencing exceptional deficits in current payments, notably the United States and Australia, and also in China, where large surpluses were corroded by the crisis. APEC is the right forum for encouraging the United States and its Asia Pacific partners to accept the large imbalances in external current payments that emerge naturally from open trade and investment policies. A large Japanese current surplus allows Japan to play its natural role in the recapitalisation of economies that have been damaged by crisis. A large US (or Australian) deficit is consistent with large gains from trade and with profitable US business leadership in the emergence of open financial sectors throughout the Asia Pacific.

The disillusionment with APEC's contribution to trade and investment expansion is premature. The contribution that is being made by APEC trade facilitation will continue to be undervalued until the region has access to the results of authoritative research on these matters. On trade liberalisation, the disappointment stems mainly from failure to recognise contributions that came mainly through influence on the domestic policy-making process, rather than through formal negotiations. Failure to recognise the APEC role in influencing domestic policy decisions led to the attempt at more formal, reciprocal negotiation of the EVSL, the failure of which is itself a major source of disappointment.

Three lessons need to be drawn from the failure of EVSL. The first is that APEC has no comparative advantage in formal, reciprocal negotiations, and should not seek a role that it cannot perform well. The second is a lesson for Japan. Japan placed at risk major national interests by granting excessive influence to sectors now of minor importance to its national performance. APEC will fail without effective leadership from Japan. Effective leadership requires the Japanese polity to assert national over minor sectoral interests.

The third is a lesson for the Asia Pacific as a whole about the United States. United States trade policy is for the time being at least deeply committed to reciprocity, delivered through formal negotiations. This is inconsistent with the APEC *modus operandi*. The United States will not quickly change, and it is neither possible nor desirable for APEC to change. The way forward is for Western Pacific APEC members, preferably with support from some American participants, to recognise the importance of maintaining momentum in their own liberalisation, and to communicate the reality of those developments into the US polity. APEC so far has failed in this communication.

US Presidential participation in Leaders' meetings, with all of the political and media attention in the United States that accompanies it, is a principal vehicle for the necessary communication. Once the US polity's attention has been engaged, an opportunity can be created to complete the implementation of the Bogor commitments through multilateral negotiations within the WTO.

One large risk of the current disillusionment is that it will encourage exclusive regional arrangements within East Asia. The East Asian Economic Caucus has enhanced credibility and new importance as a consequence of perceptions that APEC has failed. The annual meeting of leaders of ASEAN countries Japan, China and Korea is the East Asian Economic Caucus at work. Within Japan, reaction to the regional response to the Asia Fund and to failure of EVSL has given new legitimacy to discussion of East Asian regional arrangements. There is no necessary harm in regular consultation at a high level amongst East Asian governments, and possibly some good. Harm would be done, however, if discussion drifted into favourable attitudes towards a discriminatory trading bloc in East Asia. The established APEC framework is Japan's, East Asia's and APEC's best protection against East Asian economic cooperation moving fatefully towards an exclusive bloc. A Japan–Korea or Northeast Asian regional agreement need not contain any element of discrimination. It would not be discriminatory if it were premised on the APEC objective of free and open trade and investment in the Asia Pacific by 2010. But if such an agreement were not anchored on such an objective, it would be difficult to resist the introduction of elements of discrimination against outsiders. The inevitable international reaction would damage East Asian economic cooperation with the Southwest Pacific and the Americas.

Finally, APEC, as an organisation that has at its centre commitment to the success of the multilateral trading system, and many of whose actions relate closely to the work of the WTO, cannot be expected to operate successfully if such important member economies as China and Taiwan continue to be outside the WTO. The continued exclusion of China now has much to do with wider political tensions between the Asia Pacific region's two most populous countries. This is a deep problem at the heart of APEC. However clever the managers of the APEC process may be in managing the affairs for which they have responsibility, APEC will not make progress if problems in the Sino–American relationship fester, and China remains outside the WTO.

REFERENCES

Bergsten, C.F. (1994) 'APEC and the world economy: A force for worldwide liberalisation, *Foreign Affairs* 73(3).

Crawford, J. and Seow, G. (1980) *PACIFIC Economic Co-operation: Suggestions for action*, Singapore: Heineman Asia.

Drysdale, P. (1968) 'Pacific economic integration: An Australian view', in Kiyoshi Kojima (ed.) *Pacific Trade and Development*, Japan Economic Research Center, Tokyo, February 194–223.

—— and Patrick, H. (1979) 'An Asia Pacific Regional Economic Organisation: An exploratory concept paper', Washington DC: Congressional Research Service.

—— and Garnaut, R. (1989) in J.J. Schott (ed.) *Free Trade Areas and US Trade Policy*, Washington DC: Institute for International Economics.

—— (1993) 'The Pacific: An application of a general theory of economic integration', in C.F. Bergsten and M. Nolan (eds) *Pacific Dynamism and the International Economic System*, Washington DC.

——, Elek, A. and Soesastro, H. (1998) 'Open regionalism: The nature of Asia Pacific integration', in P. Drysdale and D. Vines (eds) *Europe, East Asia and APEC: A shared global agenda?*, Cambridge: Cambridge University Press.

Elek, A. (1992) 'Pacific economic co-operation in policy choices for the 1990s', in *Asia–Pacific Economic Literature* 6(1).

Eminent Persons' Group (1993) 'A vision for APEC: Towards an Asia–Pacific community', Singapore.

—— (1994) 'Achieving the APEC Vision', Singapore.

Findlay, C. and Intal, P.S. (1998) 'Beyond liberalisation of trade in goods: Alternative strategies for regional trade and investment liberalisation', in P. Drysdale and D. Vines (eds) *Europe, East Asia and APEC: A shared global agenda?*.

Garnaut, R. (1994) 'The Bogor Declaration on Asia Pacific Trade Liberalisation', paper presented at a conference organised by the Centre for Strategic and International Strategic Studies, Jakarta. Reprinted in Garnaut (1996).

—— (1996) *Open Regionalism and Trade Liberalization*, Singapore: Institute of Southeast Asian Studies.

Hawke, R. (1989) 'Regional co-operation: Challenges for Korea and Australia', speech, Seoul.

Kojima, K. (1966) 'A Pacific economic community and Asian developing countries', *Hitotsubashi Journal of Economics* 7(1).

Pacific Economic Cooperation Council (PECC) (1999) 'Competition principles: PECC principles for guiding the development of a competition-driven policy framework for APEC economies', Singapore: PECC Secretariat.

Soesastro, H. (1998) 'Economic and technical cooperation', in A. Elek (ed.) *Building an Asia Pacific Community*, Brisbane: The Foundation for Development Cooperation.

Yamazawa, I. (1992) 'On Pacific economic integration', *Economic Journal* 102 (415), November.

—— (1998) 'APEC's progress toward the Bogor Target: A quantitative assessment of 1997 IAP/CAP', PECC Japan Committee, Tokyo, March.

2 Macroeconomic interdependence in the APEC region

Akira Kohsaka

INTRODUCTION

The crisis in Asia which started in 1997 has changed its name, from a currency crisis to a financial and then an economic crisis and finally the Asian crisis. Some say that the virtual integration through trade and investment flows in the APEC region turned out to work negatively in disseminating currency and/or economic turmoil. In the European Union, by contrast, the new unified currency started to circulate and its monetary integration appeared to reach the final stage, where virtual as well as formal integration through trade and investment has been realised over the past decades. It remains to be seen, however, whether this macroeconomic integration with one monetary and multiple fiscal authorities will work well or not.

Although there have been discussions on microeconomic integration in the APEC region, its macroeconomic integration has been a relatively underdeveloped field of research. Under the general trend of globalisation of financial markets, the present crisis has grown from domestic financial crisis to currency crisis, which hit more or less all the economies in the region through volatile movements of their foreign exchange rates; subsequently real economies, including trade and investment, suffered severe damage.

In view of these recent developments, it is high time to review how far and in what way the APEC economies have interacted with one another so far in terms of macroeconomic as well as monetary dimensions; then to pursue the policy implications of future possible forms of macro-monetary cooperation, not merely defensively to prevent similar types of economic crisis, but to actively reap the potential benefit of macro-monetary integration, while minimising the possible risks.

The first section provides an overview of the development of capital market integration of the Pacific region since the 1980s. It traces an abrupt upsurge of capital inflows to the region since the end of the 1980s, and their macroeconomic implications. The second section measures the degree of integration to the international capital market of selected individual economies in the region, first examining the correlations between savings and investment ratios, to check whether the economies are facing external financial constraints. Then nominal as well as real interest rate parities are examined, in order to verify the integration through price arbitrages.

Capital market integration provides both opportunities and risks to integrated economies, particularly in the case of late-coming emerging market economies. The risk side was too greatly exposed in the case of the Asian economic crisis. The macroeconomic experiences of the crisis-hit economies are briefly discussed in the third section. There the focus is on the huge amount of destabilising capital inflows, their impact on macroeconomic management, and mutually reinforcing currency crises. Large swings in the yen–dollar real exchange rates might have played an important role in excessive risk-taking. One possible solution to the basic policy trilemma these emerging market economies are facing is monetary integration. Finally, in the fourth section, based on a framework of the theory of the optimal currency area, the nature of macroeconomic shocks and the pattern of adjustments in East Asia and Southeast Asia (hereafter, East Asia) are examined. Here, the major concerns lie in comparability with members of the European Union as well as regions within the United States, because the former gives us a present experiment toward monetary integration and the latter a post-integration example.

CAPITAL INFLOWS IN THE PACIFIC REGION

Capital market integration gives rise to very different macroeconomic properties from those in economies insulated from the international capital market. In order to examine this in the Pacific context, and before going into how to measure the degree of capital market integration, it is important to review the development of international capital movements in the region.

Private capital flows increased in the early 1990s in emerging markets in both Latin America and Asia, most of which belong to the Pacific region. The increase was literally explosive, as Figure 2.1 clearly demonstrates. This trend showed a temporary halt in 1994 because of the Mexican currency crisis, but it soon recovered and resumed. While the boom in capital flows was ignited first in Latin America in the form of portfolio investment, the flows into Asia have been mainly bank lending.[1]

The boom can be attributed to several cyclical as well as structural factors. Business cycles in industrialised economies, particularly falling interest rates, have been the strongest and the most direct driving force to realise this kind of huge capital flow to high-growth developing economies.[2] The growth of institutional investors and deregulation of their international investment in industrialised economies are important supply-side factors of investment capital, which is structural. Finally, overall economic reforms, specifically financial and capital market liberalisation in developing economies, have lured foreign capital and encouraged international risk diversification by institutional investors.

Figure 2.1 Net resource flows

Net capital inflow, East Asia and Pacific, 1970–96

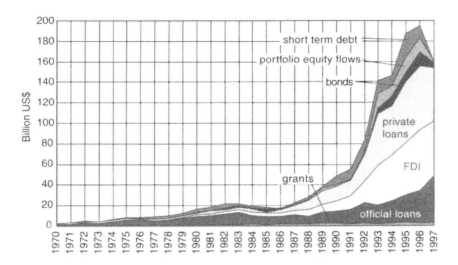

Net capital inflow, Latin America and Caribbean, 1970–97

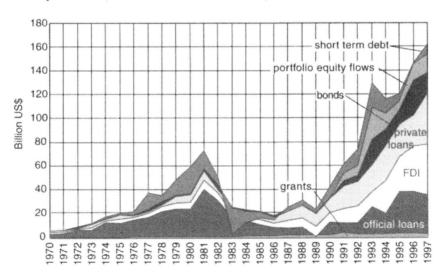

Source: World Development Finance, Global Development Finance.

The last point is crucial, because it turned out to be a double-edged sword. First, while huge capital flows in either securities investment or bank loans can relax constraints on domestic investment finance, they tend to put currency appreciation pressure on the foreign exchange market as well as inflationary pressure on the domestic financial market, through resulting monetary expansion. Second, under the general trend of financial market deregulation, these capital flows can lead to reckless bank lending and other excessive exposures without fully-fledged prudential controls by the monetary authorities, although the deregulation is, without doubt, desirable in the long run. Third, as it has turned out, these capital flows may not be reliable sources of long-term investment finance. Once the business cycle in developed economies changes, finance easily changes hands. This type of volatility should be taken into account, because emerging markets are at most marginal to those international investors looking for better opportunities in the global arena of the international capital market.

Thus, the booms and busts of private foreign capital inflows to emerging markets in the region in the 1990s have obliged the monetary authorities to face a variety of fundamental policy choices in order to insulate domestic economies from those external disturbances. One of the policy choices was how or how not to adjust exchange rates in order to minimise the possible undesirable side effects of these flows. Then, sterilised intervention in the foreign exchange market can be viewed as a combination of nominal exchange rate stabilisation and monetary control. The latter would use an open market operation, reserve requirements, and even management of public sector savings as instruments. Lastly, controls on capital inflows and/or decontrol of capital outflows would also be utilised for direct manipulation.

Optimal policy responses depend on the volatility of the flows and the absorptive capacity of domestic financial systems. The authorities can insulate domestic economies from the external impact by adjusting exchange rates, and/or resort to counteracting monetary and fiscal policies with exchange rates untouched. In fact, Pacific economies adopted a combination of policies, including exchange rate adjustments or more flexible exchange rates, monetary policies (sterilised intervention in foreign exchange and/or money markets), fiscal restraint, capital controls and even accelerating trade liberalisation.

Most economies (Chile, Colombia, Indonesia, Korea, Malaysia, Mexico, Philippines, Taiwan, Thailand) tried to sterilise the monetary impact of the capital inflows, while some (Chile, Colombia, Indonesia, Korea, Malaysia) imposed increased reserve requirements on foreign borrowing, or other capital control measures. Sterilised intervention has been said to be effective, at least in the short run, in minimising the impact on domestic monetary conditions. Some East Asian economies (Malaysia, Philippines, Singapore, Taiwan, Thailand) attempted fiscal restraint through the management of public sector savings.

Exchange rate adjustments (revaluation or appreciation) can insulate domestic financial markets from volatile external capital movements, and help promote necessary real adjustments in a less inflationary way. Chile, Colombia, Indonesia, Malaysia, Mexico and the Philippines took this option, to various degrees and timings, in the 1990s. The cost of more flexible exchange rates is its possible negative impact on trade and investment flows.

CAPITAL MARKET INTEGRATION?

As seen above, many economies in East Asia have recently become highly integrated into the international capital market. Of course, the sheer size of capital flows could be an imperfect indicator of the capital market integration. Just think of the important role played by official and officially guaranteed loans in Korean economic development in the late 1960s and the 1970s. Even though their size relative to GDP was huge, no one could claim that Korea was highly integrated into the international market at that time. Nevertheless, there are reasons that allow us to observe that emerging markets receiving these huge flows in the Pacific region have been heavily integrated to the rest of the world. One of these is that recent flows have been mostly through private sources, as shown in Figure 2.1.

Macroeconomic fluctuations are transmitted through capital markets via price (interest rates) as well as quantity (capital flows). Interactions between interest rates and capital movements in response to price differentials will be discussed here, to review and assess the developments in capital market integration in the region.

Saving–investment correlation

One measure is to observe changes in correlation between national saving and investment rates, where integrated capital markets are expected to relax liquidity constraints on borrowers, resulting in less correlation between them. In other words, the more integrated the market, the less bound are relatively low savers, with better investment opportunities from their own saving (Feldstein and Horioka 1980).

Generally speaking, East Asia has become both a high saver and a high investor since the 1960s. If we look at the relative importance of the region in terms of output, and saving and investment in the global economy (Figure 2.2), we find that, while its share in world output expanded from 5 to 10 per cent, its share in world saving jumped from 6 to 15 per cent, with the investment share increasing from 6 to 13 per cent between 1980 and 1995. Note that some East Asian economies have become net savers, while others have remained net investors. Important policy issues will therefore be whether or not the huge resources mobilised can be conduited to efficient investment uses, and through what channels.[3]

Figure 2.2 Shares in world output, saving and investment: Pacific region, 1980–95

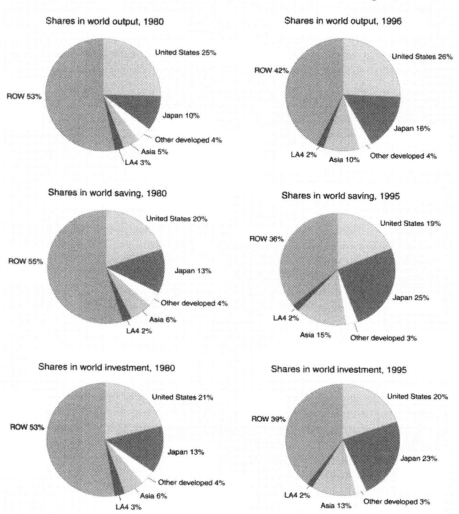

Note: LA4 are Chile, Colombia, Mexico and Peru.
Source: World Bank, World Development Indicators, 1997.

With an investment ratio to GDP (*I/Y*) as an dependent variable, and a saving ratio to GDP (*S/Y*) as an explanatory variable, the following equation was estimated by Feldstein and Horioka:

$$I/Y = a + \beta(S/Y) + e \qquad (1)$$

It can be supposed that, with the ß closer to 0 (1), the higher (lower) the capital mobility. Despite some shortcomings with this simple framework of analysis, it seems worthwhile to use it as a first step in examining the changing degree of integration of individual economies to the international capital market. (See also Dooley, Frankel and Mathieson 1987; Fry 1986; Kim 1993; Montiel 1994; and Okura 1996).[4]

Figure 2.3 shows the development of both the national saving and domestic investment ratios to GDP in eight economies in East Asia. There appear to be strong time trends in both ratios. Thus, we checked the time series properties of both saving and investment ratios (not reported here), and found that we cannot reject the existence of unit roots in the case of their levels, though we can do so in the case of their first-order differentials.[5]

Then we estimate the correlation between saving and investment by using the following equation:

$$\Delta(I/Y) = a + \text{ß} \, \Delta(S/Y) + e \qquad (2)$$

where $\Delta(I/Y) = I/Y_t - (I/Y)_{t-1}$, etc. The result of this estimation is given in Table 2.1.

First, ß is found to be significantly different from zero in Hong Kong, Indonesia, Korea, the Philippines and Thailand over the whole period, while this is not the case in Malaysia, Singapore and Taiwan. Second, even though significant, ß is estimated to be less than 0.5, except for Thailand (0.69). Note that the small value of 0.6 might be considered a 'representative' industrial-country value (Montiel 1994). In addition, if we look at the estimation results across a few sub-sample periods, ß loses its significance for the most recent period of 1980–97 in all countries except for the Philippines. On the other hand, we have mixed results on whether there is any tendency for the estimated coefficients to decline over time. There are declining trends in the 1970s and 1980s in Indonesia and Korea, but this is not the case for others.

Thus, with either insignificant, or significant but small, estimates of the coefficient ß, we can say that domestic investment has not been constrained by national savings over the past couple of years in East Asia. Moreover, the insignificance of the ß coefficient in the most recent period might suggest that East Asia has been increasingly integrated to the international capital market, in the sense that it has been freed from domestic saving constraints.

Interest rate linkages

Instead of focusing on quantities of capital flows, we can see the degree of capital market integration through their prices; that is, by looking at the extent of interest arbitrage between domestic and international counterpart assets.

Covered interest rate arbitrage. One measure is the degree of covered interest rate arbitrage (CIA), where risk-free transactions with forward cover can fully exploit profit opportunities from international interest rate differentials.

Figure 2.3 Saving and investment ratios to GDP in East Asia, 1960–97

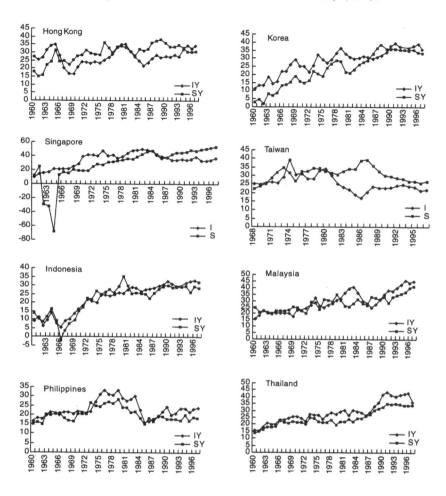

Source: IMF, International Financial Statistics, CD-ROM.

Then, the difference between the nominal interest rate on a domestic asset (*i*) and the interest rate on a comparable international asset (*i**) is equal to the forward discount on the home country's nominal exchange rate. Namely,

$$f - s = i - i^*$$
(3)

where *f* and *s* are the logarithms of forward and spot exchange rates in domestic currency, respectively. Regulatory arrangements on foreign exchange

Table 2.1   Saving–investment correlations in East Asia, 1961–97

	Estimated Coefficient β 1961– 70		1961– 80		1961– 90		1961– 97		1980– 97
Hong Kong	0.7	**	0.49	**	0.5	***	0.43	***	0.98
	−2.89		−2.74		−3.36		−2.9		−0.61
Indonesia	0.52	**	0.38	**	0.28	**	0.27	***	−0.14
	−3.1		−2.79		−2.58		−2.77		−1.26
Korea	1.08	***	0.61	**	0.46	**	0.48	***	0.23
	−4.95		−2.68		−2.45		−2.76		−1.17
Malaysia	−0.52		0.07		−0.03		−0.07		−0.3
	−1.28		−0.43		−0.20		−0.50		−1.23
Philippines	0.16		0.21		0.44	**	0.42	**	0.75
	−1.03		−1.15		−2.32		−2.43		−2.53
Singapore	−0.02		−0.02		−0.02		−0.02		0.1
	−0.59		−0.60		−0.49		−0.57		−0.33
Thailand	0.69	*	0.73	***	0.61	**	0.69	***	0.64
	−2.25		−4.19		−2.72		−3.04		−1.15

			1971– 80		1971– 90		1971– 97		1980– 97
Taiwan	—		0.12		0.04		0.05		−0.23
			−0.22		−0.13		−0.17		−0.89

Notes
a Figures below estimated coefficients are t-values.
b ***, **, * denote 1%, 5%, 10% significance levels, respectively.
c Estimated equation $\Delta(I/Y)=a+ß^*\Delta(S/Y)+e$, where I/Y, S/Y are investment and saving ratios to GDP.

transactions as well as developments of forward exchange markets affect the validity of CIA. We should note that CIA is a prerequisite for higher order interest rate arbitrage, such as uncovered interest rate arbitrage, which will be discussed later.

Drawing on several studies of CIA in Asia, such as those by Goldsbourough and Teja (1991) and Chinn and Frankel (1994), de Brouwer (1996) and de Brouwer and Gower (1996) reported tests of covered interest rate arbitrage in some Asia Pacific economies (Australia, New Zealand, Canada, Hong Kong, Singapore, Japan and Malaysia) using assets of varying maturities. They showed that CIA holds reasonably well for most of the economies on short-term assets, but not on those of longer maturity.

These results suggest that covered interest rate differentials narrowed in the 1990s, probably because of capital market liberalisation as well as innovations in technology and communications, while capital controls have been occasionally applied on a selective and temporary basis. The speeds of narrowing, however, seem to vary across economies, at least partly reflecting varying degrees of maturity of domestic financial markets. For the rest of the economies in the region, CIA cannot be checked, simply because of the lack of data, which would tend to reflect the underdevelopment of their markets.

Uncovered interest rate arbitrage. While CIA indicates a high degree of openness in money markets, it has little to do with longer-term capital movements. In fact, the results obtained by de Brouwer and Gower (1996) indicate the existence of persistent covered interest rate differentials on longer maturity assets, which may suggest there is room for developing deeper capital markets in the region. Uncovered interest rate arbitrage (UIA) observes how far foreign exchange transactions could exploit possible differentials of expected returns of investment with risks. In particular, we are concerned here with the degree of real interest rate linkages.

Prior empirical studies on real interest rate linkages include those by Glick and Hutchison (1990), Chinn and Frankel (1994) and Okura (1996). Their main conclusions are that the real interest rate linkages tend to be strengthened with financial liberalisation. In particular, in some newly industrialising economies (NIEs), the variability of real interest rate differentials has markedly decreased.

Drawing on those studies, we are going to report the development of real interest rate differentials and their components, and to examine the changes in real interest rate linkages and their background factors, using updated data samples.

The real interest rate differential between two countries (i, j) is defined as:

$$r_i - r_j = (i_i - \Delta p_i^e) - (i_j - \Delta p_j^e) \tag{4}$$

where r_i = real interest rate of country i, i_i = nominal interest rate of country i, Δp_i^e = expected inflation of country i. Equation (4) can be rewritten as:

$$r_i - r_j = (i_i - i_j - \Delta s_{ij}^e) + (\Delta s_{ij}^e + \Delta p_j^e - \Delta p_i^e) \tag{5}$$

where Δs_{ij}^e = expected depreciation of currency i against currency j. The first and the second terms of the right-hand side of equation (5) represent both the uncovered interest rate parity (UIP) and the purchasing power parity (PPP) conditions, respectively. That is, the real interest rate differential consists of deviations from UIP and PPP.

Then, assuming rational expectations and allowing for prediction errors, the real interest rate differential can be observed as:

$$r_i - r_j = (i_i - i_j - \Delta s_{ij}) + (\Delta s_{ij} + \Delta p_j - \Delta p_i) + e_{ij} \tag{6}$$

Equation (6) clarifies how the real interest rate linkages could be hampered. Persistent real interest rate differentials, which might suggest the existence of unexploited profit (investment) opportunities, could come from deviations from UIP or PPP, or both. The former reflects either risk premium in foreign exchange transactions or effective capital controls, while the latter either incomplete commodity arbitrage or relative price changes between tradable and non-tradable goods, that is, the Balassa–Samuelson effect (see Ito, Isard and Symansky 1999).[6]

The recent development of real interest rate differentials, and deviations from UIP as well as PPP in East Asia, is demonstrated in Figure 2.4, where both UIP and PPP are calculated by using US counterpart interest rates, exchange rates against the US dollar and US consumer price index (CPI) inflation.[7] At a glance, we see minimal real interest rate differentials in Singapore and Japan, while they seem either persistently or occasionally different from zero in Korea, Malaysia, the Philippines and Thailand. Deviations from UIP and PPP are not only far from negligible, but also persistent in all economies. The two deviations often appear to counter-move, mainly because of large fluctuations in nominal exchange rates.

Allowing for these deviations from the basic parity conditions, we estimate the following equation, using instrumental variables:

$$r_i = a + \beta r_j + e_{ij} \tag{7}$$

Estimation results of equation (7) are given in Table 2.2. The coefficient to the US real interest rate, β, is not significantly different from zero in Korea, Malaysia and the Philippines, while it is significant, but only a little smaller than one in Singapore and Japan. Furthermore, constant terms often turn out to be significant, which appears to imply the existence of persistent real interest rate differentials over time.

This result is not surprising, because equation (7) implicitly assumes either no deviations from UIP as well as PPP, or that they remain constant over time. In fact we knew from Figure 2.3 that these two components of real interest rate differentials show fairly volatile movements. Accordingly, next we estimate the following:

$$r_i = \alpha + \beta \, r_j + \gamma(i_i - i_j - \Delta s_{ij}) + \delta(\Delta s_{ij} + \Delta p_j - \Delta p_i) + e_{ij} \tag{8}$$

Equation (8) explicitly takes account of the impact of these two deviations on real interest rate differentials, the result of which is given in Table 2.3.

When we take account of deviations from UIP and PPP explicitly, constant terms turn out to be not significantly different from zero, suggesting no persistent real interest rate differentials in East Asia. In contrast with Table 2.2, the estimates of β become closer to one, particularly in Japan and Singapore. However, they become insignificant over the two sub-periods in Korea (1990–8), Malaysia (both 1980–9 and 1990–7) and the Philippines (1980–9), while they are significant over the whole period.

Figure 2.4 Real interest rate differentials in East Asia, 1980–98

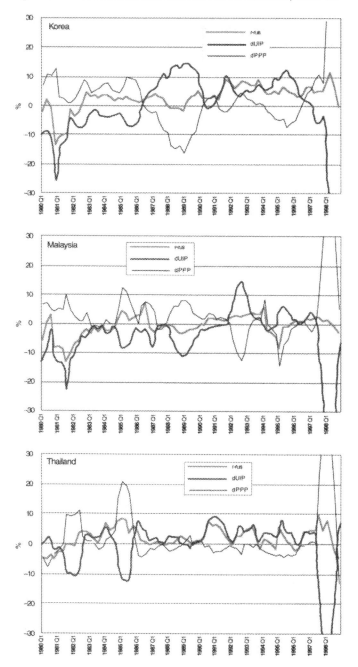

Figure 2.4 (continued)

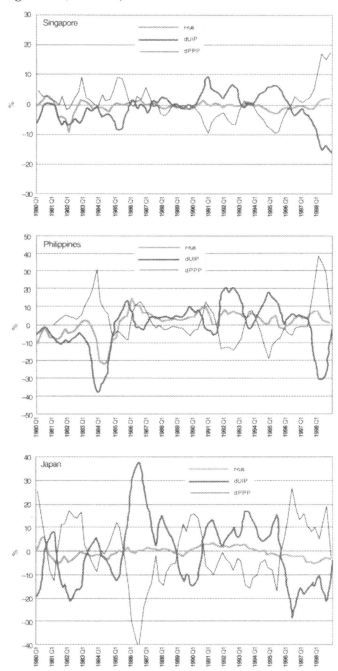

Source: IMF, IFS, CD-ROM.

Table 2.2　Real interest rate linkages in East Asia, 1980–98

	α		β	DW
Korea 1980:1–1995:4	6.525	**	−0.12	0.239
	0.968		*0.213*	
1980:1–1998:3	6.982	**	−0.142	0.316
	0.929		*0.212*	
1980:1–1989:4	3.358		0.37	0.272
	1.998		*0.364*	
1990:1–1997:2	7.742	**	−0.13	0.928
	0.644		*0.274*	
Singapore 1980:1–1995:4	0.39		0.666	**0.65
	0.428		*0.094*	
1980:1–1998:3	0.415		0.674	**0.605
	0.401		*0.091*	
1980:1–1989:4	2.041	*	0.407	*0.76
	0.833		*0.152*	
1990:1–1997:2	0.023		' 0.575	**0.518
	0.384		*0.164*	
Malaysia 1980:1–1995:4	2.823	**	−0.046	0.558
	0.844		*0.186*	
1980:1–1998:4	3.164	**	−0.083	0.539
	0.756		*0.172*	
1980:1–1989:4	2.194		0.098	0.443
	1.717		*0.312*	
1990:1–1997:2	4.086	**	−0.603	0.984
	0.948		*0.404*	
Philippines 1980:1–1995:4	6.638	**	−0.579	0.361
	1.632		*0.36*	
1980:1–1998:4	6.971	**	−0.603	#0.325
	1.457		*0.333*	
1980:1–1989:4	5.922		−0.483	0.271
	3.535		*0.644*	
1990:1–1997:2	5.483	**	0.086	0.757
	1.3		*0.554*	
Thailand 1980:1–1995:4	1.41	*	1.082	**0.455
	0.815		*0.179*	
1980:1–1998:4	1.605	*	1.069	**0.522
	0.824		*0.188*	
1980:1–1989:4	−2.263		1.691	**0.519
	1.464		*0.267*	
1990:1–1997:2	2.745	*	0.83	0.916
	1.152		*0.491*	
Japan 1980:1–1995:4	2.459	**	0.257	**0.361
	0.318		*0.068*	
1980:1–1998:4	1.588	**	0.332	**0.169
	0.453		*0.101*	
1980:1–1989:4	3.935	**	0.152	0.743
	0.56		*0.098*	
1990:1–1997:2	2.512	**	−0.145	0.151
	7.355		*0.313*	

Notes
1 Figures below the estimates are standard errors.
2 **, *, # denote 0.01, 0.05 and 0.10 significance levels, respectively.
3 Estimated equation: $r = \alpha + \beta \cdot rus + e$, where r, rus are domestic and US interest rates.

Table 2.3 Real interest rate linkages, UIP and PPP in East Asia, 1980–98

	α	β		γ		δ		DW
Korea								
1980:1–1998:3	0.586	0.871	**	0.961	**	0.964	**	2.227
	0.793	0.153		0.089		0.092		
1980:1–1989:4	0.699	0.856	**	1.01	**	1.014	**	2.138
	1.185	0.217		0.128		0.16		
1990:1–1997:2	2.649	0.578		0.687	*	0.68	*	2.358
	2.214	0.393		0.287		0.292		
Singapore								
1980:1–1998:3	0.37	0.99	**	1.405	**	1.408	**	1.98
	0.414	0.16		0.479		0.447		
1980:1–1989:4	0.208	0.996	**	1.426	*	1.551	*	1.984
	1.241	0.316		0.65		0.618		
1990:1–1997:2	0.024	1.103	**	1.29	**	1.268	**	1.954
	0.337	0.172		0.274		0.269		
Malaysia								
1980:1–1998:4	1.201	0.662	**	0.955	**	0.968	**	2.566
	0.821	0.21		0.178		0.212		
1980:1–1989:4	6.835	0.096		0.808	#	0.042		1.751
	5.257	0.608		0.401		1.225		
1990:1–1997:2	−0.389	1.095		1.375	#	1.294	*	2.839
	2.81	1.083		0.733		0.538		
Philippines								
1980:1–1998:4	0.879	0.774	**	0.967	**	0.974	**	2.186
	1.042	0.247		0.111		0.155		
1980:1–1989:4	2.418	0.546		1.033	**	1.036	**	2.466
	1.773	0.357		0.108		0.186		
1990:1–1997:2	−0.27	0.925	#	0.98	**	0.893	**	1.745
	1.999	0.539		0.282		0.276		
Thailand								
1980:1–1998:4	0.324	1.01	**	0.836	**	0.813	**	2.615
	0.696	0.157		0.183		0.187		
1980:1–1989:4	−1.076	1.226	**	0.92	**	0.852	**	2.314
	1.394	0.298		0.193		0.213		
1990:1–1997:2	1.04	0.936	*	0.659	**	0.453		2.58
	1.13	0.411		0.227		0.424		
Japan								
1981:1–1998:4	0.227	0.918	**	0.925	**	0.907	**	2.005
	0.313	0.124		0.271		0.333		
1981:1–1989:4	1.133	0.604	*	0.413		0.357		1.186
	1.143	0.274		0.379		0.441		
1990:1–1997:2	0.481	0.827	**	1.005	**	1.002	*	1.948
	0.521	0.226		0.133		0.15		

Notes
1 Figures below the estimates are standard errors.
2 **, *, # denote 0.01, 0.05 and 0.10 significance levels, respectively.
3 Estimated equation: r=a+γ*rus+*dUIP+d*dPPP, where dUIP and dPPP are deviations from
 Uncovered Interest Parity and Purchasing Power Parity, respectively.

Both deviations from the UIP and the PPP are found to be significantly different from zero in all economies over the whole period, while the PPP deviation loses significance over the sub-sample periods in Malaysia (1980–9), Thailand (1990–7) and Japan (1980–9).

From the above results, we can summarise what we have learned so far. First, real interest rate linkages to the international capital market are fairly strong during 1980–98 in East Asia, in the sense that no persistent real interest rate differentials can be detected. Second, nevertheless there is still room for foreign exchange risk premium and/or other deviations from UIP, to prevent the exploitation of potential profits implied by real interest rate differentials on the one hand, and medium-run changes in PPP exchange rates to hinder the equalisation of domestic and international real interest rates on the other.

MACROECONOMIC MANAGEMENT UNDER CAPITAL MARKET INTEGRATION

As suggested earlier, strong capital market integration has strong macroeconomic implications. We have been well aware that East Asia has become increasingly integrated with the international capital market, but it is not so clear exactly where it lies along the spectrum from autarchy to such strong integration as is found in the case of developed economies. This is one of the reasons why the monetary authorities in East Asia have failed to cope with the new environment in the Asian crisis. Since the crisis gives us a very impressive experiment (maybe too impressive) to test how to deal with capital market integration, we cannot but briefly touch upon the policy problems faced by the crisis economies.

For those concerned with developing economies, 1997 was an unforgettable year, because it proved that the Asia Pacific was not, after all, immune from the *tom yum* effect, the Asian version of the *tequila* effect. In fact, the present Asian economic crisis contains a full set of domestic banking crisis, currency crisis and contagion effects.[8] There seems to be nothing uniquely Asian in the crisis, however. In fact, one can lay the blame for the crisis on reckless risk management in the general process of domestic as well as external financial deregulation. Or one might argue that opening up the capital market tends to allow more room for domestic mismanagement, by magnifying market failure due to imperfect information problems.

The superior economic performance of developing economies in the Asia Pacific region has been characterised by increasing openness to the world economy and sustained macroeconomic stability. This characterisation holds true especially for Asian NIEs and some ASEAN economies. Among them, Korea and the ASEAN economies were hardest hit by the present crisis, while the other three capital exporting ones seemed far less affected. Consequently, the main focus will be given in this section to these four troubled economies.

As to the persistent external imbalance, the boom of the first half of the 1990s in the region eventually turned to bust. Even the remarkably high national savings could not match the excesses of private investment, which naturally resulted in persistent external imbalance. The monetary authorities tried to offset the impact of foreign capital inflow on domestic money supply via sterilisation, as well as by raising domestic interest rates and restricting external financial exposure, despite the general trend of domestic financial deregulation and external capital account liberalisation. These efforts, however, failed to prevent domestic investment from deteriorating in quality. Actually, the bust exposed the fundamental vulnerability of domestic financial systems in the region. The reverse was also true; the causality goes both ways. We have long been aware of the existence of this fundamental trilemma among monetary policy independence, exchange rate stability and free capital mobility. From this standpoint, one might say that Thailand tried, and failed, to attain the three incompatible goals simultaneously.

Large capital inflow has been often regarded as a problem for domestic macroeconomic stabilisation. Since the early 1980s, these dynamically growing economies experienced several waves of large capital inflow. Figure 2.5 shows movements of capital inflow and its components, as well as current account balances and increases in foreign exchange reserves. The figure makes it clear that, while large capital inflows were accompanied by large current account deficits, the former usually exceeded the latter, resulting in the accumulation of foreign exchange reserves.

Exchange Rate Management. Exchange rate stability had been one of the major macroeconomic policy targets in the Asia Pacific developing economies. Yet, the authorities in these economies eventually had to come to terms with the incompatibility of monetary policy independence, exchange rate stability and free capital movement. How to balance this trilemma has become a keen policy issue in the region.

Focusing on the four troubled economies in Asia, it seems that we should distinguish matters of *exchange rate risk* from those of *exchange rate levels*. On the latter, what matters here is whether the currencies in these economies have been overvalued to the extent that it aroused suspicion of depreciation/ devaluation in the near future.

As far as real effective exchange rates are concerned, there is no clear evidence of remarkable currency appreciation in these economies, at least as late as 1995–6, as discussed earlier. However, if we look at the bilateral real exchange rate with the US dollar and the Japanese yen (Figure 2.6) we observe, against the dollar, a gradual appreciation of around 10 per cent over 1990–6 for all, and then stability until the crisis (except for Korea, where the won depreciated in real terms). In contrast, against the yen, we find relatively significant depreciation of almost 40 per cent over 1990–5, and then appreciation on a similar scale over 1995–7.

Of course, this real appreciation against the yen in the recent period is because the real exchange rate between the dollar and the yen has also swung to a large extent during the period, and because these Asian economies have put more importance on dollar exchange rate stability. There does not

Figure 2.5 Current accounts, capital inflows and their composition

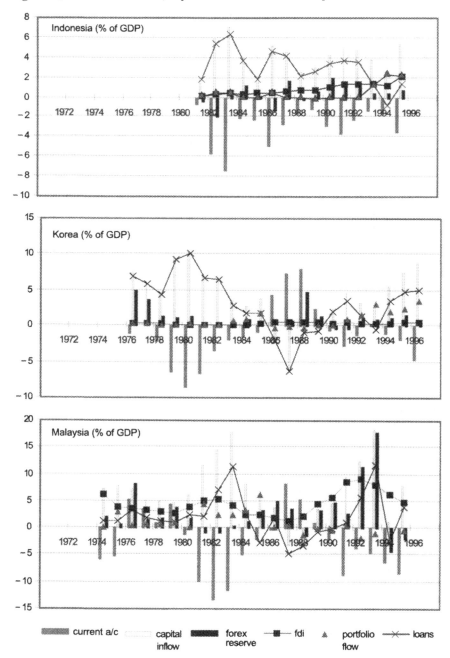

Figure 2.5 (continued)

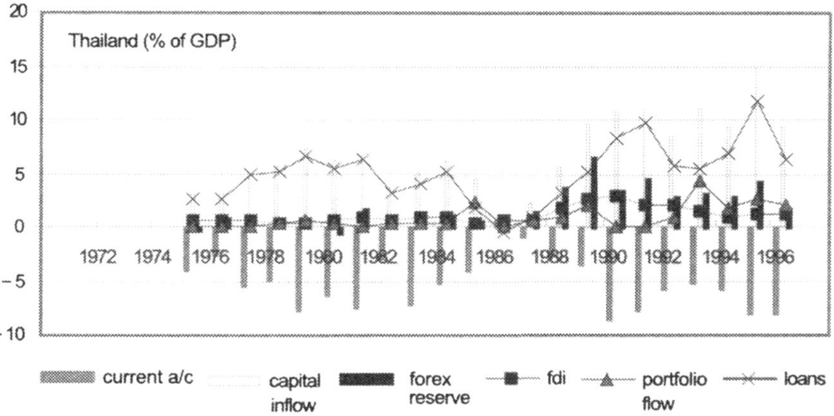

Source: IMF, IFS, CD-ROM.

appear to be any reason why this real appreciation against the yen was large enough to arouse market expectation of a depreciation in the near future. First, the real effective exchange rate would not show this much currency appreciation, since Japan's trade weight is less than 20 per cent in these economies. Second, the effect of relative price changes of this size on trade flow would not be very significant, and neither would be its impact on macroeconomic activity (IMF 1995).

Why do exchange rate policies matter in these economies? We would argue that exchange rate stability might give the wrong signals to investors, domestic as well as international. They are usually engaged in foreign exchange transactions in the US dollar in these economies (even Japanese banks do this). Exchange rate stability against the dollar means that these transactions are virtually currency-risk free. Accordingly, as long as the Thai monetary authorities stick to a virtually fixed exchange rate of the baht to the dollar, rational Thai managers would be attracted by external borrowing given significant interest rate differentials between the domestic and offshore (BIBF) capital markets. Unless alluring capital inflows generated systemic risks, there would be no problem. They did generate system risk, however.

Excess credit expansion would have been checked to some extent under more flexible exchange rate management. What matters with inflexible exchange rates in the four economies, especially Thailand, is not that the exchange rate levels were unrealistic, but that their inflexibilities distorted risk-taking transactions.

MACROECONOMIC LINKAGES

Measuring the degree of capital market integration is one way to assess the degree of macroeconomic interdependence, by focusing on transmission

Figure 2.6a Bilateral real exchange rates, Thailand, Malaysia, Korea and Indonesia
(relative to the yen)

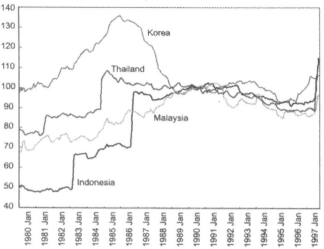

Figure 2.6b Bilateral real exchange rates, Thailand, Malaysia, Korea and Indonesia
(relative to the dollar)

Source: IMF, IFS, CD-ROM.

channels of macroeconomic impacts. Without doubt, macroeconomic
interdependence is realised not only through financial integration, but also
through real integration with external trade and foreign direct investment.
This latter aspect has been widely discussed elsewhere. Here, we examine
how macroeconomic variables affect and are affected as a result of these
increasing linkages through real and financial flows in East Asia.

In the early 1980s, developing economies, including those in the Asia Pacific region, suffered from a series of external shocks. The most serious shock, however, was the virtual severance of foreign capital inflow. This hit many developing economies in Latin America, Africa and other regions hard, but most of the Asia Pacific developing economies were fortunately either exempted or escaped quickly, with due reason.

Recently, capital exporters such as Hong Kong, Singapore and Taiwan appeared to be immune from (or at least far less affected by) the currency attacks. Only those with significant amounts of external debt have suffered. However, the market apprehends further currency depreciation in the future, because the process of currency attack is really self-realising in the case of external debtor economies. Currency depreciation magnifies the debt service burden; this deters recovery and aggravates the necessary adjustments, including currency depreciation.

How can we check or minimise the impact of this self-realising process? For the time being, we have little choice but to try every effort to prevent the abrupt severance or reversal of capital inflows to these economies. Alternatively, one might dream of monetary integration in East Asia, simply to be able to forget about currency crises. While it may sound too long a shot, it could be worth giving academic consideration to its possibility; we might then find that it is not so long a shot.

Cohesion in macroeconomic indicators

In examining this, we would like to compare East Asia with other comparable areas. Since our concern with macroeconomic interdependence in East Asia may oversee the possibility of monetary integration there in the future, it would be natural to select EU countries (hereafter, Europe) and regions in the United States (hereafter, US regions) as reference areas. Bearing in mind the theory of optimal currency area, US regions can be regarded as a post-monetary-integration area, and Europe as a pre-monetary-integration area.

As the first step towards reviewing macroeconomic interdependence, correlation and cohesion among selected macroeconomic indicators will be examined, using raw data, to present a general overview of the past and present situations in the region.

Kawai and Okumura (1996) examined correlation among such macroeconomic variables as growth rates, inflation and real exchange rates in the Pacific region (Asian NIEs, ASEAN4, China, Japan and the United States) during the period 1970–93, and found that there was a fairly high positive correlation among countries in the region in terms of some of these major macroeconomic variables. But how high is fairly high?

To answer this, the region is compared with counterpart regions. Then, the result of similar calculations for real GDP growth and domestic inflation are shown, measured by a GDP deflator, for the three distinct areas of East Asia, Europe and US regions over a few sub-periods. See Figure 2.7.

Figure 2.7 Correlations of growth and inflation

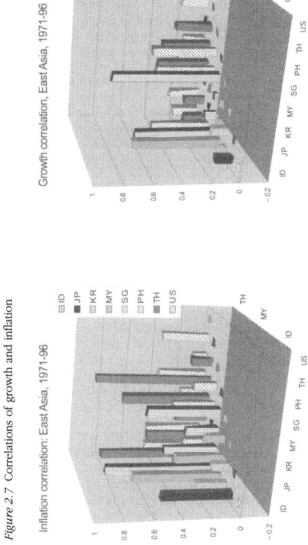

Inflation correlation: East Asia, 1971-96

Growth correlation, East Asia, 1971-96

Figure 2.7 (continued)

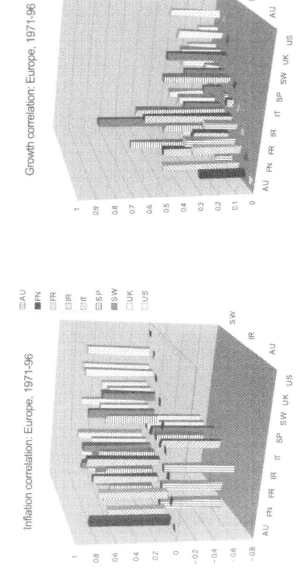

Inflation correlation: Europe, 1971-96

Growth correlation: Europe, 1971-96

Figure 2.7 (continued)

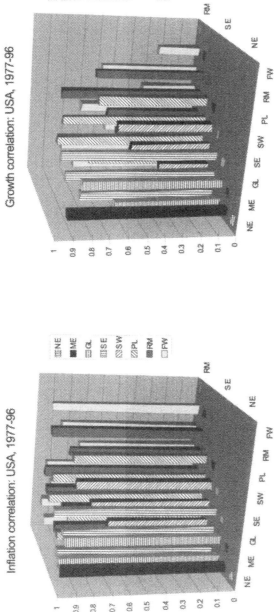

Inflation correlation: USA, 1977-96

Growth correlation: USA, 1977-96

As for inflation over the whole period, US regions show the highest positive correlation, followed by Europe. Correlation in inflation in East Asia is in fact the lowest among the three regions. Even if we divide the period into sub-periods, this general picture of East Asia does not change much, and we also find that the picture remains unchanged over time, though positive correlation reduces to a significant degree in Europe.

Turning to real GDP growth, while US regions show the highest positive correlation over the whole as well as sub-periods, positive correlation over the whole period makes little difference between Europe and East Asia, both of which show low correlation relative to the United States. One important difference between Europe and East Asia is that the correlation in the former seems to become higher in the more recent period, which is not the case in the latter.

To sum up, as far as the two macroeconomic indicators are concerned, it may be that their (positive) correlation in East Asia is far lower than within the United States, although not as high as in Europe. It is too early, however, to jump to the conclusion that East Asia is less integrated in macroeconomic terms than Europe. Observed changes in macroeconomic variables are the results of global and local exogenous shocks and endogenous responses to them. Before assessing the degree of macroeconomic interdependence, we must recognise the nature of the shocks and the pattern of the responses.

Shocks and adjustments[9]

In order to identify economic shocks, we use the structural VAR method of Blanchard and Quah (1989), decomposing a vector of first differentials of logarithmic real GDP and a GDP deflator into supply as well as demand shocks. Supply shocks are supposed to affect both real GDP (production) and GDP deflators (prices) in the long run, while demand shocks affect only prices.

Size of shocks. The larger the size of the underlying shocks, the greater the need to adjust by resorting to monetary, fiscal and exchange rate policies, and the more compelling the need for an independent economic policy response. In contrast to Bayoumi and Eichengreen (1993), we do not see any distinct features in terms of sizes of either supply or demand shocks across, as well as within, regions.[10] Their sizes are almost comparable across regions and there is little distinct regional bias within regions.

Correlation of shocks. Correlation coefficients measuring the association of supply as well as demand shocks can be compared among the three areas in Table 2.4 and Figure 2.8.

The overall picture is as follows: in both supply and demand shocks, the US regions are conspicuous in having significantly higher correlations than East Asia and Europe. Accordingly, one could say that there is not much difference between Asia and Europe as far as the degree of regional correlation among supply and demand shocks is concerned. One important difference between the two regions is that both supply and demand shocks are almost

Table 2.4 Correlations in demand and supply shocks

Correlations in demand shocks in East Asia, 1971–96	Indonesia	Japan	Korea	Malaysia	Singapore	Philippines	Thailand	USA
Indonesia	1.000							
Japan	−0.013	1.000						
Korea	0.024	−0.027	1.000					
Malaysia	0.358	0.049	0.084	1.000				
Singapore	0.500	0.059	0.227	0.522	1.000			
Philippines	0.391	−0.035	−0.030	0.447	0.284	1.000		
Thailand	−0.392	0.040	0.100	−0.500	−0.284	−0.149	1.000	
USA	−0.164	0.159	0.028	−0.122	−0.182	−0.102	0.014	1.000

Correlation in demand shocks in Europe, 1971–96	UK	Austria	Finland	France	Ireland	Italy	Spain	Sweden	USA
UK	1.000								
Austria	0.320	1.000							
Finland	0.332	0.492	1.000						
France	0.127	−0.042	0.034	1.000					
Ireland	−0.045	−0.061	−0.343	0.013	1.000				
Italy	0.085	−0.070	−0.158	0.393	0.177	1.000			
Spain	0.200	0.066	0.099	0.444	0.093	0.319	1.000		
Sweden	0.335	0.037	0.435	−0.019	0.238	−0.010	0.116	1.000	
USA	0.170	−0.006	−0.005	0.229	0.135	0.134	0.141	0.166	1.000

Correlation in demand shocks in US regions, 1977–96	New England	Mideast	Great Lakes	Southeast	Southwest	Plains	Rocky Mtains	Far West
New England	1.000							
Mideast	0.715	1.000						
Great Lakes	0.492	0.372	1.000					
Southeast	0.464	0.612	0.502	1.000				
Southwest	0.212	0.302	0.123	0.667	1.000			
Plains	0.410	0.311	0.657	0.533	0.563	1.000		
Rocky Mountains	0.491	0.475	0.700	0.585	0.374	0.662	1.000	
Far West	0.689	0.879	0.430	0.656	0.492	0.446	0.682	1.000

Table 2.4 (continued)

Correlations in supply shocks in East Asia, 1971–96

	Indonesia	Japan	Korea	Malaysia	Singapore	Philippines	Thailand	USA
Indonesia	1.000							
Japan	0.055	1.000						
Korea	−0.042	0.141	1.000					
Malaysia	−0.298	0.016	−0.023	1.000				
Singapore	0.228	0.046	0.042	−0.612	1.000			
Philippines	−0.022	0.026	0.031	−0.336	0.314	1.000		
Thailand	−0.538	−0.058	0.002	0.262	−0.413	0.137	1.000	
USA	−0.203	0.123	−0.004	0.117	−0.099	−0.063	0.110	1.000

Correlation in supply shocks in Europe, 1971–96

	UK	Austria	Finland	France	Ireland	Italy	Spain	Sweden	USA
UK	1.000								
Austria	0.009	1.000							
Finland	−0.006	0.263	1.000						
France	0.090	−0.019	−0.009	1.000					
Ireland	−0.011	−0.007	−0.186	−0.004	1.000				
Italy	−0.083	−0.064	0.048	0.134	0.143	1.000			
Spain	−0.066	0.088	0.129	−0.006	−0.119	0.018	1.000		
Sweden	0.103	−0.152	0.360	0.037	−0.129	0.111	0.040	1.000	
USA	0.125	0.072	−0.033	0.049	−0.173	−0.161	0.033	−0.078	1.000

Correlation in supply shocks in US regions, 1977–96

	New England	Mideast	Great Lakes	Southeast	Southwest	Plains	Rocky Mtains	Far West
New England	1.000							
Mideast	0.895	1.000						
Great Lakes	−0.685	−0.706	1.000					
Southeast	0.831	0.894	−0.753	1.000				
Southwest	0.478	0.589	−0.484	0.659	1.000			
Plains	−0.527	−0.635	0.640	−0.652	−0.772	1.000		
Rocky Mountains	−0.650	−0.703	0.934	−0.703	−0.565	0.673	1.000	
Far West	0.752	0.874	−0.703	0.749	0.567	−0.717	−0.772	1.000

Figure 2.8 Correlations of supply and demand shocks

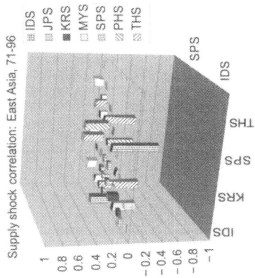

Supply shock correlation: East Asia, 71-96

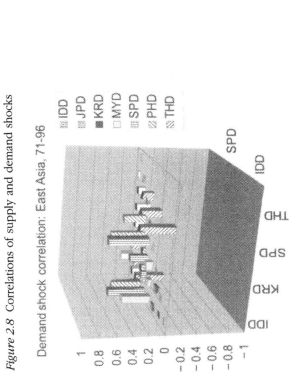

Demand shock correlation: East Asia, 71-96

Figure 2.8 (continued)

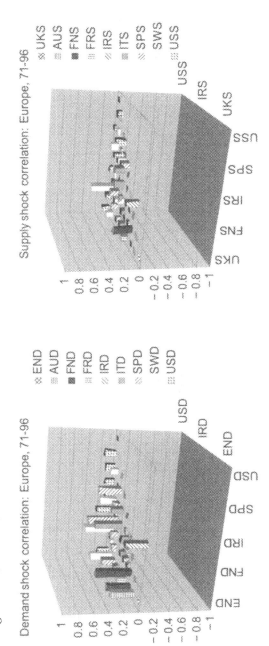

Demand shock correlation: Europe, 71-96

Supply shock correlation: Europe, 71-96

Figure 2.8 (continued)

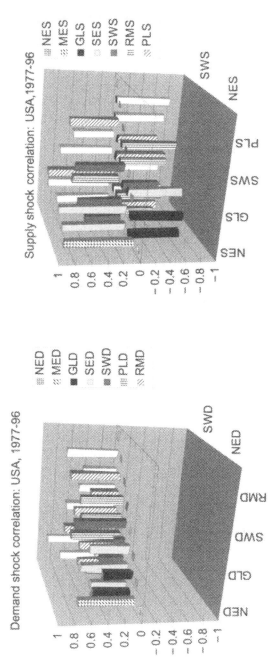

Demand shock correlation: USA, 1977-96

Supply shock correlation: USA,1977-96

Figure 2.9 Cohesion of shocks over time

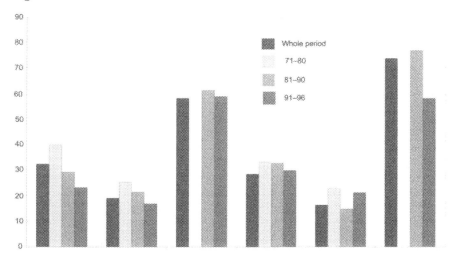

Source: Tamada (1999).

exclusively positively correlated across countries in Europe, except for Ireland, while they are often negatively correlated in East Asia.

More specifically, we can see positive correlation of demand shocks in Indonesia, Malaysia and Singapore, while their supply shocks do not show such association. Japan and Korea fail to show clear association within the region with both kinds of shocks. A similar pattern of association among shocks can be seen in Europe. Demand shocks are correlated among the United Kingdom, Sweden and Finland, and in France, Italy and Spain, but not among others within the region, while no particular correlation can be found in the case of supply shocks. In other words, with respect to correlations of supply and demand shocks within the regions, the contrast between US regions and the other two regions is clear, but this is not the case between East Asia and Europe.

Cohesion. Finally, the results of principal components analysis are summarised, for the correlation between demand and supply shocks, in Figure 2.9. For the total period, it is interesting to find that, while the shocks are explicitly more correlated in US regions than in the other two regions, they are relatively more correlated in East Asia than in Europe. Note that over the successive sub-periods, there seems to be a declining instead of increasing trend of correlation of demand shocks across all the regions, while we see no such trends in the case of supply shocks.

Patterns of adjustment to shocks. We now turn to the responses of economies to shocks. If we simplify adjustment mechanisms in the three regions, we may assume that, while US regions can be characterised by high

Figure 2.10 Impulse responses of prices

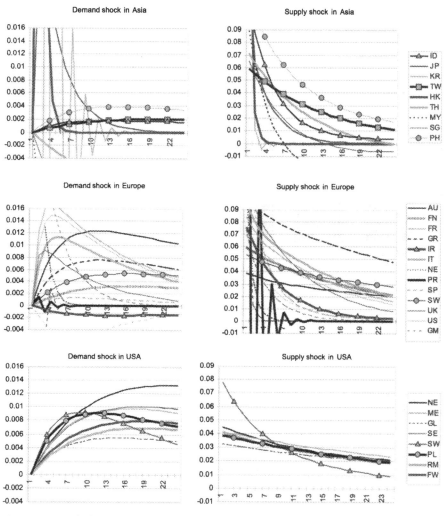

Source: Tamada (1999).

factor mobility with fixed exchange rates, and Europe by low factor mobility with exchange rate flexibility, East Asia comes in between the two. That is, though East Asia, apart from Japan, lacks labour mobility, its exchange rate flexibility is more or less limited in terms of the US dollar, but not necessarily against other major currencies (Kohsaka 1997). Under the circumstances, how can we distinguish differences in adjustment patterns among the three regions to the shocks? To do that, we use the impulse response functions associated with the structural VAR models. The impulse responses of prices

Figure 2.11 Impulse responses of production

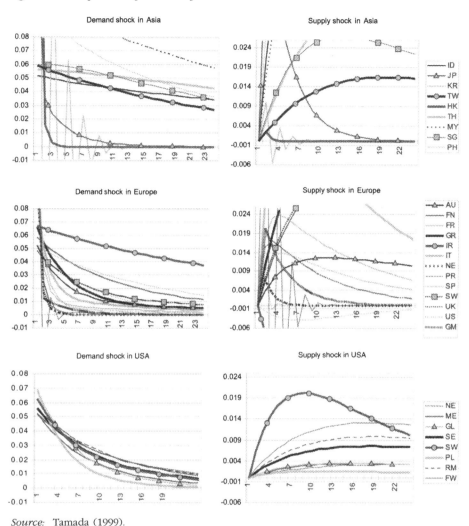

Source: Tamada (1999).

are shown in Figure 2.10, and those of production in Figure 2.11, over the total period as well as for the 1990s, in the three regions under comparison.

In the case of price responses, the speed of adjustment can be seen by looking at how soon prices converge to their long-run equilibrium levels. From Figure 2.10, we find that there seem to be fewer differences in adjustment speed across regions in the case of demand shocks than in supply shocks. While there are several countries in East Asia that show a faster adjustment speed than US regions, adjustment in the latter is generally less dispersed.

These contrasts with US regions hold true for Europe, and we see virtually no difference between East Asia and Europe.

As for responses of production, since demand shock has no long-term effect, production is expected to return to the original level over time; this is depicted by Figure 2.11, where US regions demonstrate generally faster and more cohesive adjustments to both demand and supply shocks than East Asia. This contrast with US regions appears less, this time, for Europe than for Asia, while Asia seems to need a particularly larger adjustment to supply shocks.

When we look at impulse response functions estimated over the most recent period, 1991–6, we notice that adjustment speeds appear to have accelerated recently, in the sense that more adjustment tends to be concentrated in earlier time periods; this holds for all the three regions. Nevertheless, the above-mentioned distinctions in East Asia, Europe and US regions appear to remain unchanged.

What have we learned from the above exercise? As far as the adjustment speeds of prices based on past behavioural patterns are concerned, there is little difference between East Asia and Europe in both supply and demand shock cases; both are considered to have less labour mobility but (at least, potentially) more flexible exchange rates than US regions. However, the adjustment speeds of production appear to be higher in Europe than in East Asia, which is magnified in the case of supply shocks.

To sum up, as pre-monetary-integration regions, East Asia shows little difference from Europe in terms of the size and correlations of shocks, while in terms of adjustment speed of production, we find not a small difference between East Asia and Europe. Why is this so? Is it because of differences in policy responses or in economic structures? We have no definite answer to the question. At least, however, we have found that, if Europe can afford to reap the benefit of monetary integration by converging into one Europe, like the US regions, East Asia is not totally remote from being qualified in terms of shocks and adjustment.

CONCLUSION

Private capital inflows have increased sharply since the late 1980s and/or early 1990s in emerging market economies in East Asia and Latin America. While the huge flows carry both blessings and risks, they certainly change the macroeconomic properties of those economies, forcing monetary authorities to grope for a new set of economic policy management tools. Increased integration with the international capital market appears to be ensured, not only by the larger size of capital inflows, but also by the closer interest rate arbitrage with nominal short-term as well as real medium-term financial transactions. Despite this, we find that real interest rate differentials are occasionally not insignificant, as well as persistent, mainly because of medium-run volatility in yen–dollar exchange rates.

The Asian currency crisis exposed capital market integration as a double-edged sword. Prior exchange rate stabilisation paradoxically turned out to destabilise exchange rates, by distorting risk-taking behaviours. The monetary authorities tried in vain to challenge the basic trilemma of policy goals. Binding their hands with virtually fixed exchange rates, they could not afford to free capital mobility with monetary autonomy. Their alternative options are either timely exchange rate realignments or permanent fixed exchange rates.

Regional monetary integration or collective fixed exchange rates could be one possible solution to the new reality of capital market integration in the regions of East Asia, which are closely linked together through trade and investment flows. The moot point to this solution, however, would be whether giving up monetary autonomy by adhering to one currency is a reasonable choice, in an uncertain world.

In the European Union, the new unified currency started to circulate and its monetary integration appeared to reach the final stage where virtual as well as formal integration through trade and investment has been realised over the past decades. It remains to be seen whether this macroeconomic integration with one monetary and multiple fiscal authorities will work well or not.

Comparing with pre-integration (Europe) and post-integration (US regions) cases, we found that the US regions are far better suited to monetary integration than East Asia. But we claim that East Asia is not totally unsuited to monetary integration, because there is not much difference, in terms of shock distribution and adjustment speeds, between East Asia and Europe.

Though our speculation, based on the above framework of analysis, is unavoidably of a tentative nature, since monetary integration by itself would reshape the shock distribution and the adjustment speed, it would not be fair to over-emphasise the distinctive differences between the US regions and other pre-integration regions, including East Asia. Rather, by identifying the nature of shocks and the factors behind adjustment mechanism, it may be possible to pursue a better currency arrangement to realise sustainable region-wide currency stability in the APEC region.

In view of the double-edged-sword nature of capital market integration, we must be prepared for some intrinsic self-fulfilling aspects of international capital flows:

1   On the one hand, virtually fixed exchange rates for a single major currency should be avoided, and replaced by a basket of relevant major currencies; these should, if necessary, be re-aligned in a timely and flexible manner.
2   On the other hand, capital flows should be well monitored and under adequate supervision, and excess volatility in capital flows caused by the speculative and herding behaviour of international investors should, if necessary, be checked by occasional, but minimal, capital controls.

3   Furthermore, noting the existence of regional biases in international investment flows, some sort of regional macroeconomic coordination framework may be useful, in terms not only of peer monitoring and policy dialogues, but also of currency stabilisation funds. Such a framework could be expected to provide reliable signals and a safety net to the market.

Then, given that this academic experiment may seem far-fetched and acknowledging that there are many qualifications involved, the possibility of one currency, or of monetary integration in the APEC region, is worth studying seriously.

4   Careful research should be undertaken to ensure that, as a pre-monetary-unification region, East Asia behaves with relatively little difference from Europe in terms of economic shocks and adjustments to them.

5   If this is the case, we should very carefully watch European steps, because monetary integration is one fundamental way out of the kind of currency turmoil experienced in the Asian crisis.

NOTES

1   According to Bank of International Settlements (BIS) (1997: Table VI.1), net private capital inflows to Asia amounted to US$79.8 billion in 1996 as against $70 billion for Latin America, while the inflows were $6.6 billion annually over the 1980s in Asia, as against $6.2 billion in Latin America. As for bank loans, Asia received $72.3 billion in 1996, as against $21.8 billion in Latin America (Table VII.3). Differences in patterns of capital inflows in East Asia and Latin America are discussed in more detail in Kohsaka 1996.

2   A clear negative correlation between interest rates in industrial countries and financial asset prices in emerging markets can be observed from 1993 (BIS 1997: Graph VI.1). Fernandez-Arias (1996) found international interest rates to be the most important determinant of capital flows to emerging markets.

3   Recent trends in private as well as public savings in the Pacific region are discussed in Kohsaka 1998.

4   There are several reasons why saving and investment could be correlated even if economies are highly integrated financially. See, for example, Obstfeld (1986) and Montiel (1994).

5   The result of an ADF test with both a constant and a time trend shows that all investment as well as saving ratios have a unit root at a 5% significance level.

6   Ito, Isard and Symansky (1999) find that the B–S effect is not necessarily the case in Southeast Asian economies; namely, their real exchange rates do not show any appreciation trends along with their high economic growth.

7   We use three-month Euro dollar and yen rates for the United States and Japan, respectively, and money market rates for the other economies. Since they are not exactly comparable assets, their quarterly average figures must be regarded as proxies for medium-run market-determined interest rates.

8   See Eichengreen, Rose and Wyplosz (1996) for an example of a contagion effect.

9   This and the following sub sections draw on estimation results provided by Tamada (1999). The author is grateful for her permission to quote extensively from this work.

10   Bayoumi and Eichengreen (1993) found that, over the period of 1962–88, in the case of supply shocks, peripheral countries experience supply shocks larger

than core countries in Europe, while those of US regions are similar to those in the EC core and lower than those of the EC periphery. In the case of demand shocks, however, they found that, while they are mostly the same in the EC, the US regions have larger shocks than the EC.

REFERENCES

Bank for International Settlements (BIS) (1997) *Annual Report 1996/97*, Basel.

Bayoumi, T. and Eichengreen, B. (1993) 'Shocking aspects of European Monetary Union', in F. Torres and F. Giavazzi (eds) *Adjustment and Growth in the European Monetary Union*, Cambridge: Cambridge University Press: 193–228.

Bhanupong Nidhiprabha (1997) 'Macroeconomic management and development process: The Southeast Asian perspective', paper presented at the Workshop on Comparative African & East Asian Development Experiences, Johannesburg, South Africa, 3–6 November.

Blanchard, O. and Quah, D. (1989) 'The dynamic effects of aggregate demand and supply disturbances', *American Economic Review* 79: 655–73.

Chinn, M. and Frankel, J. (1994) 'Financial links around the Pacific rim: 1982–1992', in R. Glick and M. Hutchison (eds) *Exchange Rate Policies in Pacific Basin Countries* New York: Cambridge University Press.

de Brouwer, G. (1996) 'Interest parity conditions as indicators of financial integration in East Asia', discussion paper, Canberra: Australian National University.

de Brouwer, G. and Gower, L. (1996) 'Covered interest parity in the Asia–Pacific region', paper presented at the International Symposium on Macroeconomic Interdependence in the Asia–Pacific Region, Economic Planning Agency, Tokyo, October.

Dooley, M., Frankel, J. and Mathieson, D.J. (1987) 'International capital mobility: What do saving–investment correlations tell us?', *IMF Staff Papers* 34: 503–30.

Eichengreen, B., Rose, A. and Wyplosz, C. (1996) 'Contagious currency crisis', *NBER Working Paper* no. 5681, July.

Feldstein, M. and Horioka, C. (1980) 'Domestic saving and international capital flows', *Economic Journal* 90: 314–29.

Fernandez-Arias, E. (1996) 'The new wave of private capital inflows: Push or pull?' *Journal of Development Economics* 48: 389–418.

Fry, M. (1986) 'Terms-of-trade dynamics in Asia: An analysis of national saving and domestic investment responses to terms-of-trade changes in 14 Asian LDCs', *Journal of International Money and Finance* 5: 57–73.

Glick, R. and Hutchison, M. (1990) 'Financial liberalization in the Pacific Basin: Implications for real interest rate linkages', *Journal of Japanese and International Economies* 41: 36–48.

Glick, R. and Moreno, R. (1994) 'Capital flows and monetary policy in East Asia', *Pacific Basin Working Paper Series* no. PB94-08, Federal Reserve Bank of San Francisco.

Goldsborough, D. and Teja, R. (1991) 'Globalisation of financial markets and implications for Pacific Basin countries', *IMF Working Paper* no. 34.

International Monetary Fund (IMF) (1995) 'Exchange rate movements and their impacts on trade and investment in the APEC region', *IMF Discussion Paper*, October.

Ito, T., Isard, P. and Symansky, S. (1999) 'Economic growth and real exchange rate: An overview of the Balassa–Samuelson hypothesis in Asia', in T. Ito and A.O. Krueger (eds) *Changes in Exchange Rates in Rapidly Developing Countries*, Chicago: University of Chicago Press.

Kawai, M. and Okumura, T. (1996) 'Macroeconomic interdependence in East Asia', in M. Kawai (ed.) *Asian Financial and Capital Markets*, Nihonkeizai Shinbunsha, Tokyo (in Japanese).

Kohsaka, A. (1996) 'Interdependence through capital flows in the Pacific Asia and the Role of Japan', in T. Ito and A.O. Krueger (eds) *Financial Deregulation and Integration in East Asia*, Chicago: The University of Chicago Press.

—— (ed.) (1997) *Exchange Rate Fluctuations and Macroeconomic Management*, Japan Committee for Pacific Economic Outlook, Kansai Economic Research Center, Osaka, July.

—— (ed.) (1998) *Domestic Saving in the Pacific Region*, Osaka: Pacific Economic Outlook/Structure, Japan Committee for Pacific Economic Outlook, Kansai Economic Research Center, November.

Montiel, P. (1994) 'Capital mobility in developing countries: Some measurement issues and empirical estimates', *World Bank Economic Review* 8: 311–50.

Obstfeld, M. (1986) 'Capital mobility in the world economy: Theory and measurement', *Carnegie–Rochester Conference Series on Public Policy* 24: 55–103.

Okura, M. (1996) 'Recent development of real interest rate linkages in East Asian economies', paper presented at the International Symposium on Macroeconomic Interdependence in the Asia–Pacific Region, Economic Planning Agency, Tokyo, October.

Tamada, K. (1999) 'A Possibility of Monetary Integration in East Asia', Unpublished M.A. Thesis, Graduate School of Economics, Osaka University.

3 Trade and investment liberalisation and facilitation

Ippei Yamazawa and Shujiro Urata

APEC LIBERALISATION: ITS PROCESS AND CHARACTERISTICS

In 1994 the Bogor Declaration set the ambitious target of 'achieving free and open trade in the region by 2010 and 2020'. In 1995 the Osaka Action Agenda (OAA) provided a guideline for implementing policy measures to reach this target: trade and investment liberalisation and facilitation (TILF). It adopted a unique modality for TILF: concerted unilateral liberalisation (CUL), in which individual members announce their liberalisation plans (individual action plans, IAPs) unilaterally and then watch each other's implementation so as to encourage all members to achieve the Bogor target by the set deadline. In 1996 APEC leaders adopted the Manila Action Plans for APEC (MAPA), in which all APEC members submitted their IAPs; this has been implemented since 1997.

Then the currency crisis hit the East Asian economies, halting the rapid growth of the previous decade. Governments have all struggled to overcome the economic downturn. In spite of increased domestic resistance, both the Vancouver and Kuala Lumpur APEC meetings confirmed continued efforts towards liberalisation. APEC must play its role to help Asian members restore the growth path in the long term, through strengthening the cooperative activities associated with TILF.

IAPs are the primary mechanism for the implementation of APEC's TILF agenda. However, the CUL has its merits and demerits. Its obvious merit is that APEC was able to start liberalisation and facilitation by all its members under this flexible modality as soon as two years after the Bogor Declaration. On the other hand, its demerit is that the achievement of APEC's liberalisation is not readily visible. IAPs are commitments by individual economies to liberalisation; their actual implementation needs to be confirmed by review and monitoring.

Our JANCPEC project attempted a quantitative assessment of individual members' progress toward the Bogor target, based on the 1996 IAPs and 1997 IAPs and collective action plans (CAPs) (JANCPEC 1997 and 1998). The Osaka Action Agenda defined the Bogor target in fifteen TILF areas. We scored individual economies' current state and future commitment in thirteen areas. These included tariff, non-tariff measures, services, investment, standard and conformance, customs procedures, intellectual property rights, competition policy, government procurement, deregulation, rules of origin, dispute mediation and business mobility.

Our assessment conveys mixed results. Generally speaking, with regard to liberalisation, many economies committed themselves to liberalisation in concrete figures only for a short period (up to 2000); their commitments are characterised as 'UR agreement + a'. However, 'a' turned out to be small in many economies and areas. At the Manila APEC meeting, all economies were urged to revise their IAPs every year, but their additions turned out to be minimal in 1997 and 1998. We cannot expect a big addition leading up to 2000 when the implementation of the Uruguay Round agreements is completed and the new World Trade Organisation (WTO) round starts. Individual economies tend to refrain from offering any new liberalisation commitments before new negotiations. On the other hand, the prospects are brighter in the area of facilitation. Thanks to the encouragement of the CAPs, it is likely that the objectives set by the Osaka Action Agenda will be achieved earlier than the Bogor deadline for both industrialised and developing economies.

In this chapter we apply a similar quantitative assessment to the 1998 IAP/CAPs submitted at the Kuala Lumpur APEC meeting. APEC's senior officials have been conducting their own review and monitoring of each other's IAPs since 1998, but their results have not yet been released outside the Senior Officials' Meeting (SOM). It is important for APEC to make its progress towards the Bogor target widely known to the public, in order to obtain public support for the TILF process. We hope our assessment will supplement their efforts in this direction.

Early voluntary sectoral liberalisation (EVSL) was introduced as a breakthrough during the slow liberalisation of IAPs under the Osaka Action Agenda. EVSL is also a part of collective action plans to be implemented jointly by individual economies. Its precedent, the Information Technology Agreement (ITA), aimed at removing all tariffs and non-tariff measures (NTMs) on semi-conductors and other parts and material input to information technology equipment by 2000. The ITA was adopted at the APEC Leaders' Meeting and then forwarded to the WTO Ministerial Meeting in Singapore just two weeks later, and was adopted as a legally binding treaty.

Encouraged by the success of the ITA, the Canadian chair proposed to accelerate the implementation of EVSL by two years from 2000. The Vancouver APEC meeting finally designated fifteen sectors (nine sectors as high priority) and agreed to work out their implementation during 1998. EVSL was designed to achieve not only the elimination of tariffs and NTMs, but also to implement facilitation and economic and technical cooperation (Ecotech) measures. However, its proposed modality of liberalisation has changed to a package deal with less flexibility, and was resisted by a few members. The APEC leaders failed to adopt it on consensus in 1998, and forwarded it for further negotiation at the WTO. EVSL provides a good case study to examine the nature of APEC liberalisation and its links with WTO liberalisation.

The next section examines the structure of IAPs and CAPs, and proposes a methodology for assessing them. We aim to assess the individual economies' progress in an objective and consistent manner, which is different from the conventional practice of 'focusing on highlights'. The third section applies this methodology to the 1998 IAPs and gives a score matrix of eighteen economies times thirteen areas. This will provide an objective assessment of how far individual economies have proceeded toward the Bogor target in individual TILF areas. This is followed by an analysis of the score matrix by individual economies, and shows how each economy has progressed in comparison with the APEC average. Three new members, Peru, Russia and Vietnam, participated in APEC in 1998, and they all submitted their first IAPs. However, they are not included in the foregoing assessment because of the absence of supplementary data for assessing their IAPs. Instead, we provide a brief overview of these economies.

The fifth section analyses EVSL, which was promoted to supplement the APEC liberalisation through IAPs in 1997 and 1998 but was derailed at the Kuala Lumpur APEC meeting in November 1998. It will clarify how APEC liberalisation is linked with WTO liberalisation. The final section summarises our analyses in the foregoing sections, characterises APEC liberalisation, and assesses the prospects for its probable achievements over the first five years. Several policy recommendations will be presented regarding challenges and opportunities for APEC in the twenty-first century.

STRUCTURE OF INDIVIDUAL ACTION PLANS AND METHODOLOGY OF ASSESSMENT

APEC has adopted a unique modality of implementing liberalisation and facilitation – concerted unilateral liberalisation. That is, individual member economies announce unilaterally their own liberalisation and facilitation programs and implement them in accordance with their domestic rules. However, individual APEC economies closely watch each other's liberalisation program and its implementation. They feel obliged to submit liberalisation programs as broad-ranging as their neighbours'. They are encouraged to implement in line with their commitments. APEC relies upon 'peer pressure' among members to urge all members to join in liberalisation.

This modality was regarded sometimes as unassertive in comparison with the Western approach of negotiating, as with GATT and WTO, a liberalisation agreement that is legally binding, so that the signatories will be punished and sanctioned if they fail to implement their commitments. At the initial stage of APEC, this legalistic approach was unacceptable to Asian members. However, this should not be understood as a reluctance by Asian members to commit to liberalisation. Asian members have implemented trade and investment liberalisation unilaterally for a decade since the mid-1980s and know that that era's high growth was based on their open economic policy. Continued efforts for liberalising their trade and investment are indispensable for further growth; this was reflected in their leaders' commitment to the Bogor Declaration. This new modality was based on this past experience and called for unilateral liberalisation in a concerted manner within the Osaka Action Agenda. This is a practical way of promoting liberalisation without losing the momentum enhanced by the Bogor Declaration. It would take another several years if we were to try to change APEC to a negotiating body such the WTO.

The Osaka Action Agenda is characterised as follows. First, it has a comprehensive coverage of fifteen areas, including both border and domestic measures. Liberalisation commitments take different forms between areas. Second, the eighteen APEC members differ greatly in their current level of impediments to trade and investment. Although all members started liberalising simultaneously, two tracks were set: one for industrialised members finishing by 2010 and the other for developing members finishing by 2020.

All these factors deny us any straightforward comparison of the IAPs across the eighteen members and fifteen areas. A member's IAP can only be assessed properly based on profound knowledge of its current level of impediments. Own-country assessment is highly recommended for economists in APEC member states. However, it may still be worthwhile attempting a quick comparative review of the IAPs across all economies.

Individual members' commitments to their IAPs can be assessed against the common format of IAPs in a matrix of fifteen areas times three time-frames (short, intermediate and long term). Three types of response are identified: (a) some members commit to concrete measures with a clear time frame, while others either (b) just state their intention of making efforts to achieve the Bogor target, or (c) say they will examine their current measures for possible amendment. By and large, many members committed themselves to (a) in their short-term measures, while (b) and (c) prevail in intermediate and long-term measures. Indeed, we cannot expect detailed implementation plans covering fifteen to twenty-five years. However, our assessment will be based on the short-term measures, and we will examine whether they assure us whether there is sufficient impetus to achieve the Bogor target in 2010 and 2020.

Tariff reduction toward the Bogor target

Our approach is best illustrated in the case of tariff reduction. Most members indicate their plans for tariff reduction up to 2000. Some members attach time schedules for reducing down to zero, or sectoral details. Many members commit to the Uruguay Round (UR) plus alpha, but a significant difference is observed between members.

Figure 3.1 compares a member's tariff reduction, committed to in its IAP (IAP line), with its Uruguay Round commitment (UR line) as well as the reference line connecting the current applied tariff rate with 0 per cent by

Figure 3.1 Tariff reduction toward the Bogor target

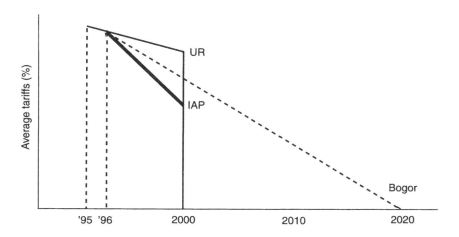

2020 (Bogor line). The UR line declines for 1995–2000, while the IAP line starts from the 1996 level on the UR line and declines faster than the UR line, representing a greater tariff reduction than the UR commitment. Furthermore, it declines faster than the Bogor line, implying that this member will achieve the Bogor target before 2020. Another member's IAP line may come above the Bogor line, implying that its IAP commitment is not big enough to achieve the Bogor target by 2020. The Bogor line for an industrialised member reaches 0 per cent by 2010. Only simple average rates for all commodities are plotted here.

Figure 3.1 reveals elements essential to our assessment task:

- the IAP commitment is quantified,
- it is compared with a similarly quantified reference path to the Bogor target, and
- both the IAP commitment and the Bogor target are compared with the current level so that it clearly shows how much still remains to be liberalised.

These elements give us clues as to how to assess IAPs in other liberalisation areas. If we can quantify NTMs and other impediments to services, trade and foreign investment, we will be able to monitor the individual members' efforts towards liberalisation. In assessing the IAPs for NTMs, services and investment, we must determine not only the future commitment to liberalisation but also the current level of impediments. Then we will be able to draw the Bogor line for other liberalisation areas, similar to those in the analysis of tariffs above. The IAPs are designed to report on the current state as well, but we often have to rely on other supplementary information. The tariff database and NTM database prepared by APEC serve this purpose.

Facilitation measures

Other areas are often grouped as facilitation measures. They are concerned with reducing the cost of doing business, by enhancing the transparency and certainty of rules, legislation and standards, and harmonising them between member economies; these are equally important to liberalisation in the APEC process. However, no agreed checklist has yet been established, and straightforward comparison is difficult.

In areas such as customs procedure, standard and conformance, and business mobility, there are some agreed checklists, and researchers can assess individual IAPs against them. Another approach is to examine the Osaka Action Agenda and the Chair's Common Format carefully, draw a scenario towards the Bogor target, and assess the IAPs against that scenario. In many areas the Bogor target results in the harmonisation of rules, legislation and standards to international norms.

In these areas, an economy has to (a) establish domestic rules or legal frameworks, (b) provide sufficient information and make this transparent to both local and foreign firms, and then (c) either mutually recognise each other's rules and framework, or adjust its own to the international rules and framework. Developed economies have already passed (a), committed to (b), and expressed their intention to proceed to (c). However, many developing economies have to achieve (a) first, and take time to proceed to (c). Thus our assessment of facilitation areas takes into consideration the current stage of preparedness of individual economies and the distance to the Bogor target, which is comparable to the Bogor line in the analysis of tariffs.

Collective action plans

The IAP drafting has improved since MAPA in 1996 in the following three respects. First, a concise summary table attached to the IAPs has enabled easier access to the IAPs. The IAPs have remained as voluminous as last year, but almost all members attached a Summary of Specific Changes to their IAPs, five- to ten-page tables of 'Commitment Achieved' and 'New Commitment Entered Into'.

Second, the CAPs have been strengthened, and have helped the IAPs to be implemented in a concerted manner. This is especially the case in the facilitation areas. CAPs were included for this purpose in the Osaka Action Agenda, and many members drafted their IAPs according to the CAP guidelines for customs procedures and standard and conformance. In 1997 the Committee for Trade and Investment (CTI) established subcommittees or expert groups, and designated convenors in charge of individual areas. The convenors have taken initiatives in urging member governments to participate in collective actions. In other words, visible progress has been made in areas under convenors with strong initiative, which is very APEC-style. Many IAPs reported on their participation in CAPs in 1997.

The relationship between CAP and IAP needs to be explained here. CAPs are concerned with joint actions but, under the APEC modality, individual members participate in them voluntarily; individual economies report on their participation in their IAPs. Participation in CAPs is often a very important step toward the Bogor target, especially in facilitation and Ecotech areas. Therefore we do not assess the CAPs themselves, but give credits to each member's participation in them in individual areas.

Nevertheless, a basic problem with the IAPs remains unresolved. This is the 'positive list formula', in which the IAPs report only the impediments to be liberalised and not the impediments which will still remain imposed. No systematic and comparable data are readily available to supplement the IAPs and provide a comprehensive list of existing impediments. This is especially the case in NTMs and services.

Assessment procedure

Our assessment procedure is as follows. For each of the thirteen areas, we first examine the Osaka Action Agenda and the Chair's Common Format, and draw a scenario toward the Bogor target for the area. The scenario often takes the form of several points against which individual economies are checked, whether they have already cleared them or not. We read the IAPs of eighteen economies and assessed them against this scenario, thus enabling consistent comparison of the eighteen economies according to the same scenario. We adopted the same grading system, with a full mark of 100. This procedure was adopted in our first assessment last year, but this year we added a common grading system, as follows, in order to secure the consistency and comparability of our assessment between different areas.

First, our assessment consists of both 'current state' and 'commitment to future liberalisation', as in the first assessment. This is consistent with APEC's modality of concerted unilateral liberalisation. Under the CUL, each economy announces unilaterally its liberalisation plan and implements it while other members watch. The IAP commitment itself is the important first step toward future liberalisation, and should be given due credit. But how shall we weigh the current state against the commitment to liberalisation?

We give a full mark (100) to a perfect current state – that is, achieving the Bogor target; and 50 points to an economy halfway to the Bogor target. We award 25 points if it commits to complete liberalisation in future; altogether 75 points. It will get the remaining 25 points only after it has actually implemented liberalisation. We identify two stages of achievement in relation to one checkpoint.

The current state plus commitment to liberalisation add up to the total score, as follows:

(a) half achieved and another half committed: 50+25=75
(b) half achieved, but no commitment: 50+0=50

(c) no achievement, but committed to complete achievement: 0+50=50
(d) no achievement, but committed to halfway achievement: 0+25=25

Using this scoring system the current state and future commitment are scored consistently.[1]

In our assessment report on the 1997 IAP (Yamazawa 1997, 1998) both current state and future commitment are scored according to this system, consistently across all areas.

ASSESSMENT OF THE 1998 IAPs: ASSESSMENT BY AREAS

The same scoring system was applied to the 1998 IAPs in this study, which resulted in a score matrix of eighteen economies times thirteen areas (Table 3.1). We scored individual economies according to a set of checkpoints for individual areas derived from the detailed examination of the Osaka Action Agenda, Chair's Common Format at MAPA, and convenors' reports on CAPs. Our methodology was elaborated in our last year's report (Yamazawa 1998, Part 2, Chapters 1–13). For the present study we adopted the same checkpoints and scoring system as for 1998, except for two areas: competition policy and deregulation. The appendix to this chapter includes the revised methodology of the two areas; 1998's report (Yamazawa 1998) should be referred to regarding other areas.[2]

The results of our quantitative assessment are summarised in Table 3.1. All the scores are measured along a scale from 0 to 100 as a full mark. The table tells us the score composition of our assessment in individual areas and the achievement of individual members toward the Bogor target. Below we shall review our assessment by areas.

Tariffs

The Osaka Action Agenda (1995) set the objective for the area of tariffs of achieving free and open trade in the Asia Pacific region by a) progressively reducing tariffs, and b) ensuring the transparency of APEC economies' respective tariff regimes.

Our assessment is mainly based on the current level of average tariffs and commitment to reduction for the next four to five years. Many economies

Table 3.1 A numerical illustration of scoring system

	Current state	Commit to achieving one step up	Commit to achieving two steps up
Complete achievement	4	—	—
Halfway achievement	2	+1	—
No achievement	0	+1	+2

reported on their tariff reduction to meet the Uruguay Round commitment (1994), but such economies as Chile, China, Indonesia, New Zealand and the Philippines are committed to a steeper reduction than the Bogor line, as is illustrated in Figure 3.1 above. Over the past three years, several economies announced their voluntary reduction of additional items, which, however, do not change our scores. Papua New Guinea introduced a comprehensive tariff reform in 1998 and announced a steep reduction, which was credited in our assessment. Almost all economies reported on their participation in the Information Technology Agreement (1997). All economies submitted Tariff Summary Tables or equivalent information. Some developing economies announced they would increase the percentage share of lowered tariffs bound to WTO.

Average single tariffs have been reduced to below 5 per cent for three economies, between 5 and 10 per cent for nine economies, and three more economies are committed to reduce to below 10 per cent in the near future. What still remains is high tariffs (more than 20 per cent) on sensitive products in eight economies, with no clear commitment made to their gradual reduction. Average tariffs of product groups in the Tariff Summary Tables often omit the existence of high-tariff items. It is time now to shift APEC's efforts from average tariff reduction to the reduction of the number of products under high tariffs.

Non-tariff measures (NTMs)

The same objective as for tariffs was given by the Osaka Action Agenda for NTMs inconsistent with WTO, but the coverage of permissible NTMs is not very clear. WTO admits NTMs for reasons of health, public morals and security, and many members reported that they impose no NTMs inconsistent with the WTO. However, the NTM summary tables, also requested by the common format, report on the existence of NTMs in many sectors. The UNCTAD NTM database tells us that industrialised members still impose NTMs of more than 20 per cent frequency on a few or several sectors (in terms of ISIC four-digit), which are, from the economist's point of view, not WTO-consistent and which aim to protect domestic producers, and should therefore be put on the liberalisation agenda.[3] Some Asian developing members impose NTMs of high frequency on many sectors. There is also the coexistence of NTMs with high tariffs. If their NTMs are imposed for WTO-consistent reasons, additional imposition of high tariffs (over 20 per cent) is not justified, and can be regarded as protection of domestic producers.

Nevertheless, the Uruguay Round negotiation achieved the elimination of two important NTMs, the imposition of tariffs and quota restrictions on agricultural products in 1995, and the gradual elimination of import quotas on textiles and clothing until 2005 under the Multi-fibre Arrangement (MFA). Japan imposed tariffs on its quota of rice imports in 1999, while Canada and the United States mentioned the elimination of the MFA quota in their 1996 IAPs.

Our scores for NTMs reflect the current high frequency of NTMs combined with commitment to future reduction. There is a big difference between member economies that rely on NTMs and those that do not, regardless of whether they are industrialised or developing economies. Papua New Guinea removed all NTMs in 1997, and the Philippines and Thailand reported in their IAPs future plans to remove their NTMs. However, other members with remaining NTMs have made no clear commitment to their reduction.

Services

The Osaka Action Agenda sets the liberalisation of the service trade by progressively reducing restrictions on market access for trade in services, and progressively providing for most-favoured nation (MFN) treatment and national treatment for trade in services. These objectives are consistent with the framework of the General Agreement on Trade in Services (GATS), and the Chair's Common Format (1996) suggested members could report against the services in the GATS classification.

Since the Osaka Action Agenda nominated four service sectors – energy, tourism, telecommunications and transport – many members reported on these sectors in their IAPs in 1996 and 1997, and these four sectors were fully covered in the 1998 IAPs; our assessment has therefore been confined to these four. Most economies reported their commitments in positive list formula, so their IAPs do not indicate how many restrictions still remain. We rely, for information regarding current states, on the frequency ratios of remaining restrictions in individual service sectors, calculated from the GATS commitment tables of 1994.[4] Three sectors other than tourism were heavily regulated, and appeared less often (indicating an absence of commitment to no restriction).

In 1997 the WTO negotiation on telecommunications and finance concluded, and quite a few economies reported on their liberalisation in these two sectors. The state monopoly of basic telecommunications was partly privatised and also opened to foreign firms, while the restriction on foreign banks' operations was partly relaxed in the financial sector. The former gained higher scores, but the latter was not counted in our assessment. In addition, professional services were also mentioned by some members in their 1998 IAPs. Several members reported with a comprehensive coverage and detailed description of current states.

Severe restrictions remain in many service sectors, and systematic and exact information on these restrictions is lacking. It has yet to be worked out how to promote the liberalisation of these service sectors, which will be left to the new WTO round. In telecommunications, some developing economies reported in their IAPs that they would first establish a regulatory body in preparation for partial removal of the state monopoly. Service liberalisation has only started at the Uruguay Round and there remains a long way to go. We are not sure how much will be achieved under voluntary liberalisation with the IAP formula. However, we have witnessed that the mentioning of four sectors by the Osaka Action Agenda, WTO negotiation of telecommunications and finance, and the inclusion of related services in the EVSL approach have encouraged individual APEC economies to report on their current state of regulation and commitment to future liberalisation of related services; this is a clear advantage of APEC.

Investment

Many APEC members have made substantial progress toward liberalisation in foreign direct investment (FDI), since they have realised the importance of attracting FDI for the promotion of economic growth. Australia liberalised FDI in the banking and telecommunications sectors. China approved some foreign banks' operating renminbi (RMB) business in Pudong, Shanghai, and is planning to improve the system of laws and regulations governing FDI. Indonesia, Korea and Mexico reduced the number of sectors in the negative list. Malaysia relaxed equity policy concerning foreign firms.

Despite substantial liberalisation carried out by APEC members, there are still significant differences in the extent of FDI liberalisation pursued among the members (Table 3.2). The members with high per capita income tend to have more liberalised FDI regimes, compared with those with lower per capita income. According to the results concerning the current status of FDI liberalisation and commitments made in the individual action plans, New Zealand, Japan, Singapore, the United States, Hong Kong and Canada scored highly, indicating that these members have already achieved very liberal FDI regimes. In contrast, Brunei, Indonesia, Chile and the Philippines still have relatively restricted FDI regimes.

Large variations can be found in performance on collective actions among the members. Hong Kong is recognised as the most active member regarding collective actions, while Australia and Thailand are not seen to be participating in any collective actions. Although performance on collective actions does not necessarily reflect the characteristics of FDI regimes, participation in collective action programs is important for APEC members, because economic assistance has an important position in FDI and trade liberalisation within APEC.

Standard and conformance

APEC announced its *Standard and Conformance Framework Declaration* in 1994. The Osaka Action Agenda emphasised specific aspects of transparency: alignment to international standards, mutual recognition of conformity assessment, and cooperation on technical infrastructure development. The Chair's Common Format requested individual members to report on their current position and future plans for further improvements. Assessment here is solely based on the IAPs.

The average scores for transparency, alignment to international standards, and mutual recognition are around 70 per cent, while it is around 60 per cent for technical infrastructure. The overall average is 70, one of the highest scores of all thirteen areas. The highest score is 82 and the lowest is 50; there

Table 3.2   Assessment of APEC's IAP 1998: summary table

	Tariff	NTM	Serv.	Invest	S&C	Cust	IPR	Comp	Gov. Proc	De-reg	ROO	Dis-pute	Bus. Visa
Australia	85	95	54	63	77	92	90	80	63	80	75	85	92
Brunei	85	85	13	43	60	54	50	25	30	35	45	56	81
Canada	80	50	57	78	73	96	90	90	85	78	60	69	72
Chile	50	60	33	59	64	75	65	70	45	65	45	75	54
China	40	20	9	58	65	67	65	45	38	60	70	62	46
Hong Kong	95	95	55	85	74	70	75	50	75	85	95	74	78
Indonesia	65	70	22	54	70	75	50	20	55	55	45	61	34
Japan	80	50	64	80	82	92	90	90	80	85	95	83	63
Korea	75	65	41	65	78	83	75	85	80	70	80	84	90
Malaysia	80	70	27	68	76	71	73	20	35	60	35	73	73
Mexico	35	70	9	68	60	79	70	75	60	75	75	64	56
New Zealand	90	85	69	75	83	83	75	70	63	90	40	77	65
PNG	25	60	6	56	50	58	30	15	10	60	30	45	47
Philippines	65	40	47	62	72	75	65	60	28	78	40	77	89
Singapore	95	95	35	77	75	79	73	25	75	70	80	85	77
Chinese Taipei	70	15	45	67	68	71	63	85	68	78	70	55	71
Thailand	45	40	26	62	57	67	65	50	25	60	40	79	53
US	85	60	84	80	80	83	95	85	80	88	45	75	69
APEC Average	69	63	39	67	70	76	70	58	55	71	59	71	67

is much less dispersion between members than in other areas. APEC economies have all made good progress in standard and conformance.

In this area, an economy first builds its own technical infrastructure, then promotes harmonisation to the international standard, and finally reaches the stage of mutual recognition. Developed members have already achieved the first two stages and are now approaching the final stage, whereas many developing members still remain at the initial stage. The scores in Table 3.1 reflect this difference, but some developing economies obtained higher scores in the middle group.

Many members reported on their efforts for achieving the four elements in the priority products designated in the Osaka Action Agenda (electrical and electronic appliances, auto-parts, and other machinery). However, a few economies reported the percentage achievement of harmonisation and indicated how much remained to be harmonised. This practice should be recommended to other economies.

Customs procedures

The APEC Sub-Committee on Customs Procedures (SCCP) has made great progress in modernising customs administration in APEC member governments over the past few years. This has included a substantial improvement in promptness, transparency and predictability in customs procedures, and an improved trade and investment environment for business across the region. Its impact will be multiplied when it is implemented jointly by as many member governments as possible. The Osaka Action Agenda set nine concrete objectives for collective action plans with target dates, as follows:

1 Harmonisation of tariff structure with the HS Convention
2 Transparency of customs procedures, customs laws, regulations, administrative guidelines, procedures and rulings
3 Simplification and harmonisation on the basis of the Kyoto Convention
4 Adoption and support for the UN/EDIFACT
5 Adoption of the principles of the WTO valuation agreement
6 Adoption of the principles of the WTO TRIPS agreement
7 Introduction of clear appeals provisions
8 Introduction of an advance classification ruling system
9 Provisions for temporary importation

In 1997, SCCP added the following three objectives to the list:

10 Harmonised APEC data elements
11 Risk management techniques
12 Guidelines on clearance of express consignments

The twelve objectives differ in their difficulty of actual implementation. Many set rules and procedures, while some require facilities or the administrative capability of customs officials for effective enforcement. The SCCP encourages technical assistance to be provided to member customs administrations on a request basis. Close collaboration with the business community is essential in order for all information about border management to be widespread and fully utilised by the latter.

The 1997 CAP report (*Convenor's Summary Report on Customs Procedures*) is the basis of the Customs Procedures CAP Implementation Matrix, which tells us the current state of each of eighteen members for each of the twelve objectives, according to four stages: (a) fully implemented, (b) to be implemented by a specific year (before target dates), (c) not applicable, and (d) actual implementation date subject to progress in the WTO. Our assessment is mainly based on this information.

Progress differs across objectives. All members have already implemented HS. Public availability of information (by sixteen members), clear appeal provisions (sixteen), advance classification ruling system (fourteen), and WTO valuation agreement (twelve), temporary importation (thirteen), and TRIPS (thirteen) have been implemented by a majority of members. On the other hand, UN/EDIFACT seems to be fully implemented only by six members, while Indonesia and Malaysia have implemented partially. Eight members have already signed the Kyoto Convention.

The average score is 76, the highest for all areas. This was achieved through the CAP under the SCCP and technical assistance provided by member governments, and also benefited from a close collaboration by business sectors. It will take a few more years to fully implement the EDIFACT by all members, and will require continued efforts for technical cooperation to late-starting members. It will help to improve the Implementation Matrix and spread the precise reporting of the IAPs to all members. It is likely that many APEC members will have implemented all of the twelve CAP objectives by the early 2000s. New objectives may be added to the Bogor target through the SCCP–business partnership so that the border management is further improved. The early achievement in customs procedures will help the liberalisation of tariffs and NTMs.

Intellectual property rights

The protection of intellectual property rights (IPR) is a prerequisite for technology and know-how to be transferred smoothly and better utilised in other countries. It is well perceived by all APEC members. The Uruguay Round agreement in 1994 included an Agreement on Trade-Related Aspects of Intellectual Property Rights (TRIPS); this has been in effect since 1 January 1995 and many developing members of APEC have become signatories. The TRIPS Agreement provides a comprehensive framework to provide a minimum protection of IPR. Industrialised members had to apply it from 1 January 1996, while the deadline for developing members was delayed until 2000. The Osaka Action Agenda set objectives to ensure adequate and effective protection – including legislation, administration and enforcement – of IPR in the Asia Pacific region, based on the principles of MFN treatment, national treatment and transparency, as set out in the TRIPS agreement and other related agreements.

Many members reported on their implementation of the TRIPS Agreement in their IAPs, following the Guidelines and Common Format. There are two elements for effective implementation of the TRIPS Agreement: TRIPS legislation, and an enforcing organisation. Many developing members detailed their TRIPS-related legislation, but reported only briefly on their enforcing mechanism, such as steps they are taking to ensure the expeditious granting of IPR and availability of effective remedies for their infringement.

We adopted the four checkpoints of (a) TRIPS-related legislation, (b) organisational arrangement for enforcement, (c) enforcement of the TRIPS Agreement by the set date, and (d) participation in technical cooperation. There is not much difference in (a) among many members, all achieving the middle stage and being committed to further implementation. However, they differ in (b), organisational arrangement for enforcing IPR. Nine members are assessed as not having implemented (b), but all of them are committed to partial or full implementation in the future. Difference also emerged in (c). Industrialised members have already implemented the TRIPS Agreement, while few developing members are explicitly committed to implement it with specific dates. Almost all members reported on their participation in technical cooperation either currently or in future, which resulted in many similar scores across members.

Competition policy

Strikingly different performance can be found in competition policies among APEC members. For overall evaluation, incorporating the current competition environment, IAP commitments, transparency, and CAP commitments, the scores range between 80 (Canada and Japan) and 10 (Papua New Guinea). Other high-scoring members include Korea, Chinese Taipei and the United States, all scoring 75, and Australia with 65, while low-scoring members include Indonesia, Malaysia and Singapore, all with 15. It is important to note that these scores are based on the characteristics of competition policies and the attitude toward cooperation on competition policies in APEC activities. If we consider only the characteristics of competition policies that are considered to indicate a competition environment, we obtain somewhat different outcomes. Australia, Canada, Japan and the United States have the highest score of 55, while Singapore and Papua New Guinea have the lowest score of 0. One should note that the evaluation is based on the documentation submitted by the members. As such, the 'true' nature of competitive environment may not be captured accurately by our evaluation. This problem is illustrated by the case of Singapore. Singapore does not have a competition law, nor does it have well-documented policies towards competition. However, liberalised trade and an FDI regime appear to have resulted in a competitive environment in Singapore. This example illustrates the difficulties associated with the evaluation of competition policies, and it also warns us to be careful in interpreting the evaluation results. Having discussed the difficulties in evaluating the policies concerning competition, our method of evaluation is useful in the absence of information such as profitability, costs and market shares, which are necessary to evaluate the level of competition in the market, for all APEC members.

Government procurement

Government procurement had long been under the 'Buy Home Product' rule, in pursuit of national security and protection of domestic production, and had been excluded from national treatment in GATT. It was only at the Tokyo Round negotiation in the 1970s, that the government procurement of commodities was opened to foreign firms (but restricted to purchased commodities over 130,000 SDRs). At the Uruguay Round Agreement in 1994, the WTO Agreement on Government Procurement was adopted, and put into effect from 1 January 1996. The opening of government procurement has now been expanded to services, and local government is also included. The Osaka Action Agenda set the objective to develop a common understanding on government procurement policies and systems as well as practices, and to achieve liberalisation of government procurement makers throughout the Asia Pacific region in accordance with the principles and objectives of the Bogor Declaration. Its guidelines urge each APEC economy to enhance transparency and to establish a government procurement information database. Both the objective and guidelines state only abstractly the direction of efforts, and lack any specific activities.

The Chair's Common Format suggested that members could report on their current state regarding legislation and procedures of government procurement and their plans to improve them. Many members followed this suggestion, but with different levels of specificity. Future plans are often designated only as short term or long term, and without specific deadlines. In our assessment we have taken into account (a) participation in the WTO's Agreement on Government Procurement, (b) implementation of legislation at home, (c) establishment of a database regarding government procurement information, (d) exchange of government procurement information, and (e) organisation of or participation in a seminar.

The overall average is 55, lower than in other areas, and with a greater dispersion, from 85 to 10. The members with high scores have half established the database in (c), and some have already participated in (a).

Deregulation

Our evaluation indicates relatively good performance by APEC members concerning deregulation, with an average score being 70 with relatively limited variations. However, it should be remembered that our evaluation tends to overestimate the extent of deregulation undertaken by the members, because we could not consider various forms of regulations applied by the member governments, due to the non-availability of necessary information. For evaluation we only considered privatisation, market access for foreign investors, and transparency. Among the members, New Zealand has the highest score of 90, followed by the United States (87.5), Hong Kong (85) and Japan (85). Brunei has an exceptionally low score of 35, while other low-scoring members include Indonesia (55), China, Malaysia, Papua New Guinea and Thailand (all with 60).

Some observations on the evaluation for separate items are in order. For privatisation, many members have achieved a high level, leaving relatively limited areas for further privatisation. Probably for this reason, only Singapore explicitly stated further privatisation in its IAP. Many members performed favourably in the area of market access, thanks to active FDI liberalisation. Furthermore, a number of members committed to further liberalisation. The members with high scores include Japan, New Zealand and the United States with 37.5, while those with low scores are Brunei (20), Indonesia (25) and Papua New Guinea (25). The scores on transparency appear to reflect the attitude of the members toward APEC activities in general, and their attitude towards deregulation in particular. It is interesting to observe that, in general, members with a low evaluation on privatisation and market access also have a low score on transparency. Specifically, Australia, Hong Kong and New

Zealand have a high score, while Brunei, Chile, Indonesia, Papua New Guinea, Singapore and Thailand have a low score. The case for Singapore does not necessarily indicate that Singapore does not provide any information on deregulation. In many cases, information on regulation/deregulation is given under different categories, such as rules and regulations on foreign trade and FDI.

Rules of origin

The Osaka Action Agenda set the objective as (a) to ensure full compliance with internationally harmonised rules of origin, to be adopted in relevant international forums, and (b) to ensure that their respective rules of origin are prepared and applied in an impartial, transparent and neutral manner.

We evaluated the performance of APEC members concerning the rules of origin, based on the following two criteria: (1) compliance with internationally harmonised rules of origin adopted in relevant international forums, and (2) preparation and application of the rules of origin in an impartial, transparent and neutral manner. Specifically, we constructed four indicators for the evaluation: (1) harmonisation of the rules, (2) participation in WTO/WCO, (3) consistency in the application of the rules, and (4) neutrality in the application of the rules. The results of our evaluation show large variations in the performance of members on the rules of origin. High-scoring members are Hong Kong and Japan, each with 95 points, while low-scoring members are Papua New Guinea (30) and Malaysia (35). This is consistent with our expectation that, in general, APEC members not belonging to regional trading agreements – China, Hong Kong, Japan, Korea and Chinese Taipei – would have high scores, while members belonging to regional trading arrangements such as NAFTA and ASEAN would have low scores.

Dispute mediation

Trade conflicts and other economic disputes have negative implications for the cooperation that APEC is designed to promote. Since APEC is not a rules-based organisation, it cannot establish a formal, binding dispute-settlement mechanism. APEC regards the WTO dispute settlement as the primary channel for solving disputes, and it has been conducting training seminars on the WTO dispute-settlement understanding, in order that its members may resort to the WTO mechanism effectively. In addition, APEC has helped to resolve and avoid disputes through non-adversarial and voluntary approaches. By confining itself to an informal mediation process, it can deal with such new sources of disputes as competition policy and environmental protection, which have not been adopted by the WTO.

The IAPs report on individual members' efforts to resolve and avoid disputes. Our scores reflect the ways in which individual members have arranged access to the international mechanism to resolve the following three types of dispute: private-to-government and private-to-private disputes are well attended by many members; fifteen members have already been signatories to the Agreement on Foreign Arbitration Judgment and Enforcement; and thirteen members have already attained access to the International Center for Settlement of Investment Disputes. Dispute settlement should be accommodated at home as well. Domestic laws and regulations to enforce dispute mediation seem to be arranged to a lesser extent. In 1998, several developing members reported on strengthening these efforts at home.

The government-to-government disputes need to be better attended. Many members have access to the WTO Dispute Settlement procedures, and have concluded bilateral agreements covering dispute settlement between the respective governments. In order to supplement the WTO mechanism, the *APEC/EPG Report* (1994) proposed an APEC Dispute Mediation Service (DMS), and the Bogor Declaration urged the SOM to work out its feasible form. Only six members have supported the DMS. On the other hand, the CTI's Dispute Mediation Experts Group (DMEG) worked on the *Principles of Dispute Mediation in the APEC Region*. Trade policy dialogue within the CTI takes advantage of its informal, off-the-record, non-adversarial procedures to exchange views on particular government-to-government disputes or issues that may lead to disputes. It will be further developed in keeping with the evolution of TILF programs and become another form of DMS.

Mobility of business people

APEC economies will enhance the mobility of business people engaged in the conduct of trade and investment in the Asia Pacific region. Promotion of business mobility within APEC is more or less concerned with the processing of visas, the procedures for this, and the term of validity. The APEC Secretariat has published the *APEC Business Travel Handbook*, by collecting and disseminating information on individual APEC members. Relying on the IAPs as well as the *Handbook*, we assessed individual member's efforts for increasing business mobility, according to the following three checkpoints: (a) feasibility of business immigration without visa, (b) procedure of processing visa, (c) participation in collective action such as APEC Business Travel Card. Point (b) includes such detailed aspects as the number of documents required; whether the application for visa must be by applicants themselves or not; the number of days required for processing a visa; the availability of multiple visas, whether valid for more than six months and extendable; uniform visa fees, and methods of payment other than in cash; and coverage of accompanying family. Only short-term business travel is covered, but temporary residency of business people is not included here.

As regards visa processing, a majority of members have already improved the situation in respect to visa application, number of documents, and multiple visas, but there remain severe restrictions on the visa period and companions. As regards entry without visa, China, Indonesia and Papua New Guinea are strict; followed by the United States, Japan, Canada, Chile and Chinese Taipei; while other APEC members are more lenient. Seven members are committed to the APEC Business Travel Card.

In summary, the average scores of eighteen members differ between areas, from 37 for services to 72 for customs procedures, but a majority of them fall between 50 and 70. That is, APEC's progress toward the Bogor target is graded as around 60 per cent at the moment. The eighteen members are divided into three groups:

(averages of 76–65) tariffs, investment, standard and conformance, customs procedures, intellectual property rights, and business mobility
(averages of 64–59) NTMs, competition policy, rules of origin, and dispute mediation
(averages of 57–39) deregulation, government procurements, and services

Roughly speaking, facilitation areas have higher averages than liberalisation areas.

The dispersion of the scores between members is greater for tariffs, NTMs, services, competition policy, government procurements, deregulation, and rules of origin – mostly liberalisation areas. In other words, APEC members have made greater progress as a group in facilitation areas. This is because of active encouragement by CAPs. To conclude, it has been shown in quantitative terms that APEC has made great progress in the area of facilitation over the past two years.

ASSESSMENT BY MEMBER ECONOMIES

In the previous section we assessed the IAPs of all eighteen APEC members in each of thirteen areas. Next, we will examine the score matrix (Table 3.2) by row, so as to obtain individual country profiles over thirteen areas. Countries' scores for individual areas are plotted along the thirteen axes, scaling outward from the origin in radar charts (Figures 3.2–3.19). The solid line connecting them represents the country's profile, while the dotted line connects the average scores of all APEC, common to all eighteen radar charts. If compared with the APEC average line, an individual member line provides a quick overview of the member's progress toward the Bogor target. The eighteen radar charts are arranged in alphabetical order.

APEC members are divided into the following three groups:

(a) Members whose radar charts are mostly located outside the APEC average: Australia, Canada, Hong Kong, Japan, Korea, New Zealand, Singapore and the United States
(b) Members whose radar charts are located around the APEC average: Brunei, Chile, Malaysia, Mexico, the Philippines and Chinese Taipei
(c) Members whose radar charts are located mostly inside the APEC average: China, Indonesia, Papua New Guinea and Thailand.

Generally speaking, industrialised members as well as Hong Kong and Singapore have gone ahead of other members towards achieving the Bogor target in many areas. The newly industrialising economy members follow them as the second tier, and other ASEAN members and China follow suit. This fits with our *ad hoc* observation and should not be regarded as surprising.

However, it is worthwhile to note that no single member has gone far ahead of other members in all areas. Each member of the (a) group falls short of the APEC average in one or two areas: Australia in investment and business mobility, Canada in NTMs and dispute settlement, Hong Kong in customs and competition policy, Japan in NTMs and business visas, Korea in investment, New Zealand in rules of origin and business visas, Singapore in services and competition policy, and the United States in rules of origin. Similarly, no single member except Papua New Guinea is lagging in all areas; China exceeds the APEC average in rules of origin, Indonesia in NTMs, and Thailand in dispute mediation. This list urges members of the (a) group to try harder in those designated areas, while it encourages members of the (c) group.

Finally, it is not sufficient to compare individual members' radar charts only with the APEC average. As is clear from our assessment criteria in Sections 2 and 3, ours is an absolute assessment in the sense that the full mark of 100 is regarded as the Bogor target. All the full-mark points of the thirteen area axes are connected so as to form a Bogor line in the radar chart. Radar charts of the (a) group mentioned above should also be compared with the Bogor line. Even the (a) group members still have a long way to go towards the Bogor target.

A brief mention is needed for three new members – Peru, Russia and Vietnam. All three submitted their IAPs to the APEC meeting in Malaysia in 1998. They have all covered all fifteen areas and have followed the common format in drafting their IAPs. They conveyed detailed explanations regarding their current states of individual TILF areas, not missing major items highlighted in CAPs. However, because of the non-availability of supplementary information, we could not go into remaining impediments and restrictions and give scores. From reading their IAPs alone, we have found no significant commitment to future implementation, especially in liberalisation areas, in any of the three. Incidentally, Vietnam mentioned reducing average tariff from 25 per cent to 15 per cent in the short term, while Russia stated its intent to specify its commitments after its accession to the WTO.

EVSL AS AN ALTERNATIVE APPROACH TO APEC LIBERALISATION

Early voluntary sectoral liberalisation (EVSL) was introduced as a breakthrough during the slow liberalisation along the lines of the IAPs. EVSL is also a part of CAP and jointly implemented by individual governments. The Osaka Action Agenda had already mentioned, in the CAPs for tariffs (and NTMs), that 'APEC members will identify industries in which the progressive reduction of tariffs (and non-tariff measures) may have positive impacts on trade and on economic growth in the Asia Pacific region or for which there is regional industry support for early liberalization' (Osaka Action Agenda 1995, Section C: 6–7)

Figure 3.2 Assessment: Australia 1998

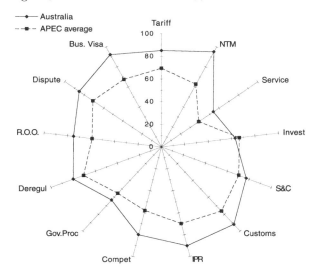

Figure 3.3 Assessment: Brunei 1998

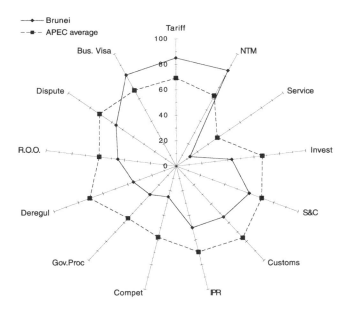

Figure 3.4 Assessment: Canada 1998

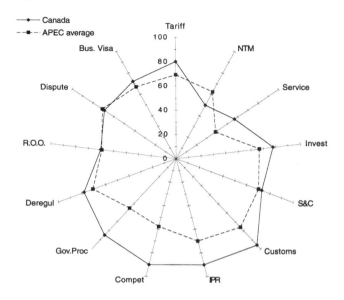

Figure 3.5 Assessment: Chile 1998

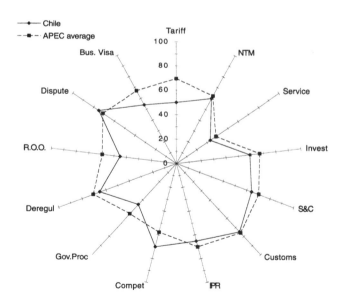

Figure 3.6 Assessment: China 1998

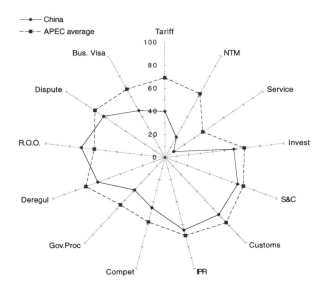

Figure 3.7 Assessment: Hong Kong 1998

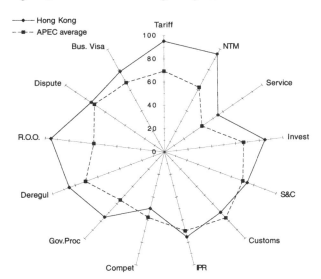

Figure 3.8 Assessment: Indonesia 1998

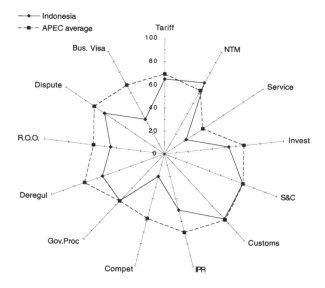

Figure 3.9 Assessment: Japan 1998

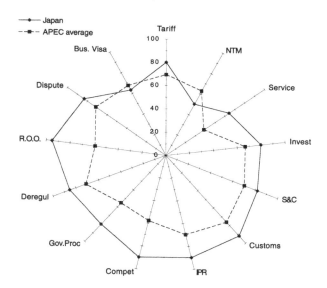

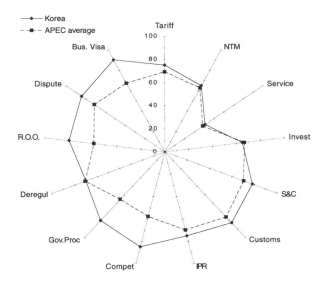

Figure 3.10 Assessment: Korea 1998

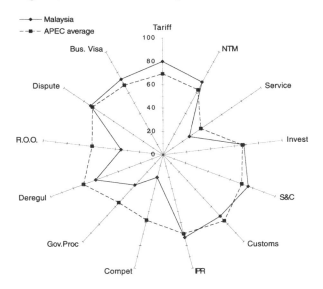

Figure 3.11 Assessment: Malaysia 1998

Figure 3.12 Assessment: Mexico 1998

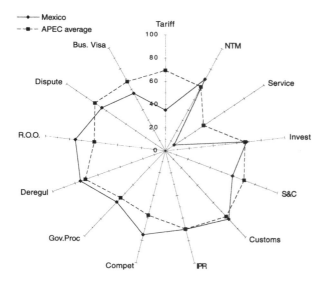

Figure 3.13 Assessment: New Zealand 1998

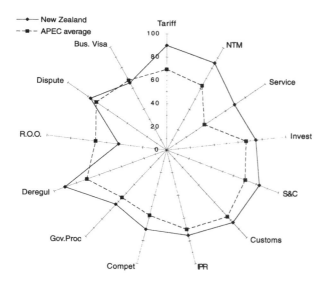

Figure 3.14 Assessment: Papua New Guinea 1998

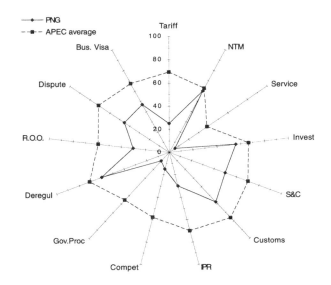

Figure 3.15 Assessment: Philippines 1998

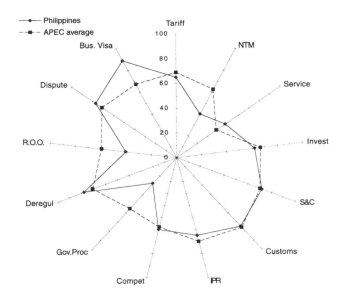

Figure 3.16 Assessment: Singapore 1998

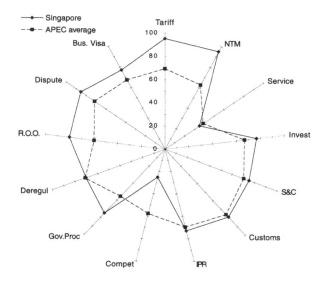

Figure 3.17 Assessment: Chinese Taipei 1998

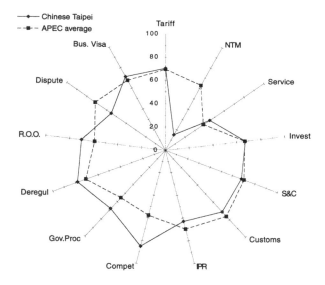

Figure 3.18 Assessment: Thailand 1998

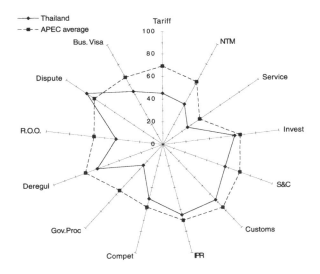

Figure 3.19 Assessment: U.S.A. 1998

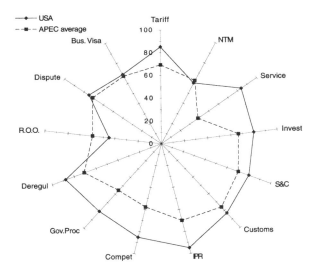

At the Subic Bay meeting in 1996, President Clinton proposed the Information Technology Agreement (ITA), under which all tariffs and NTMs on semi-conductors and other parts and materials input to information technology equipment are reduced or eliminated by the year 2000. The ITA was adopted at the APEC Leaders' Meeting and then forwarded to the WTO Ministerial Meeting in Singapore just two weeks later, and was adopted as a WTO agreement. Fifteen APEC economies signed the agreement and implemented it from April 1997. The ITA is not a voluntary liberalisation, but has become a legally binding treaty.

Encouraged by the success of the ITA, the Canadian chair proposed to accelerate the implementation of EVSL by two years from 2000. Sixty-one sectors were suggested as candidates for EVSL in 1997, and the Vancouver APEC meeting finally designated fifteen sectors (nine sectors as high priority, see Table 3.2) and agreed to work out their implementation during 1998. Each proposal had nominating economies and supporting economies, but was not necessarily supported by all economies.

The objectives of EVSL differ between sectors. Thirteen sectors aim to eliminate tariffs and NTMs, but it is yet to be elaborated how this will be implemented. In the proposals for Environmental Goods, Services, and Chemicals, it is stated explicitly that the liberalisation will be brought to WTO negotiation after a critical majority support is secured. In the Medical Equipment, Civil Aircraft, and Oilseeds proposals, there is also the intention to link with the WTO the liberalisation achieved through EVSL. But no direct link with the WTO was mentioned for other sectors. The Food proposal states that they will start with a study of the impacts of liberalisation.[5]

Facilitation measures such as Standard and Conformance and Customs Procedures are also mentioned in the EVSL proposals for several sectors, and they are the main objectives in Telecommunications, and Automotive Products. Ecotech is mentioned in eight sectors in which EVSL aims to promote the development and training of the human resources necessary to implement the facilitation measures, as well as liberalisation. What characterises the EVSL approach is that, by incorporating both facilitation and Ecotech measures, it can mitigate the adjustment cost of liberalisation, and even enhance its impacts. This is a clear advantage of APEC over GATT/WTO in promoting liberalisation, and will constitute a major value-added feature of APEC over the WTO.

At the Vancouver APEC meeting, leaders endorsed their ministers' agreement on EVSL and urged its early implementation as follows: '… action should be taken with respect to early voluntary liberalization in fifteen sectors, with nine to be advanced throughout 1998 with a view to implementation beginning in 1999. We find this package to be mutually beneficial and to represent a balance of interests'.[6]

It was scheduled that the concrete plan for implementing EVSL would be agreed upon by the Trade Ministers' meeting in June 1998. However, the

Trade Ministers failed to agree on the Chair's proposal. The implementation plan states that:

> Participation in the nine sectors and all three measures (trade liberalization, facilitation, and Ecotech) in each sector will be essential to maintain the mutual benefits and balance of interests, which Leaders had established when selecting the sectors in Vancouver.

> In order to enable finalization of the sectoral arrangements that would maximize participation, Ministers agreed that flexibility would be required to deal with product-specific concerns raised by individual economies in each sector. Such flexibility would generally be in the form of longer implementation periods. In principle developing economies should be allowed greater flexibility.[7]

The modality of liberalisation has changed to a package deal with less flexibility. The EVSL idea can supplement the IAP but this proposal of 'all nine times three in a package' seemed to be too ambitious at the current stage of APEC process.

EVSL was originally conceived to identify a few sectors to be agreed upon more easily and implemented earlier, in addition to the IAP, thereby maintaining the momentum of liberalisation within APEC. ITA was a good example, and has been regarded as a successful precedent.

Some economists warn against the EVSL approach, on the ground that it tends to lead to piecemeal liberalisation of easier sectors, leaving difficult sectors untouched. However, this criticism is not relevant to EVSL. EVSL neither aims at a full-scale package of sectoral negotiations *vis-à-vis* an across-the-board negotiation as in the Uruguay Round, nor will it replace the IAPs as the principal mechanism of APEC's liberalisation. It is only additional to the major tracks of IAPs, and whatever liberalisation is achieved through EVSL will enhance the IAPs of individual economies and should be welcome.

The modality of EVSL, as appeared in the Chair's Statement at the Trade Ministers' meeting last June, has changed from the voluntary IAP to the ITA-type negotiation, although under the same title of 'early voluntary sectoral liberalisation'. The Joint Statement of Ministers at the Vancouver APEC clearly stated:

> Recognizing the need for a balanced and mutually beneficial package, and recalling that the process of early liberalization is conducted on the basis of the APEC principle of voluntarism, whereby each economy remains free to determine the sectoral initiatives in which it will participate...

> We recommend that Leaders endorse members beginning immediately to complete the work on these proposals through finalizing the scope of coverage, flexible phasing, measures covered and implementation

schedule, including choice of measures and instruments for implementation based on existing proposals in the following sector.[8]

However, EVSL has become the package proposal of nine sectors times three measures in the Chair's Statement, as cited in Paragraph 5. The element of voluntarism has weakened, so that each economy must say either yes or no to this package proposal. The flexibility is yet to be elaborated, but it will generally be in the form of a longer implementation period, as in the same Chair's Statement. A package deal of 'mutually beneficial' and 'balance of interest' is a typical formula of the GATT negotiation and has departed far from the IAPs and their voluntary basis. Although only Japan objected to it explicitly, has this departure been accepted by all other members? If so, they should at least change the title 'early voluntary liberalisation'. Has APEC quit its unique modality of voluntarism and become a stage for negotiation?

Do the nine sectors really reflect a balanced interest? It was explained that the nine sectors were adopted mainly on the basis of exporters' interests, and were balanced in the sense that they included the interests of exporters in all APEC economies. If you count economies nominating the nine sectors in Table 3.3, you will find that the United States nominated seven, Canada, Singapore and Thailand nominated three, while five economies nominated none.

Alternatively, we could select the initial package based on importers' interests, which is consistent with the teaching of 'gains from trade'. In the reality of negotiation for liberalisation, however, resistance from domestic producers competing with imports always emerges, and we always face political economy problems of how to persuade vested interest groups at home. We could select sectors of least resistance at home, which better accord with the original idea of EVSL.

Unfortunately, we have not seen yet an analysis of the EVSL sectors which tells us how much export and import trade of individual economies are covered, and how many impediments still remain in each sector.[9] Table 3.4 compares import tariff revenues from eight EVSL sectors for nine economies. Import and tariff figures are available for only the nine economies listed in the table from WTO/IDB, and the tariff revenues were calculated by multiplying import values by trade-weighted average tariffs. If multiplied further by price elasticity, it will give an estimate of the possible increase in imports by eliminating tariffs, which is the first estimate of the impact of liberalisation, based on a static assumption.

Although with an incomplete coverage, Table 3.3 gives us an insight to a cross-economy comparison. Figures differ greatly between sectors and economies. The total figure for Japan (in the right-hand column) is never the largest, but its figures in fisheries and forest products are larger than those of other economies, mainly because of its big current imports. And it is in these two sectors that Japan faces difficult political economy problems at home. They will inevitably be associated with the WTO negotiation over agricultural

Table 3.3   Designated sectors for early voluntary liberalisation

Sectors	Objectives	Nominating economies
Environmental goods and services*	Tariffs, NTMs, Services, Ecotech	Canada, Japan, C. Taipei, US
Chemicals*	Tariffs, NTMs, S&C, Customs, Investment	Australia, HKC, Singapore, US
Medical equipment*	Tariffs, NTMs, Ecotech	Singapore, US
Energy equipment and services*	Tariffs, NTMs, Services	Australia, Thailand, US
Telecommunications*	S&C	US
Toys*	Tariffs, NTMs	China, HKC, Singapore, US
Automotive products	S&C, Customs, Ecotech	USA
Food	Tariffs, NTMs, S&C, Ecotech	Australia, Canada, NZ, Thailand
Fisheries*	Tariffs, NTMs, Subsidy, S&C, Ecotech	Brunei, Canada, Indonesia, NZ, Thailand
Oilseeds and oilseed products	Tariffs, NTMs, Ecotech	Canada, Malaysia, US
Fertiliser	Tariffs, S&C, Ecotech	Canada, Japan
Gems and jewellery*	Tariffs, NTMs	Thailand, C. Taipei
Civil craft	Tariffs	Canada
Forest products*	Tariffs, S&C	Canada, Indonesia, NZ, US
Natural and synthetic rubber	Tariffs, NTMs, Ecotech	Japan, Thailand

Notes: S&C = Standard and Conformance, Customs = Customs Procedures, Ecotech = Economic and technical cooperation, NTM = Non-tariff measures, HKC = Hong Kong China, C. Taipei = Chinese Taipei, NZ = New Zealand, * = nine priority sectors.

products scheduled to start in 2000, and it is difficult to negotiate them within APEC, separately from the forthcoming WTO negotiation. The gradual liberalisation of Japanese agriculture is necessary, but the year 1998 was not good timing for it. Was it not possible to downsize the package, by excluding a few sectors that meet with strong resistance from members? The passage of a single ITA was highlighted in Manila. Why not four to five EVSLs in Kuala Lumpur?

At the APEC ministerial meeting in Kuala Lumpur in 1998, Asian ministers supported Japan's contention and decided to forward the tariff element of the nine-sector EVSL to the WTO. Japan might have avoided being isolated in APEC, but some members may have become disappointed with the slow

Table 3.4 Estimated tariff revenues of the eight EVSL sectors in selected economies (US$'000)

Economies	Years	Env. goods & services	Fisheries	Forest	Medical products	Energy equipment & serv.	Toys	Gems & jewellery	Chemicals	Total
Australia	1995	197,636	0	190,082	23,375	347,977	9,667	14,725	227,973	1,011,435
Canada	1996	679,773	2,025	393,938	165,887	1,214,624	5,505	20,673	1,017,095	3,499,520
HKC	1995	0	0	0	0	0	0	0	0	0
Indonesia	1994	443,043	3,501	97,589	187,286	909,276	9,137	3,426	446,592	2,099,592
Japan	1995	75,038	743,298	484,628	5,588	50,017	42,527	84,898	745,591	2,240,585
New Zealand	1996	93,533	9	63,261	24,927	140,353	12,304	2,825	91,717	428,929
Philippines	1991	256,960	10,858	107,640	20,241	376,031	7,951	9,112	296,590	1,085,383
Singapore	1995	0	0	0	0	0	0	0	0	0
Thailand	1995	796,735	411,188	226,592	234,740	1,350,468	12,015	41,392	1,316,571	4,389,701
Total		2,542,718	1,170,879	1,563,730	662,044	4,388,746	99,106	177,051	2,825,558	14,755,145

Note: Tariff revenues are calculated by multiplying the amounts of dutiable imports by trade-weighted average tariffs. Imports and tariffs are calculated so as to cover precisely items included in the EVSL sectors The ninth sector, telecommunications, is excluded because non-tariff reduction is proposed.

Sources: Nine economies are selected because of their data availability in WTO/IDB.

process of liberalisation under the APEC modality. The hasty promotion of EVSL was partly responsible for their disappointment.

While the tariff element of the nine sectors of EVSL was forwarded to the WTO, the implementation of their NTMs, facilitation, and Ecotech elements will proceed under a New Zealand initiative (*Summary Conclusion of the First SOM* 1999). Facilitation and Ecotech form a WTO-plus element in APEC. EVSL aimed to push them together through liberalisation; that is, first achieve a critical mass agreement on a suitable package of liberalisation, facilitation and Ecotech within APEC, and then forward the liberalisation element to the WTO in order to link with the WTO liberalisation commitments. With the tariff element separated from the other two, the implementation of the latter may be more or less discouraged. The remaining six sectors include such broadly defined areas as food, for which a pragmatic approach is recommended for this year.

FUTURE PROSPECTS AND MID-TERM STRATEGY

APEC is now ten years old. Liberalisation has emerged as a core prime-mover of APEC over the past five years. What has it achieved so far? This chapter has aimed to examine critically the liberalisation process, assess its achievement, and point out possible reform toward the next century. Some say APEC has failed in liberalisation because of severe conflict between members regarding EVSL last year, but they are wrong.

The IAP is the primary mechanism for implementation of APEC's TILF agenda. However, its unique modality of concerted unilateral liberalisation has its merits and demerits. CUL has certainly helped APEC members to start implementing their TILF under the flexible modality in a short period of time. On the other hand, its achievement is not readily visible. The IAP packages differ between members, and its reporting in positive list formula leaves us puzzled about the remaining impediments. Peer review and monitoring of IAPs are often mentioned, but we are not assured yet how they work. We have collected supplementary information and tried to assess quantitatively how much progress individual members have made and how much still remains to be done toward the Bogor target. We examined carefully the Osaka Action Agenda and the Chair's Common Format, and selected checkpoints with which their progress can be assessed objectively and consistently. Although still handicapped by the lack of available information, and while there is still big room for improvement, we have tried to provide a fair and objective assessment of the IAPs.

Incidentally, the Pacific Economic Cooperation Council (PECC) has been commissioned by APEC to produce an independent review of the IAPs, on condition that no reference be made to individual economies. Our scoring practice is excluded by this condition. However, do the APEC senior officials understand how severe this constraint is? The PECC team has to examine the IAPs and supplementary data of individual economies similar to ours in order to give a meaningful review. Otherwise it will provide only a conventional report highlighting the liberalisation commitments, and not mentioning remaining impediments. Yet it has to produce a concise review, without mentioning specific names of economies, but nevertheless impressing readers with the objectiveness and consistency of the analysis. We have done this in a one-page table and nine pages of diagrams. We have aimed not so much at ranking individual economies as at its expository advantage, as is seen from my summary report of APEC's progress toward the Bogor target in individual areas above. The Sub-Committee on Customs Procedure has already provided the CAP implementation matrix, which is basically similar to our efforts.

Our assessment conveyed a mixed result of small and large progress. Generally speaking, many economies are committed to liberalisation in concrete figures only for the short period, and their commitment is characterised as 'UR agreement + a'. Although APEC economies are supposed to improve their IAPs every year, the additions in 1997 and 1998 have turned out to be minimal. We cannot expect a big addition toward 2000, when the implementation of Uruguay Round agreements is completed and the new WTO round starts. Individual governments tend to refrain from offering new liberalisation commitments before a new negotiation. On the other hand, we have a brighter prospect in facilitation areas. Thanks to encouragement by the CAPs, it is likely that the objectives set by the Osaka Action Agenda will be achieved earlier than the Bogor deadline by both industrialised and developing economies.

It has become evident from our experience over the past few years that APEC's TILF has achieved some results, but cannot tackle difficult sectors, which should be left to WTO negotiation. However, by revising and strengthening its guidance, we will be able to enhance the achievement of TILF. More emphasis should be given to reducing the number of high-tariff items, eliminating NTMs 'really' inconsistent with the WTO, and giving a clear indication of eliminating restrictions to services. In investment and facilitation areas, the current guidance of the Chair's Common Format and the CAP convenors' instructions should be strengthened, so that more meaningful information is provided regarding the current state and future commitments. In competition policy and deregulation, the Osaka Action Agenda itself needs to be revised, in order to give a clear direction for members' efforts.

EVSL is an 'easy sector liberalisation' and supplements the IAPs' approach through the combined elements of liberalisation, facilitation and Ecotech, a process unique to APEC. A hasty and over-ambitious approach resulted in severe conflict between APEC members last year. APEC cannot substitute for the WTO in some difficult sectors. Current EVSL programs should be promoted, with necessary modification, to achieve these aims.

APPENDIX: REVISED METHODOLOGY FOR ASSESSING COMPETITION POLICY AND DEREGULATION

Competition policy

The Osaka Action Agenda set out the objective of competition policy to maximise consumer benefits by enhancing the competitive environment in the market. To achieve the objective, APEC members agreed to carry out the following measures: (1) introduce or maintain effective and adequate competition policy and/or laws and associated enforcement policies, (2) ensure the transparency of the above, and (3) promote cooperation among APEC economies.

Based on these observations, we evaluated members' performance concerning competition policy against the following four criteria: the current competition environment, IAP, transparency and CAP. While the current competition environment refers to members' position on competition policy around 1998, IAP indicates their commitment to improving competitive environment. Transparency reflects the attitude of members to promote competition, while CAP indicates the willingness for cooperation. Using the framework adopted by Bollard and Vautier (1998), we evaluated the current competition environment and IAP by examining members' policies in the following seven areas: (1) merger regime, (2) abuse of market power, (3) horizontal agreements, (4) vertical restraints, (5) jurisdiction exceptions, (6) unfair trading, and (7) roles, enforcement, powers. Information used for the evaluation of the current position mainly comes from Bollard and Vautier, and supplementary information was obtained from the APEC Competition Policy & Law Database assembled by the Fair Trade Commission, Taipei.

The highest score is set to be 70 for the combination of present position and IAP. It is important to note that the evaluation is conducted by using the information contained in the text given in the sources above. As such, our evaluation does not assess the level of competition in the market for members. Transparency is evaluated by the documents on competition policy contained in the APEC Data Base and IAPs, while CAP is evaluated by the information given in IAPs. The highest scores for CAP and Transparency are set at 10 and 20, respectively. The highest combined score based on the four criteria is 100 (Table 3.5).

Deregulation

The Osaka Action Agenda set the following objectives concerning 'deregulation': (1) to promote transparency of regulatory regimes, and (2) to eliminate trade and investment distortion arising from domestic regulations, which impede free and open trade and investment in the Asia Pacific region. Taking into account these objectives, and also considering data availability, we evaluate the performance of APEC members on deregulation by examining

Table 3.5 Competition policy

	Merger regime	Market power	Horizontal agreements	Vertical restraint	Jurisdiction exceptions	Unfair trading	Roles enforcement	Current position	IAP	CAP	Transparency	Total
Full score	10	10	10	10	10	10	10	70	0	10	20	100
Australia	10	10	10	5	0	10	10	55	0	5	20	80
Brunei						10		10	0	5	10	25
Canada	10	10	10	5	0	10	10	55	5	10	20	90
Chile	[10]	[10]	[5]	[5]	[0]	[10]	10	50	0	0	20	70
China		5	5	5		10		25	5	5	10	45
Hong Kong, China	10							10	20	10	10	50
Indonesia								0	10	0	10	20
Japan	10	10	10	5	0	10	10	55	5	10	20	90
Korea	10	10	5	5	0	10	5	45	10	10	20	85
Malaysia						[5]		5	0	5	10	20
Mexico	10	10	10	5	0		10	45	0	10	20	75
New Zealand	10	10	5	5	0	10	10	50	0	0	20	70
PNG								0	5	0	10	15
Philippines		10			0	10	5	25	5	10	20	60
Singapore								0	0	5	20	25
Chinese Taipei	10	10	5	5	0	10	5	45	10	10	20	85
Thailand	10		5	5	0	[5]	5	30	0	0	20	50
US	10	10	10	5	0	10	10	55	0	10	20	85

Notes: Evaluation has been conducted on the following four items: current position, IAP, CAP, and transparency. Current position, which is given 70 per cent of the total evaluation, is evaluated. Evaluation in parentheses [ ] are based on the information given in APEC Competition Policy & Law Database prepared by Taiwan.

Sources: Bollard and Vautier, 'The convergence of competition law within APEC and the CER agreement', in R.I. Wu and Y.P. Chu (eds) Business, Markets and Government in the Asia Pacific, Routledge, New York, 1998, and APEC C.

Table 3.6 Deregulation

	Privatisation	Market access	Transparency	Total
Full score	40	40	20	100
Australia	30+0	30+5	10+5	80
Brunei	15+0	20+0	0+0	35
Canada	30+0	35+2.5	10+0	77.5
Chile	35+0	25+5	0+0	65
China	25+0	25+5	0+5	60
Hong Kong, China	35+0	35+0	10+5	85
Indonesia	30+0	20+5	0+0	55
Japan	35+0	35+2.5	10+2.5	85
Korea	30+0	30+5	0+5	70
Malaysia	25+0	30+0	0+5	60
Mexico	30+0	30+5	10+0	75
New Zealand	37.5+0	35+2.5	15+0	90
PNG	35+0	25+0	0+0	60
Philippines	35+0	25+5	10+2.5	77.5
Singapore	30+5	35+0	0+0	70
Chinese Taipei	30+0	30+5	10+2.5	77.5
Thailand	30+0	30+0	0+0	60
US	37.5+0	35+2.5	10+2.5	87.5
Average	31.1	32.2	7.2	70.6

Note: Privatisation is measured as 100-percentage share of state-owned enterprises in gross domestic investment. The figures are for 1990–5 and 1985–90.

Adjusted values are obtained by reducing the computed values to the nearest values with 0 or 5, in such a way that 42.5 is reduced to 40. The members not included in World Development Indicators are taken from the values shown under privatisation in the last JANCPEC report (Green book) with several adjustments: (1) full score is 50 rather than 30 (2) comparative figures with other members.

Source: World Development Indicators, World Bank, 1998.

the following three aspects: (1) privatisation, (2) market access, and (3) transparency (Table 3.6).

Privatisation is a necessary condition for deregulation. We evaluate the extent of privatisation achieved by APEC members, using information on the share of state-owned enterprises in gross domestic investment compiled by the World Bank (*World Development Indicators* 1998). Naturally, the lower the share of state-owned enterprises in gross domestic investment, the greater the extent of privatisation. The highest score for the category of privatisation is 40 points.

Privatisation is a necessary condition for deregulation, but not a sufficient condition. Even when a certain sector is privatised, that sector may be subject to various regulations such as restrictions on entry and price. In the absence of necessary information on these restrictions, we consider 'market access' for foreign firms, whose evaluation is given for 'foreign direct investment', as a proxy for the extent of regulations applied to the APEC members.

Accordingly, the outcome of the evaluation of the current position of FDI liberalisation is used to evaluate 'market access'. The highest score for market access is set at 40. Because we do not consider various restrictions, due to the non-availability of necessary information, our scores tend to overestimate the extent of deregulation achieved by members.

Transparency, which is given 20 points, is evaluated by the information presented in IAPs by the APEC members.

NOTES

1   In our earlier assessment (Yamazawa 1997) we gave 50 points to the 'current state' and another 50 points to the 'commitment to liberalisation'. However, this fixed scoring system is subject to a logical difficulty, in that an economy with a perfect current state can get only 50 points, while another economy half way to the Bogor target can get a full grade by only committing to future liberalisation, but not yet implementing it. The flexible scoring system mentioned in the text is free from this logical inconsistency.

2   Of course, the detailed scores for individual checkpoints (which were attached at the end of Chapters 1–13 of Part 2 of Yamazawa (1998)) were revised based on the 1998 IAPs.

3   The NTM database by UNCTAD identified sixty-four core NTMs; it reports which of these core NTMs are imposed on individual products (ISIC 4-digit) by each country. The NTM frequency of a product for each county is the percentage share of NTMs actually imposed on the product concerned. A 20% frequency means that a dozen core NTMs are imposed, which can include major effective NTMs and cannot be justified under any circumstances as WTO-consistent. All frequency data utilised in our assessment are obtained from PECC, Survey of Impediments, Appendix table.

4   The GATS framework identifies four modes of supply (cross-border supply, consumption abroad, commercial presence, and presence of natural persons) times two aspects (national treatment and market access) and examines in which of the eight modality X aspects is restricted for a particular service sub-sector. The frequency ratios are calculated for a particular service sector by dividing the number of modality X aspects which are still restricted by 8 (=4X2). The frequency of 100 per cent means that a service transaction is restricted in all modes and two aspects. PECC, Survey of Impediments, calculated frequency ratios of forty-two service sub-sectors for sixteen APEC member economies (except Papua New Guinea and Chinese Taipei). It shows that services trade is more restricted than commodities, and that 30–40 per cent frequency is among the lowest, while a high frequency of 80–100 per cent is not uncommon for several service sectors.

5   Based on the APEC Sectoral Liberalisation Nomination Forms for the fifteen sectors compiled at the SOM in September to November 1997.

6   APEC Economic Leaders' Declaration: 'Connecting the APEC Community', Vancouver, Canada, 25 November 1997, paragraph 6.

7   APEC Meeting of Ministers Responsible for Trade: 'Statement of the Chair', Kuching, Malaysia, 22–3 June 1998, paragraphs 5 and 6.

8   'Joint Statement by Ministers', Vancouver, Canada, 22–3 November 1997.

9   Australia published a CGE study on the EVSL issue, but from the point of view of Australian interests. P. Dee, A. Hardin and M. Schuele, *APEC Early Voluntary Sectoral Liberalisation*, Australia: Productivity Commission, July 1998.

REFERENCES

APEC (1999) *Summary Conclusion of The First APEC Senior Officials' Meeting* (SOM) for the Eleventh Ministerial Meeting, Wellington, 8–9 February.

—— (1998) 1998 *Annual Report to Ministers: Committee on Trade and Investment*, Kuala Lumpur, Malaysia, November.

—— (1997) *Individual Action Plans* (revised), submitted by seventeen members except Papua New Guinea.

—— (1997) *APEC in Action: 1997 Results Report*, Vancouver, Canada, November.

—— (1996) *MAPA 1996*, Manila Action Plan for APEC: Vol II, Individual Action Plans, and Vol. III, Collective Action Plans

—— (1996) *APEC Individual Action Plans: Format Guidelines*, provided by CTI Chair, August.

—— (1995) *The Osaka Action Agenda: Implementation of the Bogor Declaration*, Part I, Liberalization and Facilitation, Section C: Actions in Specific Areas November 1995.

APEC Committee on Trade and Investment (1997) *1997 Annual Report to Ministers*, Vancouver Canada, November. Appendix Two: Convenor Summary Reports and Collective Action Plans.

Bollard, A. and Vautier, K.M. (1998) 'The convergence of competition law within APEC and the CER Agreement', in Wu Rong-I and Chu Yun-Peng (eds) *Business, Market and Government in the Asia–Pacific*, New York: Routledge.

PECC/Trade Policy Forum (1995) 'Survey of impediments to trade and investment in the APEC region', report prepared for APEC, November.

PECC, PIDS, and Asia Foundation (1996) *Perspectives on the Manila Action Plan for APEC*, Manila, November.

Yamazawa, Ippei (1997) 'APEC's Liberalization and the WTO', *Australian Economic Review*, March.

—— (1997) 'APEC's progress toward the Bogor Target: A quantitative assessment of individual action plans', IAP Study Group/JANCPEC, September.

—— (1998) 'APEC's progress toward the Bogor Target: A quantitative assessment of 1997 IAP/CAP', PECC Japan Committee, Tokyo, March.

4 APEC and the millennium round

Peter A. Petri[1]

At APEC's tenth anniversary, global trade liberalisation is at a standstill. Although the financial crisis of 1998 has now retreated, it has undermined the momentum of global policy makers in regard to financial issues. International institutions, including APEC, have come under attack for their lacklustre response to the crisis. Meanwhile, the United States is experiencing huge trade deficits, has failed to fast-track the new trade negotiating authority, and is beginning to yield to political pressures for protection in basic industries. The European Union is similarly yielding to domestic pressures for protection, and has repeatedly confronted the WTO over rulings concerning issues of symbolic, if not economic, importance.

At the same time, recent economic trends and the global financial crisis have, if anything, increased the pay-off to integration into the world economy, at least on the current account. Thus, despite recent financial setbacks, developing countries have not retreated from liberalisation. Indeed, many have made accelerated progress, encouraged to be sure by IMF pressure. And the extraordinary boom of the 'new' economy in the United States is persuading many developed countries, including Japan, that economic integration is the key to competitiveness. In general, as globalisation attracts public attention, it stimulates new integration initiatives as well as demands for international disciplines in new areas. These are some of the reasons that account for a cautious but widespread agreement on launching a new round of global trade negotiations at the WTO's 1999 ministerial meetings in Seattle.

Despite the general support for a new round, the negotiations are not likely to move forward rapidly. The trade environment is not auspicious, and there will be inevitable jockeying for position and some initial confusion in the early stages. Uncertainty about the outcome of the presidential elections in the United States will also prevent significant progress for at least a year. But as the financial recoveries continue and the United States election is completed, a new window of opportunity will open for global agreements.

These developments thrust APEC into uncharted territory: APEC's negotiating approach must now switch from a 'between rounds' modality to a 'within rounds' modality. APEC was born in the midst of the Uruguay Round, partly to offer an alternative venue for negotiations for the United States and its Asian partners, had the Uruguay Round failed. In the lull in global negotiations since 1993, APEC provided a way to keep the 'bicycle' of trade liberalisation moving. But now the attention will shift to the Millennium Round, and APEC's members will reserve trade concessions for the round rather than making them in APEC. (Arguably, APEC's liberalisation initiatives over the last two years were already victims of the prospective round.) This chapter examines APEC's options in this new setting, including ways in which it may have to adjust its operations to the requirements of the 'within round' era.

APEC AND THE GLOBAL TRADING SYSTEM

APEC's role in the coming Millennium Round is closely conditioned by its objectives and negotiating structure. Unlike the EU, APEC is an example of a new type of regional trading arrangement (RTA) – the Euro–med Agreements and the Free Trade Agreement of the Americas (FTAA) are others – that brings together very diverse economic partners, and aims for comprehensive economic cooperation. These new RTAs typically are also concerned with broader issues such as trade and investment facilitation, social and technical cooperation, and the harmonisation of certain policies.

Moreover, APEC is unique among these agreements by its commitment to 'open regionalism'. This concept emerged at the time PECC was established in the early 1980s, and was designed to distinguish PECC from earlier proposals for a regional free trade area. In describing PECC, Masayoshi Ohira, the late Prime Minister of Japan, spoke of creating 'an open regional cooperation befitting the age of the global community' (Cheit 1992). APEC's first ministerial meeting in Canberra in 1989 also affirmed that, 'consistent with the interests of Asia Pacific economies, cooperation should be directed at strengthening the open multilateral trading system; it should not involve the formation of a trading bloc' (APEC 1989). The 1991 Seoul Declaration reaffirmed this direction by proposing that 'Asia–Pacific Economic Cooperation should serve as an exemplary model of open regional cooperation' and should 'develop and strengthen an open multilateral trading system in the interest of Asia Pacific and other economies' (APEC 1991).

But what does 'open regionalism' mean? What might be characterised as the 'Australian view' (e.g. Drysdale and Garnaut 1989) suggests that it does *not* mean preferential trade. Thus, the 'Pacific free trade area' should not 'involve discrimination within the Pacific' because that may 'provide an impetus for the accelerating movement towards liberalisation on an MFN basis, and reinforcement of the "prisoner's delight" process' of spreading reductions in trade barriers worldwide. In a recent restatement, Elek defines a concept of 'open clubs' as an arrangement that is (a) consistent with existing obligations of members, (b) transparent, (c) non-discriminatory with respect to all new measures, (d) accessible to other interested parties, and (e) subject to outside review (Elek 1998). Note that Elek's point (c) categorically excludes preferential arrangements.

An alternative 'American view' (e.g. Bergsten 1998) champions trade concessions that incorporate regional preferences, provided that they are extended (also on a preferential basis) to all partners willing to reciprocate. Under an alternative formulation, a preferential arrangement is established, but membership is automatically offered to all countries willing to subscribe to it. These interpretations lie halfway between the 'Australian view' of unconditional open regionalism and the closed preferential agreements that typically characterised earlier free trade agreements.

These conflicting views of open regionalism were vigorously debated in the Eminent Persons' Group formed to advise APEC in 1993–5, and lead to the uneasy compromise of the 1995 EPG report, which called for:

- Maximum possible unilateral liberalisation
- Continued reductions in barriers facing non-member countries on an MFN basis
- Willingness to extend regional liberalisation to non-members on a reciprocal basis
- Recognition that members can unilaterally extend liberalisation to non-members

In the event, APEC has not yet adopted any preferential measures. The somewhat ambiguous language of the Bogor Declaration ('free and open trade and investment in the region') also leaves open whether preferential regional liberalisation might be consistent with APEC's goal.

Despite this lack of clarity, APEC has made several important positive contributions to the dynamic of global free trade. It has helped to keep the Asia Pacific region free of preferential agreements and committed to outward looking policies. In addition, APEC was influential in the endplay of the Uruguay Round,[2] and subsequently in the WTO's Information Technology Agreement (ITA). And it has invented new modalities for promoting liberalisation, including the development of a striking vision for free trade and investment by a definite date.

Preventing an Asian bloc

The 1989 Canberra Conference that established APEC was the product of many years of Asian and Australian efforts to create a regional institution in the Pacific Rim. Academic proposals for a Pacific Free Trade Area were floated at the 1968 PAFTAD conference and culminated in Japanese efforts to launch formal discussions in 1980. Although that initiative resulted only in the establishment of an unofficial tripartite forum (PECC), regional interest in an inter-governmental initiative continued, albeit with little United States support.

When the proposal for a formal Pacific organisation resurfaced in 1989, the United States was preoccupied with the US–Canada Free Trade Agreement and global initiatives and was apparently caught by surprise. In fact, the United States seemed to join APEC *not* for its promise of regional economic dialogue, but because it did not want to be left out of an Asian grouping which might coalesce around Japan. The first Australian proposals for APEC in 1989 excluded the United States. Subsequent diplomatic initiatives then included the United States, and Secretary of State James Baker in turn offered US support.

Still, the concept of an Asian regional bloc continued to emerge for several years after APEC was established. Advocated by Malaysian Prime Minister Mahathir, it was first proposed as an East Asian Economic Group (EAEG) and later as an East Asian Economic Caucus (EAEC). Japan and other East Asian countries briefly flirted with these ideas, but others – notably Indonesia – were firmly opposed. The United States also made it clear that participants in EAEC would have to choose between an Asian grouping and a trans-Pacific partnership. In the end, the latter was too important for most Asian economies to risk and EAEC faded away.

Critical contributions for maintaining APEC as a Pacific-wide institution came from ASEAN. Although ASEAN leaders were concerned about APEC's institutionalisation as a possible challenge to ASEAN, they soon came to see it as an excellent forum for projecting regional views. They were offered an important role in APEC – ministerials were initially set to alternate between ASEAN and non-ASEAN countries and the secretariat was located in Singapore. In turn, ASEAN provided excellent leadership in APEC's Indonesian and Philippine years. ASEAN's support for APEC has waned in the current difficult environment, contributing to APEC's general malaise.

Overall, APEC thus helped to build the present regional framework in the Pacific: it maintained United States involvement in the region; created a loose, outward-oriented coalition of Pacific economies; supported the development of ASEAN; and prevented an inward-oriented Asian bloc – a distinct possibility in the 1990s. In light of subsequent changes in the performance of the United States and Asian economies, the current regional architecture appears fortuitous. Yet it is true that APEC did not deliver the productive partnerships that might have been expected from a stronger regional institution, either in terms of regional liberalisation or a forceful response to the financial crisis.

Competitive effects

In the early 1990s, as the Uruguay Round ran into increasing difficulty, the United States accelerated its APEC and NAFTA initiatives. On the eve of the Uruguay Round deadline in 1993, President Clinton decided to upgrade the APEC ministerial to a meeting of leaders, dramatically boosting APEC's profile. In combination with the signing of NAFTA, these initiatives signalled that the

United States was willing to create its own trading framework if Europe failed to make concessions. The threat worked and the Uruguay Round was concluded shortly afterwards.

After the Uruguay Round was concluded, APEC became an impetus for additional agreements. As Table 4.1 indicates, APEC's launch was followed by a flurry of regional trade proposals. The Enterprise of the Americas Initiative (EAI), which laid the foundations for the FTAA, was announced by President Bush in 1990, shortly after the creation of APEC and the decision to pursue the US–Mexico trade agreement that eventually evolved into NAFTA. The effort to scale up the FTAA to a fully-fledged free trade area in December 1994 in turn followed the Bogor Declaration by a few months. More generally, the FTAA's history parallels that of APEC, with each major step taking place approximately one year later. This timing sequence provides intriguing evidence of competitive pressures – either between different regional bureaus of the American bureaucracy, or across different trade partners.

The European reaction to America's regional strategies in Asia and Latin America is reflected in the ASEM and Transatlantic Economic Partnership (TEP) initiatives. Although ASEM began with the objective of a broad political dialogue, it has taken on greater economic content and now includes trade and investment initiatives. Indeed, ASEM had more to offer than APEC during the Asian crisis, as Europe volunteered a fund for Asian financial stability. Similarly, TEP is a European–American initiative designed to counterbalance APEC and FTAA. Europe's efforts to develop relations with Latin America (e.g. Mercosur) represent still another initiative designed to parallel American initiatives.

Modalities of trade policy

APEC has also made significant contributions by developing innovative approaches to trade policy and negotiations. Not all of its experiments have produced reliable results, but they have proved valuable in some settings and may be useful in APEC's future 'within rounds' role.

Leaders' meetings. By bringing heads of state together in an annual meeting, APEC 'upped the ante' on regional economic negotiations. For several years in a row, leaders could break logjams and solve problems that ministers could not. Moreover, leaders were under public pressure to produce meaningful outcomes, and were especially motivated to achieve 'spectacular' results during their terms as chair. This arrangement lent momentum to the negotiations and produced visionary outcomes. However, as vision had to give way to implementation, leaders' meetings have come under increasing scrutiny and criticism.

Vision. The Bogor Declaration – a broad vision for eliminating 'all barriers' by a certain date – remains APEC's most important contribution to the global trade policy landscape. By setting an important, yet achievable target, APEC raised the sights of the global policy community. The result came about in

Table 4.1 Super-regional integration initiatives

	World Trade Organisation	Asia Pacific Economic Cooperation	Free Trade Agreement of the Americas	Asia–Europe meeting	Trans-atlantic economic partnership
1989		APEC launched			
1990			Enterprise for the Americas Initiative launched		
1991					
1992					
1993	Uruguay Round agreement reached	Seattle Summit calls for major regional cooperation effort	Miami Summit creates 'Plan of Action' for FTAA and calls for concluding talks by 2005	EC paper on 'New Asia Policy' proposes ASEM	
1994	Marrakesh meeting sets WTO agenda and structure	Bogor Summit sets vision of free trade and investment by 2010 and 2020			
1995		Osaka Action Plan outlines an operational strategy			New Trans-atlantic Agenda announced with facilitation goals
1996	Singapore ministerial adopts ITA	Manila Action Plan introduces IAPs and CAPs, launches ITA		Bangkok leaders' meeting launches ASEM	
1997	Telecom and financial services negotiations concluded			First ministerial and Business Conference held	
1998		Year's central objective, 9-sector EVSL, fails to be adopted	Santiago Summit sets agenda up and creates 9 negotiating groups	Leaders set Asian support fund	Europe proposes free trade and services FTA; summit calls only for collaboration in WTO
1999 and beyond	Launch Millennium Round		Negotiate FTA details over next two years in Miami and then elsewhere	Develop investment promotion, trade facilitation Action Plans	

large part because President Suharto, the host of the meeting, wanted a historic outcome. Similar targets have since been set by FTAA, by the Euro–Med Agreements, were proposed by TEP, and are now under discussion for adoption in the Millennium Round. As the commitments to this vision spread, it becomes increasingly realistic to adopt the goal of complete liberalisation worldwide. Similar considerations also triggered more modest results – the Osaka Action Agenda (OAA) in 1995 and the Manila Action Plan for APEC (MAPA) in 1996.

Breadth of Coverage. APEC has pioneered the way in addressing an unusually wide range of economic cooperation issues. While the European Community, NAFTA and other highly structured economic agreements have also covered wide ground, APEC's work is significant because of the wide range of partners involved. Some areas not previously addressed in larger international fora include competition policy, investment and various facilitation issues. APEC's agenda was later reflected in a similarly broad coverage in the FTAA.

The cost of breadth, however, sometimes appears to be depth. APEC's Non-Binding Investment Principles are recognised to be weak, and even so have not been uniformly adopted. APEC's telecommunication discussions had little impact on the WTO negotiations (APEC members remained the most recalcitrant). And while considerable discussion on competition policy has taken place, guidelines still have not been offered.

Negotiation Structure. APEC has experimented with new mechanisms for collecting proposals and implementing concessions in a 'voluntary' framework. The first major approach focused on individual action plans (IAPs). The plans required members to provide details on how they plan to meet APEC goals in each of the fifteen OAA action areas. Ideally, these schedules would reflect the special circumstances of members, while targeting 'comparable' liberalisation results. The IAPs were to be accompanied by collective action plans (CAPs) on common projects. In the event, the IAPs led to frustration because the commitments listed were too distant and too general.

As an alternative, the United States proposed a sectoral negotiations structure. The approach triumphed with the successful Information Technology Agreement in 1996. In this model, APEC reached voluntary agreement on a set of liberalisation measures, and then passed the result on to the WTO to be converted into a binding agreement. This required bringing on board a sufficient number of non-APEC countries to reach a 'critical mass' of importing countries.

Unfortunately, the ITA appears to have been an exception – a sector where interests were fortuitously balanced and the sector's contribution to economic development was widely recognised. Thus, APEC shifted to a multisectoral negotiations approach. In this mode several sectors were chosen to provide balanced benefits, for a so-called 'Early Voluntary Sectoral Liberalisation' negotiation. As noted below, this attempt failed.

Running out of steam

To capitalise on the ITA agreement, the Leaders' Meeting of 1996 called for an 'Early Voluntary Sectoral Liberalisation' (EVSL) initiative that would package together liberalisation initiatives in several sectors. This initiative became a centrepiece of APEC's 1998 work program. The 1997 Vancouver summit established fifteen sectors as priorities for the EVSL initiative, and nine of these were to be adopted as a single package at the 1998 Kuala Lumpur summit (multiple sectors were needed to recreate the fortuitous distribution of benefits under the ITA). The parameters of liberalisation in these sectors were worked out earlier in 1998, and it was assumed that the package would pass APEC and then move to the WTO for binding global commitments.

The EVSL sectors were proposed, for the most part, by APEC members with export interests. For example, the controversial fish and forest product sectors that eventually doomed the agreement were proposed by Brunei, Canada, Indonesia, New Zealand, Thailand and the United States – except for Brunei, all major agricultural exporters. The overall package was balanced: for example, toys and plastics were included for countries with an advantage in labour-intensive products, while environmental equipment was included for advanced manufacturing economies. But it did not offer enough compensation to Japan for its politically sensitive forest products and fisheries sectors. The negotiations went down to the wire – until only hours before the Leaders' meeting was to start – and ended in embarrassing failure. APEC tried to put the best face on it by 'passing' the EVSL package on to the WTO anyway, where it has evolved into an 'Accelerated Tariff Liberalisation' initiative. Efforts in 1999 to address the remaining six sectors ended in a similar impasse.

APEC's current doldrums reflect several factors. The Asian crisis has diverted attention from core issues, and APEC was poorly prepared to deal with macroeconomics and finance. The failure of the EVSL showed that APEC still does not have a formula for extracting concessions from members. And APEC liberalisation needs leadership, which the United States was no longer able to provide in recent years – its presidency was under siege, its executive branch favoured global solutions to the regional problems (through the IMF and the WTO), and its legislative branch turned isolationist. Neither was ASEAN, a strong supporter of APEC in recent years, ready to continue its leadership given its vast political and economic challenges. But most importantly, APEC has ceased to be a suitable venue for trade concessions as global negotiations get underway.

Reinventing APEC

On APEC's tenth anniversary, the organisation's future is in doubt. The 1999 Auckland agenda was thin, and the Leaders' Meeting produced neither major trade or financial measures, nor a shared vision of what could be achieved in the WTO. The absence of ambitious proposals and results in 1999 was not entirely negative – expectations have consistently outpaced results at recent summits, undermining confidence. And the summit did achieve important political results by bringing China and the United States closer together and by facilitating the effort to reach a regional consensus on the East Timor crisis.

But the lack of concrete economic achievements has also led to calls for APEC's dissolution. For example, even the chairman of the Pacific Basin Economic Council recently argued that APEC should be abandoned because it was ineffective and politicised. In his view, East Asian businesses were pursuing liberalisation independently, and the collective effort through APEC was slowing the process by inducing countries to wait for reciprocity instead of moving unilaterally.

The key challenge APEC faces is to find a way to make significant, visible contributions in the shadow of the Millennium Round. Essentially, new strategies have to be developed to make APEC complementary to the WTO process. A dual strategy will be required: APEC has to find ways to support the negotiations as long as they remain on track, while threatening to offer a competitive venue should the negotiations fail. Three specific ways in which APEC could initially support the round are as follows.

Revive the IAPs. The IAPs have taken a back seat to sectoral approaches since the ITA agreement. The shortcomings of the IAPs are well understood (PECC 1999), yet they still offer the only viable, ongoing 'carrot and stick' of the APEC process: public and market reactions to country policies. The challenge now is to make the IAPs work despite the tendency for countries to withhold announcements for future liberalisation plans in light of the global negotiations underway.

We propose that APEC incorporate 'conditional programs' in the IAPs – that is, that a special section in the IAPs be established for liberalisation offers that countries are willing to implement if global agreements are reached. The sum of these offers could provide impressive testimony to the value of reaching global agreements. In addition, these offers would show that the Bogor goals remain a feasible target, provided broad support for liberalisation can be maintained.

Provide greater scope for APEC – X initiatives. Due to its diversity (indeed, increasing diversity), APEC's consensus approach to policy is increasingly an obstacle to innovation and progress. Rather, members with shared interests should be encouraged to use the APEC forum to promote initiatives in which they share interests and which they would like to project onto the global stage. A mechanism for developing and publicising APEC – X initiatives could help make APEC a force in the Millennium Round.

Inject vision into global policy making. APEC has been effective in putting vision behind its liberalisation efforts, and should continue this focus in promoting WTO action. Vision matters both on a global level – for example, by encouraging the WTO to adopt the Bogor vision – and in specific, integrated sectoral approaches. For instance, the Food Program represents an opportunity to create a plan to address the needs of both producers and consumers, through a combination of liberalisation and food security provisions. APEC's 'Automotive Dialogue' could similarly propose a broad, integrated approach to rationalise the region's automobile sector. A third example: the 'internet' economy requires significant policy commitments and extensive cooperation in building an appropriate infrastructure and knowledge base in the region.

These approaches, and APEC's options in the new era, will be examined in greater depth below. In these areas and others, APEC could play a constructive role in shaping the Millennium Round, but careful choices will need to be made about when collaboration with WTO is the most effective strategy, and when parallel efforts are the most effective.

PROSPECTS FOR THE MILLENNIUM ROUND

The new round was announced at the Quadrilateral Group's (Canada, EU, Japan and the US) meeting in December 1998, and its structure began to take shape in the Group's meetings in May 1999. The Quad called for broad-based participation in the new round, engaging the developing countries and important new applicants such as China; comprehensive coverage of issues, including areas that were not addressed in the Uruguay Round; and rapid, manageable negotiations that could be concluded in three years. These objectives were also echoed at the Auckland APEC summit in September 1999.

Content of the Round

The Quad communiqué identified a range of issues to be taken up in the round (Table 4.2). The agenda is very broad; it includes virtually all of the topics that appear on lists anticipated by experts. Analyses of a proposed new round by Anderson (1999) and Schott (1998) list similar issues. (Those studies also provide a detailed discussion of the central issues in each area, a subject outside the purview of this chapter.)

The length of the list raises questions about whether the goals of comprehensiveness, inclusiveness and speed can be simultaneously satisfied. For example, some priorities may have to be developed within the first few months of discussions, presumably leading to earlier results in a subset of fields. Agricultural and service negotiations will most likely begin early since they were committed some time ago. The liberalisation of industrial products, the customary territory of negotiators, may also move rapidly compared with other areas. Nevertheless, it is difficult to see meaningful progress in the agriculture sector without major compensations to Europe and Japan in other areas of negotiation.

Two broad tensions affect the round and the choice of topics. The first is among the major developed players (the United States, Japan and Europe) and is about agriculture and services. The second is between developed and

Table 4.2 Negotiating areas identified by the Quad in May 1999

Topic	Proposed actions
Services	Negotiations covering all sectors, including those of interest to developing countries
Agriculture	Carrying out commitments in the Uruguay Round
Non-agriculture	Negotiations on tariffs and non-tariff barriers, including those of interest to developing countries. Conclusion of ITA2
Regulation and standards	Transparency in regulatory policy and formulation of international standards, as well as acceptance of such standards
Investment	Work on investment on a progressive basis, including the development of objectives toward negotiations of WTO rules on investment
Competition policy	Consider whether negotiations are appropriate on competition laws
Trade remedies	Review concerns about the adequacy and implementation of rules
TRIPS	Implement the Agreement, noting the expiration of the transitional period on 1 January 2000
Facilitation	Implement the Customs Valuation agreement
Civil society and WTO	Improve WTO transparency, responsiveness to civil society, while preserving the government-to-government organisation
Labour	Standards should be more widely respected; ILO should promote the new Declaration on Fundamental Principles and Rights at Work
Environment	Trade policy and environment policy should be mutually supportive and environmental implications should be taken into account
Government procurement	Complete work on transparency in government procurement by November 1999; review the Agreement on Government Procurement
Electronic commerce	Continue the existing moratorium and clarify rules
Dispute settlement	Clarify rules, by the end of July, to eliminate divergent interpretations

developing countries, and involves the implementation of critical provisions of the Uruguay Round (for example, textiles) and anti-dumping, on the one hand, and new issues (investment, labour, environment, competition) on the other. Bergsten has suggested that a 'grand bargain' might involve trading assured market access to the markets of developed countries for the gradual liberalisation of the markets of developing countries. Interestingly, the membership of APEC spans both divides, enabling APEC to address critical WTO issues in a representative, but perhaps more collegial, context.

Beyond general issues, each player has its more specialised priorities. Japan is interested in investment because of its large Asian production system (MITI 1999). Japan would also like to see work on competition policy in order to check United States claims that its markets are not competitive, and perhaps also to undermine the anti-dumping provisions applied by the United States. Japan does not want, however, the forced harmonisation of competition policies, and wants to make sure that developing countries play an important role in the negotiations in order to slow down the rule-making process.

The European Union has a comprehensive work program on service liberalisation, and wants to move forward rapidly on product standards and mutual recognition, areas in which large European markets offer an important advantage. The United States also puts a high priority on services, including especially energy, environmental and express delivery services (USTR 1999). The United States is especially interested in electronic commerce, on which a WTO working program is now under way. Finally, official United States and European documents also emphasise the 'green' priorities, including labour, environment and governance.

The positions of developing countries are more diverse. Many, especially in Latin America, would have an interest in initiatives on investment, given the current investment-hungry environment. Agricultural and industrial barriers are also important to many countries. At the other extreme, developing countries will be opposed to addressing labour, environment and governance. Unless this controversy is properly managed, it could cast a shadow over the launch of the Millennium Round.

Modality of the Round

The first contentious issue to surface about the new round involves the modality of negotiations. Japan, Europe and most developing countries want the round to be a 'single undertaking'. The United States, however, has advocated other – primarily sectoral – approaches. This conflict provides insight into the objectives of the major players.

Joining issues into a single undertaking has the advantage of highlighting trade-offs across the priorities of different players. One criticism of the Uruguay Round was that critical trade-offs could not easily be made until the end because the negotiation had been compartmentalised. This is how Europe and Japan argue their position, but other motives lie beneath. It is possible that Europe and Japan believe that some urgent objectives (for example, mutual acceptance of pharmaceutical test results in the case of Europe, and stricter disciplines on anti-dumping measures in the case of Japan) will not be served by a compartmentalised, sectoral negotiation. They may also fear that the United States will be able to achieve sectoral agreements in preferred sectors (for example, technological products and electronic commerce) without making broader concessions.

The United States, on the other hand, argues that a single undertaking would be unwieldy given the breadth of the agenda and would not bring quick, significant results. It also would like to see early 'harvests' of results without waiting for a general agreement. Since the pro-market interests of exporting countries are likely to be more prominent in a sectoral forum, the United States may believe that the chances for achieving liberal results are better in a sectoral context. Finally, United States negotiators may also believe (although not publicly claim) that it will be easier to keep domestic social lobbies at bay in limited, sectoral negotiations, than in a comprehensive undertaking.

Compromises could involve dealing in a comprehensive way with clusters of issues. At one extreme, Schott (1998) has proposed 'roundups', or groups of results harvested at regular intervals. A broad schedule would be prepared for several years in advance to guide which issues would be concluded at each ministerial. In this setting, Anderson (1999) argues that the foreign investment and competition policies are too complicated to come up early, and should be left out of the earlier roundups, and Schott (1998) would shift labour and environmental issues out of the round to forums such as the ILO. At the time of writing, the best guess is that the compromise will involve taking up the traditional sectors first – industrial products, agriculture, services – as a 'single undertaking', and leaving the new issues to a later stage, or possibly out of the round altogether (except as they are addressed in the context of traditional sectors).

The role of regional forums

The major players of the Millennium Round will undoubtedly use regional institutions to advance their WTO priorities. They can do so in two ways: first by using a regional forum to generate ideas and support for an initiative, and second by using the forum to create a credible alternative (say, a potential preferential trading bloc) to the multilateral process.

The history of the Uruguay Round is instructive. The round began in 1986 in the context of two important regional initiatives – the 1985 Delors plan for a European Single Market, which eventually led to the 'Europe 1992' project; and the US–Canada Free Trade Agreement. These initiatives helped to strengthen the negotiating positions of Europe and the United States in the round, with each signaling that it was willing to 'go it alone' if necessary. No major new regional initiatives were proposed until the negotiations ran into trouble in the early 1990s and the United States took steps to complete

NAFTA and reinvigorate APEC. (APEC's launch in 1989, as already noted, was not yet motivated by global objectives.)

A similar scenario would suggest stepped-up regional negotiating activity during the next year or two as countries attempt to stake out their bargaining positions in the Millennium Round. The bilateral discussions of Japan and Korea and others already noted could represent an example.

But there is little reason to expect ambitious, early progress in the major super-regional forums. APEC has not yet found a modality that allows it to make rapid progress. Europe, in turn, offered an ambitious program for the TEP last year that would have called for date-certain tariff elimination in industrial products and a preferential free trade area in services. In the event, however, the EU–US summit adopted an ambiguous formula calling simply for collaboration in the WTO (Elek 1998). Finally, the FTAA initiative also appears to be stalled, in part because the United States has not been able to sell the concept domestically (Schott and Hufbauer 1999). Indeed, more liberalisation activity has taken place in the WTO in recent months than in the regional institutions outside it.

The longer term outlook is more interesting. If the new round gets good intermediate results – say through a sectoral negotiating approach – then each region may also feel more pressure to pursue liberalisation more forcefully. For example, regional initiatives may be justified as efforts to maintain a region's competitive position relative to other countries that are becoming more open and thus more attractive for investment and trade. If, on the other hand, the round gets into trouble, then regional initiatives will offer an alternative strategy. Not all regional groupings will represent viable venues for solving problems encountered in the WTO (which ones do will depend on the issues that cause the bottleneck), but they could well become good candidates for shaking up the global negotiating process. Thus, the regional forums might make reasonably significant contributions under several WTO outcome scenarios.

APEC's options in the Millennium Round

Among the super-regional institutions, APEC is the most substantial and experienced, and is best placed to affect the Millennium Round. To be sure, the ultimate role of APEC will depend on the priorities member governments attach to the round and to regional relationships, as well as the special characteristics and capabilities of APEC as an institution. After reviewing some of these factors, we will consider four models for an APEC role in the Millennium Round.

APEC'S ADVANTAGES

APEC's role in the Millennium Round will be shaped by central structural features of the institution and its members. Assets that help to make APEC a good venue for certain negotiations are:

- *Commitment to global trade.* APEC economies typically depend intensively on trade with distant partners and therefore do not want to limit trade to preferential partners. This is also why APEC is interested in the infrastructure of trade and in facilitation issues such as customs valuation, standards, mutual recognition, and fairness in trade remedies.
- *Diverse trade interests.* APEC is as diverse as the WTO, with members' interests ranging from agriculture to electronic commerce, from labour-intensive manufactures to sophisticated services. This means that when APEC reaches agreement on an issue, its policy framework has a good chance of attracting international support.
- *Good communications among key players.* Three of the four key players of the Millennium Round – China (assuming that it will be soon admitted to the WTO), Japan and the United States – are APEC members. The routine communications that APEC facilitates among these members, including at the highest level, should aid WTO progress.
- *Informal decision-making structure.* The characteristics that make APEC a frustrating venue for negotiation – voluntarism, aversion to commitments – are an advantage when used in parallel with formal approaches. For example, APEC could make more progress in areas such as investments, where more formal efforts have failed, and then 'serve up' blueprints that provide a starting point for negotiation.

Because of these characteristics, APEC could make useful contributions in the Millennium Round. But what exact role should it play? We now present several alternative models for conceptualising the APEC–WTO relationship. The discussion is speculative, since the round's agenda will not take shape for some months. Four scenarios are examined, representing different levels of involvement in the global process.

APEC as cheerleader

The least demanding model of involvement for APEC is to act as a vocal supporter of the multilateral process without taking a significant direct role in the negotiations. APEC will almost certainly play the cheerleader role initially; no leaders' statement will be written from now on without urging movement on the Millennium Round. But some more specific approaches that would help to improve APEC's effectiveness in a cheerleader role might include:

- Applying public and private pressure to members withholding concessions
- Adapting the IAPs to provide inducements for Millennium Round offers, for example, by creating a section within the IAPs for country offers that are conditional on WTO agreement
- Projecting visionary objectives for the negotiations as a whole, similar to the Bogor targets, or integrated liberalisation and development programs for specific sectors
- Monitoring compliance with past GATT agreements

Moreover, these and other contributions to the new round could be explicitly identified by APEC as new 'Common Action Plan' items.

APEC's role as cheerleader would not diminish the possibilities for continued direct progress in areas that the new round is not likely to cover. Thus, initiatives in facilitation and economic and technical cooperation could perhaps intensify. Even in the liberalisation area there are significant opportunities for lowering barriers below bound levels, and for developing guidelines in areas that are not likely to come under international disciplines in the near future.

APEC as laboratory

A somewhat more ambitious involvement in the Millennium Round would cast APEC as a venue for testing the 'new' areas of global negotiations. The areas selected are likely to be either those where APEC economies have significant common interests, or those in which APEC's diversity provides a good, but manageable, model of global diversity. In these areas APEC could examine, debate and propose recommendations for WTO action. This is the model of the ITA that many APEC policy makers wanted to repeat with the EVSL.

As a laboratory for the Millennium Round, APEC would:

- Adapt its work program to the priorities of the round in the areas where APEC has a comparative advantage
- Encourage APEC – X proposals on issues of special interest to a subset of APEC membership, in order to set the agenda within the WTO
- Establish closer liaison with other important players, especially Europe.

Through these activities, APEC would carve out a leadership role on issues on which it has special expertise. To be sure, if APEC acted as a formal bloc, its ability to influence non-members would rapidly diminish. Rather, as an effective laboratory, APEC would open its research and deliberative processes to non-members, and perhaps combine them with those of the WTO. These could be called 'APEC – X + Y' arrangements – initiatives that begin with a subset of APEC countries and are then extended to include like-minded advocates from around the world.

APEC's role as a laboratory would involve two types of case. First, APEC would be the right institution in areas where it has already made significant progress, such as trade facilitation, including especially customs valuation, standards, mutual recognition and competition policy. Second, APEC's diversity would create an opportunity for testing agreements on controversial issues. Investment represents one such area – APEC's Non-binding Investment Principles need to be strengthened before they can be considered a good model for the WTO. Japan is especially eager to search for solutions to this issue in APEC because some of the recalcitrant participants in a potential global debate are East Asian countries (MITI 1999). As already noted, food policy, combining elements of agricultural liberalisation and food security, could also help bridge the divides across food exporting and importing countries.

APEC as coalition

A still more rigorous role would be for APEC to form a coalition (or coalitions in several areas) along the lines of the Cairns Group in the Uruguay Round. Of course, a very high commonality of interests is essential for this role. Because of its diversity, APEC does not meet that criterion for most of the issues that are likely to be debated in the Millennium Round. Nevertheless, the APEC – X + Y principle, which allows a significant group of countries to work out common positions, could help to create new coalitions for the global dialogue.

Acting as a coalition, APEC members would:

- Develop joint bargaining objectives
- Jointly publicise positions and persuade others with whom they have special ties
- Reach out to non-members with shared interests.

While APEC's full membership may not form a coalition on any particular issue, subsets of APEC members might find the APEC process conducive to common positions. Thus, APEC might give rise to several caucuses, which in turn would reach out beyond APEC to implement their goals.

APEC as competitor

The last and least likely alternative is for APEC to emerge as a competitor to liberalisation through the Millennium Round. This could happen, for example, if APEC decided to aggressively pursue the Bogor goals with preferential free trade initiatives. Such a strategy is not likely to surface until more cooperative relationships fail, or the round runs into serious trouble. In that case, APEC may threaten to become an alternative venue for liberalisation, hopefully persuading other global players to return to serious bargaining. Because of the diversity of APEC economies and their heavy reliance on extra-APEC trade partners, it is unlikely that this scenario will materialise, except perhaps in the event of the collapse of the global round.

The four APEC roles described are not mutually exclusive – at different times and in different areas of the negotiations, APEC could play several of these roles in parallel. Each role could prove constructive and even catalytic in the global negotiating framework. Understanding these roles, in turn, will be essential as APEC seeks to adjust its internal processes to the demands of a more complex external environment.

CONCLUSIONS

Just as APEC has been helpful to global liberalisation in the past, so it could also contribute to the objectives of the new global round. Although no definitive strategy can be found for APEC until the details of the new round become clearer, this chapter has considered four models for APEC's interactions with the round:

- APEC could act as a cheerleader that encourages progress in the global negotiations, both publicly and privately through its consultative process. Broadening the IAPs to include country offers conditional on WTO agreement would provide explicit recognition for WTO concessions. The cheerleader role may not be as central as some APEC supporters would prefer, but it is APEC's most likely role in the round's initial stages.
- APEC could act as a laboratory for developing proposals in its main areas of expertise, say, in trade facilitation. And because APEC spans diverse global interests in a relatively informal and collegial way, it might be able to test agreements in difficult areas like food policy, automobile trade and communications technology.
- APEC could form coalitions. Given APEC's diversity, such coalitions are not likely to involve all members on any particular issue, but could involve APEC – X + Y approaches – groupings based on a core of APEC members plus outsiders with shared interests. Smaller developing countries might especially find APEC helpful in gaining visibility for their objectives.
- APEC could become a competitive venue to the global negotiations if the results of the new round are disappointing. For example, APEC could emerge as a competitor to the round by moving forward with its own preferential liberalisation schemes. This option is not likely, but may represent valuable leverage against difficult negotiating counterparts.

Overall, these options do not suggest a very full agenda for APEC in the near term. A period of consolidation across regional initiatives is likely to lie ahead as the new round absorbs the energies of negotiators in the key countries. In this period, political objectives and benefits may play an especially important role in keeping APEC together.

As the round gets underway, APEC's role should become more demanding, involving either activities complementary to the WTO's efforts, or competitive initiatives to promote liberalisation. The new round will engage important issues, and over time it is likely to gather the support needed to address the rapid globalisation of the world economy. A role in this effort would provide an exciting new mission for APEC, as well as a 'shot in the arm' to the Bogor commitment to achieve open markets early in the next century.

NOTES

1 The author thanks Gary Hufbauer and Ambassador Ira Shapiro for helpful conversations.
2 Since this chapter focuses on the implications of APEC for the global trading system, it does not examine the 'internal' effects of APEC on the policies of member economies. The consensus of recent evaluations (Yamazawa 1998) is that members' policies are on the path required to reach the Bogor targets. A few expectations (such as China and the Philippines) aside, however, the policy

changes reported in country Individual Action Plans represent the implementation of Uruguay Round concessions and hence cannot be regarded as 'WTO plus'.

REFERENCES

Anderson, K. (1999) 'The WTO agenda for the new millennium', Seminar Paper no. 99-01, Adelaide: Centre for International Economic Studies, University of Adelaide.

APEC (1989) 'Canberra Chairman's Statement', APEC website: www.apecsec.org.sg

—— (1991) 'Seoul Declaration', APEC website: www.apecsec.org.sg

APEC Eminent Persons' Group (1994) *Achieving the APEC Vision: Free and open trade in the Asia Pacific*, Singapore: APEC Secretariat, August.

Bergsten, C.F. (ed.) (1997a) *Whither APEC? Progress to date and agenda for the future*, Washington: Institute for International Economics.

—— (1997b) 'Open Regionalism', in C.F. Bergsten (ed.) *Whither APEC?*

—— (1998) 'Fifty years of the GATT/WTO: Lessons from the past for strategies for the future', Working Paper no. 98-3, Washington: Institute for International Economics.

—— (1999a) 'The global trading system and the developing countries in 2000', Working Paper no. 99-6, Washington: Institute for International Economics.

—— (1999b) 'A new trade liberalization strategy for APEC', Washington: Institute for International Economics, mimeo.

Cheit, E.F. (1992) 'A declaration on Open Regionalism in the Pacific', *California Management Review* 35(1): 1–13.

Drabek, Z. (1998) 'A multilateral agreement on investment: Convincing the skeptics', Working Paper ERAD-98-05, Geneva: World Trade Organisation.

Drysdale, P. and Garnaut, R. (1989) 'Principles of Pacific economic integration', in J.J. Schott (ed.) *Free Trade Areas and U.S. Trade Policy*, Washington: Institute for International Economics.

Elek, A. (1998) 'Open Regionalism going global: APEC and the new transatlantic economic partnership', *Pacific Economic Paper* no. 286, Canberra: Australia–Japan Research Centre, Australian National University.

MITI, International Economic Affairs Department, International Trade Policy Bureau (1999) 'The WTO and the Millennium Round of global free trade negotiations', *Journal of Japanese Trade and Industry*, May/June.

Quadrilateral Trade Ministers Meeting (1999) 'Chair's Statement', Tokyo, 11–12 May, mimeo.

Ruggiero, R. (1998) 'Building the framework for a global electronic marketplace', Address to the 9th International Information Industry Congress, Berlin, 17 September.

Schott, J.J. (1998) 'Launching new global trade talks: An action agenda', Special Report no. 12, Washington: Institute for International Economics.

—— and Gary C. Hufbauer (1999) 'Whither FTAA?', Washington: Institute for International Economics, mimeo.

United States Trade Representative (1999) *Trade Policy Agenda and 1998 Annual Report of the President of the United States on the Trade Agreements Program*, Washington: USTR.

Wong, J.S. (1999) 'Shipping body boss criticizes forum', *South China Morning Post*, 19 March.

Yamazawa, I. (1998) 'APEC's progress toward the Bogor Target: A quantitative assessment of 1997 IAP/CAP', PECC Japan Committee, Tokyo, March.

5   APEC's relationship with its sub-regional trading arrangements

Mahani Zainal-Abidin

INTRODUCTION

APEC is dominant in world trade: its share in global exports increased from 38 per cent in 1989 to 48 per cent in 1997 while its share in imports rose from 37 per cent to 46 per cent during the same period. With the recently enlarged membership to twenty-one countries, APEC's role in global trade is growing. However, the dynamism of APEC is in part driven by its sub-regional trading arrangements (SRTAs). When APEC was formed, it not only grouped diverse and dynamic individual members; it also grouped together SRTAs. Members that belong to SRTAs have dual commitments, to the broader grouping of APEC as well as to their respective sub-regional groups. There are three SRTAs in APEC[1]: The ASEAN Free Trade Area (AFTA); The Australia–New Zealand Closer Economic Relation Trade Arrangement (ANZCERTA); and The North American Free Trade Agreement (NAFTA).

In all, twelve APEC economies are members of SRTAs and they contribute about 85 per cent of total APEC output. In addition to share of output, SRTAs are important in terms of their share in intra-regional trade – they accounted for 72 per cent of total intra-APEC trade in 1996.

Besides the formal SRTAs, there are a number of 'growth triangles' in the APEC region where economic areas are emerging through the combination of market-led integration and supportive government policies. These include the Indonesia, Malaysia and Singapore (IMS-GT), the Indonesia, Malaysia and Thailand (IMT-GT) and the Southern China, Chinese Taipei and Hong Kong (CHT) growth triangles, where no formal arrangement exists but where regional integration is being driven by a variety of forces, including common culture, proximity, economic complementarity, and supportive government policies. This study also incorporates a review of these informal growth areas. In this chapter they are also called SRTAs.

Questions have been raised as to whether such SRTAs detract from open regionalism or whether they are building blocks towards an open multilateral trading system. Questions have also been raised as to what might be the implications of SRTAs on APEC integration. SRTAs may delay the achievements of these goals if their integration path diverges from that of APEC.

Realising the role of the SRTAs, the Bogor Declaration has stressed the need 'to review the interrelationships between APEC and the existing sub-regional arrangements and to examine possible options to prevent obstruction of each other and to promote consistency in their relationship'. The primary objective of these SRTAs is to promote free trade among members, which coincides with the overall thrust of APEC to achieve free and open trade and investment in the region by 2010/2020. These two aims may not complement each other perfectly because, in promoting free trade among members, SRTAs may increase preferential treatment to their members and not extend the same benefits to other APEC economies. Another aspect of the relationship between APEC and its SRTAs is the speed of APEC process – can the SRTAs accelerate their own liberalisation program ahead of those outlined by APEC?

Generally speaking, the determination as to whether or not SRTAs undermine or detract from a liberal global trading system is based on several considerations: what are the relative weights of the trade creation and trade diversion effects and thus the potential for resource misallocation?[2] and do SRTAs contribute to or detract from the momentum towards global trade liberalisation?

If the trade effects of SRTAs are on balance positive, then there is no serious concern about the development of such arrangements. If, on the contrary, the effects are negative, their impact on open regionalism needs to be assessed. Once APEC has reached its goals of free and open trade and investment, the preferential elements of SRTAs within APEC will cease to have any effect. Does this imply that the SRTAs are only temporarily relevant until the full realisation of the Bogor Declaration?

The first part of this chapter revisits the relationship between APEC and its SRTAs. The analysis in these sections draws heavily on materials in *The Impact of Subregionalism in APEC*, prepared by the Economic Committee of APEC. The second part examines the SRTAs' future relationship in view of the progress made and the developments arising from the current crisis affecting most of the East Asian members of APEC. A conclusion and policy recommendations are provided in the final section.

APEC PROGRESS

APEC was established in 1989 for the purpose of trade and investment facilitation and liberalisation through cooperation and consultation. Its membership is now extended to twenty-one, namely, Australia, Brunei, Canada, Chile, China, Hong Kong, Indonesia, Japan, Korea, Malaysia, Mexico, New Zealand, Papua New Guinea, Peru, Philippines, Russia, Singapore, Chinese Taipei, Thailand, the United States and Vietnam.

The objectives of APEC are:

- to sustain the growth and development of the region (and) of the world economy;

- to enhance the positive gains, both for the region and the world economy, resulting from increasing economic interdependence, including by encouraging the flow of goods, services, capital and technology;
- to develop and strengthen the open multilateral trading system in the interest of Asia Pacific and all other economies; and
- to reduce barriers to trade in goods and services and investment among participants in a manner consistent with GATT principles and without detriment to other economies.

At the Bogor Leaders' Summit in 1994, APEC set a number of specific goals and objectives, including:

- free and open trade and investment in the Asia Pacific no later than 2010/2020; and
- expansion and acceleration of trade and investment facilitation programs, to attain sustainable growth for the APEC region.

In the 1995 Osaka Meeting, the Commitment for Open Regional Cooperation was further focused by establishing definitive goals of the Osaka Action Agenda (OAA) to:

- encourage and concert the evolving efforts of voluntary liberalisation in the region;
- take collective actions to advance the liberalisation and facilitation objectives; and
- stimulate and contribute to further momentum for global liberalisation.

These definitive goals were translated into each country's own Individual Action Plan (IAP), known as the Manila Action Plan for APEC (MAPA). MAPA represented a compilation of the IAPs, as well as collective action plans for trade and investment liberalisation and facilitation, and joint activities on economic and technical cooperation.

The main features of the IAPs are:

- significant unilateral tariff reductions that provide greater market access and predictability;
- a reaffirmation of the standstill on new measures of protection;
- commitments under non-tariff measures, investment and services (including measures that complement and go beyond the GATS agreement in both coverage and depth of commitment);
- a broad range of trade and investment facilitation measures, including under customs, standards and conformance, etc.;
- greater transparency and effective liberalisation through various channels; and
- reaffirmation of Uruguay Round commitments, including those customs regulations under the GATS.

APEC agrees to deepen and broaden the outcome of the Uruguay Round, strengthen trade and investment liberalisation in the region, and facilitate regional cooperation, including in such areas as standards.

Investment liberalisation

Investment liberalisation in APEC is addressed through the agreement on non-binding investment principles. At an individual level, the policy direction taken by most APEC economies over the past two decades has generally been towards easing of restrictions on, and/or lowering or removal of barriers to, inward Foreign Direct Investment (FDI). However, some observers have argued that, notwithstanding this shift in policy direction, there has been little actual change in accessibility for foreign investors because the liberalisation of formal rules has not necessarily led to an increase in the transparency of investment regimes, and this lack of transparency is a significant barrier to inward FDI; and informal investment barriers are now more important than formal barriers.

There is considerable diversity among APEC member economies in the extent to which they have used policy on FDI as a tool to promote economic development. Despite this diversity, however, two general trends are clear from the experience of the past few decades. First, APEC member economies across the spectrum of stages of development have gradually moved toward more open investment regimes. Second, that said, investment liberalisation has been approached in a more cautious and generally less thoroughgoing fashion than has trade liberalisation.

Trade liberalisation

Rapid progress in APEC trade liberalisation has been made since the late 1980s, including significant advances on the multilateral, unilateral and sub-regional fronts. APEC members implemented unilateral reforms and deregulation programs that resulted in a significant reduction of their overall tariff rates in the 1990s. As a result of these various measures, the unweighted average tariff rate in the APEC region fell from 15.4 per cent in 1988 to 9.1 per cent in 1996.[3] Among the members, three economies have virtually zero tariffs, and only four economies had tariffs higher than 15 per cent in 1996.[4] In addition, most of the members with the higher tariffs have significantly reduced their tariff rates.

APEC members have reinforced these liberalisation trends with MAPA. Table 5.1 gives a listing of some major actions of APEC members. Five members (Brunei Darussalam, Chile, Hong Kong, New Zealand and Singapore) have indicated a target of zero tariffs by 2010/2020. China has announced a schedule of significant reduction from the current high level of 23 per cent to around 15 per cent by 2000. Two others are implementing and refining their Osaka Initial Actions by providing not only a deadline, but also the timeframe for achieving general tariff reductions.

Table 5.1 MAPA highlights – tariff action plans of APEC economies

Economy	Actions
Australia	Phase down exceptions to the 0–5% general applied tariff to 2000, including those on passenger motor vehicles, textiles, clothing and footwear, cheese and vegetables Review by 2000 general applied tariff rate and exceptions, subject to certain conditions
Brunei	Progressively reduce tariffs to zero by 2020, with some exceptions
Canada	Phase down MFN tariff rates on manufacturing inputs on 1,500 lines by 1999 Phase down GPT rates by 2004 Conclude ITA to eliminate tariffs on information technology products by 2000
Chile	Progressively reduce tariffs to 0% on most products by 2010
China	Reduce simple average tariffs to around 15% by 2000
Hong Kong, China	Progressively bind at 0% on all imports by 2010
Indonesia	Eliminate surcharges and reduce tariffs to a maximum of 5% and 10% by 2003
Japan	Expand Tariff Elimination Initiative on pharmaceuticals by 2000 Conclude ITA to eliminate tariffs on information technology products by 2000
Korea	Eliminate tariffs on ships from 1997 Consider revising tariff concession schedule
Malaysia	Reduce/abolish import duties on certain items, including canned food, dental & medical supplies, cosmetics, paper products and printed paper in 1997 Continue with unilateral tariff reductions under annual budget exercise
Mexico	Reduce tariffs on information technology products as part of ITA under negotiations starting 1999
New Zealand	All imports duty free by 2010
Papua New Guinea	Reduce to 5% tariff on basic steel, aluminium, capital equipment, machinery, basic chemicals. Chemical agricultural inputs by 1997 Revise standard rates, with a view to progressive reduction by 2000
Philippines	Progressively reduce to targeted uniform rate of 5%, except sensitive agricultural products, by 2004
Singapore	Progressively bind tariffs at 0% by 2010
Chinese Taipei	Progressively reduce average tariffs to around 6%, with about 65% at 5% or below, by 2010; review the possibility of deepening the reduction
Thailand	Regularly review import duties with a view to reducing domestic protection Review possibility of revising tariff concession schedule
USA	Proposed negotiations towards zero tariff under ITA by 2000

Source: APEC, *The Impact of Subregionalism in APEC*, Economic Committee, 1997.

Individual APEC economies are all well on track in terms of progress toward the Bogor goals. For most APEC members, the combined commitments under the IAPs, Osaka Initial Actions and other unilateral reforms will result in lower average (applied) tariffs than those committed under the Uruguay Round for the period 1996–2000. Table 5.2 shows the measures taken by countries that are beyond their WTO obligations. Average tariffs in the APEC region have declined considerably during the period 1988–96. Current tariffs for fourteen of the APEC economies are below 15 per cent, out of which twelve are below 10 per cent and seven below 5 per cent. This is due to the bold liberalisation programs, which many APEC economies have embraced and which have occurred only within the last two years as part of the APEC Initial Actions or as part of a liberalisation process, which began earlier.

Unilateral reforms undertaken primarily under the Uruguay Round Agreement have brought about a significant decline in the incidence of non-tariff measures (NTMs) on imports by APEC economies since the late 1980s. For APEC as a whole, the incidence of NTMs has been cut nearly in half, declining from 9 per cent of import coverage in 1988 to 5 per cent in 1996. The relaxation of the non-tariff measures included the removal of voluntary export restraints (VERs) by the end of 1999; removal of domestic support, export subsidies and VERs in agriculture; phasing out and integration into WTO rules of the bilateral quotas on textiles and garments; and expansion of the list of prohibited subsidies in non-agricultural trade.

The reductions of NTMs in the MAPA include the reduction of quotas and other quantitative restrictions, export controls, and licensing. Moreover, MAPA includes several important items in services trade liberalisation: in particular, the explicit statement of support for the WTO negotiating processes on services trade liberalisation, and the adoption of sets of APEC principles for the development of open markets, by the Bogor timeframe, for energy services and telecommunications.

SUB-REGIONAL TRADE ARRANGEMENTS IN APEC

This section summarises the objectives, commitment and progress in trade and investment liberalisation made under the SRTAs.

NAFTA

Objective and commitments

NAFTA came into being in two stages, first with the signing of the Canada–United States Free Trade Agreement in 1988 and the subsequent evolution of this agreement through the trilateral negotiations on Mexico's entry into the trading arrangement. The objectives of NAFTA are as follows:

- to eliminate barriers to trade in the region covered by the agreement;
- to promote fair competition within the region;
- to expand investment opportunities in the region;

- to ensure the proper protection and exercise of intellectual property rights within the region;
- to establish effective procedures for the execution of agreements and the settlement of disputes; and
- to create a framework for diversified regional co-operation among the three economies, so as to increase the benefits produced by the agreement.

Investment liberalisation

Table 5.3 shows that the share of inward FDI into NAFTA that came from other NAFTA members declined steeply in the 1980s, from 41.5 per cent in 1980 to only 22 per cent in 1990, before picking up somewhat to 23.1 per cent in 1992. The reversal of the downward trend may also reflect to some extent the effect of the Canada–US Free Trade Area. NAFTA members' inward FDI links with APEC as a whole also declined over the 1980s, but only marginally because the intra-NAFTA regional decline was almost entirely offset by an increase in FDI from other APEC members, most notably Japan and Korea, from 4.4 per cent in 1980 to 20.8 per cent in 1992. The outward FDI from NAFTA members has been directed more to countries outside APEC over the period from 1980 to 1992, as indicated by Table 5.3.

Trade liberalisation

NAFTA is one of the most comprehensive regional trade arrangements. The agreement is much wider in scope and coverage than other free trade agreements, going beyond market access in goods and services and investment, to incorporate new issues such as customs harmonisation, intellectual property rights protection, competition policy, the environment,[5] and labour (workers' rights).

With few exceptions, NAFTA will eliminate all tariffs on trade by January 2003, that is, within ten years of the date of implementation of NAFTA.[6] In addition, Chile and Mexico established a free trade agreement in January 1992, pursuant to which most products became tariff free as of 1996. The agreement is being renegotiated for the inclusion of trade in services, investment and other areas as well as for the elimination of reciprocal exceptions. Chile and Canada also signed a free trade agreement that includes trade in goods, services and investment. Since July 1997, when the agreement became effective, 92 per cent of exports of Chile and 76 per cent of exports of Canada are duty free with the rest to be liberalised in two to six years.

Under NAFTA, all non-tariff barriers to agricultural trade between the United States and Mexico were eliminated. In addition, many tariffs were eliminated immediately, with others to be phased out, resulting in full implementation of all agricultural provisions by 2008.

Recognising the differences in trade patterns between member economies, NAFTA contains separate bilateral agreements on products such as automobiles, clothing and textiles, telecommunications, and agriculture (PECC 1995). It

Table 5.2 Major IAP 'UR plus' tariff reductions

Economy	Tariff reduction: items	2000	2010
Australia	max. 5% except: passenger motor vehicles; textiles clothing and footwear; certain vegetables	current rates (0–5%) 15% 10–25% 5% (1998)	— — —
	ITA[a]	0%	0%
Brunei Darussalam	progressive liberalisation towards zero tariff to 2020	80% of total tariff lines bound at 8%	2% of total tariff lines bound at 5%
Canada	manufacturing inputs (MFN tariff rates)	Continued phase-in of unilateral MFN tariff cuts on 714 items by 1999	complete phase-in of unilateral MFN tariff cuts on 64 items by 2004
	all original equipment automotive parts and articles	0% (on 1996)	0%
	reduction in GPT rates	continued phase-in of GPT tariff cuts by 2001	completion of GPT tariff reduction
	ITA[a]	0%	0%
Chile	almost all products	8%	0%
China	simple average tariff	around 15%	further reduction
Hong Kong, China	bind tariff at 0% on all imports	about 55% of imports	0%
	ITA[a]	0%	0%
Indonesia	items with surcharges and tariffs of 20% or less in 1995 (except automotive parts)	max. 5% by 2000	max. 5% by 2003
	items with surcharges and tariffs of more than 20% in 1995 (except automotive parts)	0–20% in 1998	max. 10% by 2003
	chemicals and metal products	—	max. 10% by 2003 0% by 2005
	ITA[a]	—	—
Japan	expand Tariff Elimination Initiative on pharmaceuticals by 2000	—	—
	ITA	0%	0%

Table 5.2 (continued)

Korea	ships from 1997	% (from 1997)	0%
	ITA^a	—	0% by 2004
Malaysia	ITA^a	—	0% by 2005
Mexico	elimination of tariffs on certain electronic components and computer equipment	—	—
New Zealand	all imports	appx. 3% simple average tariff	duty free
	pharmaceutical products	0% (from July 1997)	0%
	ITA^a	0%	0%
Papua New Guinea	reduce to 5% tariff on basic steel, aluminium, capital equipment, machinery, basic chemicals. Chemical agricultural inputs by 1997	—	By 2006 bound at 30% for non-agricultural products
Philippines	all imports, except sensitive agricultural products	7.81% simple average applied tariff	uniform rate of 5%
Singapore	progressive binding of tariffs at 0% by 2010	—	0%
	ITA^a	0%	0%
Chinese Taipei	average tariffs	around 7.9% average nominal tariff rates and applied rate of 5% or lower on about 50% of tariff lines	around 6% average nominal tariff rates and applied rate of 5% or lower on about 65% of tariff lines
	ITA^a	—	0% by 2002
Thailand	ITA^a	—	0% by 2005
USA	ITA	0%	0%

Note

a Not included in IAP. Committed at the 1996 WTO Ministerial Conference or thereafter.

Source: APEC, *The Impact of Subregionalism in APEC*, Economic Committee, 1997.

Table 5.3   Distribution of FDI into and out of NAFTA

| *Distribution of inward FDI stock (%)* | | | | | | | |
Year	NAFTA	AFTA	CHT	CER	Other APEC	EU	ROW	World
1980	41.48	0.07	0.17	0.33	3.9	39.47	14.58	100
1990	22.7	0.07	0.69	1.43	16.66	47.79	10.96	100
1992	23.14	0.09	0.91	1.46	18.45	44.34	11.61	100

| *Distribution of outward FDI stock (%)* | | | | | | | |
Year	NAFTA	AFTA	CHT	CER	Other APEC	EU	ROW	World
1980	26.93	1.7	1.08	3.65	3.34	34.65	28.65	100
1990	25.16	1.7	1.81	4.02	6.22	38.54	22.55	100
1992	22.69	1.97	2.21	3.81	6.84	38.25	24.23	100

Source: APEC, *The Impact of Subregionalism in APEC*, Economic Committee, 1997.

also allows its members to phase out tariffs and non-tariff barriers over different timetables. Simple average tariffs in the NAFTA region have declined from 6.4 per cent in 1988 to 4.9 per cent in 1996.

The NAFTA member economies have the highest intra-regional trade dependence of all APEC sub-regions. As indicated in Table 5.4, over 30 per cent of NAFTA members' exports go to other NAFTA members while over 30 per cent of NAFTA members' imports are sourced from other NAFTA partners. The latter ratio has been rising since 1986, which may reflect in part the effect of the Canada–US FTA, which came into force in 1988. NAFTA members also have a high trade dependence on APEC, with over 70 per cent of their exports and imports, respectively, going to APEC partners (including NAFTA partners). Of particular note is the rising share of CHT in NAFTA trade, which reflects to some extent the natural result of the resumption of trade with China since the end of the 1970s.

In summary, NAFTA member economies have seen their trade and FDI links with other APEC members, including the trans-Pacific links as well as the intra-North American links, strengthen since the 1980s.

ASEAN Free Trade Area (AFTA)

Objective and commitments

The Association of Southeast Asian Nations (ASEAN) was established in 1967 with five founding members – Indonesia, Malaysia, the Philippines, Singapore and Thailand. ASEAN was enlarged to ten with the inclusion of Brunei Darussalam, Vietnam, Laos, Myanmar and Cambodia.

Table 5.4   Distribution of NAFTA's exports and imports to APEC sub-regions and others (per cent)

Exports

Year	NAFTA	AFTA	CHT	CER	Other APEC	EU	ROW	Sum	Total exports ($million)
1980	34.029	3.086	3.913	1.780	10.734	24.670	21.787	100.00	(326353.78)
1981	35.566	2.904	3.631	2.124	10.798	22.385	22.593	100.00	(348079.19)
1982	34.208	3.460	3.512	2.059	11.137	21.849	23.775	100.00	(330299.16)
1983	38.861	3.557	3.582	1.658	11.725	20.332	20.285	100.00	(323212.03)
1984	42.762	3.140	3.809	1.759	11.501	19.052	17.976	100.00	(357058.22)
1985	44.861	2.713	3.913	1.967	11.108	18.866	16.572	100.00	(354124.06)
1986	42.479	2.824	4.138	2.116	12.533	20.147	15.763	100.00	(353794.19)
1987	43.161	2.963	4.688	1.650	12.260	20.193	15.085	100.00	(399197.81)
1988	41.210	3.142	5.918	1.973	13.058	20.269	14.429	100.00	(483289.59)
1989	40.091	3.637	5.357	2.084	14.015	21.127	13.690	100.00	(533625.50)
1990	40.713	3.795	4.833	1.990	13.840	21.813	13.016	100.00	(582410.19)
1991	39.973	4.032	5.450	1.835	13.068	21.824	13.819	100.00	(610121.81)
1992	43.053	4.124	5.666	1.751	11.830	19.595	13.981	100.00	(673543.44)
1993	45.350	4.423	5.761	1.572	11.547	17.561	13.786	100.00	(696860.69)
1994	47.334	4.460	5.781	1.652	11.557	16.406	12.810	100.00	(787099.63)
1995	45.278	4.925	5.947	1.669	12.606	16.379	13.197	100.00	(916694.88)

Imports

Year	NAFTA	AFTA	CHT	CER	Other APEC	EU	ROW	Sum	Total imports ($million)
1980	33.730	4.196	4.665	1.070	13.377	15.372	27.590	100.00	(329242.25)
1981	34.567	3.701	5.190	0.940	14.787	16.022	24.793	100.00	(358136.63)
1982	35.375	3.808	6.261	1.020	16.179	17.562	19.795	100.00	(319399.88)
1983	36.502	4.369	6.802	0.841	17.258	16.927	17.302	100.00	(344100.81)
1984	35.906	4.030	6.967	0.798	18.941	17.529	15.828	100.00	(425233.25)
1985	35.510	3.623	6.788	0.803	20.268	19.480	13.528	100.00	(447379.69)
1986	31.727	3.354	7.955	0.808	23.419	20.142	12.595	100.00	(473688.25)
1987	32.581	3.780	8.533	0.936	22.203	19.685	12.283	100.00	(528833.94)
1988	34.409	4.144	8.265	0.965	21.690	19.395	11.132	100.00	(578826.50)
1989	34.213	4.684	8.554	0.987	21.098	18.220	12.243	100.00	(625302.31)
1990	35.222	4.680	8.027	1.078	18.971	18.641	13.381	100.00	(673206.50)
1991	36.198	5.002	8.681	1.020	19.109	17.422	12.568	100.00	(673747.19)
1992	38.704	5.462	9.207	0.961	17.957	16.878	10.830	100.00	(749221.19)
1993	38.245	5.690	9.975	0.786	17.375	16.839	11.089	100.00	(826317.44)
1994	40.100	5.976	10.036	0.692	16.738	16.645	9.813	100.00	(929084.44)
1995	40.414	6.256	9.862	0.602	15.826	16.281	10.759	100.00	(1027023.94)

Source: APEC, 1997, *The Impact of Subregionalism in APEC*, Economic Committee.

The ASEAN Free Trade Area represented an evolution of ASEAN from a forum aimed mainly at promoting peace and stability in the region to one aimed at deepening the economic partnerships in the region. AFTA evolved in three steps. First was the initiative to put into place the Preferential Trading Arrangements (PTA) in 1977. However, the ASEAN PTA covered only a small number of tariff lines and had limited scope to promote regional economic liberalisation. Meanwhile, the rapid economic development of ASEAN members in the 1980s and into the 1990s had substantially increased the volume of trade of member economies. Accordingly, the second step occurred in 1992 when ASEAN members agreed to set up the ASEAN Free Trade Area within fifteen years, using the Common Effective Preferential Tariff (CEPT) as the main mechanism. The CEPT covered many more items than had the PTA.

The 1992 CEPT Agreement excluded unprocessed agricultural products, totalling 2,025 tariff lines. However, the 1994 ASEAN Economic Ministers' Meeting decided to bring unprocessed agricultural products into the CEPT Scheme on a gradual basis. By 2003, products representing 87 per cent of tariff lines for unprocessed agricultural goods are to be brought into the CEPT Scheme and, by 2010, all products are to be in the scheme.

The original aim of AFTA was to develop ASEAN economies as a free trade area by 2008. Through AFTA, ASEAN sought to:

- secure market access within the region for its members and attract foreign direct investment;
- strengthen its credibility and negotiating weight in global and regional fora;
- enhance intra-ASEAN economic cooperation to sustain the economic growth and development of all members; and
- reduce or eliminate trade and non-trade barriers.

These goals are to be achieved by reducing effective tariffs to less than 5 per cent and removing all non-tariff barriers.

Two major economic developments prompted ASEAN to speed up the AFTA process and extend its coverage, the third step in its evolution. One was the conclusion of the Uruguay Round negotiations in 1993. The other was the declaration by APEC in 1994 of its commitment to liberalise trade and investment in APEC by 2010/2020. In 1994, ASEAN decided to reduce the implementation period of AFTA from fifteen to ten years, or by 1 January 2003.

Investment liberalisation

ASEAN countries have liberalised their investment regime, with most countries offering incentives to attract foreign direct investment. These incentives include tax holidays, exemption from import duties, training grants, support for marketing initiatives, relaxation in employment policy for expatriate employees and R&D allowances. Equally important is the capital account convertibility where FDI can freely repatriate capital, profit and dividend. Consequently, ASEAN became an attractive investment location, particularly in export-oriented manufacturing, with Japan and East Asian newly industrialised economies (NIEs) replacing western industrialised economies as the main sources since the mid-1980s. Japan and the NIEs account for half of FDI into ASEAN. Table 5.5 shows the pattern of FDI flows into and out of AFTA.

Trade liberalisation

Based on the member economies' tariff reduction schedules for products under the CEPT, AFTA estimates that 88 per cent of tariff lines will reach the goal of tariffs of 0 to 5 per cent by 2000. These tariff lines accounted for 98 per cent of intra-ASEAN imports for the year ending in June 1995. AFTA has also encouraged members to consider accelerating the tariff reduction for

Table 5.5 Distribution of direct investment stock into and out of
ASEAN (per cent)

Year	1992	1990	1980
Inward direct investment stock from:			
NAFTA	8.86	9.81	11.43
Japan	22.55	26.10	28.62
CHT	16.62	18.19	10.00
AFTA	1.23	1.20	4.36
CER	2.32	1.83	0.95
European Union	12.23	13.17	26.10
Rest of the World	36.19	29.70	18.54
Outward Direct Investment Stock to:			
NAFTA	9.82	10.05	11.39
Japan	0.21	0.03	–
CHT	18.55	23.95	29.10
AFTA	18.51	17.82	10.30
CER	5.67	7.53	4.54
European Union	20.43	2.17	0.20
Rest of the World	26.81	38.45	44.47
Total Direct Investment Stock:			
NAFTA	8.91	9.88	11.43
Japan	21.30	24.62	27.34
CHT	16.74	14.57	10.87
AFTA	2.20	2.14	1.03
CER	2.51	2.16	2.83
European Union	12.69	12.54	14.91
Rest of the World	35.65	34.09	31.59

Note: – Data not available.

Source: APEC, *The Impact of Subregionalism in APEC*, Economic Committee, 1997.

remaining products to this level by 2000, particularly for the three important sectors of machinery and electrical appliances, base metals and metal articles, and plastics. These three sectors accounted for 60 per cent of intra-regional imports in the same period. The bold liberalisation programs which many AFTA members have carried out have lowered the average tariffs of the APEC members of AFTA from 15.9 per cent in 1988 to below 9.5 per cent in 1996.

Besides tariff reduction and elimination of non-tariff measures, AFTA also seeks progress on trade facilitation. There has been varied progress made in areas such as the Green Lane System, Agreement on Customs, Common Customs Forms, and Elimination of Customs Surcharges. An alternative to the Rules of Origin for Textiles and Textile Products was introduced in 1996, allowing an exporter to select the existing 40 per cent criterion of the CEPT or the new transformation process criterion when applying for the ASEAN CEPT Certificate of Origin.

Growth in intra-regional trade has increased in recent years, with the bulk of this trade accounted for by Singapore and Malaysia. The emergence and rapid expansion of cross-border production operations by multinational enterprises has contributed significantly to this development within ASEAN. Trade between ASEAN and other regions has increased much faster than world trade in total. From 1988 to 1995, the foreign trade of ASEAN economies grew almost 1.6 times faster than that of the world as a whole. Intra-ASEAN trade has grown very fast in this period, although there has been no acceleration since 1992 (Table 5.6).

AFTA went one step further in trade liberalisation efforts when it decided to establish a Dispute Settlement Mechanism (DSM) to enhance transparency, equity and accountability in the AFTA process. The ASEAN DSM, which is patterned after the WTO Dispute Settlement Understanding, will apply to all past and future ASEAN economic agreements. An important feature of the ASEAN DSM is that rulings on disputes are by simple majority and not by consensus, the first formal use of non-consensual rule-making in ASEAN.

ANZCERTA

Objective and commitments

The Australia–New Zealand Closer Economic Relations (CER) Agreement is the oldest of the SRTAs in the Asia Pacific region, dating from 1 January 1983. It was developed to replace an earlier and more limited arrangement, the New Zealand–Australia Free Trade Agreement (NZAFTA), which was first put in place in 1965. The earlier agreement had only applied to forest products and a limited range of manufactured goods.

The original objectives of the CER agreement are to:

- strengthen the broader relationship between Australia and New Zealand;

Table 5.6 Distribution of AFTA's exports and imports to APEC sub-regions and others (per cent)

Exports

Year	NAFTA	AFTA	CHT	CER	Other APEC	EU	ROW	Total exports ($million)
1980	18.577	13.521	5.744	2.822	34.380	13.271	11.686	(74370.09)
1981	18.052	14.525	6.498	2.983	32.878	11.535	13.528	(73432.03)
1982	16.339	18.749	6.384	3.430	32.349	10.913	11.835	(74430.38)
1983	20.545	19.100	5.913	2.209	29.731	11.006	11.497	(73178.48)
1984	21.498	16.675	6.330	2.463	29.799	11.020	12.215	(79704.55)
1985	21.666	16.288	7.129	2.339	29.553	11.900	11.126	(74820.60)
1986	22.655	15.552	8.482	2.475	25.432	14.394	11.011	(70123.89)
1987	22.843	16.503	9.550	1.909	24.340	14.916	9.939	(87503.93)
1988	22.466	16.344	10.639	2.439	22.524	15.579	10.010	(106774.85)
1989	23.132	16.770	10.019	2.433	22.501	15.528	9.616	(126625.59)
1990	21.535	17.913	10.126	2.090	22.610	16.128	9.598	(146304.69)
1991	20.348	18.542	10.826	2.152	22.140	16.466	9.526	(165622.81)
1992	21.758	18.332	11.715	2.194	19.813	16.965	9.223	(188081.31)
1993	22.057	19.313	11.901	1.920	18.911	15.932	9.967	(213180.55)
1994	21.686	22.176	12.226	2.077	17.217	14.782	9.835	(256026.50)
1995	20.448	22.435	12.500	2.042	17.633	14.500	10.442	(314223.13)

Imports

Year	NAFTA	AFTA	CHT	CER	Other APEC	EU	ROW	Sum	Total imports ($million)
1980	15.122	15.098	9.169	3.369	23.125	12.555	21.561	100.00	(66598.04)
1981	14.102	14.879	9.338	3.340	23.995	11.665	22.680	100.00	(71686.02)
1982	15.176	18.531	8.890	2.956	23.258	12.224	18.966	100.00	(75305.76)
1983	15.368	18.687	8.988	2.715	23.710	12.545	17.986	100.00	(74797.08)
1984	15.634	18.535	10.128	2.793	23.344	12.552	17.014	100.00	(71706.27)
1985	15.410	19.551	12.621	3.354	23.302	14.964	10.797	100.00	(62332.76)
1986	15.898	17.353	12.266	2.878	23.835	15.025	12.746	100.00	(62845.47)
1987	14.911	18.204	12.474	2.844	24.295	14.929	12.342	100.00	(79327.82)
1988	15.383	17.678	13.001	3.308	26.229	14.746	9.655	100.00	(98716.82)
1989	16.035	17.544	12.636	3.409	26.567	13.990	9.819	100.00	(121039.02)
1990	14.164	16.795	12.665	3.553	25.970	14.507	12.345	100.00	(156049.80)
1991	14.271	17.816	12.329	3.694	28.021	14.310	9.559	100.00	(172374.95)
1992	14.473	17.965	12.143	3.987	27.473	14.566	9.392	100.00	(191915.61)
1993	14.282	19.079	11.681	3.497	28.214	16.292	6.956	100.00	(215794.20)
1994	13.169	21.297	11.404	3.217	27.184	15.499	8.230	100.00	(266603.47)
1995	13.281	20.740	11.324	2.866	27.318	15.255	9.216	100.00	(339912.00)

Source: APEC, *The Impact of Subregionalism in APEC*, Economic Committee, 1997.

- develop closer economic relations between Australia and New Zealand through a mutually beneficial expansion of free trade;
- eliminate barriers to trade between Australia and New Zealand in a gradual and progressive manner under an agreed timetable and with a minimum of disruption; and
- enhance trade between New Zealand and Australia under conditions of fair competition.

Investment liberalisation

Although there was no formal agreement to assure free and open investment between Australia and New Zealand, Table 5.7 does show a trend of growth in trans-Tasman investment. This may have resulted from the liberalisation of trade in services in the 1988 review of CER, since opportunities for services trade often result in some form of FDI to establish a commercial presence in the host economy. Nevertheless, the preferential investment relationship between the two countries has not skewed investment from other sources. Investment from outside the region is still dominant and, in particular, that from outside APEC has increased threefold from 1980 to 1992. Thus, both countries are currently following a liberal, outward-looking approach to foreign investment from all sources.

Both Australia and New Zealand have made significant progress to liberalise their investment regimes. At present, both governments have largely abolished exchange controls and have very liberal approaches to the regulations on foreign investment, especially New Zealand. To cement this liberalised approach, New Zealand has sought an investment protocol providing that national enterprises from one member should be guaranteed freedom to invest in the other as if they were nationals.

Trade liberalisation

The CER agreement originally contemplated the gradual elimination of tariffs by 1 January 1988, and of import quotas by 30 June 1995. However, in the 1988 review of CER, the Protocol on the Acceleration of Free Trade in Goods was adopted to eliminate all tariffs, import licensing, and quantitative restrictions for trans-Tasman trade in virtually all goods by 1 July 1990. The 1988 Protocol also included an agreement to replace anti-dumping arrangements with competition law effective from July 1990. The 1988 review of CER also resulted in the adoption of the Protocol on Trade in Services, effective from 1 January 1989, which brought services within CER on the basis of clearly stated rules that ensure the extension of national treatment to service providers of each member. Independently of CER, Australia and New Zealand have unilaterally reduced their barriers to trade with the rest of the world, helping to minimise potential trade diversion.

Table 5.7 Distribution of foreign direct investment stock into and out of ANZCERTA

Year	NAFTA	AFTA	Inward FDI stock (%) CHT	CER	OAPEC	EU	ROW	World
1980	39.34	0.22	1.18	5.01	5.59	39.24	9.42	100
1990	31.39	0.37	1.28	4.24	15.38	35.59	11.24	100
1992	30.90	0.41	1.57	7.85	17.46	30.77	11.85	100
			Outward FDI stock (%)					
1980	17.41	18.45	0.80	31.36	4.97	25.79	1.22	100
1990	19.30	3.37	0.65	21.00	3.61	34.45	16.62	100
1992	23.45	3.55	−2.10	26.92	4.19	40.97	3.02	100

Source: APEC, *The Impact of Subregionalism in APEC*, Economic Committee, 1997.

CER is exceptional in that it was the first SRTA to include agriculture. Both CER members are important exporters of agricultural products, and their level of protection of agriculture is in any case the lowest among the OECD economies (WTO 1995).

In terms of its effects on third economies, the CER agreement is compatible with GATT. It is also effective because it has:

- a timetable for the elimination of tariffs, quotas and export subsidies;
- a negative list approach: all goods and services are included except those specifically mentioned for exclusion;
- comprehensive product coverage;
- the imposing of disciplines on quantitative restrictions;
- replacement of anti-dumping law with competition policy;
- a rules-based system for services trade, such as the right of establishment, national treatment, etc.; and
- falling barriers to imports from the rest of the world.

Trade within CER has generally grown steadily, strengthening CER economic links, particularly from the perspective of New Zealand. In the case of Australia, the share of its total exports to New Zealand stayed more or less constant during 1983–95. Both Australia and New Zealand have experienced an increase in the share of trade with Pacific Rim economies, at the expense of the rest of the world. Table 5.8 shows that exports from CER to NAFTA increased initially, then declined in 1990. Exports to ASEAN declined gradually early in the first half of 1980s, then increased rapidly after 1986. Exports to APEC members do not show any clear-cut pattern. Exports to the rest of the world declined sharply during 1983–95.

Table 5.8 Distribution of CER exports and imports to APEC sub-regions and others (per cent)

Year	NAFTA	AFTA	CHT	CER	OAPEC	EU	ROW	World	Total exports ($million)
				Exports					
1980	12.265	7.812	6.720	6.342	26.770	16.432	23.658	100.00	(28718.36)
1981	12.014	8.547	6.506	7.085	29.436	14.579	21.833	100.00	(28014.44)
1982	11.648	7.959	7.482	6.635	29.238	15.863	21.176	100.00	(27964.52)
1983	11.441	8.031	6.761	6.802	31.755	17.117	18.093	100.00	(25288.45)
1984	11.926	7.037	8.696	7.348	30.082	15.509	19.403	100.00	(28458.87)
1985	12.210	7.110	8.495	6.495	30.753	15.943	18.994	100.00	(29407.93)
1986	12.846	6.073	9.547	6.801	30.199	16.727	17.807	100.00	(29783.78)
1987	14.137	6.446	9.821	7.433	29.171	17.880	15.113	100.00	(35004.40)
1988	13.202	7.716	5.961	7.459	34.363	17.823	13.477	100.00	(42315.77)
1989	13.101	8.762	9.137	7.640	31.706	15.520	14.132	100.00	(47085.61)
1990	13.841	10.573	7.654	7.478	30.905	14.769	14.780	100.00	(52445.32)
1991	12.721	11.792	9.683	7.310	32.747	13.359	12.389	100.00	(54003.48)
1992	12.792	13.594	10.346	7.552	30.015	14.231	11.470	100.00	(56288.73)
1993	11.631	13.523	11.313	8.274	30.329	12.747	12.182	100.00	(55804.77)
1994	10.524	14.045	11.559	9.149	30.706	12.246	11.771	100.00	(61063.28)
1995	9.385	14.782	11.731	9.660	30.727	11.722	11.995	100.00	(65897.41)
				Imports					
1980	22.663	8.185	5.767	7.104	18.036	23.256	14.989	100.00	(25637.83)
1981	24.911	7.379	5.886	6.686	20.822	20.296	14.020	100.00	(29683.89)
1982	23.146	8.691	6.173	6.316	21.515	22.125	12.035	100.00	(29379.52)
1983	22.072	6.658	6.516	7.086	23.426	22.879	11.363	100.00	(24276.12)
1984	22.011	6.880	7.040	7.328	23.818	22.988	9.935	100.00	(28535.13)
1985	23.808	5.982	6.329	6.530	24.414	26.209	6.729	100.00	(29251.48)
1986	24.105	5.587	6.850	6.521	24.200	25.993	6.744	100.00	(31061.20)
1987	21.443	5.437	8.636	8.471	23.634	25.855	6.524	100.00	(30717.16)
1988	24.526	6.696	5.032	8.117	23.541	26.945	5.143	100.00	(38885.36)
1989	23.628	6.547	8.268	7.645	22.762	24.524	6.627	100.00	(47060.57)
1990	24.268	6.403	7.559	8.213	20.603	24.981	7.972	100.00	(47751.41)
1991	24.769	7.883	8.173	8.732	21.005	22.563	6.874	100.00	(45205.41)
1992	24.038	8.411	9.396	8.663	20.862	21.956	6.675	100.00	(49070.64)
1993	21.441	8.009	10.024	9.036	22.385	23.081	6.024	100.00	(51099.11)
1994	21.363	8.738	10.278	9.177	20.583	23.629	6.232	100.00	(60872.06)
1995	21.580	9.048	9.840	8.978	18.461	24.629	7.465	100.00	(70901.18)

Source: APEC, *The Impact of Subregionalism in APEC*, Economic Committee, 1997.

Southern China–Hong Kong, China–Chinese Taipei (CHT) growth area

Two features of the CHT growth triangle that made it a very dynamic economic area are its informality – no formal negotiations have taken place among the members; and its vertical economic integration, a phenomenon observed in most growth triangles.

Although CHT was driven by the private sector and market forces, public policies have also been important in determining the extent to which the economic integration has advanced (Tang and Thant 1994: 13). For China, after economic reform and the open-door policy were initiated in 1978, Special Economic Zones (SEZs), namely Guangdong and Fujian provinces, were created to attract foreign investment. Preferential policies related to tax reduction, land use, finance, etc. were applied in these SEZs. As for Hong Kong, the government had long been implementing a very liberal economic policy, with virtually no restrictions on firms relocating their manufacturing processes to China. In Chinese Taipei, government controls on trade and investment have been gradually liberalised since 1987, a key factor in the emergence of this growth triangle.

The CHT growth triangle evolved because of the economic complementarity of neighbouring economies. This complementarity derives from the members' differing stages of development and/or factor endowments. Guangdong and Fujian are abundant in natural resources and labour. Chinese Taipei and Hong Kong have strong industrial sectors, well-established financial markets, rich 'soft' and 'hard' technological capability, a large pool of technical and managerial personnel, and plentiful capital. As a result, many manufacturing firms and labour-intensive industries in Chinese Taipei and Hong Kong have relocated their activities to Southeast China. As these industries shifted production in accordance with comparative advantage, they also brought FDI and technology to China.

CHT's dynamism is shown by its growing share in world trade, from 3.0 per cent in 1980 to about 8.4 per cent in 1996. At the same time, intra-CHT trade grew from about 10 per cent of those economies' total trade in 1978 to over 30 per cent by 1995.[7] Chinese Taipei's total indirect trade with China increased from less than US$50 million in 1978 to US$11.5 billion in 1995, with a substantial surplus in favour of Chinese Taipei. Imports from China, which are restricted primarily to raw materials, accounted for only 1.5 per cent of total Chinese Taipei imports in 1995.[8]

According to China's statistics, the cumulative value of realised direct investment by Hong Kong in China amounted to US$100 billion, accounting for 56 per cent of total external direct investment, at the end of 1996. Chinese Taipei was the second largest investor in China just after Hong Kong, accounting for about 8 per cent of total realised external direct investment. Chinese Taipei's cumulative direct investment in Guangdong alone was estimated at around US$1.5 billion. China is now the second largest external investor in Hong Kong with an investment of US$14 billion at the end of 1995.

Indonesia–Malaysia-Singapore (SIJORI) growth triangle

Singapore, the principal force behind the SIJORI triangle, possesses good infrastructure, well-developed financial markets, comprehensive sea and air transport, and advanced telecommunication facilities. It has easy access to world markets for investors and is an important financial and business services centre of the region. However, with rapid industrialisation, it faced shortages of labour, land and water as well as rising production costs. Johor (the triangle partner in Malaysia) and Riau (Indonesia), on the other hand, had low-cost land and labour available.

Singapore and Johor had had a long history of economic interaction driven mainly by market forces. By contrast, the Singapore–Riau link was created by government-led initiatives. In August 1990, a bilateral agreement between Singapore and Indonesia was signed to develop Riau jointly. As regards the third link in the growth triangle, between Johor and Riau, economic links hardly existed before 1993. However, the emerging shortage of labour in Johor led it to consider the possibility of firms in the plantation sector investing in Indonesia. Eventually, the Indonesia–Malaysia–Singapore Growth Triangle (IMS-GT) agreement was signed in December 1994 to promote development, expansion and integration in the areas of trade and transport, tourism, shipping and communications, agriculture, forestry, development of industrial infrastructure, and supporting industries.

The SIJORI triangle sought to exploit economic complementarities by reducing regulatory barriers in order to gain a competitive edge in attracting domestic and foreign investment and to promote exports. With rapid industrialisation and development, governments involved in SIJORI had to start investing in infrastructure and human resource development to meet the growing requirements of the private sector. In addition, they began work towards harmonisation and simplification of investment rules, taxes, land laws, labour market policies, and immigration and customs procedures, to improve their competitiveness and to attract foreign investment.

CONTRIBUTION OF SRTAs AND GROWTH TRIANGLES TO LIBERALISATION

SRTAs

Since the SRTAs are formal arrangements and are subject to WTO rules, their liberalisation initiatives can be assessed mainly, but not exclusively, against the WTO criteria:

1 the arrangements adhere to WTO Article XXIV;
2 the new arrangements are preceded or accompanied by MFN liberalisation, especially when protection against non-members is high;

3 exceptions are based on the negative list approach;
4 a clear timetable for liberalisation and facilitation is established to provide the private sector with a certain environment, and to prevent a reversal of policy; and, in the case of agreements which are not broadly comprehensive, a fifth criterion may be added, namely:
5 for agreements that are not broadly comprehensive, regular review of unilateral and collective actions is undertaken to push forward the process of liberalisation.

Regarding the first two criteria, given the fact that all the members of the three SRTAs considered are founding members of the WTO, it is not surprising that they comply with the key requirements of WTO, such as most-favoured nation (MFN) liberalisation and national treatment.

NAFTA would appear to meet criteria 3 and 4. It has broad coverage of sectors and issues, indeed the broadest of any of the SRTAs, and exceptions are based on the negative list approach. It has also established a clear timetable to lower, and eventually eliminate, all trade barriers among the three members. All tariffs in trade between the United States and Canada were to be eliminated by January 1998 and, likewise tariffs between Mexico and Canada and between Mexico and the United States will be phased out within ten years.

AFTA also appears to meet criteria 3 and 4. Its development of Exclusion Lists makes it consistent with the negative list approach. A schedule has also clearly been set to reduce tariffs to a maximum of 5 per cent for all products by the year 2003. Regarding criterion 5, product coverage was far from comprehensive initially but has been expanded over time. The 1995 Protocol extended the 1992 Agreement to all manufactured products, including capital goods and agricultural products. It also covers intellectual property protection and trade in services. In addition, other issues that contribute positively toward free and fair trade, such as the establishment of the DSM, have also been dealt with.

CER also meets criteria 3 and 4. It has broadly comprehensive product coverage and features a negative list approach for exceptions. It has achieved free trade in goods and is now moving towards progressive liberalisation of services and is pursuing deeper forms of integration. For example, it has replaced its anti-dumping law with a competition policy, removed regulatory barriers to trade through mutual recognition agreements and harmonisation of standards, eliminated preferences with regard to government purchasing, and established a rules-based system for services trade. Moreover, a process of regular reviews has been established.

In view of the above, it can be concluded that the SRTAs in the APEC region meet some of the criteria on global liberalisation. In fact SRTAs, like other APEC members, have included WTO-plus liberalisation in their IAPs for further tariff reduction.

Growth triangles

As noted, the growth triangles cannot be judged according to the same criteria as the SRTAs as regards their role in promoting global liberalisation. Criterion 2 would, however, appear to be relevant. In respect of this criterion, all members of the CHT and SIJORI growth triangles are part of APEC, which is based on the open regionalism concept and thus any liberalisation is extended to all trading partners.

Indeed, according to the assessment by PECC (1996), several members of these two groups (including China and Hong Kong) are considered 'champions' in their IAPs for either low tariffs or extensive tariff reductions. Hong Kong, for example, which already had zero tariffs in 1996, committed to binding tariffs at zero. The other members of these two growth triangles all have made substantial reductions in tariffs over the recent period. Between 1988 and 1996, China reduced its average applied tariff from 39.5 per cent to 23 per cent; and Chinese Taipei from 12.6 per cent to 8.6 per cent.[9]

More generally, by broadening the scope for inter-economy cooperation, growth triangles tend to promote trade among the partners and to strengthen the external orientation of their members. By exploiting scope for improved factor utilisation, they also promote growth, expanding their markets for other partners, and improve their ability to participate in formal liberalisation processes. Accordingly, while the informal growth triangles do not factor into the formal liberalisation process, they can be seen as having a positive, albeit modest, facilitating effect.

IMPACT OF THE ASIAN ECONOMIC AND FINANCIAL CRISIS ON THE SRTAs

The economic and financial crisis, which began in July 1997, has affected one SRTA, AFTA, and two growth triangles (CHT and SIJORI). Within AFTA, the economically more developed members, Indonesia, Thailand, Malaysia and Singapore, saw the most change. The impact was less severe for CHT economies: Hong Kong, China and Chinese Taipei economic growth declined but not to the extent experienced by AFTA members. China has resisted well the pressure on its currency arising from the crisis. Further afield, the non-Asian SRTAs (NAFTA and CER) were relatively unscathed and continue to enjoy robust growth.

Prolonged current account deficit has been cited as one of the causes of the crisis and this is directly linked with the movements of trade, capital flows and exchange rate. Stable exchange rates and over-investment have resulted in an upsurge of imports. Even though export growth was strong in the affected economies, it was not strong enough to support the large increase in merchandise and services imports. In addition, the liberal capital account has encouraged large inflows of short-term capital as well as allowing the accumulation of large foreign private debt.

Table 5.9 Performance of APEC economies, 1997

	GDP (US$ billion)	Real GDP growth (%)	Exports (US$ billion)	Imports (US$ billion)	FDI	In- flation rate (%)	Un- employ- ment rate (%)
Australia	406.58	3.60	63.0	68.0	US 101.2 b	1.40	8.20
Brunei	4.80	4.00	2.0	4.0	–	1.70	5.00
Canada	625.63	3.70	213.0	215.0	–	1.60	9.20
Chile	77.08	7.10	17.0	19.0	US 5.42 b	6.00	6.10
China	903.00	8.80	183.0	142.0	US 44.2 b	2.80	3.10
Hong Kong, China	173.00	5.30	188.0	209.0		5.80	2.20
Indonesia	214.99	4.60	52.0	43.0	US 33.8 b	11.05	6.00
Japan	4197.44	1.40	421.0	339.0	¥6.6 trillion	2.00	3.40
Korea	442.60	5.50	137.0	121.0	US(1.6)b	4.40	2.60
Malaysia	97.85	7.70	79.0	80.0	RM 19.2 b	2.70	2.70
Mexico	402.53	7.00	110.0	121.0	US12.1 b	20.60	3.20
New Zealand	64.50	2.30	14.0	15.0	–	1.72	6.70
Papua New Guinea	4.75	−5.40	3.0	2.0	–	3.90	–
Peru	65.20	7.20	7.0	9.0	US 2.1 b	8.50	8.60
Philippines	83.21	5.20	29.0	48.0	US 1.2 b	6.00	8.70
Russia	450.00	0.90	84.0	52.0	US 6.2 b	14.60	2.75
Singapore	96.30	7.80	125.0	133.0	–	2.00	1.80
Chinese Taipei	283.60	6.80	122.0	114.0	–	0.90	2.70
Thailand	160.50	−0.40	58.0	63.0	US 3.6 b	5.60	3.50
USA	8079.90	3.93	688.0	899.0	US 264 b	2.30	4.90
Vietnam	25.00	8.80	9.0	14.0	US 2.56 b	3.20	8.50

Going into the crisis, the affected SRTA and growth triangle economies, with the exception of Thailand, were growing steadily as indicated by Table 5.9. In 1997, real GDP growth was 7.7 per cent for Malaysia, 7.8 per cent for Singapore, 5.5 per cent for South Korea and Hong Kong, and 5.3 per cent for China. These economies ran substantial current account deficits even though their trade balances were in surplus and they received large FDI inflows. As shown in Table 5.10, South Korea's and Thailand's current account deficits were both about 1.8 per cent of the GDP, while for Malaysia it was much larger at 5 per cent. Likewise, Hong Kong, China and Indonesia had current account deficits of 3 per cent. On the other hand, Chinese Taipei recorded a surplus of 2.7 per cent while Singapore's surplus was a hefty 15.8 per cent. Inflation was low in 1997, and was less than 10 per cent in the affected economies, with the exception of Indonesia. Similarly, all these economies had low unemployment as a result of high economic growth in the preceding years.

When the downturn came, the economic contraction in the affected countries was probably the worst they had ever experienced. Indonesia's

Table 5.10 Selected economies' current account positions, (per cent of GDP)

	1997	1998	1999	2000
Advanced economies				
United States	−1.9	−2.7	−3.5	−3.3
Japan	2.2	3.2	3.6	3.4
Germany	−0.2	−0.4	−0.1	−
France	2.8	2.7	2.8	3.0
Italy	3.0	2.3	2.3	2.3
United Kingdom	0.6	−0.8	−1.2	−1.4
Canada	−1.5	−2.1	−1.6	−1.1
Australia	−3.1	−5.0	−5.4	−5.0
Austria	−2.2	−2.0	−1.5	−1.3
Finland	5.5	5.1	5.2	4.9
Greece	−2.6	−2.6	−2.5	−2.6
Hong Kong SAR[1]	−3.2	0.6	1.2	1.2
Ireland	2.8	1.9	1.9	1.8
Korea	−1.8	13.1	7.1	4.1
New Zealand	−7.1	−6.0	−6.7	−5.8
Norway	5.2	−0.8	1.4	2.9
Singapore	15.8	20.9	18.0	17.7
Spain	0.5	−0.2	−0.8	−0.8
Sweden	2.9	2.1	1.9	1.7
Switzerland	8.9	9.1	9.3	9.4
Chinese Taipei	2.7	1.3	2.0	2.0
Euro area	1.7	1.4	1.5	1.6
Developing countries				
Algeria	7.2	−2.0	−3.6	−0.6
Argentina	−3.7	−4.4	−4.3	−4.3
Brazil	−4.1	−4.5	−3.0	−2.6
Cameroon	−1.3	−2.5	−4.4	−4.4
Chile	−5.3	−6.3	−5.0	−4.9
China	3.3	2.4	1.7	1.1
Cote d'Ivoire	−4.5	−4.9	−2.9	−2.5
Egypt	0.2	−3.0	−3.9	−3.8
India	−1.4	−1.7	−1.9	−2.2
Indonesia	−3.0	3.4	2.7	1.5
Malaysia	−5.1	15.7	9.6	5.0
Mexico	1.9	−3.7	−2.0	−2.2
Nigeria	4.8	−8.4	−11.5	−5.8
Pakistan	−5.8	−2.9	−2.8	−2.6
Philippines	−5.2	2.0	2.5	1.5
Saudi Arabia	0.2	−10.4	−8.2	−6.9
South Africa	−1.5	−2.1	−1.4	−1.6
Thailand	−1.9	12.2	8.8	5.5
Turkey	−1.4	1.4	1.0	0.1
Uganda	−0.9	−2.1	−3.6	−2.6

Note: 1 Special Autonomous Region.

Source: IMF Financial Statistics, various issues.

fall, at 13.7 per cent, was the steepest, as shown in Table 5.11. But other economies were not spared – Thailand's GDP decreased by 8 per cent, Malaysia's by 6.8 per cent, Hong Kong's by 5.1 per cent and South Korea's by 5.5 per cent. The biggest decline was in the construction sector, followed by manufacturing. However, the agriculture sector performed rather well, and in some countries there was growth. These economies' exchange rates depreciated steeply, some by as much as 70 per cent, causing erosion of wealth manifested by the sharp decline in their equity markets. Another consequence was higher inflation, which brought widespread hardship for the general public, particularly the poor. For example, inflation in Indonesia had jumped sixfold from 11 per cent in 1997 to 61 per cent in 1998 and, for the same years in Thailand, it nearly doubled from 5 to 8 per cent.

As a result of collapse in demand in these economies, imports were reduced very substantially – for example in 1998, ASEAN 4 (Indonesia, Malaysia, Singapore and Thailand) imports dropped by 28 per cent, while for Korea the reduction was 36 per cent and Hong Kong, China 11.5 per cent (Table 5.12). Considering that intra-regional trade is important among APEC SRTAs and growth triangles, such an import contraction would have adversely affected their external sector. This is reflected in poor export performance. In 1998, ASEAN 4 exports decreased by 8.7 per cent in US dollar terms. South Korea and Taiwan exports also declined by 4.9 per cent and 9.5 per cent, respectively. Besides the effect on production and trade, labour flow was also disrupted. For example, Malaysia hosted a large number of Indonesian workers but many returned to Indonesia when the economy contracted. This movement has mitigated some of the effects on the Malaysian economy: the smaller employment needed for a smaller level of production is absorbed through not renewing foreign workers' contracts.

Despite the pressure on their respective current accounts due to the crisis, the affected SRTA and growth triangle economies generally maintained their existing liberal trade policy. At the beginning of the crisis, some countries in the SRTA imposed higher tariffs in some industries. For example, Malaysia and Thailand both increased the duties on imports of completely built cars. However, the threat of higher imports resulting from currency depreciation did not materialise and tariff levels were kept at the pre-crisis level, except for those early increases. The collapse in consumer demand and investor confidence, which was caused by lower income levels and erosion of wealth, had naturally reduced the demand for all categories of imports – consumer, intermediate and capital goods. Since exports from these economies use a high proportion of intermediate and capital goods, poor export performance meant less demand for these imports. In addition, these economies are trading nations, and they may not be able to take advantage of a recovery of exports if they impose a restrictive trade regime that could increase the cost of imports, especially intermediate and capital goods, or impede the smooth functioning of export activities.

Table 5.11 Selected indicators of APEC economies, 1998

	Real GDP growth (%)	Inflation rate (%)	Unemployment rate (%)
Australia	5.1	1.60	8.00
Brunei	1.0	–	–
Canada	3.1	1.00	8.30
Chile	3.1	5.10	–
China	7.8	–0.80	–
Hong Kong, China	–5.1	2.60	4.70
Indonesia	–13.7	60.70	–
Japan	–1.9	0.60	4.10
Korea	–5.8	7.50	6.80
Malaysia	–7.5	5.30	–
Mexico	4.8	16.70	–
New Zealand	–0.3	1.50	7.50
Papua New Guinea	3.8	13.50	–
Peru	0.3	7.30	–
Philippines	–0.5	9.70	–
Russia	–4.6	27.70	–
Singapore	1.5	–0.30	3.30
Taipei	4.8	1.70	2.80
Thailand	–8.0	8.10	–
USA	3.9	1.56	4.50
Vietnam	5.8	7.70	–

Similarly, the investment environment remained unchanged. FDI has proved to be the preferred form of capital in view of the volatility of portfolio flows. In light of the crisis, countries in the SRTA and growth triangles have increased their efforts to attract more FDI. For example, Malaysia has relaxed the equity requirement for foreign investment in the manufacturing sector – full foreign ownership is allowed for new investment in manufacturing sector made before 2001. Previously, the percentage of foreign ownership corresponded to the share of output exported, with full ownership extended only when all output had been exported. Singapore has introduced wide-ranging liberalisation measures for its financial sector with the aim of making the city state a leading Asian financial centre.

The APEC Leaders' Summit in Kuala Lumpur reaffirmed the group's commitment to trade and investment liberalisation and to achieve the goals previously set. APEC members consider the expansion of trade and investment as essential requirements for their recovery and therefore have stressed the need for a liberal and open market. To this end, APEC members renewed their commitment to further improve and accelerate the implementation of

Table 5.12 Selected Asian economies' macroeconomic indicators (per cent change)

	1997				1998			
	Q1	Q2	Q3	Q4	Q1	Q2	Q3	Q4
China								
Output growth[a]	9.4	9.5	9.0	8.8	7.2	7.0	7.2	7.8
Inflation	5.2	2.9	2.1	1.0	0.2	−0.9	−1.4	−1.2
Trade balance[b]	6.8	11.4	12.8	9.7	10.6	11.7	12.8	8.2
Import value growth[c]	−2.1	0.6	8.0	2.5	2.4	2.4	−2.8	−5.5
Export value growth[c]	25.8	26.8	20.6	14.0	12.6	2.4	−2.1	−7.4
Hong Kong SAR								
Output growth[a]	5.7	6.9	6.1	2.8	−2.6	−5.1	−6.9	−5.7
Inflation	6.1	5.7	6.1	5.5	5.0	4.4	2.8	−0.8
Trade balance[b]	−6.2	−6.2	−4.0	−4.1	−4.2	−4.5	−0.8	−1.0
Import value growth[c]	4.3	4.8	5.6	5.8	−5.1	−6.1	−15.5	−18.2
Export value growth[c]	2.2	4.2	2.6	7.4	−1.0	−3.1	−10.3	−13.6
Export volume growth	4.0	6.2	4.4	9.6	1.4	−0.5	−7.0	−9.6
Indonesia								
Output growth[a]	7.7	6.6	3.3	2.4	−4.0	−12.3	−18.4	−19.5
Inflation	5.2	5.1	6.0	10.1	29.9	52.2	79.7	79.2
Trade balance[b]	1.7	2.2	0.8	1.7	3.9	4.1	4.2	3.4
Import value growth[c]	11.0	−7.8	−2.6	−10.1	−31.3	−26.9	−31.2	−38.8
Export value growth[c]	10.4	7.5	9.6	2.4	−1.0	−10.5	−6.3	−22.4
Export volume growth	26.2	20.4	33.5	33.0	32.8	11.1	25.6	2.5
Korea								
Output growth[a]	4.9	6.2	5.5	3.6	−3.6	−7.2	−7.1	−5.3
Inflation	4.7	4.0	4.0	5.1	8.9	8.2	7.0	6.0
Trade balance[b]	−7.3	−1.8	−1.5	2.2	8.6	11.3	9.0	10.1
Import value growth[c]	3.9	0.8	−3.8	−14.8	−36.2	−37.0	−39.9	−28.7
Export value growth[c]	−5.6	7.1	15.6	3.6	8.4	−1.8	−10.8	−5.5
Export volume growth	16.8	24.1	35.5	23.2	32.5	20.5	10.5	−
Malaysia								
Output growth[a]	8.6	8.3	7.4	6.8	−2.8	−6.6	−9.0	−8.1
Inflation	3.2	2.5	2.3	2.7	4.3	5.7	5.7	5.4
Trade balance[b]	0.8	−1.9	0.4	0.4	2.3	3.3	4.0	5.1
Import value growth[c]	−1.1	11.2	1.5	−8.2	−19.9	−33.3	−29.3	−20.5
Export value growth[c]	6.1	0.1	2.1	−5.3	−11.4	−10.1	−10.8	4.5
Philippines								
Output growth[a]	5.5	5.6	4.9	4.8	1.6	−0.8	−0.7	−1.8
Inflation	5.4	5.4	5.9	7.5	7.9	9.9	10.4	10.6
Trade balance[b]	−2.9	−2.7	−2.8	−2.3	−1.2	−0.3	0.5	0.8
Import value growth[c]	14.2	7.9	11.1	10.4	−4.3	−17.8	−21.4	−25.1
Export value growth[c]	17.5	26.5	24.7	22.2	23.8	14.4	19.2	11.5
Singapore								
Output growth[a]	4.2	8.5	10.7	7.6	6.2	1.8	−0.6	−0.8
Inflation	1.7	1.7	2.3	2.3	1.0	0.3	−0.8	−1.6
Trade balance[b]	−0.2	0.8	−0.2	0.7	2.7	4.0	4.1	4.1
Import value growth[c]	−2.6	2.7	8.8	−5.1	−16.2	−24.9	−28.5	−23.3
Export value growth[c]	−3.2	4.0	3.2	−4.0	−7.0	−13.9	−14.9	−12.3
Export volume growth	−0.3	8.8	10.5	7.8	7.5	−2.1	−1.9	−5.4

Table 5.12 (continued)

	1997				1998			
	Q1	*Q2*	*Q3*	*Q4*	*Q1*	*Q2*	*Q3*	*Q4*
Chinese Taipei								
Output growth[a]	6.7	6.2	7.1	7.1	5.9	5.2	4.7	3.7
Inflation	1.7	1.0	1.1	−0.2	1.6	1.7	0.6	2.9
Trade balance[b]	1.8	1.7	2.0	2.2	-0.1	1.3	3.4	1.3
Import value growth[c]	9.5	7.4	19.2	11.9	0.1	−7.0	−15.4	−10.7
Export value growth[c]	5.5	2.0	7.2	6.4	−6.6	−7.9	−9.8	−12.9
Export volume growth	6.3	1.1	9.4	10.9	2.7	3.7	−0.4	−10.5
Thailand								
Output growth[a]	3.8	5.1	−3.2	−7.5	−13.4	−12.8	−9.5	−3.7
Inflation	4.4	4.3	6.2	7.5	9.0	10.3	8.1	5.0
Trade balance[b]	03.2	03.1	−0.9	2.5	3.1	2.6	3.2	3.4
Import value growth[c]	−7.7	−7.6	−11.4	−27.5	−39.8	−38.2	−34.3	−18.9
Export value growth[c]	−1.0	2.2	7.1	6.7	−2.9	−5.3	−8.7	−9.9
Export volume growth	−1.7	4.3	11.7	16.3	14.1	12.2	5.7	0.8

Notes

a GDP growth except for Thailand, where growth of manufacturing production is shown. For China, growth rates are cumulative from beginning of year.

b In billions of US dollars; on national accounts basis except balance of payments basis for the Philippines, Singapore, and Thailand, and customs basis for China; 1998: Q3 trade data for Indonesia exclude oil and gas.

c In US dollars; national accounts basis except balance of payments basis for the Philippines, Singapore, and Thailand, and customs basis for China.

Sources: IMF, *International Financial Statistics* (IFS), and IMF staff estimates.

their individual action plans. Under the pressing economic circumstances faced by many APEC members, it was not surprising that they did not make further progress on the Early Volunteer Sectoral Liberalisation Package (EVSL) for the nine remaining sectors. They instead decided to implement the agreed package for the nine sectors and continue the negotiations on the six sectors. The Kuala Lumpur Meeting did made some progress in efforts to strengthen trade and investment flows in the region. In this regard, APEC members agreed to discuss competition policy and regulatory reforms to create an environment conducive for trade and investment.

With regard to exchange rate regime, the policy responses of the affected economies in the SRTA and growth triangle were mixed. Most ASEAN countries preferred to be *de facto* pegged against the US dollar. Due to the unsustainable pressure on the bhat, Thailand floated its currency in July 1997, which triggered the crisis. Subsequently, Indonesia, Malaysia, Singapore and South Korea followed the path taken by Thailand. Hong Kong decided to continue its currency peg with the US dollar, even though there was a fierce strain on its dollar. Hong Kong had increased its interest rate in order to maintain the peg, and later this hit the property sector. Indonesia considered introducing a currency board to stabilise the rupiah but withdraw this idea owing to its small international reserves and porous border. Malaysia, on the other hand, took the reverse route when it imposed selected capital controls on 1 September 1998. The ringgit was pegged to the US dollar and the outflow of foreign holdings of Malaysian financial assets was restricted. However, policy on trade-related transactions (exports and imports) and FDI flows remains unchanged. In February 1999, capital controls were eased – outright restriction became a remittance tax to allow for a regulated flow of short-term capital.

Judging from the performance of ASEAN and the CHT growth triangle, the East Asian economic and financial crisis, in general, has not altered these countries' commitment to trade and investment liberalisation. In the case of ASEAN, although only half of its members were affected, they are the founding members, generally the bigger economies and thus have a strong influence on the whole group. The ASEAN 4 clearly signalled their intention to maintain an open trade policy and investment regime. The selected capital controls of Malaysia are short-term measures, to give the economy a breathing space from volatile capital movement. Malaysia has reiterated the underlying thrust of its economic policy, that is the strong integration with the global economy. Nor did the CHT economies (China, Hong Kong and Chinese Taipei) indicate any trade policy reversal, despite their export decline in the second half of 1998. Thus, both ASEAN and CHT, which represent the views of the other SRTAs, are sticking to the broader APEC objective, namely creating a free trade area in the Asia Pacific region.

FUTURE DIRECTIONS FOR SRTAs

Since the inception of APEC, the SRTAs and growth triangles within this regional grouping have accepted the goals set at the Bogor summit. Each of the SRTAs and growth triangles has liberalised its trade and investment regime and some have even extended their liberalisation to economies outside their grouping. These liberalisation efforts are WTO-consistent and the economies have issued timetables by which the barriers are to be reduced or eliminated. Besides these commitments, the SRTAs have gone beyond those stipulated by the WTO in order to expedite their liberalisation. For AFTA, member economies have agreed to accelerate the timetable for tariff reduction – the schedule was advanced from the original 2005 to 2003 and finally to 2000.[10] The CER trade liberalisation has been extended to include removing export subsidies, ending qualitative restriction and opening up services trade. Progress made by NAFTA is also very significant in that all tariffs among its member economies have been eliminated. Moreover, NAFTA is in the process of expanding its membership and, if successful, more free trade areas will open up. The SRTAs have liberalised their investment rules and regulations. In addition to their own individual initiatives, the SRTAs have worked as a group to attract external investment – for example, ASEAN countries have lowered investment barriers to create the ASEAN Investment Area.

The trade and investment liberalisation initiatives by the SRTAs and growth triangles have produced results. Intra-sub-regional trade and investment within each SRTA and growth triangle have increased substantially, producing a more inter-linked sub-regional economic structure. In NAFTA, the interlinkage came from the complementary nature of the member economies: Mexico provides the base for labour-intensive activities and US and Canada supply technology and capital. The economic relationship in AFTA is different because the founding members are at similar stages of economic development and they compete against one another in export markets. Interlinkage in AFTA came through foreign investment that created production chains in the region and thus promoted intra-regional trade. The CHT economic relationship is similar to that of NAFTA where Hong Kong, China and Chinese Taipei provide technological capability and capital and China is the production location.

The contribution of the SRTAs and growth triangles is often viewed in terms of whether they create or divert trade. All the SRTAs and growth triangles in APEC have become more trade-oriented and the share of trade in their GDP has increased significantly. Trade with countries outside their own regional groupings has also risen because trade and investment liberalisation is often not restricted to members of the grouping. In particular, trade and investment among APEC SRTAs and growth triangles have grown. For example, trade between AFTA and CHT has increased from 5.7 per cent in 1980 to 12.5 per cent in 1995. Likewise, CER trade with AFTA has increased from 7.8 per cent to 14.7 per cent during the same period.

The performance of the sub-regional groupings can be regarded as a key element in the progress of APEC. Their liberalisation has narrowed trade and investment policy differences among member economies, and some SRTAs may attain a free trade environment faster than the targeted schedule of 2010/2020. The response of the SRTAs to the crisis indicates the strength of their commitment to free trade. They have maintained open trade policies even under strong balance-of-payment pressure, and have reduced investment barriers to attract foreign capital. Thus, we can conclude that the SRTAs have contributed to the APEC integration and will drive efforts to attain free trade.

What will be the future for the sub-regional groupings in APEC? Realising the important role that SRTAs can play, at the onset of the APEC process the Bogor Declaration stressed the need 'to review the interrelationships between APEC and the existing sub-regional arrangements and to examine possible options to prevent obstruction of each other and to promote consistency in their relationship'. The Eminent Persons' Group in their Third Report (1995) recommended that any SRTA acceleration or linkage must be fully consistent with the WTO if it was to support and complement APEC goals. Furthermore, any new SRTA initiatives must be submitted to the WTO for confirmation and the SRTAs should be subjected to WTO surveillance and evaluation. Any SRTA acceleration or linkage should be extended to other APEC economies under the following conditions:

- they are extended on an MFN basis
- they are accompanied by a commitment to continuously reduce trade barriers
- there is a willingness to extend new liberalisation to other APEC members on a reciprocal basis
- any individual SRTA member can unilaterally extend its SRTA acceleration or linkage to other APEC economies on a conditional or non-conditional basis.

The SRTAs have definitely fulfilled these conditions but the question to be asked is 'What is the next stage for SRTAs' liberalisation and how can SRTAs' initiatives complement and promote the APEC process?' In other words, what are the additional measures that need to be introduced to maximise the SRTAs' contribution to achieving the APEC objective of a free trade area? The SRTAs have done well in terms of tariff reduction and creation of favourable investment conditions. Any further initiatives should go beyond the early liberalisation stage and venture into less clear and less quantifiable areas. The recent East Asian economic and currency crisis has shown the power of contagion in inter-linked economies. Are there new issues arising from the crisis that call for a bigger role for the SRTAs in producing a more stable economic growth that can help a more cohesive APEC integration?

Cooperation within and among sub-regional groupings is undertaken in three ways: trade and investment liberalisation; trade and investment facilitation; and economic and technical cooperation (Ecotech).

Trade and investment liberalisation

Full implementation of Individual Action Plans (IAPs) by member economies. As a consequence of the economic and currency crisis, countries may want to review the implementation schedule of their IAPs to mitigate the adverse impact of the crisis. Any slackening in the implementation of IAPs will delay the progress towards a free trade and investment regime in APEC. SRTAs can play a significant role because peer persuasion and pressure in a closer relationship can be effective. There are existing mechanisms for closer monitoring of liberalisation progress in SRTAs.

Investment codes. APEC adopted a set of non-binding investment principles in 1994. These principles represented useful first steps towards improving the investment climate in the region but the realisation of these principles can be accelerated if it is done at the sub-regional level first. ASEAN efforts to open its investment regime by developing across-the-board investment principles is a good example of how a sub-regional initiative can set the pace for further liberalisation in a larger grouping. Again, the cohesiveness of a smaller grouping allows its members to have a more active and direct negotiation, encouraging its members to lower barriers. Notwithstanding the initiative by South Korea proposed at the Kuala Lumpur Summit in 1998 to establish an encompassing set of APEC investment principles, this route may be longer than that chosen by SRTAs. Thus, other sub-regional groupings should note the example of ASEAN, and if similar advances are made in other SRTAs, they will definitely accelerate the program of an APEC investment that will make APEC a very attractive investment location.

Expanding liberalisation initiatives in services. Thus far, APEC trade liberalisation has concentrated on goods, and tariffs have fallen to low levels. Therefore, the obvious next step is to remove impediments in the services sector. Progress in this area, even at the WTO level, has proved to be slow because some services industries are strategic (such as banking), many are not competitive and some are still at an early stage of development. Another factor is the nature of barriers in the services sector – unlike goods where the barriers are represented by tariffs, in the services sector they are mostly in the form of non-tariff or informal barriers, which are difficult to quantify and thus to monitor or control. Hence, it is not surprising that the services negotiation in the GATT Uruguay Round was long, complex and not entirely successful. In this regard, the SRTAs can play a role because they involve a smaller number of countries, which have already an open relationship in trade in goods, investment and other areas of cooperation. CER is a good example of how a sub-regional grouping has advanced in services trade liberalisation. SRTAs should be encouraged to extend their liberation initiatives to the services sector. Ultimately, progress made by the SRTAs will greatly facilitate the broader APEC services liberalisation.

Expanding liberalisation initiatives in agriculture. SRTAs can also play a key role in agricultural liberalisation. There is strong resistance to opening up the agriculture sector. Even AFTA, which has made bold commitments in tariff reduction, has decided to include agricultural products only in the final stage of liberalisation. Like services, negotiation to reduce tariffs and support in the agricultural sector may be more successful at the sub-regional level.

EVSL. Although APEC was successful in lowering barriers for the information technology industry, the Kuala Lumpur APEC Leaders' Summit did not produce a breakthrough for the nine agreed EVSL sectors. One of the obstacles to a successful EVSL program is the method of implementation; in environmental goods and services, medical equipment, civil aircraft and oilseed, the agreed liberalisation proposal will be bound with the WTO program. However, in the other sectors, the mode of implementation is different. Discussion on procedural matters such as these is more likely to succeed if it is done at the sub-regional level. SRTAs have many common values: consensus on far-reaching proposals contained in some of the EVSLs is only going to be achieved by countries which have common ground. Once an EVSL has been agreed at the SRTA level, it would be much easier to present it to other APEC members.

Enlarging SRTA membership. Existing SRTAs should enlarge their membership to include other countries in the Asia Pacific region. In this way, countries that are outside any regional grouping are encouraged to lower their trade barriers and adopt a less restrictive investment policy. In return, they would receive easier market access to the SRTAs. ASEAN has extended membership to four emerging economies and they are encouraged to adopt the concept of a free trade area, albeit at a slower pace. Moves such as this are likely to encourage non-APEC countries to subscribe to the idea of free trade. These emerging countries are usually apprehensive about free trade because their economies are still at an early stage of development. But, by linking up with bigger and relatively more developed economic areas that can offer other benefits such as a bigger market, these emerging economies may be persuaded to embrace more liberal trade and investment policies.

Inter-SRTAs link-up. SRTAs can further contribute to achieving APEC's goal of free trade by extending links with each another. Each of the SRTAs has, on its own, liberalised significantly its trade and investment policy, with some SRTAs instituting more wide-ranging liberalisation than others. By linking with other SRTAs, they can extend respective benefits accruing from each liberalisation. For example, a link between AFTA and CER has been mooted. Such a relationship can begin as a forum to resolve *ad hoc* difficulties that may arise in trade and investment relations between two economic areas and to discuss areas of mutual benefit. At a later stage when the relationship has deepened, the two SRTAs can extend some of the liberalisation benefits enjoyed by one SRTA to members from the other economic area. In the case of AFTA and CER, a dialogue has started on trade facilitation matters such as a trade and investment database, environmental standards and information promotion on standards and conformance.

Trade and investment facilitation

Besides reducing tariffs, another area in which the SRTAs have made significant progress is in trade and investment facilitation through the Collective Action Plans that assist the implementations of the IAPs. They are important complements to tariff reduction and also foster a friendlier investment environment. Among the trade facilitation areas that have been under consideration are customs procedures, labelling standards for products and a tariff database. In addition to the ongoing negotiations on improving trade facilities, the SRTAs can consider the following measures:

Dispute settlement mechanism. Following the WTO model, SRTAs should establish their own dispute settlement mechanism to solve any trade contentions such as dumping and other breaches of agreed trade liberalisation provisions.

Trade and investment policy review. SRTAs can formalise a regional trade and investment policy review to ensure that members do not fall back in their liberalisation commitments. This exercise, if carried out regularly, will encourage SRTA members to fulfil their commitments as well as explore new areas that need to be opened. The review process can also be a mechanism to gauge the impact of the SRTAs' liberalisation and modify the commitments if necessary.

Non-border issues. Agreement on non-border issues such as harmonisation of standards, professional certification, investment codes and product testing would immeasurably strengthen integrated trade and investment links. Regionally accepted conformance standards will reduce the cost and transit time of traded goods, thus encouraging more trade. They are also beneficial to investors, especially those with a regional production network, because common procedures can greatly expedite investment and thus make the region an attractive investment location. To this end, SRTAs should develop a system of mutual recognition of each other's standards. This system will give mutual acceptance of products and will promote convergence based on the principle of 'approved once, accepted anywhere'. Furthermore, members of SRTAs should impose similar or identical regulatory requirements to ensure that a given product is properly tested and conforms to its stated specification. As an initial step, members can minimise or reduce this duplication.

Economic and technical cooperation (Ecotech)

Ecotech has been identified as one of the pillars of APEC cooperation but its progress has not met expectations. Ecotech can help in four areas that contribute to trade and in liberalisation and facilitation – policy development, technical cooperation, infrastructure building and financial cooperation. The approach of this cooperation is pooling of resources such as information, experience, expertise and technology, rather than one-way transfers of funds. In this context, SRTAs are in a better position to implement Ecotech because of their pre-existing close and mutually beneficial relationship. The East Asian crisis underscores the importance of Ecotech to APEC economies, especially SRTA members, because free trade must be accompanied by equitable growth. The SRTAs can lead the Ecotech initiatives in the two main areas identified: building technology capacity and forming a network of centres for upgrading technology and region-wide sharing of information about new technology. Other beneficial developments could include:

- establishing R&D centres to support up-grading of small- and medium-scale technology
- promoting education and skill development in information technology
- setting a framework to link small and medium-scale companies to be regional suppliers for larger firms
- developing human capital
- providing educational financial support
- sharing of expertise in technical training
- forming a regional university network
- expanding technical exchange programs.

In summary, SRTAs are important building blocks for the APEC process and they can advance the deployment of free trade. SRTAs have accelerated their trade and investment liberalisation and now outpace APEC. Their efforts to overcome trade impediments comply with the broader framework set by the WTO and some countries have extended the benefits of liberalisation to non-members. APEC SRTAs have also transformed their economic region into a favourable investment area, as evidenced by the large inflow of long-term foreign investment. The SRTAs' dynamism is not confined to reducing barriers, but also includes mutually beneficial linkages among members of the economic areas. Some members have provided capital and technical expertise while others have a comparative advantage in labour cost. In short, SRTAs are in the vanguard of economic development in APEC and are expected to continue to lead in three areas – extending the liberalisation process, accelerating trade facilitation and strengthening Ecotech.

CONCLUSION

The SRTAs and growth triangles have liberalised their trade and investment regimes and some have even extended these liberalisation benefits to economies outside their groupings. As the SRTAs are members of WTO, they adhere to the requirement of WTO Article 24 and their liberalisation measures are also WTO consistent. In addition to these commitments, the SRTAs have gone beyond those stipulated by the WTO in order to expedite their liberalisation process. The SRTAs and growth triangle initiatives have produced results: intra-sub-regional trade and investment within each SRTA and growth triangle have increased substantially, producing a more inter-linked sub-regional economic structure. Encouragingly, trade and investment flows with other APEC members have also increased. Their liberalisation has narrowed trade and investment policy differences among member economies and some SRTAs may even attain the free trade environment faster than the targeted schedule of 2010/2020.

The response of the SRTAs to the East Asian economic crisis indicates the strength of their commitments to free trade. As an initial response, some members of SRTAs increased tariff rates for selected goods to deal with balance-of-payment pressures. Fortunately, this type of response was very limited and the affected member countries maintained their pre-crisis trade policy regime. The affected countries, in fact, introduced further liberalisation measures to attract more foreign direct investment or to solve bad debt problems in the financial sector. Some SRTA members had implemented unilateral liberalisation in the financial sector to increase their competitiveness. At the Kuala Lumpur Leaders' Summit, APEC member countries reaffirmed their commitment to trade and investment liberalisation, but the failure of Early Sectoral Voluntary Liberalisation (EVSL) indicated that these measures alone are not sufficient for the APEC process; capacity building is another area that needs to be addressed seriously.

NOTES

1   Since the new free trade agreement (FTA) between Chile and Mexico follows the NAFTA scheme, and the Canada–Chile FTA has only recently entered into

force, this chapter will mainly focus on the three SRTAs, namely NAFTA, AFTA and CER.

2   One of the issues that SRTAs raise is the complications for the investor raised by the multiplicity of regimes. This issue has not received as much attention as the trade effect has in the literature.

3   The significant decline in tariff rates in 1996 may have partly reflected the implementation of the downpayments in the Osaka Initiative Actions.

4   The economies with virtually zero tariffs include: Brunei Darussalam, Hong Kong and Singapore. The four economies with the tariffs higher than 15% include: China; Papua New Guinea; the Philippines; and Thailand.

5   NAFTA recognises the importance of ensuring that trade rules are consistent with domestic and international environmental objectives. The Agreement allows governments to take steps to protect the environment, even when these steps conflict with their trade obligations, as long as such steps do not involve unnecessary discrimination or introduce disguised restrictions on trade. It establishes that obligations in certain international environmental agreements can override obligations in the NAFTA. It preserves the rights of governments to set high environmental standards. Any panel established to address an environmental issue will have access to environmental experts. Further, a North American Commission on the Environment was established on a parallel track. The North American Agreement on Environmental Cooperation sets out a broad cooperative work program; details the obligations of all three countries to ensure compliance with domestic environmental laws and policies; and provides a mechanism for consultation and resolution of disputes over trade-related environmental issues and recourse if a NAFTA partner fails to enforce its own environmental laws.

6   In the cases of Canada and the United States, by 1 January 1998.

7   Since there is difficulty in decomposing economy-wide data into sub-regional figures, the study used data of the respective economies to study the interdependence of the CHT area.

8   Direct trade, which consists of smuggling and 'minor trade' in ships of less than 100 tons, is also thought to have increased, although it is difficult to measure.

9   MAPA Highlights (APEC Home Page).

10   This commitment was made at the ASEAN Leaders Summit in Hanoi at the end of 1998.

REFERENCES

APEC (1995) *Implementing The APEC Vision*, Third Report of the Eminent Persons Group, Singapore: APEC Secretariat.

—— (1997) *The Impact of Subregionalism in APEC*, Economic Committee.

Ariff, M. (1994) 'APEC and ASEAN: complementing or competing?', in Chia, S.Y., (ed.) *APEC: Challenges And Opportunities*, Singapore: Institute of Southeast Asian Studies.

Garnaut, R. (1996) *Open Regionalism and Trade Liberalisation: An Asia–Pacific Contribution to the World Trading System*, Institute of Southeast Asian Studies and Allen & Unwin, Sydney.

Holmes, F. (1990) 'ANZCERTA, trade in services, and ASEAN', *ASEAN Economic Bulletin* 7(1) July.

Lopez, A.A. and Matutes, J.S. (1998) 'Open regionalism versus discriminatory trading agreements: institutional and empirical analysis', *ASEAN Economic Bulletin* 14(3), March.

Parsons, D. (1997) 'AFTA in the context of a multilateral trading system', in K.K. Hourn and S. Kanter (eds) *ASEAN Free Trade Agreement: Implications and Future Directions*, London: ASEAN Academic Press.

PECC (1995) 'Milestones in APEC Liberalisation: A Map of Market Opening Measures by APEC Economies', PECC for the APEC Secretariat.

—— (1996) Perspectives on the Manila Action Plan for APEC, PECC Secretariat, Singapore.

Smith, A.L. (1998) 'The AFTA–CER dialogue: A New Zealand perspective on the emerging trade area linkage', *ASEAN Economic Bulletin* 14(3) March.

Tang, M. and Thant, M. (1994) 'Growth triangles: Conceptual and operational considerations', in Thant, Tang and Kakazu, (eds) *Growth Triangles in Asia: A New Approach to Regional Economic Cooperation*, Hong Kong: Oxford University Press.

Yamazawa, I. and Hirata, A. (1996) *APEC: Co-operation from Diversity*, Tokyo: Institute Of Developing Economies.

6 Liberalisation of manufacturing sectors
The automobile industry in China

Ralph W. Huenemann

THE GLOBAL SETTING

The automobile industry worldwide

Worldwide, the automobile industry is passing through a period of rapid, destabilising change. There are many aspects to these upheavals, but they can perhaps be summarised in three categories: structural characteristics, capacity issues, and environmental concerns.

Structural Characteristics: Of the structural changes that are occurring, none is more striking than the recent wave of mega-mergers. The Volkswagen purchase of Rolls–Royce, the merger of Daimler–Benz AG and Chrysler Corp. into DaimlerChrysler, the takeover of Volvo by Ford, and the Renault purchase of a significant share in Nissan have all made headlines recently. Mini-mergers (such as Hyundai's bid for Kia Motors, GM's increase of its stake in Suzuki and Isuzu, Ford's control of Mazda, and Astra's search for foreign partners) are also an important part of the story. A related phenomenon is the geographical dispersion of production around the globe, with a concomitant blurring of national identities. Everyone knows that Hondas and Toyotas are now assembled in North America in large numbers, but not everyone is aware that Jeep Cherokees are now produced in Austria and China, the cheeky new Beetle is made in Latin America, and Nissan pick-up trucks sold in Australia are made in Thailand. Less visible but equally important structural changes involve moves to cut costs by building multiple vehicle models on shared 'platforms' (the basic chassis) and power units, and by increased outsourcing of parts and components. Closely related to the growth of outsourcing is the revolution in quality control and just-in-time (JIT) manufacturing.[1] All of these changes, taken together, make 'country of origin' a highly ambiguous concept.

Capacity Issues: Unsurprisingly, the recent mergers and restructurings in the world automobile industry reflect a fundamental problem – serious excess capacity. In 1996, when total world production of cars was about 50 million vehicles, the industry's capacity was about 68 million. Since 1996, the Asian financial crisis and other worries have kept world demand relatively flat, yet a number of new factories, including the Buick joint venture in Shanghai, have been brought on stream. As the *Economist* summarises the situation:

> By 2000, over-capacity will have risen from 18m to 22m units – equivalent to 80 of the world's 630 car assembly factories standing idle. Looked at another way, every factory in North America could close – and there would still be excess capacity. (*The Economist*, 10 May 1997: 22)

The stage seems set for a major price war, and big firms with lean manufacturing methods and deep pockets are the ones most likely to survive the conflict. Hence the mergers and restructurings.

Environmental Concerns: One does not have to be as grumpy as Ralph Nader to recognise that motor vehicles pollute the environment, and that the situation is particularly bad in urban areas. The culprit of course is what economists call the 'problem of the commons', in two guises, since both clean air and roadway space are collective goods. Cars spew exhaust, but cars trapped in traffic jams spew even more exhaust. Recently, scientific sampling by Beijing's Environmental Protection Bureau has confirmed what residents and visitors have long known: the air in Beijing is badly polluted and getting worse, and motor vehicle exhaust is a major contributor to the problem (*Beijing Review*, 8–14 June 1998: 11–13; Han Guojian 1999: 10–13). Other cities in China suffer from the same problems, of course.

Trade policy environment

An optimistic liberal, reviewing the history of international trading arrangements since World War II, can point to the gradual reduction of tariffs under the GATT, the creation of the WTO, and the rapid growth of world trade and investment as evidence that efforts at liberalisation have achieved major successes. A pessimistic liberal, reviewing the same history, can argue that protectionism is probably just as virulent as ever, that the reduction of tariffs has simply revealed more clearly the role of non-tariff barriers (NTBs), and that the recent demise of the proposed Multilateral Agreement on Investment (MAI) suggests that nation states are still jealously protective of their sovereignty. An ardent chauvinist could agree with the pessimistic liberal on the facts, but would add that it's a darned good thing that liberalisation has been held in check.[2]

This is an exceedingly complex environment, in which both the facts and the policy goals are contentious, yet this is the environment in which regional groupings like the APEC forum must function. The situation is rendered more complicated for APEC by the fact that China is a member of APEC but not yet a member of the WTO. So far, APEC has managed to move forward on its agenda, but arguably only because that agenda has been couched in language of 'constructive ambiguity' (Bergsten 1997: 10).

My intention in this chapter is to attempt to shed some light on APEC's dilemmas by examining the specifics of one of the region's most heavily protected infant industries – the automobile industry in China. Before turning to the specifics of this topic, however, let me frame my subject by noting that it seems to me that, as economists, we are grappling here with two basic analytical questions: First, is *regional* liberalisation, as distinct from *global* liberalisation, a good thing or not? And second, how is liberalisation of *investment* related to liberalisation of *trade*? These questions have been around for a long time, of course, yet we are still struggling to find satisfactory answers. Among economists, it seems to me, the debate is about the search for a dynamic, disequilibrium analogue to our old friend, Pareto optimality. In other words, we are seeking a more nuanced understanding of efficiency (productivity), not equity. Outside the narrow realm of economists, the debate is quite different, and in this larger realm issues of income distribution will probably always dominate the headlines. (After the first Canadian wheat sales to China, a Montreal textile manufacturer asked querulously, 'How long must we subsidise fat prairie farmers by surrendering jobs in Quebec and Ontario?' (*The Financial Post*, 10 August 1963: 2). In both realms, sensible insights depend on a good understanding of the specifics of the situation. The devil, as always, is in the details. With that thought in mind, let us turn to the specifics of the automobile industry in China.

CHINA'S AUTOMOBILE INDUSTRY

The industry before 1978

One of the first automobiles to reach China arrived in the early 1900s, a gift from the foreign community to the Empress Dowager, Ci Xi. The gift was not well received, however, for the Empress Dowager found it terribly noisy (with good reason, no doubt) and was offended by the seating arrangement (the chauffeur, out of necessity, sat with his back turned to her). Despite this unpropitious beginning, imported automobiles began to appear in China's cities over the next couple of decades. The first domestically-built car was assembled in Shenyang in 1931, just a few months before the outbreak of war with Japan. In 1936, a joint venture with a German firm was formed in Zhuzhou to produce trucks and buses, but this second effort was soon terminated by the war as well (Li and Tian 1998: 1–3).

Thus, it was not until the 1950s that China's motor vehicle industry really got started. With help from the Soviet Union, the No. 1 Vehicle Factory was built in Changchun. In 1956, this factory produced its first vehicle, a four-ton Jiefang (Liberation) truck, modelled on the Soviet ZIS-150, which was, in turn, a copy of a pre-War Ford. Construction of the No. 2 Vehicle Factory was formally authorised in 1967, but because of the disruptions caused by the Cultural Revolution, this second major factory achieved serial production of its primary vehicle, the five-ton Dongfeng (East Wind) truck, only in 1975. Production at the No. 2 Factory was hampered by the fact that it was deliberately located in the remote town of Shiyan in Hubei province, to isolate it from potential Soviet attack. Besides these two dominant factories, plants were also built in Beijing, Shenyang, Nanjing, Jinan, Shanghai and many other locations. Most were small and were meant to demonstrate the virtues of Chairman Mao's slogans of 'self-reliance' (*zili gengsheng*) and 'small but complete' (*xiao er quan*), both of which challenged the concept of economies of scale. By 1976, China had fifty-three motor vehicle factories, but all suffered from low technical quality and most had very high unit costs.[3] As Li Chunlin and Tian Shu summarise the situation, 'mistakes in guiding philosophy and mistakes in policy led to terribly wasteful expenditures'. According to Li and Tian, the two small vehicle factories at Yibing in Sichuan and Baoji in Shaanxi taken together required construction expenditures of about 400 million yuan to achieve output of 2,000 vehicles a year, for an average up-front capital cost of about 200,000 yuan per unit of annual output, compared with a cost of about 15,000 yuan at the No. 1 Factory in Changchun (Li and Tian 1998: 9).

Total domestic production of motor vehicles in China increased gradually from about 7,900 units in 1957 to about 149,100 units in 1978. Virtually all these vehicles were trucks, buses or specialty vehicles, although sedans were produced in Shanghai in small numbers beginning in 1958, and a few Hongqi (Red Flag) limousines were built in Changchun (Huenemann 1991: 464, and *China Daily* 1998b: 5).

This may be a good place to pause briefly for some clarification of terminology. In Chinese nomenclature, 'trucks' are limited to freight-hauling vehicles, so specialty trucks like fire engines and airport equipment are counted under 'other vehicles'. Also, buses (*keche*) of all sizes are included in 'other vehicles' (this category includes minivans). Finally, off-road vehicles (or SUVs, as the industry now labels them) are also included in 'other vehicles'. Thus, the Chinese category that I have translated as 'sedans' (*jiaoche*) is somewhat narrower than the North American concept of the 'family car', which these days certainly includes minivans and SUVs, but the difference is unimportant for present purposes.

In summary, by 1978 China's motor vehicle industry was well established but producing relatively few vehicles, and it was plagued by backward technology and high unit costs. Production was focused on trucks and buses; very few cars were being built. All this was about to change dramatically.

Growth of the industry since 1978

In December 1978, at the famous Third Plenum of the Eleventh Central Committee, China abandoned Maoist self-reliance and adopted a radical new policy of 'reforming the economy and opening to the outside world'. Looking back twenty years later, we can perhaps agree that the ultimate meaning of the new policy is still being explored, but that the changes to date have been profound. This is true both for the economy in general and for the automobile industry in particular. For the automobile industry, the reforms have led to sporadic waves of automobile imports, exponential growth in the number of cars produced domestically, and a proliferation of joint ventures with foreign firms, with a concomitant improvement in the quality and unit cost of the cars produced locally, but to date the reforms have not fully succeeded in bringing unit costs down to world levels, especially at the small, inefficient plants.

The overall growth of domestic motor vehicle production in China since 1980 is displayed in Table 6.1. A variety of messages can be found in Table 6.1. First, sedan production was virtually nonexistent until about 1986, but grew explosively (at about 40 per cent per annum) over the next decade, and reached 486,000 units in 1997. Second, despite this increase in the production of sedans, trucks and other vehicles continue to be important in the Chinese motor vehicle industry. Third, the growth of total vehicle production since 1980 has averaged about 12 per cent per annum. Real GDP growth averaged about 10 per cent over the same period (State Statistical Bureau 1998: 58), so the share of this industry in GDP was expanding slowly, reflecting the rising importance of the passenger sedan in the industry's product mix.

The pattern of motor vehicle imports since 1980 is also displayed in Table 6.1. A cautionary note needs to be sounded here: the data in Table 6.1 encompass only the motor vehicles declared to Customs. The number of smuggled vehicles in recent years may have been quite large, possibly reaching 100,000 units in 1997, but recent anti-smuggling efforts are said to have 'effectively plugged the illegal channel' (*China Daily* 1998d: B3). Whatever the facts may be about smuggled vehicles, *legal* imports have been rather unimportant in total supply (running between 50,000 and 100,000 units most years), but there have been two important exceptions: a surge of imports in 1985, and another surge in 1993 and 1994. In the first spike in 1985, the imports of 354,000 units came close to equalling domestic production in the same year (437,200 units). As can be seen in Table 6.1, much of the 1985 spike was 'other vehicles', many of them smallish buses like the Toyota Coaster, which were purchased by work units (which use them to transport employees and visitors). The second spike, in 1993 and 1994, was different in two ways. First, although the absolute level of imports was just as large as in 1985 (310,100 units in 1993 and another 283,100 units the next year), the share of imports in total supply was much smaller, because domestic production had grown so dramatically in the intervening decade. Second, the 1993–94 surge was dominated by passenger sedans, not buses. However, the customers were still work units, not households.

As can be seen by comparing Tables 6.1 and 6.2, the two surges of motor vehicle imports were part of a larger pattern, coinciding with years in which China's overall merchandise trade balance dipped sharply into deficit. As I will discuss in greater detail later, the Chinese authorities reacted sharply to these trade deficits, using both price measures (effective devaluation of the yuan and a sharp increase in tariffs) and administrative measures (import licences and rationing of foreign exchange) as policy tools. The impact of these measures on officially measured trade flows is clearly visible in Tables 6.1 and 6.2, though the true picture, including smuggling, is less clear.

Table 6.1 China: data on motor vehicles

Year	Domestic Production ('000 units)				Vehicle Imports ('000 units)			
	Trucks	Sedans	Other vehicles	Total vehicle pro- duction	Trucks (incl. CKD & SKD)	Sedans (incl. CKD & SKD)	Other vehicles	Total vehicle imports
1980	135.5	5.4	81.4	222.3	0.0	0.0	51.1	51.1
1981	108.3	3.4	63.9	175.6	0.0	0.0	41.6	41.6
1982	121.8	4.0	70.5	196.3	0.0	0.0	16.1	16.1
1983	137.1	6.0	96.7	239.8	0.0	0.0	25.2	25.2
1984	181.8	6.0	128.6	316.4	0.0	0.0	88.7	88.7
1985	269.0	5.2	163.0	437.2	0.0	0.0	354.0	354.0
1986	229.1	12.3	128.4	369.8	0.0	0.0	150.1	150.1
1987	298.4	29.9	143.5	471.8	0.0	0.0	67.2	67.2
1988	403.3	36.8	204.6	644.7	0.0	0.0	99.2	99.2
1989	363.4	28.8	191.3	583.5	0.0	0.0	85.6	85.6
1990	289.7	42.4	181.9	514.0	0.0	0.0	65.4	65.4
1991	382.5	81.1	250.6	714.2	0.0	0.0	98.5	98.5
1992	476.7	162.7	427.3	1066.7	0.0	0.0	210.1	210.1
1993	597.9	229.7	470.9	1298.5	0.0	0.0	310.1	310.1
1994	663.0	250.3	453.6	1366.9	0.0	0.0	283.1	283.1
1995	596.0	337.0	519.7	1452.7	0.0	0.0	158.1	158.1
1996	625.1	382.9	467.2	1475.2	0.0	0.0	75.8	75.8
1997	573.6	486.0	522.9	1582.5	0.0	0.0	48.5	48.5
1998		507.0		1630.0	0.0	0.0	39.7	39.7

Notes: Does not include motorcycles or farm vehicles.

Sources: General Administration of Customs of the PRC, China's Customs Statistics (*Monthly Exports and Imports*), various issues; State Statistical Bureau, *Zhongguo Tongji Nianjian (China Statistical Yearbook)*, various years; *Zhongguo Qiche Gongye Nianjian* (China Automotive Industry Yearbook) *1997;* State Statistical Bureau, *Zhongguo Tongji Zhaiyao (Statistical Survey of China) 1999; China Daily,* 9 January 1999: 3.

THE EVOLUTION OF FOREIGN INVESTMENT

So far, I have talked about domestic production and imports as if they are two distinct categories, but in reality this distinction is blurred, because of the role of imported components in domestic production. This is especially important in the case of joint ventures with foreign firms.

The first joint venture in China's automobile industry, agreed to in 1983, was the Beijing Jeep Corporation (BJC), a collaboration between American Motors Corporation (AMC), at that time controlled by Renault, and the Beijing Automobile Works (BAW). BAW was interested in AMC, an otherwise marginal player, because of AMC's experience with four-wheel drive technology. The conflict-laden history of BJC in its early years, which is well known from Jim Mann's book *Beijing Jeep*,[4] can be briefly summarised as follows. The American side wanted access to the domestic market, low labour costs, and perhaps an

Table 6.2 China's merchandise trade, 1980–98 (US$billion)

Year	Imports	Exports	Balance
1980	−20.0	18.1	−1.9
1981	−22.0	22.0	−0.0
1982	−19.3	22.3	3.0
1983	−21.4	22.2	0.8
1984	−27.4	26.1	−1.3
1985	−42.3	27.4	−14.9
1986	−42.9	30.9	−12.0
1987	−43.2	39.4	−3.8
1988	−55.3	47.5	−7.8
1989	−59.1	52.5	−6.6
1990	−53.3	62.1	8.7
1991	−63.8	71.8	8.1
1992	−80.6	84.9	4.4
1993	−104.0	91.7	−12.2
1994	−115.6	121.0	5.4
1995	−132.1	148.8	16.7
1996	−138.8	151.0	12.2
1997	−142.4	182.8	40.4
1998	−140.2	183.8	43.6

Sources: 1980–96 from State Statistical Bureau 1998: 621–22; 1997–98 from China's Customs Statistics (*Monthly Exports and Imports*), 1998, 12: 3.

export platform for the rest of Asia. The Chinese side wanted technology transfer (including help with designing a better military vehicle), local jobs (not just in the BJC plant, but in factories producing parts and components) and exports. These goals were not entirely incompatible, but they did lead to serious conflict, primarily because of China's overvalued and non-convertible currency.

The first Cherokee was produced at BJC in September 1985. At that time, the exchange rate was about 3.2 yuan to the US dollar, which meant that a tyre shipped from the United States cost only 284 yuan delivered in Beijing, even after paying significant duties and taxes, while a locally-produced tyre cost 465 yuan (Li and Tian 1998: 118). The same pattern applied to other local parts and components. Understandably, the American side was reluctant to use local parts and components, even assuming the quality was acceptable. At the beginning, then, Cherokees were assembled in Beijing from what the industry calls CKD ('completely knocked down') kits, which were 'cars in a box' shipped from Ohio and assembled in China. The first Cherokee produced by BJC in 1985 had a local content ratio of only 9.1 per cent, of which the labour input constituted 7.4 per cent (Li and Tian 1998: 121). Everyone smiled bravely for the publicity photos as that first Cherokee rolled off the line, but in fact both sides were deeply aggrieved – the Americans because they could not readily convert the joint venture's yuan revenues into US dollars to pay for the CKD kits or to repatriate profits, and the Chinese because a local content ratio for parts and components of 1.7 per cent was certainly not acceptable from their point of view.

A few weeks later, the Americans sent their notorious 'November telex' to the ministerial and municipal authorities supervising BAW, asking for an easing of the restrictions on CKD imports and threatening to curtail training and technology transfer if their request was not met. Predictably, the telex created enormous ill-will. And its timing was terrible, since this was just at the height of China's efforts to deal with the 1985 trade deficit. The Beijing Jeep joint venture might very well have collapsed right then, yet it did not. One important reason was almost certainly that, in the face of the flood of imported vehicles in 1985, China's balance-of-payments managers recognised that, even in the short term, CKD production used less foreign exchange than straight imports, and in the longer term held out the promise of significant import-substitution through 'localisation'. This reasoning was strengthened by AMC's promise to increase the use of local parts and components in the Cherokee as circumstances permitted. A second important reason may have been that the Beijing authorities knew that other joint ventures (with Volkswagen in Shanghai and Peugeot in Guangzhou) were being set up, and that Beijing ran the risk of losing ground relative to these rival cities. It may also have been important that the person chosen by the Chinese authorities to broker a settlement was someone named Zhu Rongji.

In the end, two secret agreements were reached that resolved much of the conflict. In March 1986, the Chinese authorities offered BJC the right to import up to 12,500 CKD kits over four years (at US $9,600 per kit, this represented a guarantee of access to US $120 million of foreign exchange), in return for a commitment from BJC to strive to reach 80 per cent local content by 1990. (The level actually achieved in 1990 was only 43.5 per cent (Li and Tian 1998: 121)). In the autumn, a second agreement gave BJC access to US $300,000 for the payment of dividends abroad.

As Beijing Jeep was resolving some of its key problems, other competitors were appearing on the scene. The most important was undoubtedly the Volkswagen joint venture in Shanghai, which produced its first Santana in 1986. As at BJC, the use of CKD kits at Shanghai in the early years was unavoidable but contentious, and foreign exchange shortage was also a problem (Woodard 1989: 40 and Harwit 1995: 92–114). Simultaneously, the Peugeot joint venture in Guangzhou was getting underway. By 1991, Volkswagen would expand its presence in China by forming a joint venture in Changchun to produce Jetta and Audi sedans, and the next year Peugeot added a joint venture in Wuhan to produce Citroens.

In the early years, Japanese car makers were reluctant to enter into joint ventures in China, strongly preferring to produce at home and export, although Toyota (through Daihatsu) did agree to a technology licensing arrangement to assist with production of the Charade in Tianjin. However, the Chinese policy environment, as it evolved over the 1980s and 1990s, created intense pressures toward FDI. At the broadest level, the sporadic but continuing devaluation of the yuan (from about 1.7 yuan/US$ in 1981 to about 8.3 yuan/US$ today) made all foreign goods more expensive in China, and the rise of the yen relative to the US dollar compounded the problem for Japanese products. The greater pressures, however, arose from policies specifically targeted at the motor vehicle industry. One aspect of this policy environment was tariffs. The duty on car imports was raised from 80 per cent to 120 per cent at the end of 1984, and then raised again to 260 per cent in 1985. Another aspect was the aggressive use of non-tariff barriers (NTBs), especially the rationing of import licences, notably the two-year moratorium on most vehicle imports imposed in 1985 (Mann 1997: 118 and 151–2).

In the 1990s, two additional elements were added to the policy pressures shaping FDI in the automotive sector. The first was the Automotive Industry Policy (AIP), issued in 1994 (Xing 1997: 8–18). Of the various provisions of the AIP, one of the most important for foreign auto companies was a stipulation that joint ventures with a local content ratio of at least 40 per cent would qualify for deep discounts on the onerous duties paid on imported parts. Another provision permitted up to 100 per cent foreign ownership in parts and components firms, compared to the 50 per cent limit in vehicle assembly firms. The AIP led to a surge of foreign investment, including Japanese investment, in parts and components supply. As one Japanese auto executive commented recently, 'We said, "What are we going to do with the [high-cost] parts?" We were opposed, but it was a national policy, and there was nothing we could do.' (Landers 1999: 51). The pressures from the AIP were reinforced the next year when the 'Provisional Regulations for Guiding the Direction of Foreign Investment' (the 'Guidelines') were issued. The 'Guidelines' explicitly identified automobile parts and components, and automobile R&D, as sectors to be 'encouraged', while engine production and final vehicle assembly were categorised as sectors to be 'restricted', which meant that 'the Chinese partner will take a leading role' (Rosen 1999: 22 and 259–78).

The cumulative impact of the Chinese policy environment on FDI in the automobile sector can be measured in various ways, but two summary statistics stand out. First, sedans produced by joint venture firms in 1996 totalled about 252,000 units, or 66 per cent of all the sedans produced in China that year (for details, see Table 6.3). This market dominance will certainly increase in the next few years as Volkswagen's joint ventures expand production and the new Honda and Buick joint ventures come on line.[5] Second, of the 444 joint ventures related to motor vehicles listed in a recent directory issued by China Business Update, only about 30 are final assembly plants for sedans, jeeps or light trucks and buses. A few more are assembly plants for motorcycles or heavy trucks and buses. All the rest are parts and component makers (*China Business Update* 1998). And parts and component makers who are not partnered with foreign firms number in the thousands (*China Business*

Table 6.3 The foreign joint ventures in China's automobile industry (sedans, jeeps, and light buses and trucks)

Chinese partner	Location	Product	Foreign partner	Foreign share (%)	Year founded	Annual production
BAIGC	Beijing	Cherokee & domestic	AMC (Renault, then Chrysler)	42	1984	71,333 ('96)
BAIGC	Beijing	Light buses	Isuzu	25	1995	
BAIGC	Beijing	Light trucks	Shoitindje (HK) & Itochu (Japan)	45	1988	
Changchun Special Purpose Auto	Changchun	Light buses & pick-ups	Sammitr Motors Ltd. (Thailand)		1993	
DMC	Wuhan	Fookang (sedan)	Citroen	30	1992	9,228 ('96)
DMC	Hangzhou	Light trucks	Nissan	50	1997	
FAGC	Qingyuan (GD)	Yuejiang (mini buses & trucks)	Baojin Industry Ltd. (HK)	18	1991	2,308 ('96)
FAGC	Changchun	Audi, Jetta & Golf (sedans)	Volkswagen & Audi	40	1992	42,000 ('96)
FAGC	Shenyang	Blazers and pick-ups	GM	50		
Fuzhou Auto Works	Fuzhou	Delica (light buses)	Chunghwa (Taiwan)	50	1997	
Guangzhou Automotive	Guangzhou	504 & 505, then Accord (sedans)	Peugeot, then Honda		1985	2,000 ('96)
Guizhou Aviation	Guizhou	Skylark (sedan)	Fuji Heavy Industries		planned	
HAIC	Haikou	Minivans	Mazda		1992	
Jiangling Motors Corp.	Nanchang	Transit (minivan)	Ford	30		<10,000 ('98)
Jiangling Motors Corp.	Nanchang	Light trucks	Lear (USA)	50	1996	
NORINCO	Chongqing	Alto (sedan)	Suzuki & Nissho Iwai	49	1993	8,455 ('96)
QAGC	Chongqing	Light trucks	Isuzu	49	1996	
SAIGC	Shanghai	Santana (sedan/station wagon)	Volkswagen	50	1985	200,222 ('96)
SAIGC	Shanghai	Buick (sedan)	General Motors	50	1997	
Sanjiang Aerospace	Xiaogan (HB)	Traffic (light buses)	Renault	45	1994	300 ('95)
TAIGC	Tianjin	Light buses	Kook-Hang Enterprise (Macao)	33	1992	2,349 ('96)
XAIC & DMC	Xiamen	Golden Dragon (light buses)	Faya Corp. (HK)	25	1988	322 ('96)
Yaxing Bus Corp.	Yangzhou (JS)	Light buses	Mercedes-Benz	50	1995	
Yuejin Automobile	Nanjing	Light trucks	Iveco (Fiat)	50	1996	
Zhangjiagang Bus Co.	Zhangjiagang	Light buses	Taisun Auto Ltd. (Singapore)	55	1993	
Zhangjiagang Dujuan	Zhangjiagang	Dujuan (light buses)	Feichi Auto Ltd. (HK)	40	1994	
Zhangjiagang Dujuan	Zhangjiagang	Shazhou (light buses)	Fansheng Auto Ltd. (HK)	48		
ZLAW & CITIC	Zhengzhou	Pick-up trucks	Nissan	30	1993	2,814 ('96)

Sources: Based primarily on information drawn from China Business Update 1998, supplemented by information from Xing 1997: 14; China Business Update 1997–98; Landers 1999: 50–52; Mann 1997; Rosen 1999: 142; Leggett and Smith 1998: 15; Shen Bin 1998b: 5; McClellan and Smith 1997: 70–71; and China Automobile Technology Research Center 1997.

Update 1997–98). In short, outsourcing has become just as important in China's motor vehicle industry as it is in the rest of the world.

CURRENT STRUCTURE OF THE INDUSTRY

The current situation in China's automobile industry can be summarised as follows: a few large firms dominate final production, surrounded by numerous uneconomic pygmies, and excess capacity is a major problem – a problem which closing down the pygmies would do little to resolve. The majors are often called the 'Big Three' (Shanghai Automotive Industry Group Corporation, Hubei's Dongfeng Motor Corporation, and Changchun's First Automobile Group Corporation), and the 'Little Three' (Beijing Automotive Group Corporation, Tianjin Automotive Group Corporation, and Guangzhou Honda). Five of the six are partnered in joint ventures with foreign majors, and it is widely predicted that the sixth will also become a joint venture when Toyota takes an equity share in Tianjin, with which Daihatsu (controlled by Toyota) has long had a technology licensing agreement to produce the Charade (*Euroweek*, 15 May 1998: 16). These six firms together produce about 89 per cent of China's sedans, while SAIGC alone has a 52 per cent share of the market (Rosen 1999: 46).

Although 'capacity' is not a precise concept, there is little doubt that excess capacity is now a major problem. Daniel Rosen estimates a capacity of 839,000 automobiles in 1996, against an actual production of 385,000, for a utilisation rate of about 46 per cent (Rosen 1999: 142). The inventory of unsold automobiles at the end of March 1998 stood at 127,000 units (Shen Bin 1998a: 5). According to a recent report in the *Beijing Review*:

> Price wars have burst out in many trades, beginning with the car market in early 1998. It was then followed by building materials, household electrical appliances, medicines, chemical raw materials, rolled steel and cashmere products. (Han 1999b: 17–18)

In mid-October, the government authorities reacted to these price pressures by imposing floor prices on automakers and dealers (Shen Bin 1998c: 5). The adverse impact of these price wars on profitability was revealed at the end of the year, when it was reported that SAIGC earned profits of 3.85 billion yuan in 1998, but the entire motor vehicle industry earned profits of only 3.44 billion yuan (Wang 1999: 3). In other words, if Shanghai is removed from the picture, the rest of the motor vehicle industry suffered aggregate losses of 410 million yuan in 1998.

Despite the growth of demand for cars, the over-capacity problem is probably getting worse. Production in 1998 was 507,000 sedans, but existing capacity was about 1.1 million sedans, with the new Buick and Honda facilities about to add another 200,000 (Han 1998: 20, and Wang 1999: 3). To illustrate what these pressures mean at the individual firm level, we can cite the recent experience of Beijing Jeep. At its production peak a few years ago, it made

80,000 vehicles; its target for this year is 35,000. The company cut its workforce from 6,000 workers to 4,800 last year, and intends to cut another 1,000 this year (Shen Bin 1999a: B2). The Dongfeng Motor Corporation faces similar pressures. It laid off 6,000 workers in 1998 and plans to lay off another 10,000 in 1999, from a total labour force of about 100,000 (Xue 1999).

EMERGING TRENDS AND ISSUES

Family Cars. Until a few years ago, virtually all automobile purchases in China were made by work units or other collective entities. For some years, however, small 'farm vehicles' (small-displacement, diesel-powered utility vehicles, usually three-wheeled) have been gaining popularity in rural areas. These are often privately owned, and function as a sometime family car in much the same way that pick-up trucks do in rural North America. Sales of these vehicles reached about 2.6 million units in 1998 (*China Daily* 1998c: 6, and Shen Liao 1999: B2).[6] More recently, urban families have also begun to buy cars. A sample survey of households in 71 cities conducted in late 1998 found that about 1.3 per cent of urban families now own a car (Han 1998: 20). The recent price wars have made cars somewhat more affordable, but prices are still high for a country where GDP per capita is about 6000 yuan (US $740), as can be seen from the following list of prices for basic models (Table 6.4).

Depending on the city of residence, a car buyer may have to spend another 20,000 yuan or more on registration fees, local taxes, parking permits, etc. Cars at the upper end of the price range will not find many private buyers. (In the words of Shanghai GM's website, 'The Buicks were designed not as consumer products, but as business tools for corporate executives and officials.') At the lower end, however, cars like the Charade and the Alto, and even the Fukang and the Santana, are beginning to attract individual buyers in significant numbers. Expansive projections of future private car sales in China are easy to find in the trade literature. Whether such projections will prove accurate depends on several imponderables: future growth rates of per capita income, developments in the real estate market (the big competitor for disposable income), the availability and popularity of bank loans for car purchases, and the evolution of environmental policies locally and nationally. Of these, the last may ultimately prove to be the most important.

Environmental Issues. Although privately-owned vehicles are still relatively rare, many of China's cities already suffer from extreme traffic congestion. To make matters worse, the technology of the vehicles is badly out-of-date. For example, one study revealed that the exhaust from Chinese-made sedans contained 14.6 times the carbon monoxide levels of American-made cars (Li Rongxia 1998: 11). Leaded gasoline, which renders catalytic converters ineffective, is still widely used. The authorities are beginning to take steps to improve the situation. Alternative fuels like natural gas, methanol and electricity are being developed (*China Daily* 1998a: 2). Leaded gasoline was banned in

Table 6.4   Prices for basic automobile models, China

	Yuan	*(US$ equiv.)*
Charade	52,000	6,300
Alto	57,000	6,900
Citroen Fukang	103,000	12,400
Santana	108,000	13,000
Cherokee Jeep	112,000	13,500
Jetta	115,000	13,900
Hongqi (Red Flag)	257,000	31,000
Honda Accord	298,000	35,900
Buick Century	300,000	36,000
Audi	330,000	39,800

Sources: Saywell 1998: 54; Landers 1999: 50; Wan 1998: 5.

Beijing from June 1997, and the ban is spreading to other cities. In December 1998 Beijing imposed the strictest regulation of exhaust emissions among Chinese cities, and in January Beijing also required all new cars sold to have electronic fuel injection systems, but the authorities are encountering strenuous resistance to a proposal that older cars be retrofitted, at a cost of 3,000 to 7,000 yuan (Lawrence 1998: 57; Han 1999a: 10; Shen Bin 1999c: B8). Subways are being built, and the revival of trams (in their modern reincarnation, LRT) is under discussion. All in all, these are worthy measures, but they are unlikely to bring about significant improvements in urban air quality if the fleet in Beijing keeps growing at 35 per cent a year. An engineer with the Beijing Public Traffic Administration (who is characterised as 'young and outspoken') has recently pointed out the obvious: people will resist parking in parkades at 3 to 5 yuan an hour if parking on the street is free (Tang 1999: 3). Various forms of pricing of roadway space for moving vehicles are also under study. But the idea of creating markets (and charging serious prices) for collective goods is still a brash one. Indeed, the Minister of Finance recently announced efforts by the tax authorities to *reduce* the financial burden of car ownership (Wang 1999: 3).

Given these developments, it seems unlikely that China will succeed in meeting its commitments on air quality as spelled out in various international undertakings such as the 1997 Kyoto Protocol. But this failure will not make China unusual in the community of nations.

THE LINKS TO APEC ISSUES

Protectionism: tariffs

Current tariff levels for automobiles have been in place since October 1997, when the most recent reductions were announced. With these latest reductions, China's (unweighted) average tariff level is now only 17 per cent.[7] But tariffs in the motor vehicle sector are well above the average. Gasoline-powered vehicles with an engine displacement up to three litres face a duty of 80 per cent, while vehicles with larger engines are charged 100 per cent (China Automobile Technology Research Center 1997: 294, and Shen Bin 1997: B2). For diesel-powered vehicles, the higher duties apply for engines greater than 2.5 litres. The duties on parts and components range from 20 per cent to 50 per cent. It is interesting to work through the arithmetic for, say, a Buick Century. The basic Century model sells for about US $18,000 in North America, so would cost perhaps US $20,000 cif at a Chinese port. The applicable tariff is 80 per cent, because the engine displacement is 2.98 litres. Beyond the tariff, the car would also attract a 5 per cent consumption tax, 17 per cent value-added tax, and 10 per cent vehicle-purchase tax (Xing 1997: 12), plus a distributor's margin. Thus the full price in the local market would be around US $50,000. But Shanghai GM is planning to price a basic Century built at the JV in Shanghai at about US $36,000. Understandably, the pricing point is being dictated, not by the delivered price of an imported Buick, but by the local competition from Honda, Audi and Hongqi. For a Honda Accord, the arithmetic is similar. The delivered price of an imported Accord is reported to be about US $50,000 (Lawrence 1998: 56), but the Honda JV in Guangzhou is planning to price the locally-assembled Accord at US $35,900.

During Zhu Rongji's April visit to Washington, the US Trade Representative's office circulated a document purporting to list the concessions being offered by China to secure WTO accession (US Trade Representative 1999). It is important to note that Shi Guangsheng, China's Minister of Foreign Trade and Economic Cooperation, has said that 'the list announced by the United States is inaccurate' (Zhang and Gao 1999: 1), and of course the concessions leaked by the USTR are not binding in any event, since in the end no deal was struck. (WTO practice, as was true in GATT negotiations earlier, is that 'nothing is definitively agreed until everything is agreed' (Abbott 1998: 11)) Still, it is interesting to note that, according to the USTR document, China is willing to reduce automobile tariffs to 25 per cent (and parts and components tariffs to an average of 10 per cent), with the reductions delivered in equal annual increments by 2005. Such dramatic cuts, if implemented (and if not rendered meaningless by non-tariff measures), would force major changes in the auto market. For example, with a 25 per cent tariff, an imported Buick Century could reach the local market for about US $36,000, as would the competition (including brands that are not being produced in China). In this context, it is an interesting question whether, as a matter of global corporate strategy, GM should lobby for WTO accession for China or sit quietly on the sidelines. As a senior executive from General Electric remarked:

> [T]he President of Volkswagen [has] argued that China should be very cautious about moving into the WTO because China's fledgling automobile industry must be allowed to develop before it is exposed to international competition. The point is that VW owned 60% of the fledgling Chinese

auto industry; self interest can distort the perspective of even the most internationally oriented companies. (Gadbaw 1998: 83)

A five-year phase-in period represents a significant grace period, however, and a company that can produce a Century for US $18,000 in North America should in time be able to produce that same car for a lot less than US $36,000 in a low-wage environment, *provided* the scale of production can be expanded toward full capacity to spread the capital costs of that US $1.52 billion investment over more cars per year. The same logic applies to Honda and Audi which, like General Motors, enjoy a mastery of technology and deep pockets. Thus, in the struggle for the luxury end of China's car market, the most vulnerable player is almost certainly Hongqi, which has no foreign partner. (Interestingly, the new Hongqi luxury sedan is produced by the First Automobile Group Corporation, which is also the joint venture partner with Volkswagen in the production of the Audi line. I am bewildered by FAGC's apparent corporate strategy of competing with itself.) Even three producers are almost certainly at least one producer too many for the high-end market, even while that market is shielded by a 80–100 per cent tariff. In the lower price brackets, similar battles for market share, also driven by excess capacity, can be confidently predicted.

A Chinese auto industry official remarked recently, 'If tariffs on complete cars were cut to as low as 50 per cent, the impact on domestic car manufacturers would be destructive' (Shen Bin 1999b: 1). Yet Zhu Rongji has offered to cut the tariffs, not to 50 per cent, but to 25 per cent. However, these proposed concessions will make no real difference if they are not matched by equally radical changes in the non-tariff barriers to trade.

Protectionism: non-tariff barriers (NTBs)

Quotas and Licences: Textbook discussions of non-tariff barriers to trade usually focus on quotas and licences, or QRs (quantitative restrictions) as they are often labelled. As documented in detail by China's 1996 Individual Action Plan (IAP) for APEC, imports of assembled motor vehicles and engines are controlled by quotas and licences as well as tariffs.[8] A recent study by Zhang Shuguang, Zhang Yansheng and Wan Zhongxin has estimated that, in 1994, when tariffs on sedans averaged about 110 per cent, the additional tariff-equivalent protection afforded to cars by NTBs was another 24.2 per cent (Zhang, Zhang and Wan 1998: 17). The administrative mechanisms for allocating quotas and import licences in China are far from transparent. Predictably, these arrangements have engendered aggressive rent-seeking behaviour, as is evident from the Hainan Island automobile scandal in 1984 and the recent accounts of rampant smuggling.[9] It may well be that some Chinese leaders see the elimination of NTBs as an anti-corruption weapon as much as a trade-liberalisation measure. Whatever the motives, China's 1996 IAP promised a phased elimination of all WTO-inconsistent NTMs by the year 2020, while the 1997 IAP accelerated this timetable to 2010, and explicitly identified motor vehicles as items on the list of NTMs subject to these commitments.

TRIMS and the Automobile Industry: The Chinese have pressed two types of performance measures on foreign firms seeking joint ventures in the motor vehicle industry: export requirements and domestic content requirements. We have seen that both played a role in the Beijing Jeep story, though the reality is that BJC has never exported Cherokees in any significant numbers, nor did BJC come anywhere near meeting its domestic content commitment of 80 per cent by 1990. When China joins the WTO, it will of course be subject in the large to the Agreement on Trade-Related Investment Measures (TRIMS), though the leaked 1997 draft Protocol of Accession suggests that the Chinese negotiators have reservations about taking on the TRIMS obligations (Abbott 1998: 10–13). Greg Mastel has argued that 'no other single issue deserves more attention in trade negotiations [with China] than performance requirements', but Daniel Rosen finds from his extensive interviewing that 'export requirements are far down the list of expatriate managers' concerns' and that domestic content requirements are 'not so onerous to foreign investors as some suggest' (Rosen 1999: 68–9).

What has happened here, I think, is that economic reality has changed dramatically, in ways that make the TRIMS issues less problematic, at least in the auto industry. Export requirements are onerous only to firms that do not want to export (many, like Beijing Jeep, would be happy to export if they could) and only if exports are uncompetitive on the world market. Thus a key issue is the level of domestic costs. (Issues around the exchange rate and currency convertibility are discussed below.) In the modern automobile industry, where so much production is outsourced, cost levels depend to a great extent on conditions outside the firm. In narrow terms, what has changed is that China's parts and components sector now involves extensive FDI from many of the big names: Delphi, Tenneco, Bosch, etc. (Murphy 1997: 47; Gardner 1997: 69). In broader systemic terms, China's shift away from central planning toward a market economy provides an essential foundation for the success of outsourced, JIT production. The earlier world of central planning, where the coordination problem between a factory and its suppliers was elegantly resolved in principle but badly handled in practice, created natural pressures for extreme vertical integration – what the Chinese call 'large and comprehensive' (*da er quan*) firms.

Sub-national Protectionism: One of the structural weaknesses of the WTO is that its members are nation states, so the WTO is built on the problematical assumption that sub-national units cheerfully accept the authority of central governments. In China's automobile industry, the reality is clearly somewhat different. The Shanghai municipal government, for example, used its regulatory powers to preserve the local taxi market for the Santana by mandating engine size requirements for taxis that discriminated against other cars. As usual, there is a pithy Chinese saying that captures the problem: 'Higher authorities have policies, but localities have countermeasures' (*shang you zhengce, xia you duice*) (Jones and Maher 1999: 29).

Non-Convertibility of the yuan: As already indicated, the yuan has gradually been devalued over the years, and various parallel changes have gradually diluted the non-convertibility of the yuan. Under the most recent reform, dating from 1996, the yuan is often said to be convertible for current account transactions, though this is not entirely true. In the words of China's IAP, the goal is to 'materialize free convertibility of the RMB under current account' by the year 2000. What the 1996 reform *did* do (and it was unquestionably an important step) was to guarantee that foreign-invested firms could freely convert their yuan revenues into foreign currencies to pay for *documented* imports or to repatriate *documented* profits. Thus, the Beijing Jeep problem of access to foreign exchange is now in principle fully resolved, though in practice there can still be significant administrative hassles over documentation.[10] The remaining controls are said to be aimed at maintaining only capital account inconvertibility, but in reality many individuals are still denied access to foreign exchange for what are clearly current account transactions, such as the payment of application fees to foreign universities. Still, the degree of convertibility that does exist means that inconvertibility of the yuan is no longer a serious non-tariff barrier to trade.

THE INTERRELATIONSHIP BETWEEN TRADE AND INVESTMENT

Let me return now to one of the two fundamental questions with which I began: how is liberalisation of *investment* related to liberalisation of *trade*? Or, to put the question somewhat differently, what happens to the insights of comparative advantage and Pareto optimality if we relax some of the classical assumptions? The pure Heckscher–Ohlin analysis, after all, deals with a world of stasis: in this model, not only are the gifts of nature immobile geographically (country X has bauxite deposits, country Y has forests, country Z has tropical weather), as Adam Smith would have understood, but the synthetic resources (machinery, skilled labour and technological knowledge) are also assumed to be immobile. Given the assumptions, it is hardly surprising that introducing one degree of freedom by permitting trade in commodities should have an efficiency pay-off, though it is also not surprising that these gains from trade are relatively small. Zhang, Zhang and Wan calculate that full trade liberalisation for China would only create annual consumer gains of about 2.6 per cent of GDP, and most of these gains would be transfers from producers and government, not pure efficiency gains (Zhang, Zhang and Wan 1998: 1).

Realistically, however, the synthetic resources are not static. Indeed, even the gifts of nature can grow (through discovery) or shrink (through exploitation). Virtually all resource endowments can change size, and most can change location as well. If we look at the world's resources as of the mid-1980s, China clearly had a serious comparative disadvantage in automobiles, and trade liberalisation would have meant a flood of imports, as the spike of imports in 1985 illustrates. But circumstances have changed substantially. The Santana assembly line, which began life in Europe, was physically moved to China, and supplemented by additional capital accumulation. Technology has been transferred and absorbed. The educational damage of the Cultural Revolution has been repaired. The list could go on. The upshot is that it is arguable that the best of China's automobile factories can now stand up to competition with the rest of the world, or will soon be able to do so. Restrictive trade arrangements (high tariffs and significant NTBs), combined with massive FDI flows and radical institutional change, may have restructured comparative advantage, as infant industry advocates have always alleged is possible.

Let me hasten to add that, in general, I am deeply sceptical of the infant industry argument. It can so easily be misused or misunderstood. Furthermore, even if the best of China's car plants can now compete globally, the mediocre certainly cannot. From the standpoint of global efficiency, it *may* be the case that Volkswagens and Buicks should be built in Mexico or China, not Europe or the United States, but that does not mean that anyone should be building the Hongqi.

One final word on efficiency. It is certainly a good idea to try to design the world's trade and investment regimes so that cars get built in the countries that have comparative advantage in that activity, recognising that the efficient geographical pattern may shift over time as comparative advantage evolves. But it is also important to recognise that the automobile industry produces two products, one good (cars) and one bad (traffic congestion and air pollution). At the end of the day, true efficiency has to include an appropriate value for collective goods.

REGIONAL ARRANGEMENTS VS GLOBAL

Let me now return to my other fundamental question: is *regional* liberalisation, as distinct from *global* liberalisation, a good thing? Or, phrased another way, what is the relationship of APEC to WTO? It is not possible to probe the depths and complexities of this question in a few paragraphs. Jagdish Bhagwati, Jeffrey Frankel, Ippei Yamazawa and others have written extensively on this issue. All I propose to do here is to discuss briefly what insights we can gather from the specifics of the automobile industry.

Perhaps the first point to be made is that the automobile sector is politically a very sensitive one. Mari Pangestu identifies Australia, Indonesia, and South Korea as APEC members where this is especially true (Pangestu 1997: 33), but her list is surely too short. My brief history has, I hope, made it clear that the automobile sector in China is also extremely sensitive in terms of protectionist politics, and I would also add that the 1965 Canada–US auto pact, later incorporated into the FTA and NAFTA, causes substantial friction with Toyota and Honda, precisely over the issue of 'closed regionalism' (Keenan and Scoffield 1998: B1, and Scoffield 1998: B1). So, although the success of the Information Technology Agreement (ITA) is frequently cited as an example of sectoral liberalisation that began at APEC but quickly moved to global acceptance at the WTO, sectoral liberalisation of automobiles does not look like a promising next step.

Another point to be made is that, for better or worse, APEC and WTO negotiations are deeply intertwined. For example, the recent Chinese offer, in the context of WTO negotiations with the United States, to reduce automobile tariffs to 25 per cent by 2005, even though unconsummated for the moment, will automatically be compared to the Bogor commitment to 'free and open trade and investment in the region' by 2010/2020. Going from the current 80–100 per cent to 25 per cent by 2005 is certainly much more ambitious than the Bogor target, however it is understood. One way to view this is to note that China is probably willing to do more to please the WTO, which it wants to join, than to please APEC, where it is already a member economy. Another way to view it is to say that the whole idea of stating goals in terms of concrete deadlines is very much a product of the Bogor spirit, for which APEC can rightly take some credit. At the end of the day, however, it is a waste of energy to argue about which organisation has the stronger claim to bragging rights on this one. What is important is that China is prepared to reduce one of its key tariffs very much faster than we previously had reason to expect.

Another point that the automobile case certainly highlights is that the *investment* side of the APEC commitment to 'free and open trade and investment' deserves more thought and attention than it seems to have had to date. In this respect, APEC has a much more ambitious agenda than the WTO. The OECD tried to draft an acceptable Multilateral Agreement on Investment (MAI) and failed dismally. One reason for this failure was that the OECD drafting group made little effort to respond to its critics. The MAI's opponents won the war of words on the Internet almost by default. Perhaps APEC, where consensus is the guiding principle, could be more successful at crafting an investment agreement that would be politically viable. Arguably, that could be far more important than whatever APEC succeeds at doing in trade liberalisation.

SUGGESTIONS FOR APEC TO CONSIDER AT AUCKLAND

1   *Competition Policy*: Competition policy issues are extremely important in China's motor vehicle industry, as a strong oligopoly has emerged with explicit government encouragement. China is at the early stages of developing a viable competition policy, and still has a notable bias toward protecting producers rather than consumers, as can be seen from the recent attempts to resolve the price wars in cars and other products by imposing floor prices. APEC seems particularly well suited to assist with this process, as part of its Ecotech activities.

2 *Environmental Issues*: Congestion and pollution are severe by-products of the motor vehicle revolution. Progress on pollution will probably require discussions in a global forum, but there is substantial expertise on issues of traffic congestion that could be shared through APEC's Ecotech mechanisms.

3 *Investment Issues*: Both analytically and politically, investment issues are even more complicated than trade issues. And the failure of the OECD's attempt to draft a viable MAI has undoubtedly made everyone doubly cautious. Nonetheless, if APEC is to take seriously the scope of the language in the IAPs (trade *and investment* liberalisation and facilitation), some serious work on investment issues is certainly required.

4 *The Relationship of APEC to WTO*: The motor vehicle industry is a politically sensitive one in many countries, not just China, and this may well mean that the WTO will have to be the venue for serious progress on trade liberalisation in this sector. However, at a more macro level, APEC may be able to play an extremely important role in the development of the WTO, since APEC is unique in one respect: both China and Taiwan are member economies. This means that APEC has a special opportunity to seek a constructive path to resolution of the question of WTO accession for these important economies.

NOTES

1   One indicator of the importance of outsourcing is the recent decision by Delphi Automotive Systems to move toward independence from General Motors by floating an IPO of 100 million shares on the NYSE. See 'The decline and fall of General Motors,' and 'Delphi closer to independence from GM'. For a discussion of JIT in the context of China's automobile industry, see Chen Shuyong and Chen Rongqiu 1997.

2   For a Canadian version, see Maude Barlow and Tony Clarke 1997; for Chinese voices in the same vein, see Song Jiang *et al.*, 1996.

3   For more detailed accounts of the period before 1978, see Li and Tian 1998: 3–10, and Ralph W. Huenemann 1991: 462–65.

4   Unless otherwise documented, my comments on BJC are based on Mann 1997. For an early Chinese account, see Jian 1985.

5   The publicity surrounding the Buick joint venture has been massive. See, for example, McClellan and Smith 1997; *Ward's Auto World*, December 1998: 23–4; Smith 1998a; Wan 1998; and http://www.shanghaigm.com. For the Honda takeover of Peugeot's failed operation in Guangzhou, see Harwit 1997, and Landers 1999.

6   Farm vehicles of this type are *not* included in the motor vehicle production figures cited in Table 6.1.

7   See China's 1998 Individual Action Plan (IAP), at http://www.apecsec.org.sg. In reality, the revenues collected as duties on imports in 1997 were 31.9 billion yuan, or a mere 2.7% of the value of imports, which measured 1180.6 billion yuan (data taken from State Statistical Bureau 1998: 274, 620).

8   The full texts of the various versions of the IAP are available at http://apecsec.org.sg.

9　One reason that smuggling is difficult to curtail is that 'some units and individuals' of the People's Liberation Army and other security forces are involved in the smuggling. See Lawrence and Gilley 1999: 22. For a very interesting analysis of the economics of smuggling, see Appendix D of Zhang, Zhang and Wan 1998. For a discussion of the possible magnitude of automobile smuggling, see Fung and Lau 1999: 22–4.

10　The hassles have become more intense since June 1998, as the Chinese authorities have cracked down on false invoicing in their attempt to stanch the illicit haemorrhage of foreign exchange. See Jones and Maher 1999 for more details.

REFERENCES

Abbott, Frederick M. (1998) 'Reflection paper on China in the world trading system', in Frederick M. Abbott (ed.) *China in the World Trading System: Defining the Principles of Engagement*, The Hague, London and Boston: Kluwer Law International.

APEC Secretariat (1996) 'Individual action plan of the People's Republic of China on trade and investment liberalization and facilitation in APEC'.

—— (1997) 'Individual action plan of the People's Republic of China on trade and investment liberalization and facilitation in APEC'.

—— (1998) 'Individual action plan on trade and investment liberalization and facilitation: People's Republic of China'.

Barlow, Maude and Tony Clarke (1997) *MAI: The Multilateral Agreement on Investment and the Threat to Canadian Sovereignty*, Toronto: Stoddart Publishing Company.

Beijing Review (1998) 'Efforts to control vehicle pollution', 8–14 June: 11–3.

Bergsten, C. Fred (ed.) (1997) *Whither APEC? The Progress to Date and Agenda for the Future*, Washington, DC: Institute for International Economics.

Bhagwati, Jagdish, Pravin Krishna and Arvind Panagariya (eds) (1999) *Trading Blocs: Alternative Approaches to Analyzing Preferential Trade Agreements*, Cambridge, MA: The MIT Press.

Chen Shuyong and Chen Rongqiu (1997) 'Manufacturer–supplier relationship in a JIT environment', *Production and Inventory Management Journal*, First Quarter: 58–64.

China Automobile Technology Research Center (1997) *Zhongguo Qiche Gongye Nianjian (China Automotive Industry Yearbook)*, Beijing: Ministry of Machine Industry.

China Business Update (1997/98) *CBU Directory of Chinese Vehicle, Component and Parts Manufacturers*, Amherst and Beijing.

—— (1998) *CBU Directory of Foreign Invested Vehicle, Component and Parts Manufacturers in China*, Amherst and Beijing.

China Daily (1998a) 'Nation keeps pace with green car technologies', 2 May: 2.

—— (1998b) 'Shanghai JV to make auto engine components', 8 June: 5.

—— (1998c) 'Juli vehicles make farmers' life much easier', *China Daily*, 30 June: 6.

—— (1998d) 'Auto smuggling', *China Daily*, 28 November: B3.

—— (1999) 'Delphi closer to independence from GM', *China Daily*, 6 February: 3.

Economist (1997) 'The coming car crash', 10 May: 21–3.

—— (1998) 'The decline and fall of General Motors', 10 October: 63–9.

Euroweek (1998) 'Daiwa to lead first T share offering for Chinese firm', 15 May: 16.

Financial Post, 10 August 1963.

Frankel, Jeffrey A. (1997) *Regional Trading Blocs in the World Economic System*, Washington, DC: Institute for International Economics.

Fung, K.C. and Lawrence J. Lau (1999) 'New estimates of the United States–China bilateral trade balances', Asia/Pacific Research Center, Institute for International Studies, Stanford University.

Gadbaw, Michael (1998) 'WTO accession: A private sector view', in Frederick M. Abbott (ed.) *China in the World Trading System: Defining the Principles of Engagement*, The Hague, London and Boston: Kluwer Law International.

Gardner, Greg (1997) 'In for the long haul,' *Ward's Auto World*, December: 69–71.

Han Guojian (1998) 'More and more Chinese own cars', *Beijing Review*, 21–27 December: 20.

—— (1999a) 'We don't want a foggy London', *Beijing Review*, 8–14 January: 10–13.

—— (1999b) 'Controversial self-restraint price', *Beijing Review*, 8–14 March: 17–8.

Harwit, Eric (1995) *China's Automobile Industry: Policies, Problems, and Prospects*, Armonk, NY: M.E. Sharpe.

—— (1997) 'Guangzhou Peugeot: Portrait of a commercial divorce', *The China Business Review*, November–December: 10–11.

Huenemann, Ralph W. (1991) 'Modernizing China's transport system', in Joint Economic Committee of the US Congress, *China's Economic Dilemmas in the 1990s: The Problems of Reforms, Modernization and Interdependence*, Washington, DC: Government Printing Office.

Jian Chuan (1985) 'Joint venture: Success speaks for itself', *Beijing Review*, 4 November: 21–5.

Jones, Thomas E. and Margaret M. Maher (1999) 'China's changing foreign exchange regime', *The China Business Review*, March–April: 26–33.

Keenan, Greg, and Heather Scoffield (1998) 'Toyota assails tariff decision', *The Globe and Mail*, 11 June: B1.

Landers, Peter (1999) 'Long, hard road,' *Far Eastern Economic Review*, 8 April 50–2.

Lawrence, Susan V. (1998) 'Roads to happiness', *Far Eastern Economic Review*, 26 November 56–7.

—— and Bruce Gilley (1999) 'Bitter harvest', *Far Eastern Economic Review*, 29 April: 22.

Leggett, Karby and Craig C. Smith (1998) 'Ford raises stake in Jiangling', *The Asian Wall Street Journal*, 9 November 15.

Li Chunlin and Tian Shu (1998) *Zouchu Kunhuo: Zhongguo Qiche Gongye Fazhan Wenti Baogao (Solving the Dilemmas: A Report on the Development of the Motor Vehicle Industry in China)*, Shenyang: Shenyang Publishing Company.

Li Rongxia (1998) 'Efforts to Control Vehicle Pollution', *Beijing Review*, 8–14 June: 11.

Mann, Jim (1997) *Beijing Jeep: A Case Study of Western Business in China*, Boulder, CO: Westview Press.

McClellan Barbara and David C. Smith (1997) 'GM's China gamble', *Ward's Auto World*, August: 70–1.

Murphy, Tom (1997) 'Aiming high for the 21st century', *Ward's Auto World*, June: 47.

Pangestu, Mari (1997) 'Assessing APEC trade liberalization', C. Fred Bergsten (ed.) *Whither APEC? The Progress to Date and Agenda for the Future*, Washington, DC: Institute for International Economics.

Rosen, Daniel H. (1999) *Behind the Open Door: Foreign Enterprises in the Chinese Marketplace*, Washington, DC: Institute for International Economics.

Saywell, Trish (1998) 'A Lease on Life', *Far Eastern Economic Review*, 26 November: 53–6.

Scoffield, Heather (1998) 'Japan to take Canada to WTO over 6.7% imported car tariff', *The Globe and Mail*, 1 July: B1.

Shen Bin (1997) 'Car sales slack despite interest and tariff cuts', *China Daily*, 22 December: B2.

—— (1998a) 'Auto sector faces bumpy reform road', *China Daily*, 28 April: 5.

—— (1998b) 'Joint venture to build sport vehicles', *China Daily*, 23 June: 5.

—— (1998c) 'Survey: Demand for cars to decline', *China Daily*, 12 October: 5.

—— (1999a) 'Marketing to restore Beijing Jeep fortunes', *China Daily*, 22 March: B2.

—— (1999b) 'Entry poses challenge to car makers', *China Daily*, 26 April: 1.

—— (1999c) 'New emission standards ruffle car makers', *China Daily*, 26 April: B8.

Shen Liao (1999) 'Official car supply reform to encourage consumption', *China Daily*, 3 May: B2.

Smith, Craig C. (1998a) 'Buick's China plant opens with a whimper', *The Globe and Mail*, 16 December: B11.

Smith, Craig C. (1998b) 'GM weighs lineup changes', *The Asian Wall Street Journal*, 21 December: 12.

State Statistical Bureau (1998) *Zhongguo Tongji Nianjian 1998* (*China Statistical Yearbook 1998*), Beijing: China Statistical Publishing House.

Song Jiang, Zhang Zangzang, Qiao Bian, Yang Zhengyu and Gu Qingsheng (1996) *Zhongguo Keyi Shuo Bu* (*China can say no*), Beijing: China Wenlian Publishing Company.

Tang Min (1999) 'Beijing to plan space for cars', *China Daily*, 7 May: 3.

US Trade Representative (1999) 'Market access and protocol commitments', 16 May: 1–22.

Wan Lixin (1998) 'Shanghai's first Buick rolls out of new plant', *China Daily*, 18 December: 5.

Wang Chuandong (1999) 'Automobile sector may pose zero growth', *China Daily*, 9 January: 3.

Ward's Auto World, 'Shanghai GM's first Buick rolls on Dec. 17', December: 23–4.

Wilson, John S. (1995) *Standards and APEC: An Action Agenda*, Washington, DC: Institute for International Economics.

Woodard, Kim (1989) 'The automotive sector', *The China Business Review*, March–April: 38–43.

Xing, Wayne W.J. (1997) 'Shifting gears', *The China Business Review*, November–December: 8–18.

Xue Cheng (1999) 'Debt for equity swap lifts weight from enterprises', *China Daily*, 28 June: B1.

Yamazawa, Ippei (1997) 'APEC and WTO in trade liberalization', in C. Fred Bergston (ed.) *Whither APEC? The Progress to Date and Agenda for the Future*, Washington, DC: Institute for International Economics.

Zhang Shuguang, Zhang Yansheng and Wan Zhongxin (1998) *Measuring the Costs of Protection in China*, Washington, DC: Institute for International Economics.

Zhang Yan and Gao Wei (1999) 'WTO: Progress Made in Sino–EU Discussions', *China Daily*, 7 May: 1.

7 Malaysia's telecommunications services Liberalisation within APEC

Sieh Lee Mei Ling and Loke Wai Heng

INTRODUCTION

Malaysia's economic structure has undergone notable changes since 1957, the year the country attained political independence. From an economy that was heavily dependent on income from mining and agricultural activities in the 1960s and early 1970s, Malaysia has seen rapid development in manufacturing, the main engine of growth in the last two to three decades. The services sector traditionally played a supporting role to primary and secondary industry. However, services sector activities have grown in importance. This is evident from the increase of services sector's 37 per cent share of GDP in 1960 to 44.9 per cent in 1997 (excluding construction services). Services are no longer regarded as supplementary activities but are recognised as significant contributors to the economy in their own right. If construction services are included, the services sector accounted for 52.2 per cent of GDP in 1998 (Economic Report 1998/99).

Telecommunications has been among the fastest growing service sub-sectors in Malaysia. A recent EPU study on the role of intermediate services in Malaysia reported that between 1990 and 1994 the telecommunications industry grew at an average rate of 12 per cent per annum, which exceeded the 8.5 per cent recorded for GDP during the period. This resulted in the telecommunications share of GDP increasing from 1.8 per cent in 1985 to 2.5 per cent in 1994. The bulk of the output of the sub-sector was consumed domestically. The 1987 Input–Output tables show that only 15.4 per cent of telecommunication output was exported. However, over the last decade, the deregulation of telecommunications, followed by the privatisation of Telekom Malaysia, saw the sole telecommunication services provider evolving from a public utility monopoly to a corporation that has to contend with several new competitors in the market.

This chapter attempts to review the Malaysian government's policies in the telecommunication services sub-sector with special reference to the APEC liberalisation program, in order to suggest APEC-consistent strategies for the near future. The chapter comprises four sections. The first provides a brief overview of the market structure, profiles of key players, and the legal and policy framework for telecommunication services within the services sector of the Malaysian economy. Analyses of Malaysia's liberalisation commitments for telecommunications, particularly within APEC, are contained in the next section. The third section discusses the likely impact and challenges Malaysia expects when implementing its commitments within the telecommunications sub-sector. Policy and strategy recommendations with regard to meeting APEC objectives for services in general, and telecommunication services in particular, are proposed in the final section.

OVERVIEW OF MALAYSIA'S TELECOMMUNICATIONS SERVICES SUB-SECTOR

Contribution to GDP and employment

Published figures on the share of telecommunications services sub-sector in GDP and employment are not available specifically for the sub-sector. Output and employment data on this sub-sector are aggregated with data for the transportation and storage sub-sectors. However, the EPU study reported that the communications sub-sector alone accounted for 2.1 per cent of GDP in 1990. The three sub-sectors, namely transportation, storage and communications, combined, contributed more than 7 per cent of the national GDP during the period 1990–8 (EPU). Together, the three sub-sectors combined to display growth of over 13 per cent per annum, exceeding the overall growth of the economy in the early 1990s. But since 1996, there has been a definite slowdown in the growth of the three sub-sectors, which in 1998 grew at only 2.6 per cent (see Table 7.1). The sharp decline in recent months is not unexpected, as the overall economy had been adversely affected by the regional economic and financial crisis since July 1997. The Malaysian economy recorded a slower growth of 6.9 per cent in the fourth quarter of 1997, compared with a growth of 8.5 per cent during the first half year. In 1998, the economy contracted by 6.7 per cent (Bank Negara Malaysia 1999).

In terms of employment, the transportation, storage and communications sub-sectors combined to contribute more than 4 per cent of Malaysia's total employment for one and a half decades prior to the slowdown, that is, within the period 1980–95. In 1998, these three sub-sectors together accounted for 5.2 per cent of total national employment. The EPU study, which analysed employment in terms of different skill levels, showed that more than 60 per cent of the jobs in communication services during 1993 were either semi-skilled or unskilled. Of this total, a significant portion was attributed to 'mail distribution clerks', since communication services include postal services. Less than 7 per cent of total employment was made up of professional and managerial personnel. It was understandable that the bulk of those employed in this sub-sector were in jobs that required electrical and electronic engineering related expertise (see Table 7.2).

Table 7.1 Malaysia's annual growth rates for GDP and transportation, storage and communications sub-sectors, selected years (per cent)

Year	GDP	Transportation, storage & communications
1990	9.7	13.40
1995	9.5	13.90
1996	8.6	9.80
1997	7.8	10.00
1998	−6.7	2.60

Sources: Malaysia's Economic Planning Unit (EPU), Bank Negara Malaysia (BNM).

Table 7.2 Employment in communication services by different skill levels, 1993

Skill category	No. employed	%
Professional & Managerial	2,930	6.71
(of which electrical & electronic engineers)	*1,616*	*55.15*
Sub-Professional/Skilled/Supervisory	11,408	26.14
(of which electronics & electrical engineering assistants and related technicians)	*9,020*	*79.07*
Semi and Unskilled/ General Workers	29,312	67.15
(of which mail distribution clerks)	*7,481*	*25.52*
Total	43,650	100

Source: Malaysia's Economic Planning Unit (EPU).

Contribution to the balance of payments

In general, the telecommunications sub-sector contributes to Malaysia's foreign exchange earnings either through the sale and purchase of equipment, or of services, that crossed national borders. In the case of equipment transactions, there are fewer difficulties, both conceptually and when recording trade data, than is the case for service transactions. For instance, telecommunication services transactions, like other services under the General Agreement on Trade in Services (GATS), may refer to trade conducted in four different ways: cross-border transactions, consumption abroad, commercial presence, and movement of personnel. It is not only more difficult to grasp the concept of trade in intangibles, but it is also more difficult to track and to keep accurate trade figures for services. As in most countries, Malaysia does not capture trade data on service transactions by the four modes. Although cross-border transactions are the most important mode of trade for telecommunication services – for example, telephone calls or electronic mail sent from one country to another – it is difficult to identify and to record other modes. To illustrate, a foreigner making an overseas telephone call from Malaysia using Telekom Malaysia's services should be treated as a Malaysian export through the 'consumption abroad' mode, and the revenue generated should be included as export revenue for Malaysia. Conversely, a Malaysian calling home from a foreign country using that country's telephone service should count as an import through 'consumption abroad'. Further, suppose an Australian telecommunication firm operating in Malaysia provides telephone services to Malaysians, such transactions should be treated as Malaysian imports through the 'commercial presence' mode of trade. Likewise, a Malaysian telecommunication firm operating in Australia and selling services to Australians should be counted as a Malaysian export. However, until now, such transactions have been treated as local sales under conventional practices for recording trade. As a result, trade data on exports and imports of telecommunication services may not reflect the full picture.

In the case of Malaysia, estimations of trade in telecommunication services are further handicapped since published trade figures are highly aggregated. The most recent data available for reference are the 1987 Input–Output Tables, in which communication services sold 15.4 per cent of its output on the export market. This reflects the fact that Malaysia's communication service producers remain relatively inwardly oriented. On the other hand, the industry has been heavily dependent on imported inputs for its operations. As much as 28 per cent of the total inputs needed for the production of communication services were imported in 1987. This percentage was significantly lower than that of four years earlier because in 1983, 47 per cent of the inputs were imported. The decline in the reliance on foreign inputs could be due to the increase in the local production of electrical and electronic parts and components during the period. By the early 1990s, most inputs of the industry, comprising mainly electrical and electronic products, were available locally, although many of the electrical and electronic firms were foreign affiliates investing in production plants in the country. The structural change in the composition of products and components manufactured by the electronics industry of Malaysia over the last decade attests to the increasing capability of domestic sources of input supply needed for the provision of telecommunication services. In 1985, over 80 per cent of Malaysia's electronics industry output were electronic components, mainly semiconductors. Less than 20 per cent of output in the industry was consumer electronics and industrial electronics. Under Malaysia's Industrial Master Plan of 1986, the government set targets to reduce the output share of electronic components and to increase the share of consumer electronics and industrial electronics. By 1993, the output share of electronic components had dropped significantly, to 43 per cent, while those of consumer electronics and industrial electronics had risen to 27 per cent and 30 per cent, respectively (Sieh 1999).

Inter-sectoral linkages

Generally, communication services have exhibited stronger intra-sectoral linkages than inter-sectoral ties. Communication services producers have been sourcing mainly from the services sector itself, with electricity and gas, and transportation as the major service inputs. In 1987, services input accounted for as much as 85 per cent of the telecommunication industry's purchases. Only 15 per cent of the intermediate inputs were obtained from the manufacturing sector.

Communication services in general have stronger output linkages with the services sector than with the primary and manufacturing sectors. In 1987, 46 per cent of the industry's output was taken up by the services sector itself, and the bulk of this was sold to wholesale and retail trade services.

Market structure

From political independence to the early 1980s, the Telecommunications Department of the Malaysian government was the sole producer of Malaysia's telecommunication services. It was believed that the granting of exclusive operation rights to a statutory body was necessary for a crucial public utility and to ensure the construction of an efficient telecommunications infrastructure in the country. Moreover, with heavy capital investment needed to develop a telecommunication network, only a state agency could continue to offer services at affordable prices. Hence, during this period, competition in the industry did not exist. Telecommunications services in Malaysia were regarded as a basic undifferentiated public utility.

The very first move to deregulate the industry came with the formation of a new company in 1985. Syarikat Telekom Malaysia (STM) was established as a result of the government's privatisation exercise to reduce direct participation of the public sector in the industry. Telekom Malaysia Berhad (TMB) was later formed in 1987 to replace STM. In the first two years of deregulation, even though direct participation from the government had been gradually reduced, the industry continued to be dominated by a monopoly that provided basic services. However, the government began to liberalise the supply of customer premises equipment even during this early stage of privatisation.

Since 1987, the market structure of the telecommunication industry of Malaysia has undergone significant changes in terms of the number of industry players and the range of service products offered. The number of licences issued by the government for different types of service reflects the rise in the number of service providers as well as the mix of services available in the market. For example, for traditional basic service of local and trunk network operations, there are now seven licences issued compared with only one licence given to TMB in 1987. The number of cellular service firms has also increased from only two in 1993 to eight firms at present. New types of service have also been developed in the industry over the years. These include Internet services and satellite broadcasting services (see Table 7.3 for a list of the number of operators in various telecommunication services).

Firms in the telecommunications industry are largely owned by Malaysian nationals. However, foreign participation has been increasing recently through joint ventures with local service producers. Currently, there are five telecommunications companies with foreign equity ranging from 21 per cent to 52 per cent. They are Binariang, DiGi Telecommunications, Technology Resources Industries, Prismanet and Sapura. British Telecommunications has recently acquired a 33 per cent stake in Binariang, a local telecommunication firm that provides various telecommunications services such as local and trunk network services, international gateway services and cellular services *(New Straits Times* 9 Nov. 1998).

Table 7.3   Number of licences issued for operating various telecommunication services in Malaysia, 1999

Type of service	*No. of licences*
Local & trunk network services	7
International network (gateway) & service	5
Cellular service/personal communication service	8
Paging services	36
Trunk radio system service	22
CT2/Telepoint Service	1
Private leased circuit telecommunication network	8
Value-added network data services	28
Premium rate interactive voice response system 600 services	7
Radio maritime services	1
Public payphone services	3
Radio leased channel service	7
Mobile satellite service	1
Satellite services	1
VSAT services	4
Radiolocation services	1
Satellite broadcasting services	1
Powerline carrier	3
Internet services provider	7
Wireless video communication network services	1
Other services	2

Source: Department of Telecommunication, Malaysia.

MALAYSIA'S LIBERALISATION COMMITMENTS FOR TELECOMMUNICATIONS

Deregulation, liberalisation and globalisation

The terms 'deregulation', 'liberalisation' and 'globalisation' have been widely used by different groups of writers, often interchangeably in similar contexts. Although these three terms are very closely connected, they may be used differently in practice. It is important to distinguish them before discussing Malaysia's commitments in liberalising the telecommunications sub-sector.

The terms 'deregulation' and 'liberalisation' basically mean reduction in market intervention by governments. However, the former generally describes decreasing levels of public sector control within a country while the latter refers to decline in restrictions to trade and market access between countries. The term 'globalisation' is often used to describe activities of multinational firms in their choice of international production locations and marketing network. However, the process of globalisation is only possible and feasible when 'deregulation' and 'liberalisation' take place. We shall follow this general usage, especially the distinction between the terms 'deregulation' and 'liberalisation'.

Malaysia's liberalisation commitments

Malaysia is involved in three main trade organisations in the process of liberalising its economy. The country participates in the WTO at the international level, in APEC at the regional level, and in the ASEAN sub-region. In the case of the WTO and ASEAN, the structure of negotiations and the resultant agreements on services are separated from those for goods. However, for APEC, services sector issues are listed along with others. Of the three, the WTO was the first to include telecommunication services under GATS in 1994. The WTO may be regarded as the most systematic in its process of negotiations, having definite time frames set out for implementation. As for ASEAN, services negotiations are conducted in a less formal and less structured manner than negotiations on goods. The process of negotiation for liberalisation under APEC is considered to be least systematic and is conducted on a voluntary basis.

Thus far, members of APEC have agreed to liberalise their markets based on voluntary initiatives mixed with elements of peer influence. It has also been agreed that member economies submit their Individual Action Plan (IAP) each year detailing their short-term and long-term plans for trade barrier reduction so as to permit greater market access. The first IAPs were made in 1996. To date, members have submitted their third IAPs in 1998; these include commitments for goods and services. Likewise, Malaysia has committed to liberalise various economic sectors including services, since the first IAP. Generally, tariff lines listed in Malaysia's IAP include those that are already committed under WTO and the Information Technology Agreement (ITA).

Basically, Malaysia's APEC commitments in the services sector are similar to those offered under the country's schedule for GATS. It is important to note that for telecommunication services, Malaysia has committed to liberalise the industry since its first IAP in 1996. In its latest IAP in 1998, Malaysia has further allowed foreign equity in telecommunication services to increase to 61 per cent.

Malaysia's communication services have been offered for market access and national treatment under GATS, along with four other service sub-sectors: business services, health-related social services, transportation services, and construction and related engineering services. For telecommunication services, Malaysia's initial schedule of offers in April 1994 listed enhanced value-added services, namely data and transmission services, mobile data services, telex and telegraph services, and audio-visual services. No limitations were imposed on market access or national treatment for trade through cross-border supply and consumption abroad for most of the telecommunication services listed. However, Malaysia's horizontal conditions that applied to all services were equally relevant to all telecommunication services. Foreign commercial presence was allowed only through a locally incorporated joint-venture corporation with Malaysian individuals or Malaysian-controlled corporations, and foreign equity – which is now limited to 61 per cent – was not to exceed 30 per cent then. In addition, movement of personnel was allowed only through intra-corporate transfers. In February 1997, Malaysia included basic telecommunication services in its GATS schedule of offers. This means that telecommunication services such as wireless and wired voice services, packet-switched and circuit-switched data transmission services, facsimile service, private leased circuit service, trunked radio services and others are included in the list of offers. However, broadcasting services have been excluded from the offers for basic telecommunications.

ASEAN members began their first round of negotiations on services in January 1996 after the signing of the ASEAN Framework Agreement on Services on 15 December 1995 in Bangkok. The negotiations resulted in two packages of commitments implemented in separate stages. Malaysia committed tourism, maritime and air transport services in the first package, which was effective from 31 March 1998. Under the second package that came into effect from 31 March 1999, Malaysia included telecommunication services in its offer together with financial services, construction services and business services. For telecommunication services, Malaysia allowed foreign equity up to 35 per cent for both basic and value-added services. The next round of negotiations on services is scheduled to begin this year and is expected to end by the year 2001.

Matters relating to technical standards and radio frequencies coordination were also discussed, especially under GATS. However, the appendix on telecommunications in the earlier part of the negotiations was finally dropped because it was agreed that other avenues were available for technical issues.

The main organisation that focuses on the coordination on technical standards, radio frequencies and other related matters is the International Telecommunication Union (ITU), where governments and telecommunication operators coordinate global telecom networks and services.

Implementation of liberalisation commitments

Malaysia's telecommunications sub-sector is generally reputed to be liberal because of its speed of deregulation and its liberalisation implementation within a span of less than ten years. Malaysia is also noted for the increase in the number of licences issued to service producers. But a recent study of the extent of liberalisation committed to by member economies, as indicated by their Individual Action Plans for 1996 and 1997, using selected criteria, showed that Malaysia's telecommunications sub-sector has relatively low market access to foreign operators (Yamazawa 1998). Most-favoured nation treatment and national treatment for foreign telecommunication service producers were found to be low relative to those of other members. The study also observed that Malaysia, as in the case of most developing member economies, ranked relatively low for its future liberalisation commitments, that is, for the next four to five years.

However, the latest IAP for 1998 demonstrated major shifts in Malaysia's telecommunication industry. With the intention of increasing the industry's capacity and of introducing new services through new technologies and upgrading of existing networks, the Malaysian government has taken a few major steps forward in deregulating and liberalising the sub-sector. At least four major changes have taken place since 1998 and these changes have propelled Malaysia's telecom sub-sector from a regulated public utility to a highly competitive industry with many private firms.

First, the enactment of the Communications and Multimedia Act 1998 to replace the Broadcasting Act 1988 and the Telecommunications Act 1950 confirms the government's policy in this sub-sector. One of the significant changes in the recent Act compared with the earlier ones is the emphasis on promoting self-regulation in the telecommunications industry. As of 1 April 1999, the Communications and Multimedia Commission was formed to replace the Telecommunication Department, with important changes that will foster convergence of telecommunication and communication. Such a bold step, believed to be the first in Asia, recognises and creates a new regulatory organisation that would create the right environment for the development of converged services.

Second, the Malaysian government has issued several licences to new operators in various telecommunications services since 1985. As licences are issued to companies for operating specific services, one firm may have several licences. This has been alluded to earlier. In line with its latest commitments in the 1998 IAP, Malaysia has approved six fixed network telecommunications operators to operate interconnectivity and equal access services, of which five started in January 1999. They were Telecom Malaysia, Celcom, Binariang, Time Telecom and DiGi Telecoms. This means that for the first time ever, the Malaysian fixed line telecommunications market will be opened to competition from several service operators. Telephone line users are now able to choose from a number of service producers to make long-distance and international telephone calls. Further, five new licences were issued in June 1998 to providers of Internet services in the country. This brings the total of Internet service providers in the market to seven.

Third, Malaysia has also facilitated access to the telecom sub-sector by reducing tariffs for most information technology products. Consistent with the commitments to WTO and ITA, Malaysia has started to eliminate tariffs for equipment and hardware necessary for producing telecommunication services, and most information technology products are expected to be tariff free by the year 2000. For example, a number of products, which had tariff rates as high as 30 per cent in 1997, will be tariff free by the year 2000. Most of them are machinery used in semiconductor production such as laser cutters for cutting contacting tracks, machines for sawing monocrystal semiconductor boules and wafers, optical stereoscopic microscopes and photomicrographic microscopes for handling semiconductor wafers.

Fourth, as from 28 April 1998, the government has relaxed foreign equity holdings in licensed basic telecommunications companies, permitting up to 61 per cent for five years. This latest liberalisation for foreign equity has exceeded the limit Malaysia imposed in its latest commitments in the ASEAN Framework Agreement on Services, where 35 per cent foreign shareholding was allowed in basic and value added telecommunication services (MITI webpage). The relaxation of equity conditions from a public statutory authority to a private corporation and then to definite majority foreign ownership of equity in several firms, all within a span of only ten years, further attests to Malaysia's commitment to deregulating and liberalising telecom services. The most recent step on foreign equity is a major step that is believed to have been prompted by the Asian financial crisis where capital shortage had to be overcome due to US dollar denominated loans taken out earlier. Nevertheless, it should be thought of as an acceleration of the liberalisation process that had already been decided upon rather than as a new direction.

Apart from the Malaysian government's policy with respect to deregulation and liberalisation, there is yet another key national objective that drives the telecommunication sub-sector: that is the eagerness of Malaysia to embark on the path of technology development. Improvements in technology not only have created new modes for delivering existing services, but also have extended the range of services offered. For example, the broad bandwidth communication network, which is among the latest technologies for telecommunication services, facilitates transmission of voice, data and images at high speed. Also, Telekom Malaysia Berhad is reported to be investing 125 million ringgit this year to provide wireless telephone service using radio waves in rural and suburban areas. In 1995, Binariang, a private telecommunication firm, had already started to venture into providing satellite services. At present, Malaysia owns two satellites with orbits covering Africa, Middle East, India and Australia besides Malaysia.

EFFECTS OF GREATER TELECOMMUNICATIONS LIBERALISATION

While Malaysia, along with other members of APEC, is expected to continue with liberalisation pledges that include the services sector in general, individual circumstances of different economies will give rise to differences in the modality and timing of carrying out those commitments. The impact on the Malaysian economy and implications for the Malaysian telecommunications industry must be examined as more players enter the domestic market.

Market, development and cost effects

Reducing barriers to market access will mean that the Malaysian industry will experience greater competition. The recent foreign equity rule of up to 61 per cent in firms providing basic telecommunication services will see greater foreign participation in the near future. In fact, the industry has already witnessed a rise in foreign equity ownership in the last two years. For instance, British Telecommunications has acquired 33 per cent stake in Binariang. Nokia Telecommunications OY of Finland has also entered into a joint venture with Malaysia's Sapura Holdings to produce software for digital switching systems. One of the main explanations for this recent trend is the East Asian economic and financial crisis that has led to sharp depreciation of most currencies in the region, including the Malaysian ringgit. On the other hand, divestment has also been observed in the industry. In March 1999, Swisscom divested its 30 per cent equity in DiGi Swisscom Berhad from Malaysia and announced its intention of focusing future operation in the European market.

Apart from the downward pricing trend due to reduced demand, the importance of competition in terms of reduced business costs is becoming evident following implementation of equal access to fixed lines. Telecommunications companies are already giving price discounts for overseas and domestic long distance calls. For example, both Maxis and Telekom are offering 12 per cent discounts, while Celcom gives 20 per cent. Price cuts began as soon as equal access started in January 1999, thus benefiting businesses with reduced telecommunications costs. However, the fear of excessive competition that may hurt investment in telecommunications in the long run may be difficult to justify because of close monitoring by the regulators in Malaysia. Also, corporate arrangements and strategies are expected to change as market forces shift along with technological innovations and regulatory amendments. Even the important dichotomy between fixed line and mobile services will become less significant as the dynamics of the sub-sector foster new ways and new relationships between users as well as among suppliers of telecommunications services.

While such liberalisation may encourage more entry into the industry, the smallness of the Malaysian market may not be attractive enough for too many foreign firms to operate in Malaysia. The limitations of market size became evident, even among domestic firms, when the government issued licences to local firms in various services in the process of deregulation. Some of these licences issued, such as for fixed lines and trunk radio system services, are not utilised in reality because firms doubt that the Malaysian market is large enough to accommodate so many firms. The risks of being unable to attain profit targets have kept licence holders from initiating operation. The government has acknowledged that the ideal number of players for Malaysia's basic telephony services should not exceed three, based on the current market of 20 million people (*The Star* 15 May 1997). Moreover, the recent Asian economic crisis led to market attrition on account of the repatriation of several hundred thousand foreign workers. For the first time since cellular services were introduced, the number of subscribers in Malaysia declined in 1998. One of the operators interviewed further indicated that overall business had declined by 45 per cent in 1998 as a result of line disconnections due to the economic downturn. In addition, the highly capital-intensive nature of the telecommunication sub-sector, together with the rapid speed of technological change, are challenges that firms in the industry need to consider before pouring in investment even when licences are granted.

Thus far APEC has emphasised liberalisation of markets. Members should recognise that the attractiveness of the Malaysian telecommunication market to foreign service suppliers also depends on factors other than market access. An important lesson from Malaysia is that APEC partners must look beyond the commitments made by Malaysia. The Malaysian case indicates that business return on investment must be sufficiently favourable for firms to start operation, even if the market has been liberalised.

While foreign telecommunication firms will find it easier to penetrate the Malaysian market with APEC commitments, business opportunities will also be created for Malaysian telecommunication services suppliers who decide to venture outwards to take advantage of those commitments. Malaysia has begun moving outward, mainly heading for other lesser developing countries. For example, Telekom Malaysia Berhad has been investing in India, Sri Lanka, Malawi, Thailand, South Africa and, recently, Cambodia. However, market entry by Malaysian firms in line with the APEC initiative remains unimpressive. Further work is needed to understand such inertia within APEC itself.

Technology and human resource development effects

As in the case of most developing countries, Malaysia depends largely on foreign investors as partners for new technologies when providing telecommunication services. A recent discussion on technology transfer in Malaysia can be found in Sieh and Loke (1998). Joint ventures and strategic alliances in various forms between local and foreign firms are expected to be important sources of technology and skills but, for this to be effective, technology transfer has to take place in an effective manner. As discussed, the recent increase of foreign equity limit from 49 per cent to 61 per cent for basic services, together with the implementation of equal access to fixed line services, are expected to stir up greater competition. In turn, the market will likely force operators to adopt newer, more cost-efficient technologies that will necessitate faster technology transfer to Malaysia in order to ensure provision of quality services that meet customers' expectations.

It is important to note that, as with other services, telecommunication service producers are highly dependent on *soft technology* such as know-how and skill, supervisory and management systems, operational or technological systems, in addition to the deployment of *hard technology* embodied in machinery and equipment. Monitoring the transfer of soft technology that is so important for telecommunication services is difficult. To ensure such transfers actually take place through joint ventures with foreign partners requires additional effort. Government agencies will need to do more to assist than simply drawing up technology transfer agreements.

Trade and investment effects

Liberalisation of the telecommunication services sub-sector is expected to increase trade and investment in the sub-sector as well as to enhance trade and investment in other sectors. For example, Electronic Data Interchange (EDI) technology that facilitates trade transactions in various sectors through speedier and more efficient port and freight forwarding services cannot be implemented smoothly without a reliable and sound telecommunication service system. Malaysia's Port Klang has improved markedly since an EDI port community system went into operation, and a reliable telecommunication system is crucial.

A telecommunication services sub-sector also constitutes basic, but critical, infrastructure for attracting foreign direct investment (FDI). As multinational firms globalise their activities, segments of their production chains are sited in different locations across countries and regions. Telecommunication services provide the network linking up the segments, as well as facilitating the intra-firm trade that is induced by such globally dispersed production facilities. Telecommunication services will act as lubricants in intra-corporate production, marketing, financial linkages and also as cement within management for steering global corporate entities afloat and ahead.

Linkage effects

The communication services sub-sector has strong output linkages with the services sector as a whole and with wholesale and retail trade services in particular. Hence, any change as a result of deregulation and liberalisation in this sub-sector is likely to have a significant impact on the rest of the services sector, especially the distributive trades. Lower prices, together with improved service quality following increased competition in the telecommunication sub-sector that result from liberalising the telecommunication services market, will benefit telecommunication users, especially wholesale and retail trade services, and transportation services. To ensure that these benefits trickle down to final consumers, it is important that the forward linked industries are also open to competition.

POLICY AND STRATEGY RECOMMENDATIONS FOR TELECOMMUNICATION FIRMS

Prepare for intensifying competition

The liberalisation of Malaysia's telecommunications sub-sector under APEC and other trade agreements, such as AFTA and GATS, means intensifying competition for domestic firms and MNCs that choose to have a presence in the market. To prepare for more competition in the near future, telecommunication firms will have to plan strategically on improving their competitiveness. Strategies are needed that help to attain higher levels of production and cost efficiencies, and also that improve firms' abilities to offer and deliver service types at attractive prices that meet quality standards expected by the market. A major challenge facing local firms will lie in their ability to acquire the technologies needed for the provision of services that are competitive in all respects. The Telekom University established by Telekom Malaysia Berhad is an important institution that can be utilised as a centre for producing the skilled professionals needed by the industry as well as for conducting much-needed design and development, and for proceeding towards research and development.

Work with government for global links

Within a liberalised environment, the onus of responsibility with regard to major investment decisions will shift entirely to telecommunication firms. The timing of heavy investments and decisions about which service products to offer will be as important as finding the right business partners, technology sources and suppliers of hardware and software. Despite the role of the Malaysian government in deciding on national economic affiliations, such as through membership of groupings based on regional proximity or other criteria, business decisions on whether to enter specific markets and on the mode of entry will remain with the firms. Nevertheless, operators must continue to maintain close relationships with the government, who will be able to assist in bilateral, plurilateral and multilateral matters that impinge on the satisfactory performance, or otherwise, of the telecommunication sub-sector.

   An active industry association should be established within the country for all telecommunications services, to help settle disputes within the industry and to deal with regulators, especially in heading off potential disputes within the country and with external markets. Until now, cross-border control appears nebulous for issues related to licensing and tariff decisions. The APEC Advisory Business Council (ABAC) should serve as a useful starting point for intra-industry meeting points within the region. An immediate concern in the industry relates to bilateral negotiations on accounting rates and settlement charges, which were not endorsed by ITU when they were first established in the 1930s and 1940s. However, the extent to which ABAC can help alleviate tensions due to excess capacity remains unclear. Corporations need to devise strategies by themselves or with each other for long-term competitiveness and sustainability.

Develop Malaysian brand names for goods and services packages

Greater effort in developing and nurturing Malaysian brand names both for telecommunication products and services will be a prerequisite for long-term sustainability of market presence either domestically or beyond the local market. This will require alliances with electronic firms that manufacture industrial electronic-based telecommunication products, and close linkages with software producers that make up the packages of tangibles and intangibles needed for service delivery. Within APEC, opportunities should be explored among member economies for all stages of development of such telecommunication goods–service product packages. Such firm-level initiatives should be encouraged and obstacles, if any, among member economies should be brought forth for appropriate remedy at the level of governments, either through industry associations or the firms themselves. This will amount to ASEAN-like cooperation, although with a larger membership of greater diversity and interests. Telecommunications within APEC may need to find a more suitable way of getting businesses to converge than is presently available. The focus is not to have governments displacing private sector leadership in business, but to put in place policies that support firm-level intra-APEC activities and to remove hindrances to business cooperation among economies of the grouping. Interweaving support between governments and service producers is needed. For this public–private reinforcement to materialise for extracting regional benefits, businesses need to recognise and make use of APEC as a possible avenue to alleviate intra-APEC hardships. Issues of standards across economies within APEC should be taken up in this way.

POLICY AND STRATEGY RECOMMENDATIONS FOR POLICY MAKERS

Focus on ensuring market forces and healthy competition work

The above discussion leads into the policy and strategy issues for the Malaysian government. It has never been an easy task for policy makers to draw up effective plans for the development of any industry. The task is made more difficult in the case of telecommunication services, where ever-changing technological developments drive not only businesses but also regulators. For Malaysia's policy makers, this task is further challenged by the industry's relative inexperience when dealing with the incessant waves of new technologies that demand heavy infrastructure investments. Nevertheless, two general guidelines are believed to be important references when drafting and implementing policies. First, under liberalised conditions, policies should be used mainly to assist and complement the functions of market forces. In this regard, the Malaysian government should concentrate further on creating an environment conducive to attracting FDI and traders, while removing or reducing constraints that impede the workings of the market. Second, government policies should promote a healthy competitive environment for the industry. New service product entry and exit conditions should not be overly burdensome to would-be investors, especially when compared with neighbouring economies in the region. While playing its part in ensuring consumer protection, the government should also be mindful of the social and economic costs when much-needed efficient telecommunication services developed through new technologies that are available elsewhere are not offered in Malaysia. Excessive supply regulations either from state or local administration or from the central government should be avoided.

Discard unnecessary hang-ups

This chapter has reviewed the commitments that Malaysia has made in APEC and in other international and regional agreements for telecommunication services. It is clear that the Malaysian telecommunication sub-sector is among the most liberalised among developing countries. The government has recognised the need to allow a high degree of openness in this sub-sector in order to keep up with the industry's rapid developments, and because of Malaysia's technology deficiency. Liberalisation of telecommunication services is also inevitable in an increasingly interdependent world where demands of foreign investors for up-to-date services must be met. There is, however, one apparent concern for the Malaysian government: that is, the need to determine the optimal number of industry players for different telecommunication services in the economy. We believe that this is an unnecessary 'hang-up' that should be left to market forces, as will be discussed shortly below. This issue might have arisen out of the criticisms levelled at the government when licence holders failed to realise their intended proposals and did not start operations. The scramble for licences in the early days of deregulation led to the over-valuation of the licences themselves; hence the criticisms. Against a policy of deregulation and liberalisation, the criticisms themselves are illogical and unjustifiable. Similarly, pricing flexibility for new packages of different services purchased from the same supplier would help promote efficiency among competing firms. The need to 'prevent a price war' may be another hang-up in a liberalised environment.

Develop a culture of greater transparency

Instead of being preoccupied with determining the optimal number of operators for each type of telecommunication service, the government should divert its attention towards helping the private sector in their business decisions. An important step is to begin providing accurate, up-to-date and timely information that is relevant for industry strategists. It is also important for the government to strive towards developing a culture of greater transparency in the way its policies are implemented and decisions made. Until recently, telecommunication firms had been voicing dissatisfaction over the absence of data on the licences awarded for various services. Part of their holding back on investment, which would have been high for capital equipment, was attributed to the lack of transparency over the number of possible competitors they might have to face after committing capital.

There is evidence that certain telecommunication services such as cellular services have been overcrowded with service suppliers, while fixed-line services have been facing shortages especially in suburban areas, even though seven licences have been issued to firms to provide such services. Apart from Telekom Malaysia Berhad, others granted licences for fixed-line services are not fully utilising their rights, as is evident by the fact that new fixed lines are connected only in selected lucrative areas.

Review strategies for competing for FDI within context of commitments

The experience of Malaysia suggests that even though the telecommunication industry has been deregulated to allow more participants and that liberalisation has extended beyond expectations, market access alone is insufficient for investors, who need to satisfy a host of conditions before placing a stake in any economy. An important point shown by the Malaysian case is that its market size, which is small and does not allow too many service providers for certain services, is an important limitation. In addition to the need for firms to explore strategies to overcome such constraints – for instance, by considering the potential for broadening their market perspectives within APEC – the Malaysian government should encourage domestic firms to prepare themselves for strategic alliances with foreign investors, particularly those from APEC who are interested in markets within the Asia Pacific region. The government, which has been actively seeking ways to compete for FDI, should constantly review its own strategies in competing for FDI. Whether investment from APEC sources should be viewed differently, that is, more favourably than others, remains a question, because without a more formalised arrangement, APEC may run into WTO inconsistencies.

POLICY AND STRATEGY RECOMMENDATIONS FOR SERVICES WITHIN APEC

Need for a separate APEC services agreement

For APEC to see meaningful results as far as the services sector is concerned, several important steps must be seriously considered by member economies. First, a more systematic effort to secure commitments on services liberalisation may be possible if a separate agreement on services is negotiated. As almost every APEC member is a party to the WTO, the first step would be along individual members' GATS offers, with the understanding that members should strive for better commitments than GATS in a smaller regional grouping, to the extent possible. While referring to service products, the structure of the APEC services agreement would serve the region better if based on time period to market admission targets, with flexibility for adjustments of those targets if expected conditions change. In other words, while incorporating the clarity of GATS in indicating intended directions, the APEC services agreement would retain the time elasticity of actual implementation if the voluntary principle were retained. The size of APEC may not lend itself to the consensus style practised by ASEAN. Nevertheless, indications of directions would provide guidance to members' future development and investment policies in the services sector. Besides guidelines on time targets for liberalisation, the APEC services agreement should focus on principles of how to push GATS and on exceptions, particularly to enable less-developed members to work out alternative revenue sources for their fledgling telecommunications companies.

In order to have a separate APEC services agreement, the urgency of compiling services data based on new definitions and classifications cannot be overemphasised. It is also crucial that concessions for relatively less-developed members be provided in terms of service types, offer conditions and time targets for full implementation of liberalisation. Technical assistance through Ecotech programs for least-developed members, for development of the sector by more advanced members, should be considered in preparation for meaningful two-way services trade. This would include services that involve established technical standards; for example, telecommunications, accounting services, and environment engineering services. Assistance towards the development of producer or intermediate services such as telecommunication, transportation, and professional and business services – particularly finance and insurance – in the less developed economies, would enable them to engage in future trade of those services. With the high degree of intra-sectoral linkages for services, an APEC services agreement might also accelerate indirect services trade through such linkages.

Emphasise factors other than market access

It follows from the above discussion that it is important for individual economies, as well as APEC as a whole, to start paying more attention to competition beyond issues of market access. Much time has been spent on tariffs, non-tariff measures, service types offered for entry, modes of trade, and conditions that go with each mode. While such deliberation should continue, the story of Malaysia's telecommunications demonstrates that market liberalisation is but one of the many dimensions that matter for businesses. As potential market sizes are stretched to cover regions and sub-regions – hence the usefulness of APEC – technological issues that necessitate international cooperation are expected to become more complex as more satellites are launched by APEC members and non-members, to permit greater volume and higher speed multi-directional flows. The existing framework for telecommunication technical agreements through ITU is almost indispensable, and APEC should be put to work for its members after its house is put in order within the grouping. This means that intra-APEC discords over technicalities should be straightened out either bilaterally or multilaterally, notwithstanding ITU. Technical and administrative issues should not be allowed to become barriers to trade in telecommunication services among member economies, as illustrated by the friction between two larger APEC members several years ago in this very sub-sector. Intra-APEC cooperation in services is believed to have much room for future expansion, with attention paid to issues beyond market access.

Build complementary ties within APEC

Until now, the spirit of cooperation among APEC member economies remains weak in telecommunications, in the services sector and even in other sectors. The nature of telecommunication activities itself accords extremely good opportunities for the group to seek and develop operational linkages between and among members for the industry and for the users of telecommunication services. Taking into account the differences in the maturity of the telecommunication industries in the different economies, complementarity should be encouraged through inter-corporate alliances. This applies to other services as well. Here we cannot but encounter the North–South divide. It is inevitable that issues beyond trade and economics must be dealt with, although they have been by and large excluded from APEC thus far. Examples include international relations and human security – which are beyond our scope of discussion and should be taken up elsewhere. Nevertheless, it is too obvious to point out that for APEC to bear fruit, and for telecommunications and the services sector to draw benefits from and to make contributions to the Asia Pacific region, strong political will is needed to foster closer ties than what is now seen. Policies should also be implemented to promote intra-APEC ties and complementation targeted at specific activities within specific sub-sectors or industries. For telecommunications, research and development will be a good starting point.

CONCLUSION

The experience of Malaysia's telecommunications sub-sector with respect to market liberalisation within APEC is still too new for solid lessons to be drawn for other economies and other services. Nevertheless, even with the difficult business and economic conditions attributed to the financial crisis that have affected APEC members on the Asian side of the Pacific since mid-1997, Malaysia has been able to hold on to its commitments. In fact, in the field of telecommunications, where demand has dropped, Malaysia had accelerated liberalisation. This does not mean that the market opening process was trouble free. On the contrary, there were problems that ranged from technical issues to fairness to producers and to consumers. There was also the need to balance foreign and local interests, which was necessary for external relations and to safeguard domestic sensitivities. In spite of the drawbacks and worries implementing its market access commitments, Malaysia is confident of reaping future benefits in the telecommunication sub-sector and in the services sector. In turn, through backward and forward linkages, liberalised telecommunication industries in Malaysia are expected to bring net positive effects to the rest of the economy and the APEC region as a whole. We strongly believe that the proposals contained in this chapter are important for the realisation of such results.

REFERENCES

Asia–Pacific Economic Cooperation (APEC) webpage, http://www.apecsec.org.sg/
Association of Southeast Asian Nations (ASEAN) webpage, http://www.aseansec.org/
Department of Telecommunication (Malaysia) webpage, http://www.jtm.gov.my/
General Agreement on Tariffs and Trade (GATT) (15 April 1994) *Final Act Embodying The Results of The Uruguay Round of Multilateral Trade Negotiations,* Geneva: GATT Trade Negotiations Committee.
General Agreement on Trade in Services (GATS) (April 1994) Malaysia's Schedule of Specific Commitments (GATS/SC/52), Geneva: GATT.
International Telecommunication Union (ITU) webpage, http://www.itu.int/
Malaysia (1994) *1987 Input–Output Tables,* Kuala Lumpur: Department of Statistics.
Malaysia (1999) *Bank Negara Malaysia Annual Report,* Kuala Lumpur: Bank Negara Malaysia.
Malaysian Government/Asian Development Bank (1993) 'Study on the role of the services sector in the economic development of Malaysia : the contribution of intermediate services', (unpublished report).
Ministry of Finance, Malaysia, *Economic Report,* Kuala Lumpur, various issues.
Ministry of Energy, Communications and Multimedia (Malaysia) webpage, http://www.ktkm.gov.my/
Ministry of International Trade and Industry (MITI) (Malaysia) webpage, http://miti.gov.my/
Prime Minister's Department Malaysia, *Malaysian Economy in Figures,* Kuala Lumpur: Economic Planning Unit (EPU), Prime Minister's Department, various issues.
Sieh, L.M.L. (1999) 'Malaysia's Electronics Industry' in Findlay, C. (ed.) *Switching On – the Effects of Liberalisation in Asia's Electronics Industry: Studies in APEC Liberalisation.* Adelaide: University of Adelaide.
Sieh, L.M.L and Loke, W.H. (1998) 'FDIs in Malaysia: Firm level characteristics', in *Papers and Proceedings of International Symposium – Foreign Direct Investment in Asia,* Tokyo: Economic Planning Agency, Government of Japan.
World Trade Organisation (WTO) webpage, http://www.wto.org/
Yamazawa, I. (1998) *APEC's Progress Toward The Bogor Target: A Quantitative Assessment of 1997 IAP/CAP,* Tokyo: Pacific Economic Cooperation Council, Japan Committee.

8 Liberalisation of the rice sector in Japan, Korea and Taiwan

Tsu-Tan Fu

INTRODUCTION

In the Uruguay Round Agreement on Agriculture, concluded in 1993, Japan and South Korea agreed to open up their rice markets by allowing minimum market access, despite strong opposition from local farmers' groups. In a special clause to the agreement, Japanese rice is exempt from tariffs for the period 1995–2000. Under its rice import commitments, Japan had to initiate minimum access for rice imports in April 1995 equivalent to 4 per cent of domestic rice consumption, to increase by 0.8 per cent annually until the year 2000, when 8 per cent of domestic rice consumption must be imported. Korea, which participated in the Uruguay Round Agreement as a developing country, has been granted a ten-year rice import scheme, covering 1995–2004. According to its provisions, Korea must import 1 per cent of domestic rice consumption in the base year as the minimum market access. The annual increments of the import quota are 0.25 per cent for the years before 2000, and 0.5 per cent thereafter. By 2004, the import quota for rice in Korea must reach 4 per cent of base year domestic consumption.

In order to soften the impact of opening up the rice market on the domestic rice sector, the Japanese and Korean governments have implemented various policy reforms on rice production and distribution as well as on the structure of rice farming. The degree of effectiveness of these measures will be critical for both governments in gaining support from farmers' groups in time for the next round of multilateral negotiations, to take place in the next millennium, when further opening of the rice market is expected to be requested by rice exporting countries. It is interesting to note that Japan decided to abandon the minimum market access scheme, a special treatment for rice imports, and will apply the tariff scheme starting from April 1999; this decision was due to unexpected negative market responses to market opening, the minimum market access scheme and related policy measures. Taiwan, in its latest bilateral negotiations with the United States, committed to apply the minimum access scheme for rice imports once Taiwan is allowed to enter the WTO, as did Japan. In accordance with WTO trading rules, Taiwan is currently also implementing various policy measures in advance, to soften the impact of market opening on Taiwan's rice sector and rice farmers.

Why the Japanese government decided to accept a tariff regime, and whether or not the Korean or Taiwanese government will follow in Japan's footsteps or will instead opt for the minimum access scheme for rice imports are interesting and complicated questions that deserve further investigation. This chapter attempts to analyse these issues by examining the structure of the agricultural sector, market responses to rice imports, and the effects of adjustment policies on the three economies of Japan, Korea and Taiwan. By comparing different policy measures, we hope to find a suitable way of liberalising national rice sectors that is consistent with the demands of the WTO and APEC.

CHARACTERISTICS OF THE AGRICULTURE AND RICE SECTOR IN JAPAN, KOREA AND TAIWAN

The importance of agriculture in the national economy

Agriculture is regarded as the bedrock of the early stages of economic development in East Asian countries. The contribution of agriculture to the national economy comes through the supply of foodstuffs, through increases in gross national product, in the labour supply for non-agricultural sectors, in capital generation, and through the conservation of the environment and the preservation of tradition.

Although the remarkable economic growth seen in Japan in 1955–70 and in Korea and Taiwan in the 1980s and 1990s can be mainly attributed to rapid industrial development, the proportion of GDP generated by agriculture, though decreasing, is still significant. In 1995, the contribution to total GDP by agriculture was 6.6 per cent in Korea, 3.6 per cent in Taiwan and 2.1 per cent in Japan. The total value of agricultural trade accounted for between 15 per cent and 24 per cent of the total trade value of these three economies in the same year (Table 8.1). While industrial products comprise the bulk of export goods for these countries, the import of farm products accounted for 23 per cent of total imports in Japan, 11 per cent in Korea and 9 per cent in Taiwan in 1995. These economies can thus be regarded as important agricultural importing economies in the Asian region. Although the overall population and workforce in Japan, Korea and Taiwan have steadily increased over time, the proportion of the population involved in farming has been decreasing with the decline in the importance of the agricultural sector. In 1995, the proportion of agricultural workers to the total workforce was 5 per cent in Japan, 12.5 per cent in Korea and 11 per cent in Taiwan.

While being characterised as small owner-operated farming, over the last several decades the average cultivated area per farm has remained at around one hectare for each of these three economies. The agricultural sectors have also faced continual labour shortages in the last two decades, resulting from rapid industrial growth that has been poaching labourers from the farming

Table 8.1 The role of agriculture in Japan, Korea and Taiwan

	Japan 1980	Japan 1990	Japan 1995	Korea 1980	Korea 1990	Korea 1995	Taiwan 1980	Taiwan 1990	Taiwan 1995
GDP (US$ billion)	1,083	3,252	5,833	58	254	447	41	160	261
GDP growth rate[a]	3.5	4.8	0.9	3.7	9.5	8.9	7.3	4.9	6.0
GDP per capita ($)	9,143	24,436	41,220	1,597	5,883	10,037	2,344	8,111	12,439
GDP from agriculture (%)	2.4	1.8	0.8	12.7	7.4	6.6	7.7	4.2	3.6
Agricultural products									
Exports (US$ million)		3,540	4,274		2,988	4,272	2,251	3,661	5,639
Imports (US$ million)		52,478	76,811		9,564	15,298	3,089	6,088	9,764
Share of agricultural trade to total trade									
Exports (%)		1.2	1.0		4.6	3.4	11.4	5.5	5.1
Imports (%)		22.3	22.8		13.7	11.3	15.6	11.1	9.4
Total population (thousand)	117,060	123,611	125,569	38,124	42,869	44,606	17,805	20,353	21,304
Farm household population (%)	18.2	13.8	12.0	28.4	15.5	10.8	30.3	21.1	18.5
Total workforce (thousand)	55,520	62,800	64,570	13,683	18,036	20,377	6,547	8,283	9,045
Farming workforce (%)	9.1	6.2	5.1	32.4	17.5	12.5	19.5	12.9	10.6
Full-time farmers (%)	13.4	12.3	12.4	76.2	59.6	56.6	9.0	13.0	12.8
Non-agricultural income to farm household income (%)	78.9	82.4	79.1	34.8	25.8	31.8	70.4	64.8	61.2

Notes

a The GDP growth rate for Japan was 3.6% in 1996, 0.1% in 1997, and −0.5% in 1998; in Korea it was 7.1% in 1996, 5.5% in 1997 and −1.0% in 1998; and in Taiwan it was 8.5% in 1996, 8.8% in 1997 and 6.0% in 1998.

sector. Consequently, part-time farming, where farmers take regular jobs in non-agricultural sectors and practise farming on a part-time basis or only during busy farming seasons, has become a common feature of farming activity in the region. However, there are noticeable differences between Korea and the other two economies in terms of the share of full-time and part-time farmers. In Japan and Taiwan, the proportion of full-time farmers to the total number of farmers was around 12–13 per cent in 1995, whereas this figure was 57 per cent for Korea. Meanwhile, the proportion of the income of farming households generated purely by agricultural activity was 48 per cent in 1995 in Korea, while it was only 21 per cent in Japan and 39 per cent in Taiwan. Therefore, the contribution of farming-generated income in farming households seems to be larger in Korea than in Taiwan and Japan. This suggests that the impact on Korea as a result of the liberalisation of the agricultural sector will be greater than that in Taiwan and Japan.

Production and consumption of rice

Rice is a staple food and one of the most important crops for most countries in Asia. Rice production has also provided an importance source of income for farming families. Therefore, ensuring a sufficient supply of rice for the population has been very important for social and political stability in Asia. Food security for major crops, especially rice, has long been regarded as a major policy objective of the region as a whole. Import restrictions and price supports are the major policy measures for ensuring a stable supply of cheap rice in Japan, Korea and Taiwan.

In Taiwan (and Japan) in the 1990s, about 23–27 per cent (40–42 per cent) of cultivated land was used to grow rice (Table 8.2). This ratio was over 50 per cent in Korea. The acreage of land planted for rice has, however, decreased over time in Korea and Taiwan, whereas in Japan it has increased during 1990–7, partially due to a serious rice supply shortage in 1993. Rice consumption has decreased over the last two decades, which is reflected in a negative income effect for Japan, Korea and Taiwan. Figure 8.1 shows per capita rice consumption in Japan, Korea and Taiwan has followed different trends. It can be seen that rice consumption per capita over time has steadily decreased in Korea and Japan, while in Taiwan there was a drastic decline in the 1980s, and stability in the 1990s. In 1995, Korea had a higher rice consumption per capita (106.5kg) than Japan (67.8kg) and Taiwan (59.1kg). Such relatively high rice consumption meant that there was a lower probability that Korea could meet its total demand for rice, except in the late 1980s and early 1990s, as shown in Figure 8.1. The self-sufficiency rates for Taiwan and Japan, meanwhile, tend to be over 100 per cent for most of the 1970s.

The contribution of the rice sector to agricultural production can also be shown by indicators of rice production value to total agricultural production value and average rice receipts to household farming receipts. As indicated in the preceding section, farming activity accounted for 68 per cent of the average farm household's income in Korea in 1995. Receipts from rice farming

Table 8.2 Rice statistics for Japan, Korea and Taiwan

	Japan			Korea			Taiwan		
	1980	1990	1995	1980	1990	1995	1980	1990	1995
Acreage planted (1,000 ha)	2,377	2,074	2,118	1,233	1,244	1,056	638	455	363
Production (polished) (thousand tons)	9,751	10,499	10,748	3,550	5,606	4,695	2,118	1,626	1,518
Total consumption (polished) (thousand tons)	11,209	10,484	10,485	5,402	5,444	5,200	1,954	1,650	1,480
Rice consumption per capita (kg)	78.9	70.0	67.8	132.4	119.6	106.5	105.5	65.9	59.1
Trade quantity (polished)									
Imports (thousand tons)	27	50	495	580	—	—	0.1	5.1	5.6
Exports (thousand tons)	754	0	581	—	—	—	266.1	109.5	192.1
Rice land/total cultivated land (%)	43	40	42	56	59	53	36[a]	27[a]	23[a]
Rice self-sufficiency ratio	87	100	103	95.1	108.3	96.3	113	99	103
Rice production/total agricultural production (%)	29.8	28.6	30.4		36.9	26.1	26.5	17.0	12.9
Rice receipts/on-farm receipts (%)	28.6	28.6		41.8	48.2	34.0		27.4	22.8

Note

a Rice in Taiwan grows two crops a year. The percentages used in this table for rice land/total cultivated land were calculated from the first rice crop. For the second rice crop, those percentages were 34 per cent in 1980, 24 per cent in 1990 and 19 per cent in 1995.

Figure 8.1 Per capita consumption of rice in Japan, Korea and Taiwan

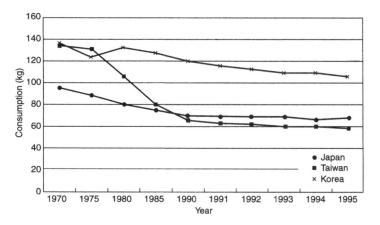

have accounted for more than one-third of on-farm receipts for Korean farmers. A lower proportion of farming income is accounted for by rice production for the average Taiwanese farmer, at about one quarter. The share of rice production value to total agricultural production value in Korea has been roughly double that of Taiwan so far in the 1990s.

Recent changes in rice policy

In accordance with the Uruguay Round Agreement on Agriculture, for Japan and Korea, rice is exempt from tariffs and these countries are granted a minimum access commitment. In addition, the level of the aggregate measurement of support (AMS) will be subject to a 20 per cent cut for Japan in six years' time and a 13.3 per cent cut for Korea in ten years' time. To soften the impact of these commitments on the farming sector and farm households, various reform policies have been undertaken. They are briefly analysed below.

THE IMPLEMENTATION OF RICE IMPORT COMMITMENT

Minimum market access and tariffs

The importation of rice has long been strictly controlled by the governments of Japan, Korea and Taiwan. According to the schedule of minimum market access (MMA) commitment as shown in Table 8.3, Korea had to import 192.4 billion tons and Japan 1,365 billion tons of rice by 1997. Both countries fulfilled these commitments. As for Taiwan, if it is allowed to enter the WTO in 1999 and applies the same scheme as Japan, then it would have to open its rice market and import 7.2 per cent of domestic rice consumption in the base year 1999. In 2000, Taiwan would have to import at least 8 per cent of the base year rice consumption.

Table 8.3 Schedule and implementation of minimum market access for rice

Year	1995	1996	1997	1998	1999	2000	2001	2002	2003	2004
Korea										
Import quota for MMA (1,000 tons, milled)	51.3	64.1	77.0	89.8	102.6	102.6	128.3	153.9	179.6	205.2
Share to base year domestic consumption (%)	1	1.25	1.50	1.75	2.00	2.00	2.50	3.00	3.50	4.00
Actual imports	51.3	63.9	77.0	NA	NA	NA	NA	NA	NA	NA
Japan										
Import quota for MMA (1,000 tons, milled)	379	455	531	606	682	758	NA	NA	NA	NA
Share to base year domestic consumption (%)	4	4.8	5.6	6.4	7.2	8	NA	NA	NA	NA
Actual imports	379	455	525	NA	NA	NA	NA	NA	NA	NA
Tariffication (1999)[a]										
Import quota under tariffication (1,000 tons, milled)	NA	NA	NA	NA	650	682	(Tariff equivalent =1,100%)			
Share to base year domestic consumption (%)	NA	NA	NA	NA	6.8	7.2	(Tariff reduction=15%)			
Taiwan (if entering WTO in 1999)										
Import quota for MMA (1,000 tons, milled)	NA	NA	NA	NA	127	144	NA	NA	NA	NA
Share to base year domestic consumption (%)	NA	NA	NA	NA	7.2	8	NA	NA	NA	NA

Note
a Japan decided to apply tariffication on rice imports on 1 April 1999.

Figure 8.2 Self-sufficiency rate of rice in Japan, Korea and Taiwan

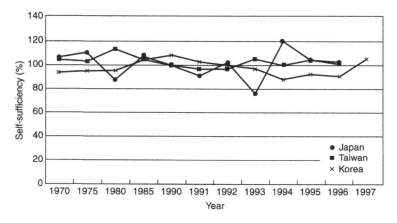

The tariffication scheme for rice that Japan has accepted starts from 1 April 1999. By applying this scheme, Japan has to import 6.8 per cent of base year rice consumption in 1999, 0.4 per cent lower than the amount required by the minimum access scheme. Therefore, by adopting this new scheme, Japan may reduce its required rice imports by a total of 114 billion tons, equivalent to 1.2 per cent of base year rice consumption in 1999 and 2000. Although Japanese rice imports are subject to a tariff reduction of at least 15 per cent for six years, there will be no induced imports since the tariff equivalent has been set high. The tariff equivalent will be 351.17 yen per kilogram in 1999 and 341 yen per kilogram in 2000, which is approximately equal to an 850–1,170 per cent tariff rate, according to estimates from the report of Japan Central Agricultural Association (Japan Central Agricultural Association 1998).

State trading/imported rice distribution

In order to prevent imported rice from impacting on the domestic fresh rice market and to stabilise domestic market prices, Korea has implemented a state trading scheme by assigning its food agency, the MAFF, responsibility for the management of rice imports. In addition, all imported rice by minimum market access is to be used for processing only. Japan has also adopted a state trading scheme for imported rice. Of the total 1,370,000 million tons of milled rice imported to Japan up until April of 1998, 4.5 per cent was used for food, 38 per cent for processing, 12 per cent for animal feed and the remainder for emergency food aid to other countries (Table 8.4).

The impact of rice imports

A precise measurement of the impact of rice importation on indigenous agricultural sectors or on farm households is difficult to obtain. The impact simulation results also depend upon the assumption of some critical

Table 8.4   Major changes in rice policy

Policy instrument	Japan	Korea	Taiwan
Border measures:			
Import commitment	MMA(1995–9) Tariffication (1999–2000)	MMAI	MMA ([a])
State trading	90% of MMA imported by MAFF; 10% of MMA by SBS[b]	100% of MMA imported by MAFF	65% of rice imported by government; 35% by private sector
Import rice distribution	most used for processing, feed and food aid	all used for processing	–
Domestic policies:			
Administered price	price support to government purchased rice; auction price for voluntary rice	price support to government purchased rice (1984; 94) deficiency payment (1995–)	price support to government purchased rice (1973–)
Supply control	government procurement rice diversion subsidy; set-aside subsidy; rice gross revenue insurance program	government procurement	government procurement; rice diversion subsidy; set-aside subsidy

Note
a Taiwan has agreed to apply MMA in bilateral trade negotiations with the United States.
b SBS is 'Simultaneous Buy-Sale System'.

parameters. Inelastic supply and demand elasticity for rice have been the key parameters used in simulations. Kako, Gemma and Ito (1997) predict that unless a rice diversion program can fully meet target levels, then the market price of rice will fall fast as a result of an increase in supply. Large-scale rice farmers in Japan will thus suffer from a sharp drop in income and may even move out of rice production. In fact, due to four consecutive bumper rice harvest years since 1994, rice reserves in Japan reached 3.7 million tons in 1998, creating a downward pressure on the price of rice. Such stockpiling also offset progress made by the set-aside program. The increasing amount of minimum market access rice used for processing caused the market price of low quality Hokkaido rice to drop by about 20 per cent in 1997. It was such huge and unexpected negative impacts on the market that made Japan's government switch its rice import strategy from the minimum access scheme to tariffication. Because of this change, Japan is required to import less rice, at least in 1999 and 2000.

Korea suffers from insufficient rice production. Farmers' groups, however, remain opposed to the opening up of Korea's rice market. Korea has only had to import a relatively small amount of rice in the last few years, which was used for processing. Thus there has been no significant impact on its rice market. Moreover, the state trading scheme has also minimised the impact on the market price of rice in Korea. As for Taiwan, the Council of Agriculture has estimated that the WTO agreement on its rice sector could hurt the Taiwanese rice sector to the tune of around US$100 million in the first six years.

ADJUSTMENT OF DOMESTIC SUPPORT IN JAPAN

In addition to border measures on rice supply in Japan, policy reform pertaining to the rice sector has also targeted the adjustment of domestic supports, specifically the price support program, the marketing and distribution system and income support measures. The results of such changes can partially be revealed by the changes in the producer subsidy equivalent (PSE) and AMS measures.

Rice production adjustments

In Japan, rice production has been adjusted to meet the declining domestic rice consumption through the rice diversion program for more than thirty years. Under the reduction quota for the acreage of land used for rice cultivation, rice growers are compelled to meet rice acreage reduction quotas drawn up by both the government and agricultural cooperatives. However, starting in 1996, the government implemented a rice diversion program in cooperation with the agricultural cooperatives. The diversion quota is under the control of the government, which will purchase rice only from those farmers who participate in the diversion program. To facilitate the attainment of the diversion targets, diversion subsidies are paid to program participants. Funding for these diversion subsidies comes jointly from farmers and the government. A mutual compensation program has been set up by the agricultural cooperatives, in which those farmers who divert their paddy fields away from rice production obtain more financial assistance than those who do not (Kako *et al.* 1997). A structural improvement policy, with rice farming at its core, has also been promoted by the Japanese government. This policy has led to a reduction in rice production costs of about 20–30 per cent by promoting the aggregation of farmland and by promoting a commissioned or entrusted farming system, which results in economies of scale.

Rice price support and distribution

The price of rice in Japan has long been supported by a government price support program, which has led to rapid growth in rice production since the early 1960s. In 1969, a subsidised paddy land diversion program was first introduced as a means of coping with a huge rice surplus. In the 1980s, the set-aside program was also used to reduce the mounting rice surplus. Until October 1995, under the Food Control Law of 1947 the marketing of rice and its purchasing and selling prices had been under government control. However, upon accepting the Uruguay Round Agreement in 1994, the Japanese government introduced a new rice policy in 1995. The 'Law for the Stabilisation of the Supply, Demand and Price of Staple Food', first applied to the 1996 rice harvest, introduced major modifications to the price support regime for rice. Under the law, the administered prices (government purchase and sale price) of domestic rice will only be applicable to government rice, or about 14 per cent of consumption. For the remainder of rice production, which is largely sold as so-called voluntary marketed rice, support is provided mainly by border protection. Since 1990, the price of voluntary marketed rice has been determined through a tender system, sponsored by the Price Finding Organisation for voluntary rice, which is a subsidiary of the Food Agency of Japan (Kako *et al.* 1997). The voluntary rice is a higher quality rice that commands a higher price than the government price. As a result, the price of voluntary marketed rice is generally around 40–50 per cent higher than the government procurement price.

Under the Food Control Law of Japan, only designated agents could participate in the marketing of rice, where prices were regulated by the government. In 1969, rice marketing came under direct government control and voluntary rice systems. To increase the share of voluntary rice, the government also paid subsidies to rice producers for rice sold through voluntary rice channels. As a result of such promotion, the proportion of voluntary rice production to total rice production reached around 40 per cent in 1988, and increased to 70 per cent in 1994 (Kako *et al.* 1997). The voluntary rice, however, was mainly traded through the agricultural cooperatives system under the supervision of the government, and can thus be regarded as semi-controlled rice. Government procured rice has accounted for around 15 per cent of total rice production in Japan in recent years. It should also be noted that the share of rice sold to the market directly from farmers or private companies has been increasing in recent years.

Another new provision on rice distribution in Japan pertains to government purchase of rice reserves. In order to reduce the government's huge rice reserves to a reasonable level (from 3.7 million tons in 1998 to 2 million tons in 2000), regulations on government purchase and sale of rice were put in place. First, the amount of rice purchased must be lower than that sold. Second, there must be no purchase of those rice varieties generally not sold in the market.

Japan's Rice Gross Revenue Stabilisation program

Including the adoption of the concepts of insurance and cross-compliance, the Rice Gross Revenue Stabilisation Program was introduced in late 1997 in Japan as part of its new rice policy. The introduction of this income stabilisation policy replaced the traditional price stabilisation-type policy employed for years in Japan. This program, which requests that farmers fully cooperate with paddy field diversion programs, was launched to mitigate short-term fluctuations in the income of rice farmers and to promote production adjustment. This program is funded jointly by rice farmers and the government. When the market price of rice is lower than the average market price of rice in the preceding three-year period, farmers will be compensated for 80 per cent of the difference between the two prices. However, compensation is limited to those farmers who fulfil their requested production adjustment in the paddy field diversion program. Participation in this insurance program is voluntary. However, to date, the registration rate for farmers to this program has been as high as 80 per cent.

ADJUSTMENT OF DOMESTIC SUPPORT IN KOREA

Rice production adjustments

Rice production in Korea has been on the decrease since the late 1980s due to its relatively low profitability per acre as compared with fruits and vegetables. Increased conversion of paddy land into factories and other industrial uses has also been observed in recent years. In 1996, the Korea Ministry of Agriculture, Forestry and Fisheries set securing a stable supply of rice as its first policy objective. Korea will not suffer from an oversupply of rice even if the mandatory imports of rice as requested by the WTO increase every year.

Rice price support and distribution

In Korea, the government operates a dual pricing system, setting prices and volumes for rice purchases from producers while taking account of inflationary trends, budgetary circumstances and national economic objectives; and then, at least until recently, reselling at a lower price. However, following recent changes in policy, price purchases are now made through a competitive bidding system managed by the national agricultural cooperatives.

Beginning in 1984, the Korean government also partially mandated the government price purchase to the National Agricultural Cooperative Federation (NACF). The average share of government rice purchase to total government rice purchase via NACF was about 26.3 per cent in 1990–7. Such rice purchases were based on the government purchase price until 1994. Since 1995, the government has paid the price difference between the market price and the government purchase price. In the long run, the government plans to hand over the purchase program to the NACF and to provide financial support to the NACF. Government purchase prices and quantity are decided by the government after consultations with the Grower Marketing Commitment and are then submitted to the National Assembly for approval.

In recent years, around 30 per cent of total rice production in Korea has been purchased by the government, the remainder being either consumed by farmers or marketed through private channels (Table 8.5). A buffer stocking arrangement has been adopted to facilitate price stability and orderly marketing. The government's purchases had been financed by the Grain Management Special Fund (MSF), which was raised by issuing food grain public bonds and by government contributions. The release prices of rice were lower than the buying prices. The deficit comes from such price differences and other handling costs. The MSF suffered a huge deficit of US$11 billion in 1995, 44 per cent of the annual sum used for buying rice. Some measures designed to reduce government support for rice have been introduced in recent years. The gap between grain purchase and selling prices is to be lowered gradually and new income-compensating programs are to be developed in line with changes in grain purchase policy (Korea MAFF 1996).

ADJUSTMENT OF DOMESTIC SUPPORT IN TAIWAN

Rice production adjustments

Taiwan has been facing the problem of a rice surplus since the 1970s. Beginning in 1984, the government implemented a six-year paddy field diversion program that successfully reduced the extent of rice production areas by around 26 per cent and annual rice production by 25 per cent. Crop diversion subsidies and price difference subsidies for the purchase of dry land crops were introduced to facilitate farmers' adjustment. The rice production adjustment and rice field diversion program has been in place since 1990. Major policy measures include the continuation of paddy land diversion and the implementation of the farmland set-aside program. In addition, a paddy–dry crop rotation system has been implemented in some production areas in order to increase the long-term productivity of the land as well as to reduce rice production. Subsidies to farmers who participate in these rice field diversion, farmland set-aside and crop rotation production programs are offered by the government. Moreover, the government also promotes the production of high quality rice varieties. The target is for the

Table 8.5 Share of government-purchased rice to total rice production (per cent)

	1990	1991	1992	1993	1994	1995
Japan	17.6	12.1	15.4	0.3	17.7	15.8
Korea	21.5	22.7	25.9	30.3	29.9	29.3
Taiwan	30.0	23.0	24.8	24.7	30.7	21.9

production of high quality rice to exceed 30 per cent of total rice supply in Taiwan by the year 2000.

Rice price support and distribution

In Taiwan, a portion of the rice produced is purchased by the government at a guaranteed price that is used to exceed market prices. In recent years, the government has procured around 20–35 per cent of output. The cost of this price support program has been around NT$7–10 billion annually, which accounts for a large proportion of its agricultural budget. The guaranteed rice price has been frozen in the past few years. Under the WTO agreement, with its demands for rice imports, the rice price in Taiwan will be under pressure to fall in coming years.

The rice not purchased by the government all goes to market through private channels. The market price is determined by the market supply and demand of rice. The main farmers' organisation in Taiwan is the Farmers Association, and not cooperatives. The Farmers Association assists the government in its rice purchases and in rice storage. However, the Farmers Association operates as a township-type decentralised organisational system, and thus it has only a limited influence on the market price for rice.

PSE/AMS

The Producer Subsidy Equivalent (PSE) has been widely used as a measurement of the value of money transfers to the agricultural sector resulting from agricultural policies. Tsujii (1998) shows that the PSE for Japanese rice from 1986 to 1988 was 92 per cent. It was 95 per cent in 1992, 91 per cent in 1993, 97 per cent in 1994, and 88 per cent in 1995. In Taiwan, the PSE for rice was as low as 28.1 per cent in 1982–6. However, there are no updated PSE figures available for Taiwan. The PSE figures for Korean rice were 97 per cent in 1995 and 92 per cent in 1996. The MAFF in Korea (1996) has indicated that Korea intends to make sufficient adjustments in order to meet the AMS bound level by the year 2004, that is, a 13.3 per cent reduction to the level of the base year.

FACTORS AFFECTING POLICY CHOICE

Several factors that may affect policy makers' decisions are discussed below. Among these factors are such as food security concerns, income support to farmers and the environmental/social function of rice cultivation, all of which are politically important to citizens in Japan, Korea and Taiwan. Governmental budget constraints and allocation, as well as the question of rice quality, are economically important to policy makers.

Food security concerns

The food security issue will be one of the most pressing problems confronting policy makers in the coming century. Although Japan, Korea and Taiwan are high-income countries and far from poor, their governments are still responsible for implementing food security policies so that national food demand can be met. Part of the reason for such concern over food is the serious food shortages that these nations experienced either during the Second World War, the Korean War or the Chinese Civil War. Moreover, the world food crisis of the early 1970s, the United States soybean embargo on Japan to the Soviet Union, and the Chernobyl nuclear power station incident have given these governments a strong incentive to ensure food security and to be ready for unexpected turns in the world food market.

Effective food security policies consist of food imports, reserve stocks and self-sufficiency. In discussing the food security problems of importing countries such as Japan, Korea and Taiwan, it should be noted that exporting countries are not obligated to supply agricultural products and that the embargo of agricultural products as well as the regulation of agricultural exports are not prohibited in the GATT Uruguay Round agreement. When there is a food shortage, food-exporting countries tend to introduce export regulations to prevent increases in domestic prices. This means importing countries have to pay an extremely high price for their food supply over the shortage period to meet their food demands. Therefore, until the WTO can provide stable-supply regulations, importing countries will continue to maintain a certain level of food self-sufficiency in order to ensure a stable food supply. This is particularly important for staple foods such as rice in Japan, Korea and Taiwan. The low level of self-sufficiency rate in cereal production in recent years, 30 per cent in Japan and Korea and 58 per cent in Taiwan in 1995, has also prompted calls for higher self-sufficiency in rice. From the policy makers' point of view, maintaining self-sufficiency in rice production and stability in rice prices are important political objectives since rice is regarded as a thin market, where less than 5 per cent of world rice production is traded in the international market. Such thin market characteristics makes the world rice market highly sensitive to shortfalls in the domestic production of major rice consuming countries such as China, India and Indonesia.

Income support to farmers

In the early stages of their economic development, Japan, Korea and Taiwan adopted a strategy of taxing agriculture to support industrial development. However, this strategy has switched back to supporting agriculture in the later stages of economic development over the last few decades. To narrow the gap between agricultural and non-agricultural incomes resulting from unbalanced growth between the agricultural and non-agricultural sectors as well as in small-scale farming, these governments have implemented different policy instruments such as rice purchase at a guaranteed price coupled with border control measures. Such measures have been in place since the 1960s in Japan, the 1970s in Taiwan and the 1980s in Korea. Income transferred from consumer and government budgets via price supports has become a major source of farm income. In addition, active lobbying for continuing price support for farmers by farmers' groups has been very effective, since the farmer vote yields considerable influence with politicians wishing to be re-elected. Therefore, it would be politically unfeasible to reduce price supports without providing a compensation scheme or alternative income support measures. For this reason, alternative direct income payment programs, which are consistent with WTO regulations, have been implemented in order to fully or partially compensate farmers' economic losses due to reductions in the government support of rice.

Government budget constraints and allocation

Budgetary data provide a picture of the direction and magnitude of government expenditure on agriculture. In Taiwan, since the 1980s, price support and subsidy has accounted for 30–40 per cent of the total agricultural budget. However, over the 1990s it has decreased, whereas expenditure on public infrastructure investment and farmer welfare programs, such as farmers' pensions and medical insurance programs, has increased. In Japan, expenditure on 'Rice and Wheat Control Costs and Price Stabilisation of Other Products' decreased from 44 per cent of total agricultural expenditure in 1960 to 8 per cent in 1995, whereas expenditure on 'Agricultural and Rural Investment and Agricultural Research and Extension' increased from 24 per cent to 54 per cent during the same period. That share also declined from 12 per cent in 1995 to 8 per cent in 1995, reflecting the policy adjustments on reducing price support and the liberalisation of the agricultural sector following the Uruguay Round Agricultural Agreement. In Korea, investment on structural development dominates the budget, accounting for 62 per cent of total expenditure on agriculture in 1996.

The above budgetary figures seem to indicate that the governments of Japan, Korea and Taiwan are currently directing their agriculture policies toward less government price support but a more sustained and productive production base. In fact, under WTO regulations, the AMS for agricultural products, including rice, will be subject to a 20 per cent cut in six years' time for Japan and a 13.3 per cent cut in ten years' time for Korea. Therefore, the extent of government purchase of rice and the level of support prices will shrink over time. Recently, Korea and Taiwan have both been having to face an enormous government deficit in the rice purchase programs, which has accelerated moves towards the reduction of the support price and a decrease in rice production. Reduced funding of rice supply control and price stabilisation could also indicate a slow change in border controls on rice. The speed of changes in the border controls on rice will depend on the government's ability (or budget) to shift transferred income (to farmers) from consumers to the government (or taxpayers) while maintaining the same level of income support for farmers.

The environmental and social function of rice cultivation

Agriculture plays a fundamental role as the source of a stable, continuous supply of a basic foodstuff to a nation. However, as described by Nagata (1991), once a society becomes richer and more mature, more people recognise that agriculture is no longer simply a food and raw materials industry, but an industry that supplies society with many multilateral benefits. This new role of agriculture lies in the various social benefits it contributes, stemming from agricultural land use and normal agricultural production.

Under this new emerging role, the social benefits from farming include the preservation of water resources, flood control, soil erosion prevention, the prevention of landslides, soil purification, health and recreation, wildlife protection, the supply of oxygen, air purification, the provision of verdant land and beautiful landscapes, and the conservation of rural villages and regional culture. Although the value of these external economic effects of agriculture is difficult to assess through the market mechanism, in the case of Japan a rough figure, which is equivalent to around 15 per cent of Japan's current GNP and three times the gross product of its agricultural and forestry industries, has been estimated by the Ministry of Agriculture, Forestry, and Fisheries of Japan (Nagata 1991). In addition, the social stability resulting from agricultural activity and the maintenance of rural villages is also regarded as an important benefit to Japanese society (Egaitsu 1991).

The importance of paddy fields, mainly used for rice production, in serving an environmental protection role, is receiving more and more attention these days from the governments and citizens of Japan, Korea and Taiwan. If the externalities of rice cultivation become popular, then the maintenance of an appropriately sized rice sector will be necessary.

The quality dimension of rice

Since the income elasticities of rice in Japan, Korea and Taiwan have all been negative in recent decades, the declining trend of rice consumption per capita in these countries is likely to continue in the future. The share of daily household expenditure on rice is, moreover, insignificant in these three relatively developed economies. Yet growing numbers of consumers in these countries have been demanding higher quality rice in recent decades. As a reflection of such growing market demand, safer foods, such as organic and pesticide residue-free products, have been gaining an increasing market share in the fresh food markets. The share of high quality rice to total rice production has also increased substantially in Japan recently.

Currently, the government of Japan (and Taiwan) is employing rice land diversion programs to reduce rice production. This comes in response to a decline in rice consumption and an increase in imports of foreign rice. However, if consumer demand for high quality rice that is locally grown continues to strengthen, then the rice market will become segmented according to quality. Since imported rice is of a relatively low quality and is prevalent in the processing market but not in the fresh rice market, promotion of the cultivation of high quality rice could be a means of maintaining rice cultivation in the developed economies of Asia.

CONCLUSION

In accordance with their WTO agreements on agriculture, Japan and Korea have fulfilled their minimum access rice import commitments since 1994. Almost all of the rice imported went to state trading and the processing market. In Korea, with its insufficient domestic production and relatively small volume of imports, no significant impact from market opening was felt. A series of bumper rice harvests and relatively large amounts of rice imports had led to stock piling and a rice price decrease for low quality rice after 1994 in Japan. Such an unfavourable response from the Japanese rice market also led to changes in its border measures for rice – there was a switch from the minimum access scheme to tariffication in April 1999. This switch to tariffication is consistent with WTO and APEC regulations. However, Japan's change in policy choice has also provided the policy makers of other rice importing economies, such as South Korea, Taiwan, China and other Asian countries, an opportunity to re-evaluate their best choice of import scheme for rice, in addition to the minimum access scheme.

In order to lessen the impact of market opening on the rice sector, the governments of Japan, Korea and Taiwan implemented several adjustment policies in the 1990s. Among these policies, changes in the rice pricing and distribution system, production adjustment, income support schemes and structural adjustment are analysed in this chapter.

Policies for rice pricing and distribution tend to induce more rice production via the free market by phasing out food control laws (Japan) and reducing the amount of government procurement. Although a good deal of rice production and distribution will remain under government control, governments will also allocate more room for market forces to play a role. In fact, the role of government in the rice market in the 1990s has been limited to price stabilisation by means of buffer stock operations. In 1995, the share of government-purchased rice to total rice production was only 16 per cent in Japan, 30 per cent in Korea and 22 per cent in Taiwan. Although a considerable amount of the market supply of rice has been traded through agricultural cooperatives, which are strongly influenced or even supervised by the Japanese and Korean governments, the supply of rice through private channels has increased over time. The price of non-government procured rice is mainly determined by market forces.

To cope with the excessive rice supply problem, partially due to good crop years and a decline in the per capita consumption of rice, the Japanese and Taiwan governments have implemented production adjustment measures including paddy land diversion and set-aside programs. These production adjustments help reduce the acreage of planted rice and rice production.

Shrinking market demand and the impact of oversupply from importation have made such measures necessary.

These supply management strategies are coupled with government subsidies to serve as incentives for promoting producers' participation in the programs. Thus, these kinds of subsidy payments can be regarded as direct income payments. However, in facilitating the achievement of diversion targets, the concepts of cross-compliance and mutual compensation have been adopted in Japan in recent years. The so-called 'Rice Gross Revenue Stabilisation Program', which is jointly funded by the Japanese government and farmers, has also been in operation since 1998. This program was designed to stabilise rice farmers' income in a way that is more consistent with the WTO agreement.

Last, but not least, structural adjustment policy is analysed in this chapter. This policy, which has long been in place, has received a large share of the agricultural budget in Japan, Korea and Taiwan in recent years. Farmland consolidation, infrastructure investment as well as measures for expanding farming not only enhance international competitiveness in the agricultural sectors, but also improve the quality of the rural environment as well as farmers' quality of life.

Cross comparison and evaluation of policies between countries is a very difficult and complicated issue since every country has its own different economic and political environment. In this chapter, factors that affect policy makers' decisions are analysed. Among these factors are food security concerns, income support to farmers and the environmental/social function of rice cultivation, all of which are politically important to citizens in Japan, Korea and Taiwan. Governmental budget constraints and allocation, as well as the question of rice quality, are economically important to policy makers.

In view of the above analysis, the following policy recommendations are put forward:

1 Under the 1994 WTO agreement on agriculture, Japan, Korea and Taiwan have adopted several kinds of adjustment policy to soften the potential impact of liberalisation on their rice sectors. The policy effect of these adjustment measures is very positive. However, the marginal effect of some policies such as paddy diversions or set-asides seems to decrease, and reach a limit. Further liberalisation of the rice market will be difficult under current WTO and APEC modality, that is, unilateral liberalisation with peer pressure. More incentive alternatives are required to facilitate the smooth transition of the rice sector.

2 Concerns over whether the domestic supply of rice will become more stable after the opening up of the rice market, which are consistent with food security concerns, are the key factor affecting the attitude of policy makers and civilians in rice importing economies towards further liberalisation of the rice sector. It is thus important for rice-exporting countries to provide some kind of guaranteed rice supply commitments to the rice-importing countries. Such a commitment or agreement could

alleviate rice importers' worries about possible future uncertainty in the rice trade and also help with the implementation of a long-term rice production plan in these importing countries. APEC should act as coordinator of its major rice consumption and production members, to come up with an acceptable scheme for such a commitment.

3   APEC has to expressly understand and respect its members as to their means of accommodating to rice market liberalisation. That is to say, APEC should adopt a minimal- or non-intervention principle, out of respect for its members' choices on adopting domestic assistance measures. In this way, rice-importing countries will be allowed more flexibility in their choice of adjustment policies, which will also help the further liberalisation of their rice markets.

4   In responding to increasing demand domestically for high quality foods, Japan, Korea and Taiwan should promote the production of high quality rice. Through such market promotion, Japan, Korea and Taiwan could vouchsafe their rice farmers' income through the production of high quality rice, which would also lessen any impact from the rice importation.

5   APEC needs to recognise the importance of the environmental and social functions of rice cultivation in its member nations. APEC policy study groups should invest in and suggest ways of reconciling the liberalisation of the rice sector with traditional indigenous lifestyles that are centred around the cultivation of rice.

6   It is also suggested that APEC should form a study forum to provide a closer dialogue between rice consumers and rice producers; potential rice-importing countries including China, Indonesia and the Philippines should also be invited to participate in such talks.

REFERENCES

Council of Agriculture (Taiwan) (1997) *The Cross-Century Agricultural Development Program*, June.

Egaitsu, F. (1991) 'Income disparities between agricultural and industrial workers, and price-support policies for agricultural products', Tokyo: University of Tokyo Press.

Hayami, Y. and Godo, Y. (1995) 'Economics and politics of rice policy in Japan: A perspective on Uruguay Round', *Working Paper* no. 5341, NBER.

Japan Central Agricultural Association (1998) *Basic Outlook of Next Round WTO Agricultural Agreements: Choices and Strategies for the Special Treatment of Rice*, November (in Japanese).

Kako, T. (1997) 'Projections and policy implications of supply and demand of rice in South Korea, Taiwan, Japan and United States', *Final Report of International Scientific Research Program of Ministry of Education, Science and Culture, Japanese Government*, March.

Kako, T., Gemma, M. and Ito, S. (1997) 'Implications of the minimum access rice import on supply and demand balance of rice in Japan', *Agricultural Economics* 16: 193–204.

Lee, Yuan-ho (1996) 'Rice production and consumption, and rice policy in Taiwan', *Industry of Free China*, April.

Ministry of Agriculture, Forestry and Fisheries (Korea) (1996) *Korean Agriculture*.

Nagata, K., (1991) 'The maturation of the Japanese economy and the role of agriculture', Tokyo: University of Tokyo Press.

Park, Sang-Woo (1998) 'Agricultural policy adjustment in Korea with trade liberalization under the WTO', paper presented at the International Symposium on Agricultural Policy for the 21st Century, 15–16 June, Taipei, Taiwan.

Shih, J.T. and Fu, T.T. (1992) 'The adjustment of Taiwan's agricultural policy to trade liberalization', *Industry of Free China*.

Sombilla, M.A. and Hossain, M. (1998) 'Rice and food security in Asia', paper presented at Conference on the East Asia Food Security Issues in the 21st Century, 16–17 April, Taipei; Taiwan.

Tsujii, H. (1998) 'Changes in rice and agricultural policies in Japan after The GATT Uruguay Round agricultural trade liberalization', paper presented at International Symposium on Agricultural Policy for the 21st Century, 15–16 June, Taipei, Taiwan.

9 Ecotech at the heart of APEC
Capacity-building in the Asia Pacific

Andrew Elek and Hadi Soesastro

INTRODUCTION[1]

The financial crises of 1997 and 1998 reminded everyone in the Asia Pacific region that sustained economic development requires careful attention to its foundations. The institutions of several East Asian economies proved inadequate, especially in terms of financial sector management. These weaknesses, combined with great instability in international capital markets, led to a severe and widespread economic downturn in activity in the region, shaking confidence in the prospects for further rapid improvements in living standards as well as in the prospects for effective economic cooperation in the Asia Pacific.

Up to 1997, rapid growth was taken for granted and the success of Asia Pacific Economic Cooperation (APEC) was measured largely in terms of reducing barriers to trade and investment. When the economic environment changed, the process was not prepared for its new and very different challenge. It has become evident that economic cooperation needs to be far more broadly based than the interaction of regional governments to dismantle obstacles to trade and investment. Undoubtedly, all economies can benefit from further progress towards the Bogor 2010/2020 targets for free and open trade and investment. At the same time, there are many other opportunities for economic cooperation to strengthen the human, institutional and technological capacity for sustainable and rapid economic development.

The worst of the financial crisis appears to be over for most of the region, but much needs to be done to shore up the foundations for resumed rapid growth and to limit the risks of similar crises of confidence. Cooperation among Asia Pacific economies can help to accelerate and facilitate the costly, short-term effort needed to restructure and recapitalise severely damaged financial sectors as well as the multi-year human resource development and institutional capacity-building effort needed to create better managed and more robust financial sectors for the future. It has been recognised that these are essentially tasks of economic and technical cooperation among Asia Pacific governments, in either a regional or global context. This perception will help to convince the region's leaders that economic and technical cooperation is at the heart of the APEC process, rather than a distraction from the drive towards free and open trade and investment. But greater recognition of the importance of such cooperation will not guarantee satisfactory outcomes.

First, it will not be easy to develop a model of economic and technical cooperation that anticipates the massive changes expected in the political economy of the region. Some of the economies which currently have the greatest need for capacity-building will be among the most influential in the region by the middle of the twenty-first century. The experience of 1998 showed how hard it is to escape from an expectation that the currently richest and most powerful can insist on, and even consider themselves to be responsible for, imposing their opinions and conditions on those who need urgent short-term support. Second, there will always be excess demand for cooperative arrangements to enhance the potential of Asia Pacific economies for sustainable growth, so it will be important to have realistic expectations. Third, APEC will need to define its role in the 'market' for economic and technical cooperation. APEC leaders will need to build consensus on where the process may have comparative advantage: either in terms of identifying gaps to be filled, or in terms of direct or indirect involvement in filling such gaps.

In addition to these difficulties, APEC will also need to solve a self-imposed problem, generated during its first ten years. APEC set out with the broad aim of sustaining the momentum of successful economic growth in East Asia and the Pacific. However, the process has come to be dominated by the issue of trade and investment liberalisation and facilitation (TILF). Within this broad effort to reduce obstacles to trade and investment, pre-eminent attention has been given to traditional issues of trade liberalisation. There is a widespread perception that APEC is essentially a trading arrangement, albeit not a preferential one, with some other ancillary activities designated as Ecotech.[2]

An early focus on trade policy issues was appropriate, since the defence of an open and non-discriminatory multilateral trading system is the most important shared economic interest of Asia Pacific economies. But that need not mean the neglect of other ways to enhance the capacity of Asia Pacific economies for sustainable economic growth – it is a matter of setting and balancing different priorities for cooperation.

ECOTECH'S ENTRY INTO APEC

Initial resistance

Finding an appropriate balance among APEC's priorities has been hampered by the early resistance of some participants to including it in the agenda. As chair of APEC in 1994, Indonesia insisted that the APEC agenda should not be focused on trade and investment liberalisation alone. While Indonesia promotes and, in fact, gave birth to the Bogor goals of free and open trade and investment in the region, it has also made it clear that liberalisation must be accompanied by facilitation measures and 'development cooperation'. It saw these three aspects of economic cooperation as essential for the APEC enterprise. It was well understood by the developing members of APEC that the APEC process can help them sustain, and even accelerate, the already established momentum of trade and investment. It was not difficult for all APEC members to see that facilitation measures complement liberalisation. Yet, some members did not immediately appreciate the need for development cooperation.

Indonesia has articulated the importance of the acceptance of development cooperation as the 'third pillar' of APEC, in order to enhance the capacity of developing economies to take an active part in the process, including the liberalisation agenda. Its inclusion would demonstrate a kind of solidarity on the part of developed members towards developing members. Such solidarity would help assure both governments and the public in the developing members that they could participate confidently in APEC's liberalisation initiative.

The rather negative reactions to this proposition were perhaps motivated by a concern that the inclusion of development cooperation in APEC's agenda would weaken the liberalisation program that had just taken off. Comments were heard from such countries as the United States that APEC was all about trade and investment liberalisation. Other comments pointed to the problems of nurturing mutual respect if APEC members regrouped themselves as donors and clients as well as to the undesirability of turning APEC into yet another aid organisation.

Whatever the arguments were for rejecting the inclusion of development cooperation, it boiled down to a concern by some members that it would divert APEC's attention from trade and investment liberalisation. This was certainly a short sighted and narrow view of what APEC is all about. It failed to understand the need to accommodate the interests of all members. In that sense, a balanced agenda is essential to the ultimate objective of community-building in the region through APEC.

It needs to be recalled that economic cooperation was the main reason for Ministers to come to the inaugural meeting in Canberra in 1989. In that meeting the ministers identified broad areas of cooperation, including economic studies, trade liberalisation, investment, technology transfer and human resources development, and sectoral cooperation as the basis for the development of APEC's work program. The work program, which has been translated into a set of work projects, is meant to:

- produce tangible benefits;
- progress beyond agreement on general principles;
- develop a habit of cooperation among such diverse members; and
- demonstrate that an Asia Pacific community can be nurtured.

Initially, seven work projects were designated and work began following the second Ministerial Meeting in Singapore in 1990. Three more work projects were added a year later at the third meeting in Seoul. The number of sub-projects under those work projects soon proliferated. By the time development cooperation was accepted as APEC's third pillar in the 1994 Bogor Declaration, there were about 200 projects.

In Osaka in 1995, the term 'development cooperation' was officially changed to 'economic and technical cooperation'. The Osaka Action Agenda noted that facilitation and liberalisation were indivisible components of work towards the Bogor vision of free and open trade and investment. On the other hand, it contained an Ecotech agenda which was quite clearly identified as parallel to, but separate from the TILF agenda.

Three additional broad Ecotech work projects were introduced, so that the Ecotech agenda now covers thirteen areas (broad work projects) of economic and technical cooperation, namely: trade and investment data, trade promotion, industrial science and technology, human resources development, regional energy cooperation, marine resources conservation, fisheries, telecommunications, transportation, tourism, small and medium enterprises (SME), economic infrastructure, and agricultural technology.

The Osaka Action Agenda also proposed three essential elements in the implementation of Ecotech: the development of common policy concepts, collective action, and policy dialogue in individual areas. It also defined the modality of cooperation, which emphasised a departure from the conventional donor–recipient relationship, consistency with market mechanisms, and encouragement of private sector participation.

By the time of the meeting in Manila in 1996, the work projects had further proliferated to a total of 320. The largest number of work projects was in human resources development (86), followed by energy (43), industrial science and technology (41), and agricultural technology (35). These numbers, however, did not give any indication of what was going on in each of the thirteen areas and of the priorities for APEC: the many projects were inherited from a largely incoherent process. Yamazawa (1997) observed that a typical Ecotech activity was a 'pet project' proposed and coordinated by one particular APEC member, financed mainly by the proponent, and partly supported by APEC's Central Fund. A closer examination of the work projects showed that they were mostly seminars, studies, or information gathering. Such activities have their value, but they can be undertaken (perhaps more efficiently) by public or private agencies outside APEC. Yamazawa explained this poor performance as resulting from a lack of practical guidelines which permitted the dominance of pet projects of individual members and from a failure to involve conventional donor and multilateral aid agencies.

Yamazawa argued that Japan's Partners for Progress (PFP) proposal[3] was meant to boost Ecotech beyond studies and seminars by formulating an overall program, providing some seed money (¥10 billion) and establishing an agency within APEC to administer it. This proposal failed to gain acceptance and eventually it was watered down to an initiative that involved technical cooperation in improving administrative capability and transferring technology in just three specific areas of TILF (standards and conformance, intellectual property rights, and competition policy).

The 1996 Manila Declaration

A more serious effort to provide a conceptual and operational framework for economic and technical cooperation and to achieve a new consensus on the balance of APEC's activities began in 1996. Under Philippines leadership, APEC leaders adopted the Manila Declaration on an Asia Pacific Economic Cooperation Framework for Strengthening Economic Cooperation and Development. That declaration set out the objectives, guiding principles and priorities for promoting economic and technical cooperation, defining a model of cooperation based genuinely on mutual respect as well as mutual benefit. The nature of cooperation promoted by APEC is different from 'foreign aid'; that is, transfers of funds from donors to clients, often conditional on some surrender of political sovereignty. Instead, the new model seeks to take advantage of the enormous scope for cooperation by sharing the region's richly diverse resources of information, experience, expertise and technology for the benefit all Asia Pacific economies.

The Manila Declaration stipulated that Ecotech should be goal-oriented with explicit objectives, milestones and performance criteria. Furthermore, it could combine government actions, private sector projects and joint public–private activities, with the public sector playing a direct or indirect role in creating an enabling environment for private sector initiatives. Ecotech should also draw on voluntary contributions commensurate with member economies' capabilities, and generate direct and broadly shared benefits among APEC member economies to reduce economic disparities in the region. The six priority areas identified for joint cooperative activities to be promoted by APEC were to:

1   develop human capital;
2   develop stable, safe and efficient capital markets;
3   strengthen economic infrastructure;
4   harness technologies for the future;
5   safeguard the quality of life through environmentally sound growth; and
6   develop and strengthen the dynamism of small and medium enterprises.

Recent developments and dilemmas

At present, there are 274 ongoing Ecotech projects. An Ecotech sub-committee of the APEC SOM was established in 1997, with the aim of coordinating and managing Ecotech to ensure focused outcomes. The committee has produced a set of principles and, in reviewing proposals, will consider those that have value added. The committee has proposed that specific members of APEC be designated to act as coordinator for each of the six priority areas. This is a significant development which could result in greater coherence in the Ecotech agenda. In Vancouver in 1997, infrastructure was elevated to the attention of the leaders. In Kuala Lumpur in 1998, human resources (skills) development and industrial science and technology were brought to the highest level of policy. It remains to be seen whether these initiatives will bring concrete results in the not too distant future.

In their 1997 Vancouver Declaration, Connecting the APEC Community, APEC leaders have committed themselves to a balanced agenda and pointed to the indivisibility of the different pillars of the APEC agenda. Despite the increased attention to Ecotech, more needs to be done to develop a coherent and integrated view of the nature of economic and technical cooperation and its place in the overall APEC process.

As discussed in this chapter, there have been constructive moves, by the business/private sector as well as by governments, to turn that conceptual framework into a new operational model of development cooperation. Several hundred activities have been proposed by APEC committees and working groups, mostly involving the exchange of information and expertise. Some of these are already under way, with some being supported by the private sector as well as by existing development agencies. Nevertheless, the total number of potential activities is growing more rapidly than the small number being implemented. A sense of frustration and several misunderstandings persist.

One set of problems is that there are widely varying and incompatible expectations about the nature of the cooperative activities which could be promoted collectively by APEC governments and about how these could be financed and implemented. That is being compounded by an inadequate appreciation of the current and potential role of existing agencies, such as the Asian Development Bank (ADB), in promoting the new ideas for economic and technical cooperation emerging from the APEC process.

In that context, Morrison (1997) suggested that APEC members should view Ecotech broadly as a process by which they work together to develop the entire region in mutually agreed ways. It is in this sense that the activity is a collective action. Morrison proposed that the modality of cooperation in the Ecotech area be developed along the modality adopted for TILF. Work programs should primarily be national ones. Individual member economies should make and compare their own national action plans for economic and technical cooperation to achieve regional goals (such as efficient regional transportation networks, world-class telecommunication links, human resources for economic growth, and protection of the regional environment). APEC governments, as a group, would then seek to supplement and strengthen these individual efforts by sharing information and experience as well as concerting national efforts and formulating joint endeavours which would involve the private sectors as well as the existing development agencies of APEC economies. Such a sense of strategy has yet to emerge.

Ecotech versus TILF?

A further serious problem for the APEC process is the unduly sharp dichotomy which has come to be drawn between work to promote TILF and other forms of cooperation. Moreover, economic and technical cooperation activities are being seen as residual and not part of the drive towards free and open trade and investment. That is an incorrect perception, which underestimates the potential contribution of economic and technical cooperation to all of APEC's efforts to enhance the capacity for sustainable economic growth, including through trade and investment policy reforms.

The current perception of Ecotech as an alternative to TILF (and even as a competitor) leads to unhelpful debates about their relative importance. The developing economies in APEC believe, correctly, that more open international trade and investment is just one of several ingredients for sustained growth. Accordingly, they are pressing to move the emphasis away from TILF. At the same time, the currently more wealthy APEC economies perceive less benefit to themselves from activities other than TILF. There is a risk that reluctant support for economic and technical cooperation will be seen as the 'price' the currently more developed economies have to pay to persuade the others to pursue trade and investment policy reforms. Such perceptions make it difficult to distinguish Ecotech from old-style 'foreign aid'. They also tend to erode mutual respect and weaken APEC's ability to promote a sense of community in the diverse Asia Pacific.

If Ecotech and TILF continue to be seen as separate strands of the APEC process, it will be hard to build a sense of shared economic interests and mutual respect. Unless Ecotech is understood to be an essential ingredient of TILF as well as of other cooperative activities, TILF can be too easily viewed as an adversarial negotiating process, rather than a joint cooperative effort with all-round benefits. The frustrating experience with early 'voluntary' sectoral liberalisation (EVSL) in 1998 indicated a drift towards a perception that trade policy reforms are 'concessions' Asia Pacific governments must make to preserve the credibility of the APEC process. Such a drift will rapidly erode APEC's potential contribution towards more open global trade and investment. As a voluntary process of cooperation, APEC has no comparative advantage over the WTO as a forum for traditional trade negotiations.

AN INTEGRAL APPROACH: ECOTECH AT THE HEART OF APEC

For these reasons, this chapter advocates an integrated view of the APEC process. As expressed in the 1991 Seoul APEC Declaration, the primary objective of Asia Pacific economic cooperation is:

> to sustain the growth and development of the region for the common good of its peoples and, in this way, to contribute to the growth and development of the world economy. (APEC 1991, Clause 1(a))

In that context, all the cooperative activities promoted by APEC can be seen as ways to strengthen the capacity of Asia Pacific economies to reach their full potential for sustainable economic growth.

The challenge is to enhance the capacity of all Asia Pacific economies to increase their productive resources and to allocate them in an increasingly efficient and sustainable way. Cooperation among APEC economies can help by sharing the information, experience, expertise and technology needed to design and administer a progressively more efficient set of economic policies to achieve these ends. Cooperation which improves the ability of Asia Pacific governments to reduce impediments to trade and investment through unilateral or coordinated reforms (that is, TILF) is just one important part of this overall cooperative effort.

As set out in this chapter, there are many potential cooperative arrangements among APEC governments and/or their private sectors that can help all Asia Pacific economies enhance their institutional and technological capacity. Some of these cooperative arrangements will be more directly related to international economic policy, while others will relate more to enhancing the economic environment, including the policy framework within individual Asia Pacific economies. However, progress on both fronts is complementary.

It is widely recognised that, as economies become increasingly interdependent, the evolution of policies to manage and strengthen domestic economies will have increasingly significant indirect effects on the costs and risks of international and domestic economic transactions. Divergent ways of regulating domestic economic activity tend to increase the impediments to international commerce. Conversely, cooperative activities among Asia Pacific economies in all types of institution-building can reduce the costs and risks of international trade and investment. Cooperative policy development can improve the capacity of Asia Pacific governments to anticipate the international implications of the way all of their policies are made and administered. Enhanced communications among the region's policy makers should also lead towards more compatible and, in some cases, more convergent approaches to economic management in all Asia Pacific economies. All such cooperative activities will contribute, more or less directly, to TILF.

Turning to TILF itself, efforts to reduce impediments to international economic transactions involve several stages:

1   to identify particular impediments (or sets of impediments);
2   to identify policy measures which cause these impediments;
3   to understand the policy objectives being pursued by these policy measures;
4   to estimate the effects of these policy measures on economies; particularly on the economies which impose these measures;
5   to identify alternative policy combinations which can achieve the same policy objectives more efficiently, while reducing impediments to international economic transactions;

6   to develop the expertise and institutional capacity to implement alternative policy options; and
7   to persuade Asia Pacific governments to adopt such alternative policy combinations.

APEC participants can undertake each of these steps individually. In practice, TILF was well under way before APEC was established. However, economic and technical cooperation among Asia Pacific economies can help at each of these stages. In reality, much of APEC's potential contribution to achieving free and open trade and investment is through cooperative policy development and technical cooperation.

Some impediments, such as tariffs, are deliberate policy measures which are intended to raise the cost of international economic transactions relative to comparable domestic transactions. In many other cases, impediments may be due simply to a lack of awareness of the costs (or risks) they impose, or a lack of attention to reducing or eliminating them.

For example, differences in commercial regulations (such as disclosure or auditing requirements) may be due to historical factors in various economies, but can add to the costs and risks of international commerce, without any direct intention of doing so. Once the nature and effects of such differences are understood, it is usually possible to find ways of amending regulations or procedures to reduce needless differences and to make them more transparent and less arbitrary. In the case of costly international transport or telecommunications links, it is often possible for trading partners to identify the policies (or absence of them) which make it difficult to link up the transport and telecommunications networks of different economies. One early form of practical technical cooperation in APEC has been to harmonise the procedures for gathering and processing customs information, thus reducing the cost of international trade. Work is also under way to build the institutional capacity needed for a successful program of mutual recognition of product and process standards.

More generally, economic and technical cooperation can encourage, then enable, Asia Pacific governments to reform policies which currently impede trade and investment. Sharing the policy-making experience of Asia Pacific economies and sharing the expertise needed to estimate the effects of alternative policy options can help change perceptions about the merits of policies. Clearer insight into the effects of policy instruments and alternative ways to achieve policy objectives can encourage governments to reduce impediments through voluntary unilateral policy reforms, including unilateral trade liberalisation.

In many cases, economic and technical cooperation taking place in APEC committees and working groups is already helping to change perceptions. That is leading to continuing improvements in the scope and depth of Individual Action Plans (IAPs) to dismantle impediments to international economic transactions. Further economic cooperation in the form of coordinated enhancement of IAPs, consistent with the principles of the Osaka Action Agenda, can also assist Asia Pacific governments to overcome short-term resistance to change within each of their economies.

Economic and technical cooperation will not always prove sufficient to change perceptions. If certain border barriers continue to be perceived as of net political benefit to particular governments, they will not reduce them voluntarily. They may do so through negotiations, but it does not follow that APEC is an appropriate forum for such negotiations.

As a voluntary process of cooperation, APEC is not likely to provide an effective framework for negotiating and enforcing involuntary reforms of trade and investment policies. Moreover, if reforms are regarded as 'concessions' to others, it is difficult to negotiate lower border barriers to trade or investment in line with the principle of open regionalism. There will be continual pressure to deny the benefit of reforms to those not involved in the negotiations. Therefore, if negotiations are required to agree on trade or investment policy reforms, it is more sensible to conduct these negotiations in the WTO where:

- all significant non-APEC trading partners are automatically involved;
- the framework and procedures for negotiations are well established;
- there are agreed procedures, including dispute settlement procedures, for monitoring and enforcing adherence to agreements.[4]

Against this background, it is somewhat artificial to try to distinguish TILF from Ecotech. Most opportunities for cooperation among Asia Pacific economies to promote free and open trade and investment are, in practice, opportunities for economic and technical cooperation. It may be more useful to separate APEC's facilitation and liberalisation efforts into two components; namely: TILF which is economic and technical cooperation and TILF which is the negotiation of involuntary trade or investment liberalisation. For the latter type of TILF, the time has come for APEC to adopt a more efficient strategy.

Rather than attempting to mimic WTO negotiations within the region, it would be preferable to accept that the negotiation of involuntary reforms should be left to the WTO. At the same time, there is considerable scope for economic and technical cooperation among APEC governments to prepare the ground for successful WTO outcomes. Part of that task is to promote a progressively more accurate perception of the economy-wide benefits of what are still regarded as 'concessions'; the other is to exercise joint leadership in the WTO to set the principles, priorities and objectives of future WTO negotiations.

To sum up, all cooperative activities promoted by APEC can be seen as enhancing the capacity of participants to devise and adopt more efficient and compatible policies for economic management and to enhance their capacity to administer them. Such cooperation for capacity-building can serve to advance all the objectives which have been set out in the Seoul, Bogor and Manila declarations of APEC.

The APEC process provides a new means of interaction among Asia Pacific political leaders and officials which can lead to innovative ideas and opportunities for cooperative policy development and technical cooperation. That does not mean that APEC should be seen simply as one more development cooperation agency, alongside the many which already exist. There is no project or program for enhancing the capacity of Asia Pacific economies for sustainable growth which could not, in principle, be financed and managed by the ADB, by various UN agencies, by the development agencies of many individual APEC participants or by the private sector.

Just as APEC should make use of and complement the WTO, not imitate it, APEC should motivate and steer the extensive development cooperation effort already under way, rather than compete with it. It follows that APEC should not try to assess its contribution to capacity-building in Asia Pacific economies in terms of projects directly financed or managed by any new APEC mechanism, such as APEC-funded dams, bridges or training institutes – that would certainly not be in line with comparative advantage. Nor should APEC seek to measure progress in terms of the additional amounts contributed to APEC by its member governments. At a time of tight budget constraints and 'aid fatigue', such funds would, most likely, be simply diverted from resources of other development agencies.

Compared with the business sector or Asia Pacific governments, the APEC process has, and is always likely to have, very modest funds at its direct disposal. These can be used to fund, at most, a small proportion of the many economic and technical cooperation opportunities it has already identified. This need not imply a passive role for APEC, but a serious effort to concentrate on its comparative advantage and to complement the work of others.

Having built up new channels for region-wide communications, APEC leaders and officials do have a comparative advantage in designing options for economic and technical cooperation which can draw on information, experience, expertise and technology from throughout the region and make it available widely to many Asia Pacific economies. The next challenge is to develop a strategy for using these ideas as a catalyst for cooperation; APEC leaders should be able to evoke a positive response to such new ideas from the business/private sector and from Asia Pacific governments. Such a strategy for encouraging their involvement, advocated in this chapter, can be summarised as identifying carefully selected regional public goods to create an environment in which:

- more of the vast pool of private savings being generated within the region is steered, through sensible policies and market signals, into capacity-building investments to boost the growth potential of Asia Pacific economies; and

- the activities of all existing, as well as any new, government-sponsored programs of development cooperation come to be increasingly consistent with the shared objectives and guiding principles of a new Asia Pacific model of development cooperation.

The following sections explain how economic and technical cooperation among Asia Pacific economies is already contributing to enhancing their capacity for sustained growth and development, helping to:

- strengthen domestic and international financial markets;
- facilitate trade and investment;
- liberalise traditional border barriers to trade;
- defend and strengthen the multilateral trading system;
- develop the capacity of economic infrastructure;
- promote human resource development; and
- enhance technological capacity.

In continuing all of these efforts, it will be essential to distinguish what the APEC process itself can be expected to contribute, either directly through its committees and working groups or its own limited budget, or in terms of mobilising and/or redirecting the resources of the private sector and existing development agencies to promote these objectives.

STRENGTHENING FINANCIAL SECTORS

APEC was slow to react as the financial crisis deepened dramatically soon after Asia Pacific leaders met in Vancouver in late 1997. Nevertheless, by November 1998, there was a worthwhile set of initiatives for economic and technical cooperation to help overcome the crisis. Economic activity has begun to recover in most of the economies worst affected, but there is plenty of scope for further economic and technical cooperation to strengthen the recovery and to lessen the probability of future financial crises.

Restoring confidence – policy development

In the aftermath of the crisis, APEC leaders have agreed to adopt internationally recognised principles for financial sector management and supervision. That will help provide a framework for sounder financial management, but further cooperative policy development is needed. Experience in many economies has shown that it is not sufficient to rely on fixed parameters to avert problems. There will be continuing scope to exchange information and experience with gradually more sophisticated and flexible forms of financial risk management.

An important challenge for cooperative policy development by APEC governments is to build the foundations for coping with international financial movements. The Bogor objective of free and open trade and investment cannot be realised without a high degree of capital mobility. On the other hand, the experience of 1997 and 1998 demonstrated that the policy framework and/or the institutional capacity of several Asia Pacific economies was not yet able to manage international capital movements, particularly short-term movements.

There is widespread agreement that 'pegged' exchange rates contributed substantially to the crises, by creating unsustainable expectations of exchange rate stability. Some economies may follow the Hong Kong precedent of a permanently fixed exchange rate, which would need to be backed by the expertise to manage currency board type arrangements and to adapt all other aspects of macroeconomic management to the lack of any exchange rate flexibility. More Asia Pacific economies are likely to adopt freely floating exchange rates; these will require strong demand management and an adequate international coordination of macroeconomic policies to avoid erratic fluctuations of exchange rates. Helping to put effective macroeconomic management into practice is one of many important opportunities for ongoing economic cooperation and cooperative policy development among Asia Pacific economies; APEC finance ministers and officials have already initiated cooperative arrangements for sharing information about macroeconomic developments.

Strengthening institutions – technical cooperation

An institution-building effort is needed to back up understandings on parameters and methods for financial sector risk management. A correspondingly significant program of technical cooperation can help to strengthen institutional capacity and to train the people who are going to make these systems work, both as parts of the regulatory or policy-making system and as part of the private sector institutions which will implement the new financial systems of the Asia Pacific region.

The types of information needed and the basis for decision making will be very different in the financial systems of the future. A massive human resource development program is needed; firstly to pool the wide range of experience and expertise available in the Asia Pacific; secondly to provide appropriate training for those directly involved in the financial sector and for those who supervise them.[5]

Such training efforts need not be financed by APEC itself. The ADB has already lent money to support reform and restructuring of financial systems – it and the development cooperation agencies of APEC governments can be urged to do more along these lines. Coordination among APEC governments can increase the effectiveness of training programs by encouraging region-wide programs which can make the best expertise in the region available to all economies which are interested in strengthening their financial sectors. The establishment of an IMF Regional Training Institute in Singapore is a positive example.

Restructuring financial sectors

APEC governments can also speed up the process of rescheduling or writing off the very substantial amounts of private debt which certainly cannot be serviced at anything like current exchange rates. A very large amount of capital will be needed to recapitalise the reformed and strengthened next generation of financial institutions – most estimates of the cost of 'working out' from the current debt crises are over 20 per cent of the GDP of the economies most heavily affected. The private sector will make a direct contribution by rescheduling or writing off some debt, but many of the funds will need to be raised by governments.

In late 1998, the Japanese Government announced a US$30 billion fund to support economic recovery. This was followed, in Kuala Lumpur, by an initiative announced by the United States and Japan, in conjunction with the World Bank and the ADB, to contribute a further US$10 billion. These funds have the potential to accelerate the restructuring of corporate debt and the recapitalisation of the region's banks, both of which are unavoidable and urgent in restoring growth and the return of investor confidence.

Strengthening international capital markets

In the wake of the events of 1997–8, there is already broad agreement on the need for a fundamental reassessment of the nature and mandate of international institutions to help prevent a recurrence of such problems. The debate has moved beyond whether international capital markets are regulated. It is becoming evident that all markets, domestic and international, are regulated; the practical issue is the nature of regulation and the means of administering them while continuing to strive to improve their effectiveness.[6] As noted earlier, unsustainable exchange rate regimes were partly to blame for the crisis, by encouraging excess borrowing on short-term global capital markets. But the problem of excessive lending also needs to be addressed.

It is beyond the scope of this chapter to canvass specific proposals for improving international capital markets.[7] Nor is it up to APEC governments alone to resolve the problem; these are global issues which are most efficiently addressed by global understandings and institutions, but APEC governments can cooperate to help ensure timely, constructive reforms. International consultations on the future international financial architecture will continue for several years. Close consultations among APEC governments can help the nature of any new international institutions, and the regulation of international capital markets reflects the needs and interests of developing, as well as the already developed, economies.

FACILITATING TRADE AND INVESTMENT

Since its establishment in 1989, APEC has sought to promote closer and mutually beneficial economic integration in the Asia Pacific, consistent with the overriding interest of all participating economies in a rules-based multilateral trading system. The Osaka Action Agenda sets out the very broad scope of the challenge of free and open trade and investment by no later than 2020 – thus setting the agenda for a comprehensive drive to facilitate trade and investment by dismantling obstacles to trade and investment. As described below, economic and technical cooperation, in the sense of pooling the region's diverse resources of information, experience, expertise and technology, is an essential ingredient of all aspects of facilitation, including the liberalisation of border barriers to trade and investment.

Capacity-building and facilitation

The experience of 1997 and 1998 has demonstrated the need to ensure that the foundation of institutions and the way they are managed keeps pace with the challenges of rapid economic growth and structural change. Strengthening and maintaining these foundations requires much more than a response to market signals. Individual economic agents cannot be expected to meet the needs for institution-building and human resource development, which extend well beyond the financial sector.

Massive investment is needed in what are essentially public goods; some of them international public goods. Individual businesses cannot be expected to set up effective public regulatory institutions to meet economy-wide needs for education and training. Similarly, it will not always be efficient for Asia Pacific governments to design and administer such institutions or human resource development programs in isolation. In many cases, international economic cooperation can realise economies of scope; in some cases cooperation among governments may prove to be essential to implement options for reducing impediments to international economic transactions.

There should be scope to create mechanisms for new forms of economic cooperation among Asia Pacific governments and new opportunities for pooling the resources and capabilities of existing development cooperation agencies to promote institution-building and human resource development. As discussed below, there are very positive signs that the business/private sector is willing to become involved, collectively, in the provision of some of these international public goods.

Facilitating international trade and investment by reducing transactions costs usually involves institution-building in the economies which wish to encourage closer economic integration and the establishment of effective and confident communications among parallel institutions in these economies. As illustrated by the following examples, economic and technical cooperation to share and disseminate the region's best available administrative and technical practices, is an efficient way to promote such capacity-building.

Harmonisation of customs procedures

APEC governments are already well on the way to implementing a harmonised approach for the collection, electronic transmission and processing of customs information. This approach promises very significant economic returns, not only by reducing costs and delays in processing, but also by reducing the need for new investment in infrastructure at ports and airports, thus allowing existing facilities to operate more efficiently. Implementing the new system has been, essentially, an exercise in economic and technical cooperation. The policy development work of APEC working groups has led to the design and acceptance of new parameters and software for processing the vast amounts of data handled daily. That was followed by technical cooperation to help Asia Pacific governments to develop the capacity to install, test and operate the new system. Such cooperation represents the supply of an international public good with mutual benefits, which can only be created by cooperation by several governments.

APEC-wide work has concentrated on cargo-handling, but some APEC governments have also cooperated to design and install more efficient systems for the issue and processing of business travel visas, lowering transaction costs for business people and reducing congestion at airports. 'APEC channels' are appearing in more and more customs halls and, through further technical cooperation, the experiment is likely to spread to much of the region in the next few years.

Mutual recognition of standards

Free and open trade among any group of economies requires acceptance of the principle of 'tested once, tested everywhere'. That need not rely on the creation of new, let alone uniform, product and process standards. Commercial realities are driving producers to conform to existing globally widespread standards (such as ISO standards) and placing pressure on governments to develop credible means of monitoring conformance with their national standards for quality, performance and environmental or other safeguards.

The response to these pressures is already laying the groundwork for a potentially comprehensive region-wide agreement on mutual recognition of product and process standards. For such a system to operate sustainably and efficiently, without excessive need to resort to litigation, products users will need to have a high degree of confidence in the ability and integrity of all the institutions in the region that monitor compliance with standards. Such confidence requires, in turn, a high degree of mutual respect and mutual trust among the network of parallel institutions.

Establishing and sustaining such trust needs both policy development and technical cooperation. The legislative frameworks need to be adequate, and internationally accepted as being adequate, for effective monitoring of standards. Mutual confidence in the capacity to use such regulatory powers depends on well-trained staff. This is an ongoing technical cooperation challenge as those trained move to, or are promoted to, other occupations.

Policy development and technical cooperation

The above are just two examples of the thousands of opportunities for cooperation among APEC governments to design compatible approaches to a wide range of commercial regulatory issues. Taking up such opportunities is a technically difficult challenge. A complex set of changes to a very wide range of domestic commercial policies is required to achieve anything like free trade in services, for example, by moving towards full national treatment of international investment, which is often an essential vehicle for trade in services.[8]

Dealing with these issues is, once again, essentially a matter of cooperative policy development backed up by ongoing technical cooperation. For example, a thoughtful evolutionary approach will be essential to develop competition policies within economies, let alone to deal with their international implications. Many aspects of competition policy, of which competition laws or 'anti-trust' laws are just one component, will need to be dealt with internationally. There is much more to be done than attempting to 'deal with' competition policy in the WTO, especially since the WTO deals with government actions, while many competition policy issues relate to private actions. As noted in PECC (1996a), a much clearer understanding of the linkages between trade and many aspects of competition policy is essential, starting with building consensus on the objectives of competition policy and some basic guiding principles for its evolution.[9]

More generally, a close examination of issues of trade in services and international investment demonstrates the importance of working consistently to address the current problems that have been identified as business priorities. These problems go well beyond cross-border barriers; they are inherent in international business due to interacting sets of legislation and regulations in each economy including competition policy, company laws and tax laws. It may prove useful to adopt a general evolutionary approach to dealing with an increasing range of issues which used to be regarded as purely 'domestic', in order to facilitate international economic transactions while respecting the autonomy of all governments over their policies. The first steps involved are to promote transparency and then to foster mutual understanding.

Mutual understanding of the issues and of the motives of current policies, once achieved, can lead to the mutual respect needed for governments to agree on objectives and non-binding guiding principles or norms for various aspects of economic or commercial policies. These involve the pooling of the region's resources of information, experience and expertise; it is yet another challenge for cooperative policy development.

Efficient policy norms or guiding principles for the many aspects of commercial policy are likely to incorporate, in each case, the fundamental concepts of transparency, non-discrimination and national treatment. Once desirable region-wide norms are agreed, they can then be the basis for:

- individual governments to use such principles, if they wish, in the ongoing reform of their domestic policies;
- mutual recognition; or
- where considered efficient and desirable, some convergence or harmonisation of approaches.

Such an evolutionary approach is already being applied by APEC to facilitate trade and investment by improving the efficiency of customs procedures and by its work on product and process standards and conformance. A similar approach can also be used to encourage the acceptance of shared principles for the conduct of other commercial policy.

Promoting gradually more compatible and potentially convergent approaches to a wide range of commercial policies and regulations will need extensive cooperative policy development. That challenge is already being tackled by APEC's working groups. They can draw on the international cooperative policy development work of others including the Pacific Economic Cooperation Council (PECC). They, in turn can draw on research and experience from the rest of the world, for example by the OECD, adapting it to the realities of a diverse Asia Pacific.

Once new principles and policies are accepted by some Asia Pacific economies, they will need to be backed by efforts to strengthen relevant institutional capacity, then by ongoing training. Communications among APEC leaders can create the opportunities for region-wide training efforts. Such cooperative activities can capture economies of scale and scope as well as create a sense of mutual respect and mutual trust among the region's administrators. This is essential for such new policies and institutions to be effective in terms of facilitating international trade and investment.

The preceding examples of options for facilitating trade and investment demonstrate that their implementation relies on building the capacity of institutions and strengthening human resources through economic and technical cooperation. In other words, Ecotech is an essential ingredient of, not an alternative to, facilitation. As discussed below, Ecotech is also an essential ingredient of serious efforts to promote trade liberalisation by APEC governments.

TRADE LIBERALISATION

Cooperative policy development work by officials, particularly in the Committee for Trade and Investment (CTI), has underpinned APEC's progress towards trade liberalisation to date and will be needed to sustain progress. The Bogor Declaration and its vision for free and open trade and investment would have remained no more than a vision in the absence of valuable work by the CTI and senior officials to define the guiding principles of tangible progress towards dismantling border barriers, consistent with the principles of open regionalism and voluntary cooperation. The concepts of concerted unilateral liberalisation and voluntary collective action to facilitate trade and investment were developed jointly through consensus-building among APEC officials, then endorsed by Ministers in the 1995 Osaka Action Agenda. That was followed by intensive work to draw up Individual Action Plans for market opening and deregulation as set out in the Manila Action Plan for APEC and subsequently updated.

Trade liberalisation is technically easy to implement – unlike the extensive capacity-building needed for facilitation, it does not require much technical expertise to abolish or change tariffs and non-tariff barriers to trade. On the other hand, concerted unilateral liberalisation relies on APEC governments continuing to perceive that further voluntary liberalisation is in their self-interest. The challenge for cooperative policy development and analysis is to build, then to sustain, the political support for liberalisation, by demonstrating the advantages of 'opening to the outside world' and of doing so in concert with other APEC participants.

Enhancing political support for trade liberalisation

The greatest gains from liberalisation flow to those undertaking the reforms. That has been demonstrated by the experience of recent decades. In the three decades from 1965 to 1995, those economies which have opened their economies to international competition and taken advantage of opportunities to specialise in line with their evolving comparative advantage spectacularly outperformed those which sought to follow an inward-looking strategy concentrating on import substitution and sheltered domestic markets. That remains true despite the very severe setbacks of 1997 and 1998. However, the crisis has shaken confidence about the long-term gains from further market opening and strengthened the hand of protectionists in uncompetitive sectors who would lose from further liberalisation.

In these circumstances, it would be useful for APEC officials to commission economic analysis which puts the long-term net gains of liberalisation into perspective, under different assumptions about the length and severity of the current downturn. Moreover, the increased questioning of the costs of exposure to global competition points to the ongoing need for economic and technical cooperation among Asia Pacific economies to share their experience in liberalisation, particularly the experience of coping with the short-term strains of adjustment to wider competition in a somewhat unpredictable international economic environment.

Future voluntary liberalisation can also be promoted by sharing information and experience gained, either in terms of the benefits of past policy reforms, or the long-term problems of inefficiency caused by decisions to shield particular sectors from competition. The region-wide dissemination of expertise and technology can also foster mutual trust and confidence that the drive towards free and open trade and investment is designed to enhance, not undermine, the capacity of emerging economies to upgrade their technological capability.

Political support for concerted unilateral liberalisation can also be enhanced by confidence that all APEC governments are, or remain, committed to progressive elimination of border barriers to trade, since 'home economy' gains from liberalisation can be magnified if an economy's main trading partners are also opening their markets. Correspondingly, both forms of gain will be forgone if the failure of some APEC participants to meet their commitments induces other governments to follow suit by slowing down, or turning away from, liberalisation. Moreover, arguments against liberalisation are easier to counter if other APEC governments are also reducing the protection given to their producers.

Economic cooperation among APEC participants to sponsor objective and independent assessment of progress is vital to sustain region-wide confidence in continuing commitment to the process of concerted unilateral liberalisation. Independent studies by PECC served to lay the foundation for concerted unilateral liberalisation. One of these (PECC 1995a) documented the substantial progress most Asia Pacific economies had already made in terms of unilateral liberalisation even before their Bogor commitment, providing confidence that such a trend could be expected to continue, especially if all APEC governments acted in concert. The other study (PECC 1995b) documented the barriers that remain, especially in terms of border barriers to trade, setting a basis for monitoring progress. A subsequent (PECC 1996b) analysis of the Manila Action Plan for APEC indicated that, at that time, individual APEC economies were well on track towards their Bogor goals and that their actual, or committed, tariff reductions were mostly faster or deeper than their commitments under the Uruguay Round.

On the other hand, there have been only very modest new commitments to trade liberalisation since then. As Bogor target dates loom closer and the sectors that remain to be tackled are increasingly sensitive, it is becoming more evident that voluntary cooperation alone will not achieve free and open trade and investment by 2010/2020. Nor does the 1998 experience with EVSL provide any grounds for confidence about the prospects for WTO-style negotiations among APEC governments.

Dealing with sensitive sectors

An urgent challenge for cooperative policy development among APEC governments is to develop a credible strategy for sustained progress towards dismantling traditional border barriers to trade, not just in the region, but globally.

Having learnt the lessons of 1998, it would not be helpful for APEC simply to try even harder to convert itself into a negotiating forum. As already emphasised, a voluntary process of economic cooperation has no comparative advantage over the WTO in terms of negotiations in which trade liberalisation is regarded as a 'concession' to others. Any attempt to change the basic principles of APEC, to make it a treaty-based process which could enforce reforms, would place the 2010/2020 targets for trade liberalisation well beyond reach.

A possible compromise might be to seek a restructuring of APEC so that while most cooperative arrangements and activities remained voluntary, traditional trade liberalisation would no longer be expected to be voluntary. Instead, trade liberalisation within APEC would proceed by means of negotiating binding commitments. Even if that were acceptable to all participants (which is doubtful) and could be agreed quickly (also doubtful), it would still not change APEC's lack of comparative advantage over WTO-based negotiations on border barriers to trade. More importantly, such an attempt would also be likely to undercut any current comparative advantage in terms of other options to facilitate trade and investment.

As demonstrated by earlier examples, facilitating trade and investment essentially involves a patient search for more compatible and/or convergent approaches to often complex matters of commercial policy. Moreover, it is more than a matter of adopting new regulations; it also requires the capacity to implement them and the willingness to do so in good faith. Cooperative arrangements for mutual recognition of standards or harmonised customs procedures will not deliver anything like their potential benefit if there is frequent need for litigation about the way these arrangements are being implemented. Sustained progress in terms of facilitation to reduce many of the costs and risks of international commerce requires a high degree of mutual respect and mutual trust. These crucial ingredients cannot be expected to be nurtured in the shadow of high profile negotiations and disagreements about a few traditional trade barriers.

Changing perceptions

A more effective strategy is to accept that there are some sectors, such as parts of agriculture and some labour-intensive manufacturing in different Asia Pacific economies, where protection has become deeply entrenched. In most of these cases, governments are aware of the long-term advantages of dismantling protection, both to their own economies and the credibility of their commitment to APEC, but these potential gains are perceived to be outweighed by the short-term political risks of reform. In these cases, there is some room for changing public perceptions over time, but free and open trade and investment in these sectors by 2010/2020 is most unlikely to be achieved, except through negotiations. This points to the need for APEC governments to cooperate to increase the prospects of dealing with these sectors in the WTO. Enhancing the likelihood of success in the WTO involves far more than accumulating either leverage or bargaining chips.

In some other sectors of some Asia Pacific economies, there are genuinely held concerns about the risk of reliance on international markets. There are some products, such as foodgrains, fertilisers, steel and energy, where concern with the security of supply (and/or the capacity to pay for them) can outweigh the potential benefits of international specialisation. Free trade in such products, which would allow all economies to benefit from the efficient location of production, will not be achieved until these concerns are dealt with.

Much work is needed to create an environment in which economies which are potentially large net consumers can be confident about regular supplies being available on international markets at reasonably stable prices. Correspondingly, potentially large net suppliers will not risk long-term investment to supply unstable or unreliable international markets; these problems are likely to be acute for sectors with strong economies of scale and long investment lead times. Despite the obvious complementarity of Asia Pacific economies due to very different resource endowments, long-term decisions for efficient location of production will only be possible if these underlying problems are addressed and there is good reason to be confident about stable demand and supply conditions. There is ample scope for APEC officials and policy-oriented researchers around the region, for example in PECC, to engage in cooperative policy development to create the confident international market environments, which are necessary for serious commitment to free trade in some of these vital commodities.

Steel products provide an example. For large potential net importers to consider free trade, they would need comprehensive assurance, not only of secure supplies, but also that potential suppliers are not seeking to retard either the technological capacity of domestic steel industries in general, or defence capabilities in particular. For sustained success in exporting, potential exporters will need to be seen to be willing to bolster, not undermine, the domestic capacity of potential importers. That could be demonstrated by willingness to transfer technology and to invest in production in the net importing economy. Without such assurances of cooperation as well as competition, potential suppliers will continue to face the risk of disruption of their markets due to policy changes by importers. They will be aware that appeals to peer pressure by APEC governments, or even recourse to time-consuming WTO dispute settlement mechanisms, cannot assure the commercial survival of large-scale export-oriented investments.

Some essential ingredients of an understanding which might pave the way for confident agreement on promoting the growth of mutually beneficial large-scale international trade in steel and steel products in the Asia Pacific region, have been outlined by Drysdale (1992: 13) as follows.

> recognising the central importance of the steel industry in the continuing industrialisation and development of East Asia, participants in such an agreement could be required to: 1. Encourage the expansion of production and efficient use of resources in all facets of steel production so as to contribute to raising standards of living in the region and in other countries. 2. Assure stable and continuing supplies of raw materials and open access to markets for raw materials on a commercial basis. 3. Promote free trade in steel products among participants on terms which in no way disadvantage third parties. 4. Facilitate the flow of investment into the steel industry on a commercial basis, including the flow of foreign investment through provision for national treatment of foreign investors and exemption from such national laws and regulations as inhibit foreign investment. 5. Foster internationally acceptable safety and related conditions of labour in the steel industry and related raw materials industries in the region and encourage schemes for exchange and training. 6. Promote the continuing development and transfer of new technologies

on commercial terms in all aspects of production, environmental impact of the production and use of steel products. 7. Have regular consultations for the purpose of reviewing developments in regional steel trade and production and providing an opportunity for comment on any measures taken by governments or international agencies to assist the industry or its adjustment and, if appropriate, make proposals for such assistance, from the viewpoint of their consistency with the objectives of the agreement. 8. Encourage research and development on both technical and economic aspects of the development of the steel industry in the region. 9. Insure, collectively, private investors against loss from breach of the steel community agreement by one or more governments.

Most of these ingredients can only be 'supplied' by joint policy development and technical cooperation among potential participants in such an understanding, while the last point emphasises the potential need for financial cooperation to facilitate the growth of trade.

Similar types of confidence-building policy development and technical cooperation will also be needed to permit serious consideration of free trade in other vital commodities. Garnaut and Ma (1992) and Garnaut (1993) set out some similar issues relating to the prospects for substantial growth in international trade in wool, textiles and grains. Such issues need to be addressed constructively to avoid the prospect of substantially reduced potential for economic growth and trade in the region, and globally, if large and densely populated East Asian economies consider it necessary to be largely self-sufficient in basic agricultural products like foodgrains.

Based on an assessment of resource endowments and likely comparative advantage, China could quickly emerge as the largest trader in many commodities. Large-scale imports of many raw materials and foodgrains would permit a more efficient allocation of China's resources and create huge opportunities for potential suppliers. However, these opportunities will be severely restricted unless China becomes a member of the WTO. While accession continues to be blocked, China cannot have the level of confidence in the international economic environment for it to take full advantage of global export opportunities and, in turn, create correspondingly large new market opportunities for others. A very important short-term option for economic cooperation among most APEC participants is to make it clear to the United States that it is the only member which is opposed to the immediate membership of China in the WTO, based on its already demonstrated record of outward-looking policy reform.[10]

Capacity-building and trade liberalisation

To sum up, much of APEC's potential contribution to trade liberalisation is cooperative policy development, backed by support of objective economic analysis to:

- improve the understanding of currently distorted markets;
- find ways of reducing uncertainties;
- estimate the potential effects of trade liberalisation; and
- monitor the progress towards free and open trade and investment achieved and expected from the progressive enhancement of IAPs.

Each of these is a form of economic and technical cooperation. Once the important role of Ecotech as a necessary ingredient of trade liberalisation is accepted, that should resolve the past difficulties in integrating Ecotech into the APEC agenda, where it has tended to be seen as separate from, and competing with, TILF.

The recently introduced APEC Joint Fora Meetings can be seen as a positive step. It is important, however, that the meetings not only help coordinate the various activities in APEC but also contribute to their effective integration. This means that the Ecotech agenda must be relevant for TILF and *vice versa*. An attempt at integration was made in the EVSL initiative in which the reduction of impediments to trade in specific sectors calls for facilitation measures and Ecotech cooperation. It is unfortunate that the EVSL framework has been misguided, lapsing into adversarial trade negotiations, which meant that the various sectoral initiatives could not be implemented successfully.

APEC's contribution to trade liberalisation will be to help governments increase their capacity to reduce barriers, either unilaterally or in the course of WTO negotiations. Once efforts to liberalise border barriers to trade go beyond such capacity-building to attempt formal negotiation of 'concessions' within the APEC process, APEC no longer has comparative advantage. The region's scarce resources of policy-making capacity and goodwill can be allocated more productively to strengthening, rather than duplicating, the WTO-based multilateral trading system.

STRENGTHENING THE MULTILATERAL TRADING SYSTEM

The recent financial crisis has demonstrated that the potential benefits of highly mobile international capital will only be realised in an appropriate policy environment. In the absence of adequately managed and supervised domestic banking systems and international institutions able to respond to emerging signs of instability, short-term capital movements can be greatly destabilising and detrimental to economic growth.

Correspondingly, the potential benefits of free trade in goods and services can only be realised in the context of a rules-based and non-discriminatory multilateral trading system. The examples discussed above indicate that, in the absence of confidence about the likely behaviour of trading partners, the risks of interdependence can sometimes outweigh the potential benefits of international specialisation along lines of underlying comparative advantage. Hence the overriding shared economic interest of Asia Pacific economies to sustain and defend the WTO based rules for international trade. Free and open trade will only be achieved if the integrity of the WTO-based system is respected by all significant economies.

In that context, the resurgence of new and serious trade disputes between the United States and the European Union is a cause for serious concern.[11] The refusal of the European Union to abide by recent WTO rulings threatens to weaken the usefulness of the dispute settlement mechanism adopted by the WTO. If that mechanism is not respected, there is a high probability that the United States will once again resort increasingly to unilateral judgements about the appropriateness of the trade policies of other governments, backed by threats of trade retaliation inconsistent with WTO disciplines. The potential erosion of adherence to WTO disciplines and determinations poses a far more serious threat to the prospects of continued outwardly-oriented rapid development in the Asia Pacific than the remnants of protection provided to some sectors of steadily declining relative importance.

The growing complexity of international economic transactions and of WTO articles, coupled with political pressures, makes it inevitable that there will be problems in meeting all WTO commitments. Disputes will continue to arise, pointing to the need for an effective dispute settlement mechanism. To defend the new dispute settlement mechanism of the WTO, a worthwhile option for cooperation among APEC leaders would be for them to make an unequivocal commitment to abide fully and promptly with any determinations by WTO dispute settlement panels. To add weight to such commitment, it would be desirable to set a timetable for enacting domestic legislation to provide for such compliance. Such commitments would form a valuable new component of IAPs aimed at achieving free and open trade and investment.

In addition to defending the current form of the WTO, there are many opportunities for economic cooperation among APEC participants to deepen, broaden and widen the capacity of the organisation. The need for widening membership has already been discussed. Even if China is admitted in the near future, there will be some APEC participants who are not members of the WTO and such a situation may persist as APEC admits new participants. An important contribution of economic cooperation within APEC would be for their governments to undertake that all other APEC participants will be treated no less favourably in terms of trade policy than WTO trading partners.

Since the end of the Uruguay Round, increased attention has been given to the links between trade and other policy areas, including investment, competition policy, environmental management and labour standards. These will need to be addressed, but it does not always follow that they should all be dealt with in the WTO; otherwise that organisation would also stray away from its comparative advantage. There are opportunities for Asia Pacific governments to set positive WTO-consistent examples for others to follow, though not necessarily within the explicit context of the WTO.

It should be possible to adopt gradually more precise guiding principles for the conduct of policies, such as competition policies, which have implications for trade policy. In each case these guiding principles can incorporate the fundamental WTO principles of transparency, non-discriminatory and national treatment. At the outset, cooperative policy development can encourage the adoption of non-binding principles; once such principles prove useful, APEC governments can be encouraged to incorporate them in relevant domestic legislation. Cooperative development of approaches to new policy areas can also help ensure that appropriate account is given to the diverse needs of economies at different stages of development.

There is also scope for deepening by dismantling the remaining border barriers to trade in areas already covered by the WTO. APEC governments can contribute to that effort most effectively by setting positive examples. A strong political commitment to the full liberalisation of information technology products by APEC leaders in November 1996 led to swift agreement on binding schedules for the WTO-wide dismantling of protection in a sector where free trade can help boost economic development and where several APEC economies are highly competitive. However, the information technology precedent has not proved easy to follow.

Early voluntary sectoral liberalisation

In November 1997, APEC leaders agreed to the early voluntary sectoral liberalisation of nine sectors.[12] By early 1998, the 'V' had disappeared from EVSL and the process turned into a GATT-style trade negotiation to establish a balance of the short-term political costs of trade liberalisation among participants. By November, sixteen out of eighteen APEC participants had agreed on concerted action in terms of trade liberalisation, facilitation and technical cooperation for seven out of the nine sectors nominated.[13] Despite this progress, almost all the reporting about trade liberalisation at the Kuala Lumpur meeting focused on the refusal by Japan – already a large importer of fisheries and forest products – to open these particular markets further.

Much less attention was given to the reality that the US administration has no legal authority to deliver on any EVSL commitments. EVSL cannot remain viable without such authority, but that is only likely to be granted if the European Union is willing to match such commitment. APEC governments have agreed to table the agreements they have reached on EVSL as an 'offer' in the WTO; these offers should be sufficient to test the willingness of the European Union to respond by comparable offers. If there is such a response (as there was in the case of information technology products), all APEC and EU governments could bind their reductions in protection in the WTO. This would be an extremely significant step towards global free and open trade and investment.

EVSL has led to some progress, but transforming part of the APEC process into a negotiating forum carries risks. With widening membership, it will be increasingly difficult to set up 'package deals' to balance an ever-wider range of diverse sectoral interests. It would also be counter-productive to recreate a false perception that 'opening to the outside world' is a concession to others, rather than of intrinsic benefit to the economies that undertake these reforms. Nevertheless, it may be possible to identify, cooperatively, some sectors where a significant number of APEC participants can see a shared interest in early, and genuinely voluntary, liberalisation.

This approach would accept that EVSL is not the vehicle for attempting to negotiate involuntary liberalisation of sensitive sectors. Instead, it would be more productive to concentrate on sectors where protection has not yet become entrenched, as was the case for information technology. While the immediate economic gains would not be large, it would help ensure that these do not evolve into the sensitive sectors of the future and would also help APEC governments to show joint leadership in the WTO. It may also be possible to identify some sectors, especially energy-intensive sectors, where the original reasons for protection have been weakened by changes in circumstances.

STRENGTHENING ECONOMIC INFRASTRUCTURE

Border barriers to trade and investment and costs imposed by divergent approaches to commercial regulation are not the only transaction costs on international economic transactions. There are also natural barriers of distance and poor communications. Shortages of economic infrastructure, or inefficient operation of existing capacity, can also impose heavy costs on international trade and investment.

A recent estimate by the World Bank (1995) indicated that the developing East Asian economies alone would need between US$1.2 trillion and US$1.5 trillion for infrastructure investment in the decade ending in 2004. Additions to infrastructure ranging from ports, telecommunications, power generation to sewerage facilities and enhancing the efficiency of their operations will be vital for sustained economic growth in general and for TILF in particular. An important component of any program to facilitate trade and investment is to reduce the costs currently imposed by transport and communications bottlenecks.

The current slump in activity might temporarily reduce the urgency of investment in economic infrastructure, but trillions of dollars will still need to be found and spent on infrastructure projects in the near future. It is widely accepted that such amounts are far beyond the capacity of Asia Pacific governments' savings, let alone their 'windows' for concessional financing. The bulk of these essential infrastructure investments will need to be financed with private risk capital.[14]

Nevertheless, there is a great deal that governments can do to help ensure that the necessary private investment occurs at the time it is needed, rather than after costly bottlenecks develop. Policy development is also necessary to try to minimise the costs and risks of such investment, which are ultimately passed on to users. Moreover, the design and implementation of sound policies towards infrastructure can be enhanced through economic and technical cooperation.

The customs procedures and passport control examples discussed above illustrate how the need for new physical investment can be reduced by more efficient operation of existing facilities based on policy development and technical cooperation among Asia Pacific governments. Technical cooperation can also help attract, on reasonable terms, the risk capital which will still be needed on a large scale to build new economic infrastructure.

Cooperative policy development work by APEC officials, combined with technical cooperation, can improve the framework for attracting commercial investment, including by strengthening financial markets, or by creating the policy environment needed in cases where several Asia Pacific economies may need to cooperate in order to facilitate investment in infrastructure (e.g. sub-regional power or irrigation schemes).

APEC is already seeking ways to enhance the prospects for large-scale private investment in economic infrastructure. In November 1997, APEC leaders endorsed the Vancouver Framework for Enhanced Public–Private Partnerships in Infrastructure Development. Such partnerships will be essential to finance and manage the enhancement of economic infrastructure needed in the Asia Pacific region in order to meet its economic, environmental and social goals.

Within this framework, multilateral financial institutions are to catalyse and support efforts by each APEC economy to enhance their policy environment for facilitating flows of private capital while continuing raising private capital on their own account to finance infrastructure development. Several export credit agencies and export financing institutions have signed a protocol for mutual cooperation to enhance the attractiveness of private sector investment in infrastructure. There is also scope for redesigning the lending rules of multilateral development cooperation agencies to make it simpler for them to raise funds for activities in several neighbouring economies.

Region-wide technical cooperation can also help to gather and disseminate information on best practices for policies to facilitate large-scale private investment in economic infrastructure. Much information has been gained about the design of effective and transparent tendering procedures and about options for sharing risks between investors and users, for example, through combinations of performance guarantees, pricing and risk sharing. Potential investors would also welcome the establishment of a region-wide data base describing current policies of Asia Pacific governments which are relevant to their commercial assessments. Following a Canadian initiative, an APEC Infrastructure Facilitation Center is expected to be established in the near future (Potter 1998).

Economic cooperation can also contribute on the demand side. The present slump in East Asian economic activity provides the breathing space to ease some severe infrastructure bottlenecks, but the financial sector problems make it relatively less likely that investors will be attracted to new infrastructure projects. But, even on very pessimistic estimates of the time taken for rapid growth to recommence, many infrastructure projects with long lead times remain potentially commercially viable. Credible economic forecasting work by APEC committees and working groups can foreshadow the need for further timely investments in economic infrastructure.

ENHANCING INSTITUTIONAL AND TECHNOLOGICAL CAPACITY

The preceding sections have sought to demonstrate the many ways economic and technical cooperation among Asia Pacific economies can contribute to financial recovery, to economic infrastructure and to continued progress in terms of TILF. Many of these activities are already under way; these as well as potential opportunities for cooperation are essentially exercises in capacity-building by means of cooperative policy development and technical cooperation. The opportunities for technical cooperation involve pooling the information, experience and the best available expertise and technology in the Asia Pacific, then disseminating it throughout the region in order to enhance institutional and technological capacity.

Such cooperative policy development and technical cooperation, with considerable emphasis on human resource development, are also the main ingredients of cooperative efforts to enhance the management of all sectors. Cooperative policy development has been carried out by APEC's committees and working groups since 1990, contributing to progress in cooperation in many sectoral activities to improve information and reduce transaction costs. The work performed by these groups is reasonably similar to the sectoral policy analysis and development work of the OECD, but requires far fewer resources and carries far fewer bureaucratic overheads.

APEC governments are financing, and should continue to finance, the bulk of the costs of policy development, partly by sending relevant officials to working meetings, but also by devoting resources to substantial preparations for these meetings. They can, and do, make use of relevant policy development work by others, such as PECC task forces. In addition, APEC committees have drawn on APEC's modest 'central' budget to commission specialised tasks of data gathering or policy-oriented research, especially when there is a need for evaluation and interpretation of options and of achievements by independent analysts.

Technological capacity

Turning to technical cooperation, there is considerable scope for cooperation to reduce the environmental costs of rapid economic development by helping to ensure that all of the region has access to and the ability to make use of the least-polluting technology for a wide range of industries. Yamazawa (1996) lists a series of 'model projects' to encourage fast-growing Asia Pacific economies to adopt clean coal and efficient energy use technology. These projects are designed to adapt an environmentally-friendly technology developed in one Asia Pacific economy; then to install it in a plant of another economy and to provide the training needed to use it.

Typically, such products transfer technology between a pair of economies. The existence of APEC can provide a framework in which industry managers from anywhere in the Asia Pacific can be familiarised with and trained in the use of the most efficient technology available in the region. A regional approach can create greater efficiencies of both scale and scope than a proliferation of bilateral projects.

There are many other ways in which Asia Pacific governments can cooperate to enhance the capacity of their researchers and producers to absorb and adapt and disseminate new technologies as well as to begin to build the capacity for basic research. Governments could also contribute to technological development by creating a competitive environment which encouraged innovation. Those in the region can also draw, to some extent, on the relevant experience of European governments. Several Asia Pacific governments, including Korea, Singapore and Taiwan, have already set up centres for promoting technological capacity-building. There is scope for linking such initiatives through a network of National Innovation Systems, which can share the technology and experience gained by each centre in terms of developing and disseminating new technologies.

Human resource development

Technical cooperation relies very heavily on the design and delivery of human resource development programs. The success of many options to facilitate trade and investment, such as the mutual recognition of standards, depends on confidence in the willingness as well as the capacity of each APEC economy to ensure compliance with their own domestic standards. That, in turn, requires a massive training effort.

The need for enhanced institutional capacity to support sustained economic growth goes well beyond cooperative activities to support TILF. For example, the financial crisis highlighted the desirability of well-structured bankruptcy procedures to sort out the after-effects of financial shocks. Cooperative policy development can help each economy identify the type of bankruptcy legislation and procedures suited to each Asia Pacific economy, drawing on the experience of others. But once new procedures are legislated, there is an even greater human resource development challenge to ensure that new institutions are staffed by competent people.

Similar institution-building and training needs arise in all sectors. In many Asia Pacific economies, there is an urgent need to upgrade the ability to administer, as well as update, commercial legislation and regulations. That needs to be supported by training in the administration of sectoral policies, for example to provide and manage a policy environment which can encourage private sector investment in economic infrastructure.

As noted earlier, the need for training for managing new institutions and implementing new policies is an ongoing task, as those trained move to, or are promoted to, other occupations. Meeting these needs provides an excellent opportunity for region-wide cooperation. Each Asia Pacific economy could implement its own training programs. However, there are significant economies of scope to be gained by having staff with potentially similar future responsibilities undergoing their training together as a way of fostering mutual respect and trust in each others' competence.

Implementing technical cooperation

Cooperative policy development can be implemented using the existing structure and modest financial resources of APEC committees and working groups, drawing on (and perhaps commissioning) policy research by others, such as PECC. By contrast, widespread benefits to Asia Pacific economies from technical cooperation will need substantially greater resources than the funds at the joint disposal of APEC Ministers. The very large number of ongoing training programs that could be usefully established on a region-wide basis will all need resources such as buildings, training materials, payments for the design and updating of curriculums and for trainers. Such costs are in addition to the direct and opportunity costs of the time of those being trained.

All APEC governments can benefit from financing such activities. But that should not lead to the establishment of a new regional Ecotech bureaucracy with a large central budget. There is now widespread agreement that APEC should play a catalytic, rather than direct role in implementing projects which APEC leaders jointly identify to be of region-wide benefit. The challenge is to forge partnerships with existing development cooperation agencies as well as with the business/private sector to turn ideas into tangible cooperative activities.[15]

Re-orienting development cooperation agencies

Many APEC governments already manage development cooperation agencies which provide resources for institution-building, human resource development and upgrading technological capability. In most cases, these are carried out on a bilateral basis. As already explained, there are large economies of scope as well as scale to be gained by cooperation among several governments to set up regional, rather than economy-specific activities. Such a cooperative approach can ensure the dissemination of the best expertise and techniques available anywhere in the region. Moreover, human resource development activities to support the implementation of cooperative arrangements for trade or investment facilitation will be most effective if regional administrators receive at least some of their training together.

To take advantage of such opportunities and potential gains from coordination, APEC governments will need to review the priorities of their own international development agencies. This may involve some diversion of resources from bilateral activities to regional projects which are designed to benefit several (ideally all) Asia Pacific economies and which are more consistent with the principles of the 1996 Manila Declaration on economic cooperation and development. Some existing agencies have already taken responsibility for implementing activities proposed by APEC working groups and more agencies can be encouraged to consider shifting their emphasis to supporting projects of region-wide significance emerging from APEC, rather than projects with a narrower, bilateral focus. The recent Australian government initiative for enhancing the capacity for economic governance in the region provides a positive example.

Once APEC governments have set priorities for technical cooperation, they will have considerable potential collective influence over the priorities and activities of multilateral development agencies, particularly the ADB. Such development agencies have the institutional capacity to raise the funds required and to select firms best qualified to construct physical facilities and for the day-to-day management of technical cooperation projects.

Engaging the business/private sector – Partnership for equitable growth

In its 1997 report to APEC leaders, the APEC Business Advisory Council (ABAC) confirmed the willingness of the business sector to give direct support to APEC's economic cooperation and development agenda by establishing a Partnership for Equitable Growth (PEG). PEG is to serve as a new framework to encourage business participation in economic and technical cooperation activities, noting that the private sector can add value by undertaking projects in areas where neither the market nor governments currently meet regional needs. This initiative by ABAC was welcomed and endorsed by APEC leaders in Vancouver and should commence its activities in 1999.

PEG is expected to facilitate project funding by coordinating partnerships and/or joint ventures involving private capital, multilateral development cooperation agencies and foundations. Activities for potential support through PEG would be selected in accordance with the objectives, guiding principles and priorities expressed in the Manila Declaration on an Asia Pacific Economic Cooperation Framework for Strengthening Economic Cooperation and Development. In selecting cooperative activities for support, PEG intends to focus on activities that:

- will benefit at least two Asia Pacific economies in order to reflect the community-building goal of APEC and Ecotech;
- can be financially self-sustaining and business/private sector led in execution; and
- are endorsed by governments of APEC economies, in order to underline the importance of forging partnerships between governments and the business/private sector.

PEG itself is to be a business/private sector oriented organisation, designed to act as a 'merchant bank of ideas' by forming partnerships or joint ventures to implement particular Ecotech projects. These are likely to include activities to promote human resource development, technological capacity and education in information technology. Each activity is expected to be implemented initially on a small scale, then possibly expanded if it proves successful and financially self-sustaining.

SUMMARY AND RECOMMENDATIONS

The financial crisis has clarified both the limitations and the potential of APEC. While trade and investment issues are important, it has become evident that economic cooperation needs to be far more broadly based in order to nurture a sense of community.

There are some welcome signs of recovery from the crisis, but much remains to be done to shore up the foundations for resumed rapid growth and to limit the risks of similar crises of confidence. Cooperation among Asia Pacific economies can help to accelerate and facilitate the costly, short-term effort of restructuring and the multi-year capacity-building effort needed to create better-managed and more robust financial sectors. It has been recognised that these are essentially tasks of economic and technical cooperation among Asia Pacific governments, in either a regional or global context. This perception will help to convince the region's leaders that economic and technical cooperation (Ecotech) is at the heart of the APEC process.

Since the signing of the Manila Declaration on an Asia Pacific Economic Cooperation Framework for Strengthening Economic Cooperation and Development there have been constructive moves, by the business/private sector as well as by governments, to turn that conceptual framework into a new operational model of development cooperation. Several hundred projects are under way, but a sense of frustration and several misunderstandings persist.

There remains a wide range of incompatible expectations about the nature of the cooperative activities which could be promoted collectively by APEC governments and how these could be financed and implemented. That is being compounded by an inadequate appreciation of the current and potential role of existing agencies in promoting the new ideas for Ecotech emerging from the APEC process.

A further serious problem is the unduly sharp dichotomy which has come to be drawn between work to promote TILF and other forms of cooperation. Economic and technical cooperation are often seen as residual activities which are not part of the drive towards free and open trade and investment.

If Ecotech and TILF continue to be seen separate, competing strands of the APEC process, it will be hard to build a sense of shared economic interests and mutual respect. The difficult experience with EVSL in 1998 showed that

TILF can quickly come to be perceived as an adversarial negotiating process, rather than a joint cooperative effort with all-round benefits. To avoid such problems, this chapter advocates an integrated view of the APEC process within which all cooperative activities are seen as ways to strengthen the capacity of Asia Pacific economies to reach their full potential for sustainable economic growth.

The basic challenge is to enhance the capacity of all Asia Pacific economies to enhance their productive resources and to allocate them in an increasingly efficient and sustainable way. Cooperation among APEC economies can help by sharing the information, experience, expertise and technology need to design and administer a progressively more efficient set of economic policies to achieve these ends. The PECC Competition Principles provide a valuable reference point for cooperation to encourage and enable all Asia Pacific economies to adopt more efficient policies for all markets. Economic and technical cooperation which improves the ability of Asia Pacific governments to reduce impediments to trade and investment through unilateral or coordinated reforms (that is, TILF) is an important part, but only one part, of this overall cooperative effort.

The chapter sets out the opportunities for cooperative policy development and technical cooperation to:

- strengthen domestic and international financial markets;
- facilitate trade and investment;
- liberalise traditional border barriers to trade;
- defend and strengthen the multilateral trading system; and
- develop the capacity of economic infrastructure.

Many of these challenges in these areas, including those recommended by other chapters in this volume are, in large part, challenges of capacity-building through economic and technical cooperation.

Recommendations for implementing Ecotech

General objective: to encourage and enable Asia Pacific economies to continue to strengthen their economic policy framework in order to enhance their available productive resources and promote their efficient allocation. This can be achieved by means of a combination of cooperative policy development and technical cooperation, with particular emphasis on human resource development and institution-building.

Cooperative policy development among APEC economies parallels what the OECD is seeking to promote in a very different context. APEC governments should continue to follow an evolutionary approach which is less bureaucratic, less expensive and less centralised. APEC committees and working groups, which are already engaged in such work, should be encouraged to draw more intensively on existing networks such as the PECC and APEC Study Centres. There is no need for a large new bureaucracy.

Technical cooperation should focus on a small number of well-defined priorities, such as:

- strengthening financial sectors;
- promoting progressively closer adherence to principles based on the PECC Competition Principles, which are likely to be endorsed by APEC leaders;
- sectoral analysis to help demonstrate the significant long-term net benefits of reducing impediments to trade in key sectors such as financial services, air and maritime transport, iron and steel products and foodgrains.

Long-term programs for technical cooperation should be developed in each of these areas, focusing on human resource development and institution-building. Once such programs are endorsed by APEC leaders, they should invite APEC governments, regional and multilateral development banks as well as the business/private sector to mobilise resources to finance the technical cooperation programs jointly identified by APEC and to make arrangements for their ongoing implementation.

The APEC Business Advisory Council (ABAC) has already indicated how the business sector can support APEC's Ecotech agenda by establishing a Partnership for Equitable Growth. The PEG is to serve as a new framework to encourage business participation in technical cooperation activities. APEC leaders should continue to encourage such innovative contributions.

APEC governments should be encouraged to include their commitment to promote specific aspects of the priority technical cooperation programs endorsed by APEC leaders as a significant part of their IAPs. This would emphasise the organic link between the policy reform aspects and Ecotech aspects of promoting progress towards the Bogor vision of free and open trade and investment. Where possible, APEC governments should be encouraged to promote technical cooperation projects jointly: their contributions to such cooperative activities could be included as part of APEC's Collective Action Plans (CAPs).

It is also important to note that APEC governments, collectively, are well placed to direct regional and multilateral development banks to take up significant components of long-term human resource development and institution-building programs endorsed by APEC leaders.

NOTES

1 The authors would like to acknowledge the contribution of The Foundation for Development Cooperation, based in Brisbane Australia. With its support, a group of Asia Pacific researchers (including the authors) and officials in their private capacity met several times between 1995 and 1998 to consider opportunities for economic and technical cooperation to be promoted by APEC, as well as to design a conceptual framework which helped to shape the 1996 *Manila Declaration on an Asia Pacific Economic Cooperation Framework for Strengthening Economic Cooperation and Development.*

A previous version of this chapter was presented to an international conference on APEC liberalisation and the Chinese economy in Beijing, in October 1998.

The authors are grateful for the comments received at that time and subsequently from Professor Ippei Yamazawa.

2   See for example, Pomfret (1998).

3   See JICA (1995).

4   Such a strategy was advocated in Bora and Findlay (1996).

5   These remarks on technical cooperation opportunities in financial sectors draw on Petri (1998).

6   See Stiglitz (1998).

7   Some of many recent proposals, including for 'bailing-in' lenders in the event of financial crises, are reviewed in Elek and Wilson (1999).

8   See PECC (1996a).

9   PECC (1999) proposes a set of competition policy principles for consideration and adoption by APEC governments.

10   The United States will also need to be persuaded to repeal current legislation (the Jackson–Vanek amendment) which prevents an assurance of unconditional MFN treatment of imports from China. The US Administration and China agreed on the policy reforms for China's accession to the WTO in late 1999, but at the time of publication, the US Congress had yet to debate the repeal of the Jackson–Vanek amendment.

11   See *Economist* (1999).

12   The nine sectors were: environmental goods and services, fish and fish products, toys, forest products, gems and jewellery, chemicals, energy sector, medical equipment and instruments, and telecommunications mutual recognition arrangements.

13   Mexico and Chile did not participate in the EVSL exercise as they are already committed to a schedule for elimination of border barriers across the board.

14   See Intal, in Elek (1997).

15   The following remarks on technical cooperation draw on FDC (1998).

REFERENCES

APEC (1991) *Seoul APEC Declaration*, Ministerial Declaration, Seoul, November.

—— (1994) *Bogor Declaration of Common Resolve*, Second APEC leaders meeting, Bogor, November.

—— (1995) *Osaka Action Agenda*, Ministerial Declaration, Osaka, November.

—— (1996a) *Manila Declaration on an Asia Pacific Economic Cooperation Framework for Strengthening Economic Cooperation and Development*, Ministerial Declaration, Manila, November.

—— (1996b) *Manila Action Plan for APEC*, Manila, November.

—— (1997) *Vancouver Framework for Enhanced Public–Private Partnerships in Infrastructure Development*, Vancouver, November.

APEC Business Advisory Council (ABAC) (1997) *APEC Means Business: ABAC's Call to Action*, 1997 report to APEC leaders, APEC Secretariat, Singapore, November.

Bora, B. and Findlay, C. (1996) 'Introduction and overview', in B. Bora and C. Findlay (eds), *Regional Integration and the Asia–Pacific*, Melbourne: Oxford University Press.

Drysdale, P. (1992) 'Next steps in Asia Pacific Economic Cooperation: An East Asian steel community', in P. Drysdale (ed.), *East Asia, the East Asia Steel Industry*, Research School of Pacific Studies, Australian National University, Canberra.

Economist (1999) 'Free trade in peril' and 'World trade' 12 and 19–23, 8–14 May, London.

Elek, A. and Wilson, D. (1999) 'The East Asian crisis and international capital markets', *Asian–Pacific Economic Literature*, vol 13, no. 1, Blackwells.

Elek, A. (ed.) (1997) *Building an Asia–Pacific Economic Community: Development cooperation within APEC,* Brisbane: Foundation for Development Cooperation.

Foundation for Development Cooperation (FDC) (1998) 'Forging new partnerships: economic and technical cooperation and the APEC process', Report of meetings and recommendations to APEC and ABAC, Kuala Lumpur, 2 December 1997 and 10 August, 1998, Foundation for Development Cooperation, Brisbane, December.

Garnaut, R. and Ma, G. (1992) *Grain in China,* East Asia Analytical Unit, Department of Foreign Affairs and Trade, Canberra, Australia.

Garnaut, R. (1993) 'Strategies for growth in the Chinese wool textile industry and the role of Sino–Australian cooperation', Keynote address to the Symposium, Wool – Australia and China: The natural partners, Beijing.

Intal, P. (1997) 'Towards strengthening development co-operation in the Asia Pacific: Hardware *vs* software', in Elek (1997).

Japan International Cooperation Agency (JICA) (1995) APEC Partners for Progress (PFP), Research Report, Tokyo.

Morrison, C.E. (1997) 'Development cooperation in the 21st century: Implications for APEC', in Elek (1997).

Petri, P. (1998) Role of Asia–Pacific governments in supporting Ecotech activities identified by APEC, remarks to the Second APEC Dialogue on Economic and Technical Cooperation, Kuala Lumpur, 10 August.

PECC (1995a) *Milestones in APEC Liberalisation: a map of market opening measures by APEC economies,* PECC Secretariat, Singapore.

—— (1995b) Survey of Impediments to Trade and Investment in the APEC region, PECC Secretariat, Singapore.

—— (1996a) Road Map for APEC and the WTO: Business priorities and policy leadership, report of Trade Policy Forum IX, Seoul, PECC Secretariat, Singapore.

—— (1996b) *Perspectives on the Manila Action Plan for APEC,* PECC Secretariat, Singapore.

—— (1999) 'Principles for guiding the development of a competition-driven policy framework for APEC economies', report of Trade Policy Forum Competition Principles Project, Singapore.

Pomfret, R. (1998) 'Regionalism in Europe and the Asia Pacific economy', in P. Drysdale and D. Vines, (eds), *Europe, East Asia and APEC: A shared global agenda?,* Cambridge, 1998.

Potter, P. (1998) 'APEC infrastructure facilitation center: A mediating structure for interdependent nonconvergent political economy', paper to Conference on Regionalism and Global Affairs in the Post-Cold War Era: the European Union, APEC and the new international political economy, International Institute for Asian Studies, Leiden University and the APEC Studies Center, University of Washington, held in Brussels, March.

Stiglitz, J. (1998) 'Must financial crises be this frequent and this painful', McKay Lecture, Pittsburgh, Pennsylvania, September 23. Available at <http://www.worldbank.org/html/extdr/extme/js-092398/index.htm>

World Bank (1995) *Infrastructure Development in East Asia and the Pacific: Towards a new public–private partnership,* The World Bank, Washington D.C.

Yamazawa, I. (1997) 'APEC's economic and technical cooperation: Evolution and tasks ahead', in Elek (1997).

Yamazawa, I., Nakayama, S. and Kitamura, H. (1996) 'Asia–Pacific cooperation in energy and environment', in *APEC: Cooperation from Diversity,* I. Yamazawa and A. Hirata (eds), Institute of Develooping Economies, Tokyo.

10 Competition and deregulation policy areas in APEC

Kerrin M. Vautier and Peter Lloyd[1]

INTRODUCTION

Competition Policy and Deregulation were two of the fifteen specific areas identified in APEC's Action Plan framework for achieving the Bogor goals (APEC 1995). Both Individual and Collective Action Plans were required as part of a mechanism for assessing progress in each of the various policy areas. The APEC Committee on Trade and Investment (CTI) noted the central role of competition policy in enhancing economic efficiency but also realised that business globalisation is creating new challenges for this policy area. As noted in the PAFTAD 25 Conference program, the competition area is a 'highly complicated issue'. Complexity is added by the increasing flow of cross-border economic transactions and by the Region's economic diversity. Trans-national markets in which business is conducted combine with national jurisdictions in which policy is conducted (see Lloyd and Vautier 1999). Technology and business organisation are also changing rapidly. As a consequence of these developments, the ability of an individual sovereign power to regulate business either within or beyond its jurisdiction is diminishing. Whether or not there is a need to regulate is a separate question.

Reflecting on the considerable discussion of APEC's role at the first Senior Officials Meeting in 1999, Hawke (1999a), as a PECC Observer, reports:

> There is clearly a desire to find something which is not merely aggregating what governments are doing individually, and which is also different from what is done by other international organisations ... [T]here is no source of an APEC view other than the consensus of the members. APEC is therefore a forum for cooperative action ...

An important area for cooperative action is to continue the building of informed APEC-wide dialogue on competition and regulatory issues.

In its 1998 Annual Report to Ministers the CTI reaffirmed that 'Competition Policy [at the international level] is a relatively new and challenging work area'. Because of this, 'APEC members' views on how exactly to achieve the objectives of the Osaka Action Agenda on Competition Policy are still developing'. The most important element of this Collective Action Plan in the long run is the mandate to consider developing non-binding principles on competition policy and/or laws in APEC (although we are mindful of the concern that a narrow interpretation of this mandate would not be a major advance). The Collective Action Plan for Deregulation contains a mandate to 'examine the possibility of establishing non-binding APEC guidelines on domestic deregulation' (although this would be better extended to regulatory reform).

The CTI foresaw benefits from the interrelationship between competition policy/law and deregulation, and in February 1996 agreed to combine these work areas under a single convener, although Action Plans for these areas have remained separate. They both continue to have a major focus on information sharing, dialogue and study, which is entirely appropriate. Generally, the Individual Action Plans reveal a lack of agreement on the core objective of 'competition policy' and widely divergent views on the scope of this policy area. Herein lies a major challenge for APEC in the twenty-first century, especially when considering competition principles and deregulation guidelines.

The complexity of the issues lends support for an over-arching and principled policy framework for guiding approaches to them, and for encouraging convergence in policy objectives and policy direction while avoiding the risks inherent in attempts to devise 'one-size-fits-all' policy prescriptions. This is consistent with APEC's decentralised approach and unilateralism.

We believe that the central issue for APEC in respect of competition/ deregulation/regulatory reform is to achieve convergence around policy *objectives* and policy *direction*, not *rules*. Such cooperative endeavour is of critical importance in the context of APEC's overall goals. It goes beyond 'merely aggregating what governments are doing individually' and also differentiates APEC's approach. It has the potential to add real value at this time when the focus on competition, deregulation and the strengthening of markets is becoming increasingly internationalised in recognition of the links between contestable markets, economic growth and wealth creation. Further, convergence around a competition-driven policy framework is totally in line with the outcome of PECC's Competition Principles Project (PECC 1999) and with the recent statement on competition-driven policy in the context of APEC's vision (Panel of Independent Experts 1998).

APEC 1999 provides an immediate challenge for APEC Leaders, Ministers and officials as well as for those groupings such as PECC, PAFTAD and ABAC that seek to influence APEC's progress. That challenge derives from one of the unifying themes for APEC 1999, namely cooperative efforts to strengthen the functioning of markets, including financial and capital markets; as well as from one of the specific deliverables for 1999, namely developing a framework of non-binding competition and regulatory principles for endorsement by

APEC Leaders (APEC 1998a).[2] We believe that this focus on general *market strengthening* (as distinct from particular market outcomes), on *policy framework building* (as distinct from policy prescriptions), and on *principles* (as distinct from rules) is the preferred course for cooperative action in the APEC forum.

This course involves a more comprehensive approach to competition issues than might at first appear. Far more important than policy labelling and attempts to fit emerging issues into traditional policy compartments is the extent to which a competition dimension finds expression in all market-related policy areas covered by the IAPs. It is interesting to note that in the CTI's Dialogue on Competition Policy (APEC 1999a) the following areas were touched upon in presentations from ten member economies: trade policy, regulatory policy, competition policy, regulated natural monopolies, market concentration, entry barriers, competition law, cartels, anti-dumping measures, intellectual property, corporate restructuring, mergers and standards. Thus, a comprehensive approach to competition issues is emerging as is concern about policy compartmentalisation and the lack of complementarity between competition, regulatory and trade policies.

MULTI–NATIONAL APPROACHES TO THE PROMOTION OF COMPETITION IN GLOBALISING MARKETS

The APEC discussion of competition principles needs to be viewed in the light of global developments that affect market competition. In almost all countries in the world economy there has been a major shift towards more market-oriented policies during the last decade or so. This applies to developed and developing countries alike and it applies to all APEC members. Deregulation of industries is one of the measures which countries have adopted, along with privatisation, corporatisation, liberalisation of trade and FDI and other measures. In many industries, deregulation is believed to be important precisely because it will improve the efficiency of markets. However, in some industries, deregulation raises new issues of competition law and policy as new private competitors may possess undue market power or engage in anti-competitive conduct. This applies particularly to industries in which there are natural monopolies, including networks such as power distribution and telecommunications.

One aspect of these developments is the need for some countries to develop their regulatory capacity, covering the making of laws and rules and their enforcement. At the same time, the experiences of other countries that have successfully deregulated industries may provide lessons. However, not all deregulation successes are transferable.

Unlike trade liberalisation where the ultimate goal is zero border restrictions on trade, there is no universal goal of zero regulation. The optimum degree of regulation will vary from market to market. The markets for many goods and services have been lightly regulated but the markets for other goods and services may require more extensive regulation. Market regulations should be designed to correct market failures due to natural monopolies, the presence of public goods, major environmental effects or other market failures. This implies that countries that have had a recent history of heavy regulation will be generally deregulating, that is reducing the extent of regulations, while other countries that have had lighter regulation may actually be increasing the extent of regulations, at least in some industries. An example of the latter is financial services in some East Asian economies where the Asian crisis has drawn attention to the need for tighter prudential and governance controls.

In this environment, policies to promote competition among private competitors play an important role. The promotion of competition is necessary for efficient production and distribution in all markets. The complexity of competition issues in globalising markets is indicated by the array of simultaneous initiatives for dealing with them at national, bilateral, regional and multilateral levels as well as by a noticeable absence of such initiatives in some countries or regions[3] (Lloyd and Vautier 1999). Some of these issues (for example, a major trans-national merger) obviously span national jurisdictional boundaries; others (for example, a domestic cartel) may, but less obviously, also span national borders. At the regional level, competition issues prompt three categories of response:

- the development of national competition policies with the potential for convergence between them;
- approaches to competition problems that cross national borders but reside within a defined regional area;
- approaches to intra-regional competition problems whose source is outside a defined regional area.

Elements of one or more of these categories are present in the EU, CER, NAFTA, Andean Community, Group of Three, MERCOSUR and Canada–Chile Regional Trading Arrangements (RTAs), largely in response to general developments in competition-promoting policies in the 1990s. The Free Trade Area of the Americas (FTAA) also promises an advance in competition-promoting policy at the Hemisphere level. (For a general review of competition policies in the RTAs and the FTAA, see Lloyd and Vautier 1999: Part Three.)

But variations abound in respect of competition provisions and institutional arrangements. The European Union has developed broad policies to promote intra-area competition as well as specific area-wide competition law. It has a powerful supra-national competition authority.[4] CER has also taken a broad approach to the promotion of competition, including a comprehensive competition law in each member country. There is, however, no supra-national authority. Unlike the European Union, its (limited) cross-border competition provisions are competition- and efficiency-oriented rather than trade-oriented. Canada–Chile and the Group of Three can be grouped with NAFTA, as the provisions and wording of their agreements closely follow those of NAFTA.

Their explicit competition provisions are much more limited than either the European Union or CER. MERCOSUR and the Andean Community have each developed strong competition-promoting policies and have put some institutional arrangements in place, but these have yet to be implemented. Differences also abound in the treatment of anti-dumping, subsidies and countervailing duties, cartels and mergers – all matters of significance to the competitive process.

Trite as it might seem, competition-promoting policies at the RTA level very much depend on the competition culture within it. As well, attitudes to inter-government cooperation at both a policy and institutional level, to the principle of subsidiarity and how this might be applied, and to the balance between national and global welfare are all particularly important. Generally, the achievements of RTAs in respect of region-wide competition-promoting policies are noteworthy (as a product of competition advocacy, including in relation to the role of national competition law) but limited.

However, alternative bilateral and multilateral approaches to trans-national competition issues also have severe limitations. The number of countries covered by bilateral agreements is less than the number covered by RTAs; these bilateral agreements rely on voluntary cooperation and are limited by constraints on information sharing and enforcement. (For a review of the bilateral experience, see Lloyd and Vautier 1999: chapter 3.)

The OECD has been active over many years in exploring the linkages between anti-competitive business practices, competition law and international trade. It has sought to encourage national competition laws and their convergence, and to promote cooperation among national competition agencies, most recently in respect of eliminating/deterring 'hard core cartels'. (See Lloyd and Vautier 1999, chapter 8, for a review of OECD work on 'competition policy'.) The OECD is exploring the notion of 'core principles' in relation to competition law, its procedures and enforcement, reflecting a preference for what might be termed a rules framework rather than specific rules (www.oecd.org).

The role of the WTO in promulgating binding competition rules has been limited to the international trade of state trading enterprises and monopolies and to the regulation of certain government actions, mainly in respect of services. Ceding powers to the WTO to negotiate and enforce multilateral rules to deal with private business conduct would be fraught with difficulty and at risk of sectoral unevenness. Continued and comprehensive trade liberalisation by governments is likely to remain the WTO's most pro-competition strategy. (For reviews of WTO 'competition policy' elements, see WTO 1997: chapter 4; and Lloyd and Vautier 1999: chapter 10.)

Competition issues in trans-national markets warrant a complementary multi-track approach. Even though much more effort is required to determine the comparative advantages of each track, it is clear that well-functioning markets will depend first and foremost upon cooperative national strategies based on a range of competition-promoting policies relevant to globalising markets. In the words of the Osaka Action Agenda for APEC (APEC 1995): 'APEC economies will enhance the competitive environment in the Asia–Pacific region by introducing or maintaining effective and adequate competition policy and/or laws and associated enforcement policies ...'.

THE APEC APPROACH

PAFTAD 24 saw promise in APEC (which is not an RTA) as a less formal and non-threatening forum for education and sharing of information and policy ideas in the complex area of 'competition policy' (Wu and Chu 1998: 334). Essentially this learning should reinforce, not substitute for, comprehensive trade and investment liberalisation by APEC economies; and, indeed 'most participants agreed the best antitrust policy was free trade'. Most also agreed that a 'common starting point of principle for [trade/investment/competition] policies was non-discrimination between domestic and imported (or exported) goods and services, and national treatment of foreign and domestic firms'.

Convergence *vs* harmonisation

The exploration at PAFTAD 24 of harmonisation in the Competition Policy area strongly suggested that harmonisation was not a central issue. Harmonisation was certainly not an end in itself and may not even be desirable; its benefits were uncertain; and there could be no guarantee that it would deliver 'best' standards or efficient and welfare-enhancing outcomes. APEC has made no commitment to harmonisation of competition or regulatory policies/laws across APEC economies. However, implicit in the whole Action Plan process is an invitation to consider opportunities for economic cooperation and strategy/policy *convergence* within each of the policy areas (although we argue that these policy divisions are becoming increasingly strained and inhibiting convergence around a broader policy direction).

Wu and Chu in their Introduction (1998) suggest that regulatory reform involved 'convergence to a particular mode of government deregulation of the markets and privatisation of state enterprises'. They also suggest that the competing hypothesis of 'pluralism' means that 'different economies should choose a competition policy that is best for them ... [which] could mean the absence of policy'. For regulatory reform, pluralism means 'the coexistence of different patterns or paths taken by the authorities ...'. Wu and Chu go on to say that, with the gradualism of institutional change in the region, coupled with the different starting points in respect of economic systems and stages of development, pluralistic development can be expected. But convergence is not precluded.

We do not propose to discuss this categorisation here, but wish to make three points that arise from it. First, there is a definitional problem. We note that in their paper (1998: 188), Wu and Chu define competition law and policy as:

the set of laws, regulations and institutions which control restrictive business practices, including domestic cartels and horizontal restraints among competitors; dominant firm behaviour or monopolisation; anti-competitive mergers; and other restrictive business practices.

They point out (191) that this definition is broad in that it embodies effective enforcement. But, from our perspective, their definition is not broad enough, in that it does not include government regulatory and other interventions that might also be antithetical to the competitive process. In effect, their definition around business conduct means that 'competition law' is substituted for 'competition policy'.

Second, one might contemplate some aspects of competition law, for instance, merger or takeover procedures, as being quite amenable to (beneficial) harmonisation, particularly at later stages of economic integration (Bollard and Vautier 1998: 140), whereas general harmonisation to tight standards would be neither possible nor beneficial. Trebilcock (1998) is even more forthright in his reservations about highly standardised rules of competition. While efficiency-inducing effects are acknowledged, Trebilcock ranks highly the difficulty involved in reaching consensus at the regional level (he cites NAFTA), let alone at a multilateral level.

Third, as far as competition-related policies are concerned (that is, not just competition law), there is in our view considerable room for and need for *convergence of direction* in the Asia Pacific Region, consistent with variations in national policies. Once again the definitional issue can obscure rather than enlighten. Wu and Chu (1998) themselves go some way to bringing other policies, notably trade policies, into what we call a competition framework. Indeed, they state that trade policy – in the sense of removing entry barriers to enable producers to compete across borders – 'should form an integral part of a general policy aimed at fair competition' (178). They are clearly alert to the adverse effects that trade measures, particularly anti-dumping, can have on competition, and indeed go so far as to recommend that anti-dumping remedies be withdrawn in favour of 'competition policy [= law]' controls (194). They also specifically acknowledge intellectual property right issues.

Action plans for competition policy and deregulation

The underlying theme of the Competition Policy and Deregulation Action Plans is the ascertaining of appropriate cooperation initiatives and arrangements in respect of transparency, information gathering and sharing, consultation among competition authorities and technical assistance. Also envisaged at the outset were non-binding principles on competition policy and/or laws and the possibility of guidelines on domestic deregulation.

The convenor's summary report on Competition Policy and on Deregulation (APEC CTI 1999b) reinforced the short-term and ongoing focus on information sharing, dialogue and study, transparency of existing policy regimes and

---

BOX 1

COMPETITION POLICY

Objective

APEC economies will enhance the competitive environment in the Asia–Pacific region by introducing or maintaining effective and adequate competition policy and/or laws and associated enforcement policies, ensuring the transparency of the above, and promoting cooperation among APEC economies, thereby maximising, *inter alia*, the efficient operation of markets, competition among producers and traders, and consumer benefits.

Guidelines

Each APEC economy will:

a. review its respective competition policy and/or laws and the enforcement thereof in terms of transparency;
b. implement as appropriate technical assistance in regard to policy development; legislative drafting; and the constitution, powers and functions of appropriate enforcement agencies; and
c. establish appropriate cooperation arrangements among APEC economies.

OSAKA ACTION AGENDA

---

reform processes, and policy inter-relationships as important first steps in building a common understanding of these policy areas within APEC. Continuing activities and maintaining dialogue with other international organisations (notably the WTO and OECD) in respect of competition policy and law were also highlighted as 'collective actions achieved'. A particular ongoing collective action is to continue to respond positively to the WTO Working Group on the Interaction Between Trade and Competition Policy, thereby ensuring information sharing on APEC's Competition Policy/Deregulation work. One implementation step commenced in 1998 was a study on the advantages and disadvantages of competition law for APEC's developing economies.

Another step is examining 'the possibility of establishing non-binding APEC *guidelines* on domestic *deregulation*' (emphases added), which guidelines seem to link back to the mandate for APEC economies to identify common

---

BOX 2

COMPETITION POLICY

Collective Actions

APEC economies will:

a. gather information and promote dialogue on and study, starting from 1996:
   i) the objectives, necessity, role and operation of each APEC economy's competition policy and/or laws and administrative procedures, thereby establishing a database on competition policy;
   ii) competition policy issues that impact on trade and investment flows in the Asia–Pacific region;
   iii) areas for technical assistance and the modalities thereof, including exchange and training programs for officials in charge of competition policy, taking into account the availability of resources; and
   iv) the inter-relationship between competition policy and/or laws and other policies related to trade and investment;
b. deepen competition policy dialogue between APEC economies and relevant international organisations:
c. continue to develop understanding in the APEC business community of competition policy and/or laws and administrative procedures;
d. encourage cooperation among the competition authorities of APEC economies with regard to information exchange, notification and consultation;
e. contribute to the use of trade and competition laws, policies and measures that promote free and open trade, investment and competition; and
f. consider developing non-binding principles for competition policy and/or laws in APEC.

OSAKA ACTION AGENDA

---

priority areas and sectors for deregulation and for the provision of technical assistance related thereto. This is in addition to the medium-term implementation step to:

> promote dialogue and understanding within APEC, through focused discussion, on the experiences of APEC economies and on the principles applied to, and best practices in, regulatory reform (drawing on the short-term information gathering exercise) (APEC CTI 1998b: 77)

BOX 3

DEREGULATION

Objective

APEC economies will:

a. note the transparency of their respective regulatory regime; and
b. eliminate trade and investment distortion arising from domestic regulations which not only impede free and open trade and investment in the Asia–Pacific region but also are more trade and/or investment restricting than necessary to fulfil a legitimate objective.

OSAKA ACTION AGENDA

BOX 4

DEREGULATION

Collective Actions

APEC economies, taking into account work done in other areas of APEC activity, will:

a. publish annual reports detailing actions taken by APEC economies to deregulate their domestic regulatory regimes; and
b. develop further actions taking into account the above reports including:

   i) policy dialogue on APEC economies' experiences in regard to best practices in deregulation, including the use of individual case studies to assist in the design and implementation of deregulatory measures, and consideration of further options for a work program which may include:
   – identification of common priority areas and sectors for deregulation;
   – provision of technical assistance in designing and implementing deregulation measures;
   – examination of the possibility of establishing APEC guidelines on domestic deregulation;

   ii) regular dialogue with the business community, including a possible symposium.

OSAKA ACTION AGENDA

That appears to be an attempt to build up a set of regulatory principles from a consensus as to what constitutes 'best practices' in respect of both deregulation and new regulation. It should be noted that conformity with competition principles will generally be a prerequisite for 'best practice' in these areas.

Competition principles

APEC's Annual Workshop on Competition Policy and Deregulation has itself facilitated progress on APEC's collective commitments in these two policy areas, including in respect of competition and regulatory principles. In Quebec 1997 (PECC (TPF) 1997) and Kuantan 1998 (PECC (TPF) 1998) the PECC Trade Policy Forum was invited to report on its Competition Principles Project; and in February 1999 (PECC (TPF) 1999), a presentation on this Project formed part of a special Competition Policy Dialogue in the CTI. The CTI was informed that the proposed Competition Principles for APEC economies were seen as a necessary response to the demands of APEC's long-term goals as well as a necessary part of a coherent policy response to the Asian crisis. Fundamental elements of PECC's approach were described as follows:

- the role of the Competition Principles is to promote or defend the whole process of competition in globalising markets, through creating and maintaining those conditions that will allow and encourage the competitive process to work;
- the Principles therefore cover a range of government actions as well as business actions that impact on globalising markets;[5]
- traditional policy compartments are breaking down as they are becoming a barrier to policy coherence around a competition focus;
- promoting competition is not simply about increasing or maximising international trade, but is important because of its role in stimulating markets to operate more efficiently in the interests of all consumers.

In outlining its Principles for guiding policy development in APEC economies, and the rationale for them, PECC's Trade Policy Forum stressed the linkage between the Competition Principles and the APEC Leaders' theme of strengthening the foundations for sustainable growth through cooperative strategy. In endorsing the Principles, PECC's TPF had been motivated by the impetus they could give to building a competition-driven, liberalising, growth-oriented and welfare-enhancing policy framework for APEC. But their adoption by APEC would clearly rely on cooperation in overall policy direction. The PECC Standing Committee, which subsequently endorsed the Principles, accepted their compatibility with the APEC model of concerted unilateralism and general non-negotiated concessions over time.

The PECC Competition Principles featured at APEC's 1999 Competition Policy and Deregulation Workshop in support of the market-strengthening theme and the interest in developing a framework of competition (and regulatory) principles for endorsement by APEC Leaders. Also, their application to financial markets was the subject of a paper (Grimes 1999) presented to a joint session between the Workshop and APEC's Group on Services. The 'Agreed Outcomes' from the Workshop (APEC 1999b) acknowledged that the PECC Principles provided the foundation for consensus building on a competition and regulatory reform-driven framework for APEC. The PECC Principles were seen as a reference point for developing, in the short term, a set of core principles together with related actions. They were also seen as an important reference document for integrating the Principles into Individual Action Plans, which itself could inform the further development of 'the APEC principles'.

Action plan objectives

The core objective of any competition-related policy is the promotion or defence of the competitive process. That is not to say that competition (let alone atomistic competition) is an end in itself but, rather, it is the preferred means of moving APEC economies towards achievement of their collective goals. An efficiently functioning competitive process is the basis for 'maximising the efficient operation of markets'; and it is efficiently operating markets that will best guide the quantum and composition and attributes of the total supply of goods and services produced and consumed. It is important to distinguish between the efficiency and welfare aims for Competition Policy and Deregulation, and one or more other objectives sometimes assigned to these areas: for example, fair trade, eliminating trade and investment distortions, zero impediments to trade, and guaranteed market access.

APEC's Competition Policy Objective (see Box 1) links the enhancement of the competitive environment – by means of transparent, effective and adequate competition policy and/or laws and their enforcement – with maximising the efficient operation of markets, competition among producers and traders, and consumer benefits.

The basic objective of market efficiency is clearly recognised. There is a logical link between the Objective and the mandated collective action to 'contribute to the use of trade and competition laws, policies and measures that promote free and open trade, investment *and competition*' (emphasis added) together with the requirement to 'consider developing non-binding principles on competition policy and/or laws' (Box 2).

By contrast, the stated Objective for the Deregulation policy area is not expressed in *competition* terms but is directed specifically at the removal of domestic regulations that *distort/impede/over-restrict free and open trade and investment* (Box 3). (Over-restriction is defined in terms of a distortion that is more than necessary to fulfil a legitimate objective.) Having merged the work areas of Competition Policy and Deregulation, it is unsatisfactory that each area has retained the original separate and conflicting objectives. In our view, the Deregulation area should adopt the same objective as Competition

Policy, namely market efficiency. Although the two areas involve different policies, they should both serve the same end.

Review of individual action plans

The 1998 Individual Action Plans reflect a range of views on what is encompassed by APEC's Competition Policy and Deregulation policy areas. This should not be a surprise, since the IAP process, underpinned by consensus on the importance of transparency, will inevitably reveal different perspectives arising from differences in economic development and market orientation. More problematic is the lack of consensus on the objectives and essence of 'Competition Policy' and presumably therefore on the role it can play in achieving APEC's overall goals. The present lack of consensus in this regard complicates the task of suggesting improvements to the Individual Action Plans.

The objectives stated by individual economies for the Competition Policy area vary markedly, from a clear focus on efficiency and consumer welfare to free and fair competition and the protection of small firms. Where fairness means protection for producers in general or for particular producers, this is generally not helpful either to the cause of trade liberalisation or to market strengthening aims. The IAPs suggest that APEC economies are still some distance from converging around the competition–efficiency–welfare (not just producer welfare) paradigm although there is increasing recognition of it.

In respect of Deregulation, the IAPs highlight two dimensions:

(i) liberalisation/privatisation/corporatisation, that is, more private sector investment and reduced government involvement in running the economy;
(ii) reduction or elimination of regulations in order to cut the cost of doing business and to increase efficiency (and competitiveness), innovation and market access.

Where the emphasis lies in an Individual Action Plan depends in part on the extent of current government involvement in the economy. In economies where significant privatisation has already occurred, the focus is more on reducing regulation. Economies that have extensive government involvement are more focused on privatisation as their first step in the deregulation process. Many economies deal with both of the dimensions described.

It is important to read each economy's Competition Policy plan in conjunction with its Deregulation plan in order to get a better sense of the extent to which competition and efficiency objectives are embedded in domestic policy. A reading of the US plans, for example, reveals that deregulation is an important part of that economy's *competition* agenda, whereas the US treatment of so-called Competition Policy is relatively narrow.

When read in conjunction, most of the Competition Policy and Deregulation IAPs are geared towards creating the most favourable market *conditions* as distinct from particular market *outcomes*. Some economies show a mixed focus on market conditions and market outcomes.

On the interconnection between the Competition Policy and Deregulation areas, the PECC Trade Policy Forum submitted the following (PECC (TPF) 1997):

> APEC's Competition Policy Workshops have emphasised the important links between competition policy and deregulation. Put another way, they have been focussing on a competition-based approach to regulation and an entry barrier approach to competition. However, the IAPs themselves tend to place more emphasis on linkages between deregulation and trade/market access. This approach in the IAPs reinforces concerns that traditional views on trade and market access, which give insufficient weight to competition and efficiency considerations, have been given undue prominence.

Our review of the Deregulation area of the 1998 IAPs suggests that there is now less emphasis on trade and market access and somewhat more emphasis on the link between deregulation and competition/efficiency (and competitiveness).

THE PLACE OF COMPETITION LAW

Even where two economies share the same objectives for Competition Policy, their means of achieving these can vary markedly. Competition law is a case in point. Some Individual Action Plans give considerable prominence to the role of competition law; and for those economies that presently have competition laws, some common elements emerge:

- prohibitions on certain forms of private anti-competitive conduct;
- acceptance of the desirability of competitive neutrality through applying domestic competition rules to all producers;
- identification of special issues relating to utilities and natural monopolies.

With the exception of Singapore and Hong Kong, whether or not a competition law is in place and its degree of sophistication generally depends on the level of economic development. Those economies with general competition laws also have consumer protection laws and a body (often a single body) responsible for enforcement of both laws. There are some economies with no present law (or with unsophisticated laws) or enforcement authority, while some are investigating the need for, or improvement or implementation of, such law and enforcement.

Discussions within both APEC and PECC indicate that resistance to having a general competition law arises for two main reasons: first, a belief that general competition law is not necessary (although industry-specific regulation might be) in an economy relying on free trade and generally open and deregulated markets to foster the competitive process. This issue has yet to be resolved. Second, there is a perceived sequencing problem in developing economies, giving rise to questions about the priority that should be accorded to competition law relative to other measures aimed at liberalisation and deregulation.

Discussion on competition law at PAFTAD 24 also focused on the sequencing problem (although some scepticism was expressed) and cautioned on pushing developing economies too fast or prematurely, especially on industry structure, prior to further deregulation/reforms and some playing out of technological change. Discussion also emphasised the need to strengthen institutions and legal and enforcement mechanisms through transparency, independence, accountability and resources.[6] There was an attempt to link the competition law sequencing issue for an economy with the competitiveness of that economy (as distinct from competition in markets); and a perceived conflict between a 'market structure' approach to competition policy and industrial and trade policies was mentioned.

In our view, the sequencing issue too has not been resolved and needs careful examination, especially since there is an argument that developing economies also need some disciplines on anti-competitive business conduct as part of the mix of measures to make these economies more open and competition oriented. It is hoped that the study commissioned by APEC on the advantages and disadvantages of competition law for APEC's developing economies will take the debate forward. It may well be that the question 'to have or not to have a competition law' is wrongly formulated and has been driven in part by contrasting a zero base with a fully developed US-type anti-trust law and enforcement. Perhaps more consideration should be given to appropriate starting points for developing economies (or, as some would say, minimum standards) and how the number and type of competition rules and associated enforcement requirements might be accommodated during a transition period and assisted by capacity-building initiatives.

Trade-related issue?

In the main, international discussions on 'competition policy' have been stimulated by its promotion as a 'new trade-related issue' and its relevance to what Lawrence (1996) called 'deep integration' via policies 'beyond the border'.[7] There is no doubt that competition policies (or lack thereof) may positively reinforce (or negatively impinge on) international trade. Removing all border/market access restrictions affecting cross-border trade in goods and services does not assure non-discriminatory access for foreign supplies if other policies, including domestic regulations, discriminate against them. Indeed, as border barriers to foreign trade have been lowered, the spotlight has shifted to the role and influence of a range of other policies (now relatively more important) and especially to the ways in which and the extent to which those policies discriminate against internationally traded supplies or discriminate in favour of domestically owned or operated production.

In particular, the spotlight has shifted to the potential for private business conduct to introduce another distortion into enlarging markets in response to reductions in government barriers to border/market access. At the multilateral level, there is concern that embedded or new business practices within or across economies might nullify the benefits of negotiated trade concessions. Indeed, this concern was reflected in the establishment of a special Working Group in the WTO to study the interaction between trade and competition policy.

Interest in this linkage between international trade and restrictive business practices is in fact long-standing,[8] so much so that 'competition policy' was becoming synonymous with competition law (covering prohibitions on certain unilateral and collusive conduct and mergers/takeovers) and associated legal remedies.

Support for a trade-related rationale for 'competition policy' tends to be manifest in the 'market access' objective often assigned to this policy area. One problem with attributing a 'market access' objective to competition policies is that it risks importing traditional trade policy concerns about *country* access. The term 'market access' is strongly associated with the WTO and with its focus on trade-related negotiated concessions between countries. Australia's presentation at the CTI's Dialogue on Competition Policy and Deregulation (APEC 1999a: 5) suggested that trade policy experts adopt a broad approach to 'market access', namely, the totality of government-imposed conditions under which a good or service may enter a *country,* while for competition policy experts, 'market access' means the opportunity to compete effectively in a *market* (emphases added). As Hawke (1999b) says:

> APEC is taking us away from the idea that national markets are matters of pride and national value so that access is provided to foreigners only as a concession in return for something equally valuable from them. This legalistic ideal is the best that could be attained in 1947 when GATT was formed. It is giving way in APEC to the economic idea that world income is maximised when there are as few barriers as possible to resource allocation irrespective of national boundaries.

As long as competition-related policies are seen to drive off *trade-related* and *country* concerns rather than *competition* and *market* concerns, there will be difficulty in advancing the Competition Policy and Deregulation areas within APEC.

Our extensive research on the linkages between international trade and various approaches to the promotion of competition has led us unequivocally to the conclusion that 'competition policy' is not simply or even primarily a trade-related issue.[9] (Neither should international discussions in this policy area be confined to competition law.[10]) We do not accept that the primary objective of international competition policies is to maximise the benefits of free trade through combating government or private actions seen to nullify or impair negotiated trade concessions. (For discussion, see Vautier and Lloyd 1997: Part I.) Competition in markets is desirable independently of trade liberalisation, because of its contribution to efficiency and welfare. Welfare economics teaches us that competitive behaviour and free international trade are two separate conditions required for the efficient allocation of resources in the world economy. Trends towards adoption of more pro-competition policies in areas such as deregulation, privatisation and foreign direct investment reflect the converging view that the competitive process is the primary and preferred means for promoting efficient resource allocations both in individual economies and in trans-national markets.

In theory the apparent paradigm difference between trade and competition policies should not matter, given their shared ultimate aim of promoting efficient production and consumption in the world economy. However, in practice, we cannot be so sanguine.

Fair competition?

Wu and Chu (1998) postulate that 'fair competition' is the general principle that brings trade and competition policies together. They elaborate on how they view policy fairness:

> The concept of what is 'reciprocal is fair' and what is 'level (as in a playing field) is fair' has taken root and will not be done away with. Therefore, countries can no longer use the excuse 'it is purely domestic' when they choose not to discuss the impacts of regulatory, purchasing or competition policy regimes.

This notion of policy fairness and of the underpinning notions of reciprocity and equality of access do not sit comfortably in the APEC model of open regionalism and concerted unilateralism. The notion of 'fairness' in competition, as with 'fairness' in trade, risks being construed as a distributive policy to promote the interests of particular traders or competitors as distinct from promoting efficiency in the process of trade and competition.

The key meaning of fairness in the area of Competition Policy is competitive neutrality. Competition amongst producers on the basis of merit, coupled with greater transparency and accountability in policy formation and application, are likely to be fairer than market positions secured by special government-endowed privileges, protection and shelters, with their discriminatory impacts both within and between economies. Our view is that building and implementing a competition-driven policy framework for APEC has the hallmarks of a fairer approach to policy and markets. More open, competitive and well-functioning markets will generally be fairer markets. Merit-based competition is an impetus for business to pursue opportunities on behalf of customers/consumers and to manage the risks of doing so. Competition-promoting policies are best directed at generally fostering these opportunities to participate in economic activity rather than seeking to provide guarantees of particular market positions, structures or outcomes. As many commentators recognise, industrial and regulatory policies can have negative impacts on opportunities to compete. At the same time, competitive endeavour will usually be modified to some extent by appropriate social constraints and responsibilities. In short, in globalising markets, transparency/accountability (including in corporate governance) and non-discrimination/competitive neutrality contribute to fairness. In this sense we see no contradiction in the call for fair and efficient markets.

In policy making, an important consideration is the question as to which policy instruments are best assigned to the achievement of agreed policy objectives. If individual policy instruments, competition law for example, are assigned multiple and inherently conflicting objectives, one or more of the objectives are compromised from the start. Efficient policy targeting, to deal separately with, say, efficiency and income distribution objectives, is likely to be more conducive to successful policy outcomes. Supporting an efficiency–welfare orientation for competition principles and policies does not deny the existence of other legitimate non-efficiency goals; but it is a matter of policy makers assigning instruments that deal most systematically and directly with such goals.

Competition principles should be helpful for addressing 'market access' and 'fairness' issues, especially where market access is taken to mean country access and fairness is confused with the interests of particular exporters/ producers. If market access and fairness are regarded as the objectives of competition policies – reflecting a tension between trade and competition perspectives – conflicts between trade policy and competition will continue. From a competition perspective, these conflicts should be resolved in favour of protecting the competitive process as distinct from trying to guarantee or prevent a particular trade flow. It is important for the integrity of a competition framework for APEC that disputes over market access and fairness in trade are distinguished from disputes over the efficiency of the competitive process. Many of these disputes will be seen in trade-related terms: parallel importing, export cartels and intellectual property, for example. However, an impact on exports does not itself constitute a cross-border competition problem warranting intervention or retaliatory action.

Underlying all of this is a broad shift in emphasis from policies that unduly favour producers to policies that give more weight to the interests of consumers/buyers in terms of their real incomes, the choices available to them, and the search for innovative responses to their demands. However, there is not really a consumer versus producer dichotomy here. If there is a competition-driven policy approach and if concerted unilateralism works, the loss of protection for producers within economies can be compensated by the expansion of opportunities for competitive business in markets that are enlarging and liberalising.

The comprehensiveness principle

Any competition framework for APEC economies needs to be underpinned by the principle of *comprehensiveness*. Comprehensiveness, along with *non-discrimination/competitive neutrality*, *transparency* and *accountability*, comprise the core Competition Principles advocated by PECC. First of all, the promotion of competition is relevant to goods and services from all modes of supply including trade, but also home country production and inwards and outwards foreign direct investment (which is of special importance to service industries requiring a commercial presence). Second, comprehensiveness in relation to supply means that foreign and domestic suppliers, and large as well as small suppliers, are covered by the framework, as are all economies irrespective of their particular stage of development. As PECC puts it (PECC 1999), there should be a competition dimension to all policy making that impacts on goods and services markets. Exceptions from reliance upon well-functioning market mechanisms and from merit-based competition should be minimised.

The General Principle of comprehensiveness as it is expressed in the Osaka Action Agenda envisages that 'all impediments to achieving the long-term goal of free and open trade and investment' will be addressed in APEC's liberalisation and facilitation process. The term 'impediments' has thus gained some currency in the context of the Bogor goals, and there have been major studies (see PECC 1995, for example) directed at identifying impediments to trade and investment liberalisation in the region. Business firms too tend to be responsive to the language of 'impediments' and willingly submit what they regard as impediments to their trade and investment efforts, particularly those that raise transaction costs.

Once again, this is not the language of *competition* analysis. An actual or perceived 'impediment' need not cause a distortion to the competitive process and may not therefore justify government intervention in the marketplace. Having identified regulatory or other impediments to trade or investment, some assessment is required of their severity in terms of impact on the competitive process. A 'competition scanner' should be applied in order to assess which impediments constitute a risk to the competitive process, as distinct from individual competitors. Does an impediment on its own, or in conjunction with others, matter in competition terms?[11]

We do not interpret the comprehensiveness principle, as expressed in the Osaka Action Agenda, as a mandate for pursuing all impediments to trade and investment, irrespective of competition considerations.[12] We do not believe that this principle was intended to mean that trade maximisation is a superior objective to all others. It is for this reason that trade policy needs to be treated as an integral part of any competition framework, so as to align better the objectives of competition-related policies. APEC economies should be encouraging policy thinking to move beyond traditional policy divisions and to cohere around competition principles so that competition can become a unifying theme for policy development in the region, including for trade policy.

Following the debate on Competition Policy and Deregulation that has already occurred, APEC has clearly come some distance in linking trade, competition, deregulation and welfare. However, a problem with the present Individual Action Plan process is that it imports the policy fragmentation that still typifies policy development in individual APEC economies. As part of its development of a framework for thinking about competition issues in globalising markets, APEC could use the IAP process to facilitate greater coherence around the unifying theme of promoting and defending the competitive process.

PECC has been stressing the importance of 'competition scanning' in relation to a whole range of government actions or inactions that can and do impact upon market conditions and the competitive process. International trade policy and foreign investment policy are particularly important in this regard, but so too are other policy areas such as Standards and Conformance, Intellectual Property Rights and Government Procurement. PECC's core competition principle of comprehensiveness requires a competition dimension to be reflected in all relevant areas of policy development.

The importance of this generic approach to promoting competition; the role of Competition Principles in building a competition framework;[13] a competition dimension being embedded in the Individual Action Plans as a unifying theme for policy development; and of the role that Competition Principles can play in cross-border dispute resolution cannot be over-stated, given APEC's aspirations for continuing economic and social advancement.

CHALLENGES AND TASKS FOR APEC IN THE TWENTY-FIRST CENTURY

1 The present lack of consensus around the objectives and scope of APEC's Competition Policy and Deregulation areas, and the policy fragmentation observed within the IAP process, underlie the importance of the CAP requirement that APEC economies should consider developing non-binding principles relevant to the promotion of competition and regulatory reform. These Principles should reflect clear objectives consistent with APEC's growth and welfare aims. Adopting and operationalising a coherent set of competition principles – specifically, the PECC Principles (PECC 1999) – for building a competition-driven policy framework, is the primary challenge.

2 Recognition that application of the core competition principle of comprehensiveness covers:

- all modes of international supply;
- a range of policy instruments including trade policy;
- public as well as private actions;
- small as well as large economies;
- developed as well as developing economies; and
- small and medium-sized enterprises as well as large enterprises.

3   In respect of transparency, we agree with the PECC TPF submission to APEC's Competition Policy and Deregulation Workshop (PECC (TPF) 1997) that the IAPs could usefully include:

- a clear and authoritative statement of all relevant laws and regulatory interventions;[14]
- a clear description of decision making/enforcement procedures;
- a clear definition of the considerations which will guide administrative discretion on all regulatory matters, including competition law.

Transparency of policy implementation also requires a clear exposition of the reasoning behind actual decisions where discretion is involved (as it is in competition law).

4   Guided by the PECC Competition Principles, which are generally applicable, each APEC member should devise its most effective means for promoting the role of competition

- across traditionally separate policy compartments, and
- amongst those groups, notably business and consumers, most immediately affected by a comprehensive approach to the promotion and defence of competition.

Many of the ingredients are already present. But the process of incorporating competition principles into and throughout the IAPs for each APEC economy will take time. While this process will be accompanied by awareness building, a pro-active competition advocacy role will be essential. This will tend to have a national focus but it can be given impetus by APEC Economic Leaders and Ministers (not just Trade Ministers) and via peer as well as independent reviews of IAPs.

5   It is clear that APEC officials cannot be isolated from the wider policy development processes within their domestic economies. This point is of general relevance and importance. APEC began with Foreign Affairs and Trade Ministries and continues to draw heavily on these for Senior APEC Officials. But economic, financial and other expertise will increasingly need to be drawn from other agencies as the business of APEC turns more to *how* member economies get to where they have said they want to go. This observation is also pertinent in effecting better linkages between macro, financial and competition-related (including trade) policies.

6   A competition framework based on competition principles is, in our view, essential to the 'how' question. It would provide a direct response to the purposes of APEC in dealing with welfare aims. A key challenge is to build the level of comprehension about what this framework entails and how it can guide concerted unilateralism. Essentially, that comprehension must rise above the classification of tariffs, facilitation, Ecotech, financial issues and social issues as discrete policy arenas (Hawke 1999b).

7   The Individual and Collective Action Plan process needs to be responsive to this challenge. This comes to the heart of the implementation issue:

how, if competition (and regulatory) principles are endorsed by APEC Economic Leaders, do they become integrated into the Action Plans? Review methodology is important in this context, since there is a risk that continuing with the present basis for review of each of the individual policy areas will reinforce the traditional divisions and approaches to them. The PECC Competition Principles provide a new reference point for Action Plan Reviews.

8   A primary challenge for APEC is to link capacity-building aims more directly and tangibly with the key requirements for giving effect to competition principles, and hence with economic integration in the region.

9   Training of specialists is mandated in the Collective Action Plan and clearly fits with growing recognition of the need for capacity building as an essential stimulus for both policy development and implementation.[15] The CTI's efforts in promoting the sharing of information and experiences are applauded and encouraged. But APEC officials need more assistance to formulate effective policy dialogue. This has been described as a process intermediate between PECC's annual *Pacific Economic Outlook* exercise, which is an effective networking of forecasters, and determining negotiating positions (Hawke 1999a).

10 The Osaka Action Agenda envisaged APEC economies exploring the possibility of taking joint initiatives under the WTO, including initiatives for WTO Ministerial meetings (APEC 1995). Obviously, any mutually reinforcing opportunities to enhance liberalisation and the open trading system should be taken. The promotion of competition principles at the WTO level is a case in point. But it would be a great pity if APEC were distracted from its gestating and non-binding approach to competition principles and policies by the prospect of negotiating trade-related 'competition' rules and specific concessions. This is especially so, given the constraints on the WTO taking a comprehensive approach to competition issues. Of paramount importance for APEC at this stage is to continue efforts to build support for competition principles and their application in APEC economies. The more that APEC builds and applies its own principled competition framework, the stronger its position to influence the WTO's approach to issues such as anti-dumping, export and import cartels and government procurement, all of which are relevant to trade and competition and the efficient operation of globalising markets.

CONCLUSION

It was suggested (note 7) that the distinction between 'at the border' and 'beyond/within the border' was not particularly robust insofar as competition policies were concerned. We reaffirm that view. The comprehensive promotion of effective competition in globalising markets needs to address:

•   entry conditions affecting access into a country;

- impacts of domestic policies on the conditions facing business within that country; and
- cross-border spill-overs of government or business actions that unduly undermine the competitive process.

Ultimately, a competition-driven policy framework for APEC economies would encompass all those policies and government and private actions that cause anti-competitive distortions to domestic and inwards and outwards flows of goods, services and investment.

Over time, the building of a comprehensive competition framework should allow the phasing out of a separate Competition Policy area in the IAPs. Competition law could be combined with other aspects of regulatory policy, also subject to competition principles.

To date, APEC could properly claim that its distinctive and relatively informal approach is helping to shape a constructive response to the relatively new and complex area of competition-related policies for globalising markets. Its interest in competition and regulatory principles is encouraging. APEC can certainly add value if it proceeds to embrace a set of competition principles for guiding (not prescribing) policy development within individual member economies. The willingness of APEC Economic Leaders to adopt a clear and coherent set of competition principles is the necessary starting point. Ministers and Officials will then be responsible for ensuring that these principles are integrated over time within the Collective and Individual Action Plans, that they are used as a reference point for Action Plan Reviews, and adhered to in practical situations. All of this would be a major demonstration of Leaders' vision and of APEC's credibility as an engine for well-functioning markets and economic and social progress. Adoption by APEC of the PECC Competition Principles, and giving effect to them within member economies, would certainly qualify as 'best practice'.

There will be continuing debate on the issue of non-binding versus binding principles. To be realistic, non-binding principles are the order of the day in APEC. This approach is advantageous if it avoids undermining the principles by negotiation and thereby enables adoption of a sharper and fuller description of the principles and the requirements for upholding them in practice. The purer the principles adopted by APEC economies as a group, the more effective they will be as a guide to policy development in individual economies. Inevitably there will be compromise and pragmatism in actual policy design and implementation. But if the principles themselves (including objectives) are compromised and pragmatised they will have little value.

The history of non-binding multilateral agreements in the area of competition law and policy is not encouraging, as there has been no incentive for or means of enforcing them (see Lloyd and Vautier 1999). Similarly, APEC is a consensus forum with no incentive or means of enforcing non-binding principles. Thus, for adherence to any agreed competition principles, APEC must rely on the concerted unilateralism and peer pressure it espouses, as well as effective independent and peer review.

NOTES

1   We gratefully acknowledge the considerable research assistance provided by Vanessa Bruton, a solicitor with Hesketh Henry, Auckland, in analysing the 1998 Individual Action Plans of APEC Economies.

2   In line with Leaders' instructions from Kuala Lumpur (APEC 1998b), work in this area will also address institutional weaknesses and capacity shortages, particularly skills shortages; strengthening social safety nets; and needs in the area of economic governance.

3   Discussion at PAFTAD 24 (Wu and Chu 1998: 332) suggested that the complex interaction between competition policy and traditional trade and industrial policies made international agreements on competition policy difficult to achieve.

4   Trebilcock (1998) argues that interest in the European Union model as a general paradigm, and given its supra-national institutions, is misguided since such a model arises out of a particular set of geopolitical circumstances.

5   At PAFTAD 24, Janow (1998) argued that one of the Competition Policy issues 'that could usefully receive priority international attention' is the 'broad spectrum of government actions that can negatively impact on the ability of firms to compete in a market – for example: exceptions to competition laws; industrial policies; and government procurement practices'. She goes on to say that these 'important and difficult areas need to be more fully addressed in an international context because they have been and are likely to continue to be sources of international economic and trade tension in the future'.

6   Without these characteristics, competition law itself could be misapplied with negative impacts on the business sector (331).

7   The distinction between 'border' and 'beyond-the-border' policies is not accurate in relation to competition policies since these apply both within and across national borders.

8   See Lloyd and Vautier (1999: Part Four) for a review of non-binding approaches, for example, UNCTAD's Set of Multilaterally Agreed Equitable Principles and Rules for the Control of Restrictive Business Practices.

9   Certainly there are some competition issues that are very much trade-related, for example, anti-dumping, and they should be dealt with multilaterally in the 'trade-related' WTO.

10   General discussion at PAFTAD 24 (Wu and Chu 1998: 329) agreed: 'The meaning of competition policy should be taken in its broad sense in creating a competitive environment and not taken narrowly to mean antitrust and competition laws'.

11   There is an analogous question in the policy harmonisation debate: do identified policy differences between APEC economies interfere with the competitive process (or even with trade facilitation) to such an extent as to warrant policy adjustment?

12   Similarly, only those 'private restraints' that actually or potentially distort the competitive process warrant a regulatory response.

13   The relevance of the principles of *comprehensiveness* and *non-discrimination/competitive neutrality* to a competition-driven policy framework will increasingly come to the fore as governments become less involved in economic activity and as opportunities are enhanced for 'foreign' sources of goods and services supply and investment.

14   Growing acceptance of transparency has contributed to clear and authoritative statements in the IAPs although the level of inclusiveness will depend on each member's test of 'relevance'.

15   'The idea has never been as important as the execution' (*Economist*, 1999).

REFERENCES

APEC (1995) *The Osaka Action Agenda – Implementation of the Bogor Declaration*, November, Japan.

—— (1998a) 'APEC 1999: New Zealand objectives', background paper, APEC Task Force, November: Wellington: Ministry of Foreign Affairs and Trade.

—— (1998b) 'APEC Economic Leaders Declaration', 18 November, Kuala Lumpur.

—— (1999a) CTI 'Trade Policy Dialogue', February, Wellington.

—— (1999b) CTI 'Convenor's Report – Competition Policy/Deregulation', May, Christchurch.

APEC CTI (1998) *Annual Report to Ministers*, Committee on Trade and Investment, November, Singapore.

Bollard, A. and Vautier, K.M. (1998) 'The convergence of competition law within APEC and the CER Agreement', in Rong-I Wu and Yun-Peng Chu, eds, (1998).

Grimes, A. (1999) 'Competition Policy: Application to Financial Services', paper presented to APEC Joint Session between Competition Policy and Deregulation Workshop and the Group on Services, May, Christchurch.

Economist (1999) Letter to the Editor, 20–6 March, London.

Hawke, G. (1999a) 'Reflections by a PECC observer', First Senior Officials' Meeting, 8–9 February, Wellington (unpublished).

—— (1999b) Oral Submission to Foreign Affairs, Defence and Trade Committee Inquiry into the Implications of New Zealand's Participation in APEC, 25 March.

Janow, M. (1998) 'Policy approaches to economic deregulation and regulatory reform', in Rong-I Wu and Yun-Peng Chu, eds, (1998).

Lawrence, R.Z. (1996) *Regionalism, Multilateralism and Deeper Integration*, Washington DC: Brookings Institution.

Lloyd, P.J. and Vautier, K.M. (1999) *Promoting Competition in Global Markets: A Multi-National Approach*, UK: Edward Elgar Publishing Ltd.

Panel of Independent Experts (1998) August (unpublished).

PECC (1995) *Survey of Impediments to Trade and Investment in the APEC Region*, Singapore: PECC.

—— (1999) *PECC Principles for Guiding the Development of a Competition-Driven Policy Framework for APEC Economies*, June, PECC.

PECC (TPF) (1997) 'Comments on competition policy area of MAPA', APEC Workshop on Competition Policy and Deregulation, Quebec City, 18–19 May.

—— (1998) Presentation at PECC Trade Policy Forum Workshop on Competition Principles Project, 4 September, Kuantan.

—— (1999) 'International cooperation through Competition Principles: The role of Competition Principles in building a competition framework for policy development in APEC', APEC CTI Trade Policy Dialogue, 5–6 February, Wellington.

Trebilcock, M.J. (1998) 'The evolution of Competition Policy: Lessons from comparative experience', in Rong-I Wu and Yun-Peng Chu, eds, (1998).

Vautier, K.M. and Lloyd, P.J. (1997) *International Trade and Competition Policy: CER, APEC and the WTO*, Wellington: The Institute of Policy Studies.

World Trade Organisation (WTO) (1997) *Annual Report 1997*, vol. 1, Geneva: WTO.

Wu, Rong-I and Chu, Yun-Peng (eds) (1998) *Business, Markets and Government in the Asia Pacific*, London: Routledge.

—— (1998) 'Trade and Competition Policy', in Rong-I Wu and Yun-Peng Chu, eds, (1998).

11 Application of CGE modelling to analysis of environmental measures in APEC

Kanemi Ban

INTRODUCTION

Worldwide energy-related CO_2 emissions have risen steadily since the Industrial Revolution. Presently, atmospheric concentration of CO_2 is responsible for more than half of greenhouse effects. The reduction of CO_2 emissions has thus become one of the major environmental policy objectives of most countries. At the June 1992 Earth Summit in Rio de Janeiro, more than 150 countries signed a treaty aimed at stabilising greenhouse gases, mainly CO_2. Most industrial countries have adopted a national target for stabilising CO_2 emissions at 1990 levels by the year 2000. Unfortunately, CO_2 emissions by OECD countries have steadily increased. The level of CO_2 emissions in 2000 is estimated to be higher than that of 1990 by more than 12 per cent. The rate of increase in non-OECD countries is less than that of OECD countries, which is mainly due to the former USSR. If the former USSR is excluded, the rate of increase in non-OECD countries is much higher than that of OECD countries. In the case of APEC Asia, except for Japan, the level of CO_2 emission in 1995 is higher than that of 1990 by 32 per cent.

Figure 11.1 illustrates the CO_2 emissions from fuel combustion by regions during two decades from 1975 to 1995.[1] The level of CO_2 emissions has increased by 37.2 per cent in APEC, 1.8 per cent in the EU and 69 per cent in the Rest of the World during the recent two decades. As illustrated in Figure 11.2, the share of CO_2 emissions in the EU decreased from 19 per cent in 1975 to 14 per cent in 1995, while that of the Rest of the World increased from 17 per cent in 1975 to 22 per cent in 1995. On the other hand, the share of APEC countries has been stable at around 64 per cent. These facts imply that APEC countries have been significantly responsible for CO_2 emissions during the two decades.

Figure 11.3 illustrates CO_2 emissions in APEC countries. Total share of APEC countries in the world has been stable, but the share of each country and region has changed drastically (Figure 11.4). The share of the former USSR has declined from 28 per cent in 1975 to 17 per cent in 1995. This is mainly due to the effects of economic transition. The GDP in the former USSR, based on 1990 US dollars, was $945.7 billion in 1990, while it was $475.4 billion in 1995. On the other hand, the share of APEC Asia including

Figure 11.1 World CO$_2$ emissions by region

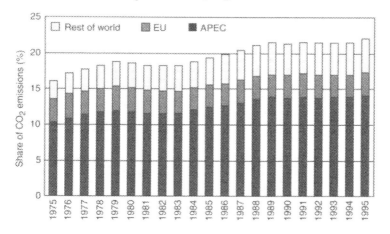

Figure 11.2 Share of CO$_2$ emissions by regions, 1975 and 1995

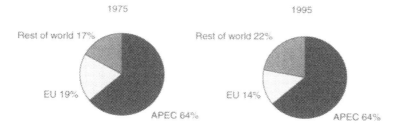

China, NIEs and ASEAN countries, has increased from 13 per cent in 1975 to 29 per cent in 1995. These facts imply that APEC countries have to begin to contribute an increasing proportion to stabilise CO$_2$ emissions in the world.

Figure 11.5 illustrates the ratio of CO$_2$ emissions to GDP based on 1990 US dollars, using exchange rates. The unit is expressed in kilograms of CO$_2$ per 1990 US dollar. According to the figure, energy usage in the former USSR and China is tremendously inefficient compared with other countries.[2] Energy usage in most APEC countries is much higher than the world average. These facts imply that technological innovation is likely to be a key element for reducing CO$_2$ emissions. It is reasonable, therefore, to ask whether there are any policies to promote technological innovation to save energy usage, and whether the pace of technological innovation is likely to be accelerated by policies selected. However, we shall not discuss policies for energy saving, but rather the impact of exogenous technological innovations on energy usage and the economy.

Figure 11.3 APEC CO_2 emissions by region

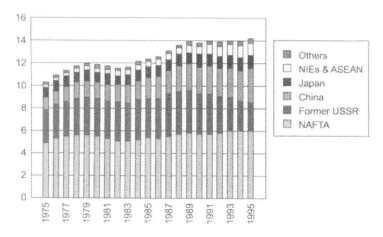

Figure 11.4 Share of CO_2 emissions by APEC region, 1975 and 1995

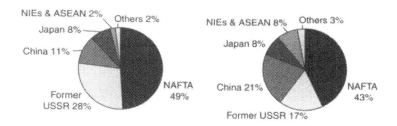

In this chapter, we study the impact of introducing carbon taxes and technological innovations on the economy. The idea of imposing a carbon tax has been advocated in recent years. A carbon tax would raise fossil fuel prices. As a result, demand for fossil fuel would fall. The problem is that CO_2 emissions are a global externality, but a carbon tax is levied by individual countries. Some countries might not be willing to participate. OECD countries have agreed that some sort of limit should be placed on CO_2 emissions, but have been reluctant to adopt a carbon tax. It is theoretically possible for the introduction of a carbon tax to result in a net increase in CO_2 emissions in the world, if production in participating countries were to move to non-participating countries, which have less efficient energy technology.

On the other hand, there is another policy option to reduce CO_2 emissions. As illustrated in Figure 11.5, energy efficiency in developing countries is lower than that of developed countries. Of course, technologies employed in

Figure 11.5 Energy efficiency by country (kilogram per 1990 US$)

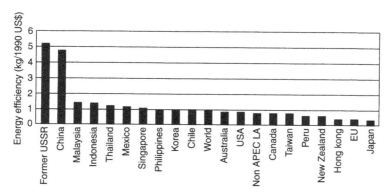

each country depend on cost minimising behaviour. That is, the choice of energy technologies reflects a long line of historical decisions, governed by price structure or institutional barriers. Simulation results from technological innovations in this chapter advocate policies for promoting technological innovation in energy use.

In this chapter, we use the Global Trade Analysis Project (GTAP) Model Version 4.1 (Hertel and Tsigas 1997). The model is a multi-country, multi-industry Computable General Equilibrium Model that includes a database of world input–output tables with trade and tariff matrices on forty-five individual countries and regions and fifty commodities.

GTAP MODEL

Tables 11.1 and 11.2 show the regional and commodity aggregation for this chapter. The APEC regions are disaggregated, but non-APEC regions are aggregated. Table 11.3 shows factor endowments treated in the model.

According to our previous study using the GTAP model, sensitivity of parameters on model properties is an essential aspect in model development (Ban, Kawasaki and Tsutsumi 1997). There are three types of behavioural parameters in the GTAP model: elasticity of substitution in demand and production functions, transformation elasticity on mobility of endowment factors across sectors, and flexibility of investment allocation across regions. Simulation results are sensitive to Armington parameters, which reflect the assumption of imperfect substitutions. Sensitivity analysis suggests that the model properties are almost linear as concerns Armington parameters. Simulation results also depend on key assumptions on capital movement. In this chapter, international capital movements are allowed in the model.

CARBON TAX

It has been argued that taxing and subsidising energy distorts consumption and production decisions and has adverse consequence for the local and

Table 11.1 Regional aggregation

Abbreviation	Description
ANZ	Australia and New Zealand
JPN	Japan
ASA	Indonesia, Malaysia, Philippines and Thailand
CHN	China
NIE	Korea, Singapore, Hong Kong and Taiwan
USA	United States
ONA	Canada and Mexico
SAM	Central and South America
WEU	Western Europe
FSU	Former Soviet Union
MEA	Middle East
ROW	Rest of World

Table 11.2 Commodity aggregation

Abbreviation	Description
AGR	Agriculture, forestry and fishing
COL	Coal
OIL	Oil
GAS	Gas
MNP	Minerals and mineral products
FDP	Food products
PCP	Petroleum and coal products
CHM	Chemical products
MTL	Metals and metal products
OMF	Other Manufacturing
MEQ	Machinery and equipment
EGD	Electricity and gas distribution
TTR	Trade and transport
SRV	Service

Table 11.3 Endowment aggregation

Abbreviation	Description
Land	Land
UnSkLab	Unskilled labour
SkLab	Skilled labour
Capital	Capital
NatRes	Natural resource

global environment. Table 11.4 illustrates tax rates on fossil fuels in OECD countries in 1995. According to the table, tax rates on petroleum are higher than those on coal and natural gas. Gasoline and diesel oil are highly taxed, but coal and natural gas are less taxed or not taxed. In the case of developing countries, subsidies (measured as the difference between domestic and world prices) are quite pervasive. In some cases, restructuring the energy pricing regime would yield rich dividends in terms of higher economic welfare and reduced CO_2 emissions.

Economists have long argued that restructuring the energy price regime or introducing a carbon tax makes good sense in the reduction of CO_2 emissions from the point of view of both the economy and the environment. Unfortunately, this kind of policy has rarely been adopted. Developing countries are often unwilling to participate. Even in the OECD countries, many people believe that the introduction of a carbon tax would result in a net increase in CO_2 emissions in the world, because production in developed countries would move to developing countries, which have less efficient energy technology.

In this chapter, we undertake three different simulations for introducing a carbon tax, and evaluate their impacts on the world and national economy. In the simulations, a level of tax rate on each fossil fuel is figured out mechanically as follows. The figures are proportionate with carbon content.

- Coal   20 per cent
- Petroleum   16 per cent
- Natural Gas   12 per cent

We conducted the following three simulations:

1 Carbon tax is levied in the OECD such as ANZ, JPN, USA, ONA, WEU and FSU;
2 Carbon tax is levied in the OECD, Former USSR, and APEC Asia such as ASA, NIE and China;
3 Carbon tax is levied in the entire world. Each country is supposed to levy a carbon tax on both domestically produced and imported fossil fuels, but to exempt exported fossil fuels from the carbon tax. We use the three policy variables, *to(i,r)*, *pms(i,r,s)* and *txs(i,r,s)*, in the equations of the GTAP model.

to(i,r) is included in the equation which links pre- and post-tax supply prices for all industries:

$$ps(i,r) = \quad to(i,r) + pm(i,r)$$

    ps(i,r)   supply price of commodity *i* in region *r*
    to(i,r)   power of tax on output of commodity *i* in region *r*
    pm(i,r)   market price of commodity *i* in region *r*

tms(i,r,s) is included in the equation which links domestic and world prices:

Table 11.4 Tax rates on fossil fuels in OECD countries

	Coal	Gasoline			Diesel		Petroleum Kerosene		Fuel		Gas	
		Premium	Regular	Unlead	Comm.	Non-com.	Industry	Home	Industry	Elec.	Industry	Home
Australia	0	58.1	56.8	54.6	26.5	61.2	22.8	39.4	43.1		0	16.7
Austria			68.7	67.2	52.1	60	9.5	24.9	6.5	6.5	0	21
Belgium		74.7		72.3	58.5	64.8						
Canada	25.4		47.5		41.3							
Denmark	30	72.2	70.8		46.5		8.5	64.4	18.4			20
Finland	0	82.2		74.2	57.6	65.2	17.9	32.7	22.9	22.9	9.2	25.6
France		76.9	78.4	80.2	67	72.4	36.4	41.1	14.2		0	16.4
Germany				76.3	63.7	68.4	22.7	32.8	14.2	27.2	14.1	19.2
Greece		74		69.9	60.8	66.7	57.5	64	26.7	26.7		
Ireland	0	67.2		66.3	53.2	61.1	24.4	27.7	12.1		0	11.1
Italy	2.9	75.8		73.2	65.2	70.7	67.5	72.7	16.5	13.9	9.6	44.5
Japan			52.8		50.6		2.9	2.9	2.9		2.9	2.9
Luxembourg		70.5	67.2	67.2	58.3	63.8		13.5	5.7			5.7
Netherlands		75.9		74.1	51.3	58.5	3.1	42	21.5		7	19.3
New Zealand		47.8	47.7		1	12	0		0		6.2	14.5
Norway		70.2		66.4	59.2	47.4	20.3	33.8	31.8			
Portugal		74		70.9	61.9	63.7	61.9	63.7	21.2			
Spain		69.2		67.6	59	64.6	35.3	44.2	9.5	0	0	15.1
Sweden		78.3		73.5	48.9	59.1	16.8	61.3	27.7	9.5		
Switzerland	5.6	72.6		70.8	79.2	70.4	9.8	13.7	9.5	0	1.3	6.8
Turkey	13	67.8		66.6	60.8			62.5	44	44	7.4	7.4
UK	0	75.9		73.6	68.4	73.1	18.9	22.9	18.8		0	7.4
US	0		33.3	28.6		39.7						

Source: IEA Energy Prices and Taxes.

$$pms(i,r,s) = tm(i,s) + tms(i,r,s) + pcif(i,r,s)$$

$pms(i,r,s)$ market price by source of imported commodity i from source r to destination s

$tm(i,s)$ power of import tax on commodity i in region s

$tms(i,r,s)$ power of tax on imported commodity i from source r to destination s

$pcif(i,r,s)$ world cif price of imported commodity i from source region r to destination s

$txs(i,r,s)$ is included in the equation which links agent's and world prices:

$$pfob(i,r,s) = pm(i,r) - tx(i,r) - txs(i,r,s)$$

$pfob(i,r,s)$ world fob price of exported commodity i from source r to destination s

$tx(i,r)$ power of tax on exported commodity i from source r

$txs(i,r,s)$ power of tax on exported commodity i from source r to destination s

We implement the following two new variables in the model. The first variable is quantity of total used of commodity i in region r, which is defined as follows:

$$qdm(i,r) = (1 - SHRVIM(i,r)) * qds(i,r) + SHRVIM(i,r) * qim(i,r)$$

$dqm(i,r)$ quantity of domestic sales and imports of commodity i in region r

$qds(i,r)$ quantity of domestic sales of commodity i in region r

$qim(i,r)$ quantity of imports of commodity i in region r

$SHRVIM(i,r)$ share of imports of commodity i in region r

The second variable is quantity of total commodity used in the world, which is defined as follows:

$$quse(i) = sum(s,REG, SHRUSE(i,s) * qdm(i,s))$$

$quse(i)$ quantity of total commodity i used in the world

$SHRVIM(i,r)$ share of total commodity i used in region r

If a carbon tax were imposed, its revenue would be extremely large. Taxes distort decision making in general, and create losses for both consumers and producers. In the simulations, revenue-neutral introduction of a carbon tax is supposed, where tax revenue is redistributed with no change in existing taxes. That is, all additional tax revenue is used for government spending. In the GTAP model, allocation of the spending across sectors is determined by the Cobb–Douglas assumption of constant budget shares.

Table 11.5 shows the impact of a carbon tax on fossil fuel use and economic welfare by region. In the case of coal, the amount of coal used in the world declines by 1.46 per cent by introducing a carbon tax in all countries, while it declines by 0.89 per cent by introducing a carbon tax only in advanced countries. In the case of oil, the amount of oil used in the world declines by 2.04 per cent by introducing a carbon tax in all countries, while it declines by

1.34 per cent by introducing a carbon tax only in advanced countries. In the case of natural gas, the amount of natural gas used in the world declines by 2.06 per cent by introducing a carbon tax in all countries, while it declines by 1.84 per cent by introducing a carbon tax only in advanced countries.

If a carbon tax is levied in OECD, former USSR and APEC Asia, its impact depends on fossil fuels. The participation of APEC Asia in carbon tax regimes succeeds in improving worldwide CO_2 emissions from coal, but fails in reducing worldwide CO_2 emissions from natural gas. In the case of oil, it improves worldwide CO_2 emissions slightly.

We can gain some insight into 'leakage' problems. Most global carbon tax regimes appear unworkable in practice, in view of the difficulties of getting nations to agree on a common tax framework. Some countries negotiate an agreement to reduce their CO_2 emissions, while all other countries do not participate in the agreement. If the non-cooperating countries increase their emissions despite the abatement undertaken by the cooperating countries, leakage rises. Leakage is transmitted through trade. Suppose that the reduction in emissions is realised by a unilateral carbon tax on fossil fuels. Then the cost to domestic manufacturers using fossil fuels will rise relative to their foreign competitors, and comparative advantage will be shifted from cooperating countries to non-cooperating countries. As the non-cooperating countries produce more tradable carbon-intensive goods, their CO_2 emissions will rise. If the unilateral carbon tax reduces world demand for fossil fuels, and their world prices decline, then the non-cooperating countries will increase CO_2 emissions even more.

According to Table 11.5, the amount of fossil fuels in the cooperating country declines, but those of the non-cooperating country increase. This means that there is some leakage. However, the amount of reduction in fossil fuels in the cooperating countries dominates that of the non-cooperating countries. As a result, even if a carbon tax is levied on only the OECD and former USSR, the total amount of fossil fuels used in the world declines.

In Table 11.5, it is shown that, in the case of coal, worldwide cooperation is more effective than that of a subset of countries. This result reflects that coal is a cheap and plentiful fossil fuel in developing countries. In the case of China, coal is responsible for more than 85 per cent of CO_2 emissions. On the other hand, the cooperation among the OECD and the former USSR is enough in the case of natural gas.

If a carbon tax is levied, regional real GDP usually declines, but its magnitude is extremely small. GTAP also computes regional equivalent variation (EV) measures. The values in Table 11.5 are in 1995 $US million. In any case, both Japan and USA benefit from introducing carbon tax regimes, while fossil fuel producing countries such as ANZ, the former USSR and the Middle East lose. APEC Asia benefits from introducing a carbon tax in advanced countries only, while it loses by introducing a carbon tax in its own countries. However, fossil energy use in APEC Asia has resulted in serious air pollution, including heavy smoke dust pollution and acid rain and, consequently,

Table 11.5 Impact of carbon tax on fossil fuel use and economic welfare by region

	World	ANZ	JPN	ASA	CHN	NIE	USA	ONA	SAM	WEU	FSU	MEA	ROW
Carbon tax is levied in OECD and former USSR													
COL	-0.89	-2.37	-0.15	0.18	0.04	0.11	-1.51	-0.07	0	-2.1	-0.54	0.81	0
OIL	-1.34	-3.15	-0.35	0.68	0.22	1.15	-3.61	-4.01	1.88	-3.52	-0.27	0.91	1.11
GAS	-1.84	-1.91	-0.34	0.19	0.14	0.47	-3.59	-2.65	0.88	-2.17	-2.02	0.32	1.01
GDP		-0.07	0	0	0	0	-0.01	-0.02	0.02	-0.03	-0.05	-0.02	0.01
EV		-214	449	85	2	169	81	-647	221	-2049	-423	-1645	39
Carbon tax is levied in OECD, former USSR and APEC Asia													
COL	-1.22	-2.03	-0.11	-0.47	-1.01	-2.65	-1.5	-0.01	0.06	-2.07	-0.51	1.32	0
OIL	-1.48	-2.62	-0.24	-2.85	-0.66	-1.95	-3.53	-3.93	1.94	-3.42	-0.21	1.59	1.32
GAS	-1.83	-1.63	-0.32	-1.11	-0.37	-1.11	-3.5	-2.64	0.94	-2.14	-2.02	0.59	1.19
GDP		-0.06	0	-0.01	-0.11	-0.02	-0.01	-0.01	0.02	-0.03	-0.05	-0.01	0.02
EV		-88	817	-707	-1450	-229	661	-618	351	-1304	-333	-1599	199
Carbon tax is levied in the entire world													
COL	-1.46	-1.94	-0.17	-0.41	-1	-2.45	-1.53	-0.02	0.04	-1.98	-0.48	-1.51	-2.36
OIL	-2.04	-2.45	-0.19	-2.19	-0.55	-0.76	-3.17	-3.07	-1.31	-2.7	-0.01	-2.19	-1.27
GAS	-2.06	-1.55	-0.36	-0.97	-0.34	-0.67	-3.15	-2.5	-2.37	-1.93	-1.97	-1.25	-1.22
GDP		-0.05	0	0	-0.1	-0.01	-0.01	-0.01	-0.01	-0.01	-0.04	-0.22	-0.05
EV		-37	1676	-745	-1417	-178	874	-434	-414	700	-189	-3227	-2099

governments in APEC Asia have begun to pay more attention to solving environmental problems.

Tables A11.1 to A11.6 in the Appendix illustrate the impact of introducing a carbon tax on industrial outputs and their market prices in each country.

TECHNOLOGICAL INNOVATIONS

Figure 11.5 shows that energy efficiency in developing countries is lower than that of developed countries. Increasing energy productivity is a necessary condition in order to realise sustainable development in the worldwide economy. Increasing energy productivity also yields other environmental benefits in the form of improved air and water quality. However, the choices of energy technology in each country have some microeconomic aspects. Business firms and households have selected energy technology as a result of cost-minimising behaviour. A shift from higher energy intensive technology to lower energy intensive technology would depend on the structure of relative prices. The cost effect strongly depends on the elasticity of substitution between energy and capital. In some cases, higher energy prices may not necessarily increase the cost of using energy. That is, technological change is to a large extent an endogenous phenomenon in an individual economy. For this reason, additional policies may be needed to stimulate demand for energy-efficient technologies.

Despite the importance of endogenous technological innovations, we examine the impacts of exogenous productivity innovation in using fossil fuel in APEC Asia, including the ASEAN countries (ASA), China (CHN) and Asian NIE countries (NIE). The shock applied to the GTAP model is a 10 per cent increase in intermediate input augmenting technical change for fossil fuels, that is, $af(i,j,r)$ in the following equation:

$$qf(i,j,r) = \quad - af(i,j,r) + qo(j,r) - ESUBT(j) * [pf(i,j,r) - af(i,j,r) - ps(j,r)]$$

$af(i,j,r)$ intermediate input i augmenting technical change in sector j of region r

$pf(i,j,r)$ demand price of commodity i for firms in sector j of region r

$ps(j,r)$ supply price of commodity i in region r

$qf(i,j,r)$ quantity of composite tradable commodity i demanded by firms in sector j region r

$qo(j,r)$ quantity of commodity i output in region r

$ESUBT(j)$ elasticity of substitution for output j

Table 11.5 illustrates the impact of productivity innovation in using fossil fuels in APEC Asia on the aggregated real GDP, Equivalent Variations, and the demand for commodities in each country. In the case of China, total demand for each fossil fuel declines by around 8.5 per cent, respectively. Table A11.8 in the Appendix shows that technological innovation reduces the market prices of fossil fuels by 10.8 per cent in the case of coal, 6.86 per cent in the case of oil and 8.9 per cent in the case of gas. These tendencies are observed in ASEAN and Asian NIEs. At the same time, factor prices of natural resources decline in the entire world. It is sometimes said that if technological innovations for using fossil fuels were realised in some region in the world, the decline in demand for fossil fuels would reduce the price of fossil fuels, and other countries might increase their demand for fossil fuels. As a result, CO_2 emissions might increase. Fortunately, according to the simulations, the worldwide demand for fossil fuels also declines by 2.39 per cent in the case of coal, 0.85 per cent for oil, and 0.35 per cent in the case of gas.

Table 11.6 also shows that the real GDP of APEC Asia increases, while that of fossil fuel producing countries such as ANZ, FSU and MEA declines slightly. From a point of equivalent variation, APEC Asia, JPN, USA and WEU benefit, while other regions lose.

SUMMARY AND POLICY IMPLICATIONS

In the chapter, we have examined the impact of introducing carbon taxes and technological innovations on the economy. The idea of imposing a carbon tax has been advocated in recent years. The problem is that CO_2 emissions are a global externality, but a carbon tax is levied by individual countries. Some countries might not be willing to participate. OECD countries have agreed that some sort of limit should be placed on CO_2 emissions, but have been reluctant to adopt a carbon tax. On the other hand, we have another policy option. Energy efficiency in developing countries is lower than that of developed countries. The choice of technologies for energy usage reflects a long line of decision making, which was governed by price structure or institutional barriers. According to the estimates, energy usage in most APEC countries is relatively inefficient as compared with the world average. In particular, energy usage in the former USSR and China is tremendously inefficient. In the chapter, we illustrate that technological innovation is likely to be another key element for reducing CO_2 emissions.

We use the GTAP Model to evaluate the impact of policy options to reduce CO_2 emissions. Economists recommend introducing a carbon tax, but it has been rarely adopted. Developing countries might not be willing to participate. Even in the OECD countries, it is sometimes believed that introducing a carbon tax in developed countries might increase worldwide CO_2 emissions, since production in developed countries would move to developing countries, where less efficient energy technology is used.

We undertake simulations to evaluate the impact of introducing a carbon tax with or without worldwide cooperation. According to the simulation results, even if a carbon tax on fossil fuel coal is levied only in the developed countries, the amount of CO_2 emissions will be reduced. This fact implies that even if the non-cooperating countries increase their emissions despite the abatement undertaken by the cooperating countries, and leakage rises as a result, CO_2 emissions will decline in the world. However, imposing a carbon tax on coal in all countries is more effective than in only developed countries.

Table 11.6 The impact of productivity innovation on demand for commodity in APEC Asia

	ANZ	JPN	ASA	CHN	NIE	USA	ONA	SAM	WEU	FSU	MEA	ROW
GDP	-0.01	0	0.31	0.83	0.28	0	0	0	0	-0.01	-0.09	0
EV	-336	1822	1588	5917	3906	723	-311	-180	1012	-364	-3754	-365
AGR	0.22	0.02	0.06	0.18	0.09	0.03	0.05	0.01	0.01	0.07	0.01	0
COL	0.17	-0.08	-8.6	-8.38	-6.51	0	0	-0.01	0.02	0.02	0.47	-0.23
OIL	0.15	-0.06	-5.42	-8.39	-7.34	0.16	0.25	-0.07	0.23	-0.07	0	-0.51
GAS	0	0.03	-7.36	-8.56	-8.11	0.14	0.09	-0.06	0.04	0.09	-0.14	-0.01
MNP	0.05	-0.02	0.44	0.65	0.2	-0.02	-0.03	-0.02	-0.04	0.07	0.22	-0.02
FDP	0.01	0.01	0.11	0.41	0.19	0	-0.01	-0.01	0	-0.01	-0.42	0.01
PCP	0.48	0.04	1.13	0.18	0.61	0.4	0.23	0.14	0.34	0.02	0.17	-0.02
CHM	0.11	0.03	0.11	0.18	0	0.02	0.08	0.04	-0.01	0.08	0.29	0.04
MTL	0.17	-0.03	0.15	0.53	-0.33	0.01	0.07	0.02	-0.02	0.1	0.56	0.1
OMF	0.03	0.03	0.06	-0.33	0.06	0.01	0.05	0.03	0.02	0.03	-0.22	0.1
MEQ	-0.05	0.02	0.14	0.68	0.01	0	0.05	0.01	0.01	-0.04	-1.35	0.17
EGD	0.12	0.03	0.44	0.16	0.22	0.13	0.04	0	0.07	0.04	0.08	0.02
TTR	-0.03	0.01	0.25	0.35	0.14	0	-0.02	-0.01	0	-0.03	-0.6	0
SRV	-0.08	0.02	0.31	1.11	0.34	-0.01	-0.05	-0.02	0	-0.06	-1.01	0

In particular, the participation of APEC Asia in carbon tax regimes succeeds in improving worldwide CO_2 emissions from coal.

Energy efficiency in APEC Asia and the former USSR is lower than that of other countries. Despite the importance of endogenous technological innovations, we examine the impacts of exogenous productivity innovation in using fossil fuel in APEC Asia. The shock applied to the GTAP model is a 10 per cent increase in intermediate input augmenting technical change for fossil fuels. Simulation results illustrate that productivity innovations in using fossil fuels in APEC Asia improve not only the amount of CO_2 emissions, but also the aggregated real GDP and Equivalent Variations (EV).

Governments in APEC Asia have begun to pay more attention to solving environmental problems because fossil energy use in the region has resulted in serious air pollution including heavy smoke dust pollution and acid rain. According to the simulations in this chapter, we can propose two policy options. One is a carbon tax and the other is technological innovation. In many developing countries, huge subsidies for fossil fuels result in a massive discrepancy between domestic and world prices. Subsidising distorts consumption and production decisions and has adverse consequences not only for government revenue but also for the protection of the local environment. Taking these facts into account, we can propose imposing a carbon tax for the developed APEC countries, and removing subsidies for the developing APEC countries. As for the other policy option, technology transfer in the field of fossil energy use among APEC region is also recommended. Its impact on reducing CO_2 emissions is reliable, because energy efficiency in developing APEC countries is lower that in the world generally. Moreover, the economic and political costs of implementing the policy might be lower than those for a carbon tax.

NOTES

1   The Figures are based on IEA Statistics on CO_2 Emissions from Fuel Combustion 1972–95, OECD 1997.
2   IEA released other figures based on the 1990 US$ using PPP, where the same basket of goods and services are used for currency conversion. According to these figures, it is 2.61 for the Former USSR, 0.92 for China, and 0.75 for World.

REFERENCES

Ban, K., Kawasaki, K. and Tsutsumi, M. (1997) 'Diagnostic analysis of CGE modeling: the property of APEC trade liberalization', Discussion paper no. 81, Economic Research Institutes, Economic Planning Agency.

Ban, K., Otsubo, S., Kawasaki, K. *et al.* (1998) 'Applied general equilibrium analysis of current global issues: APEC, FDI, new regionalism and environment', *The Economic Analysis* 156, Economic Research Institutes, Economic Planning Agency.

Hertel, T.W. and Tsigas, M.E. (1997) 'Structure of the standard GTAP model', Chapter 2 in T.W. Hertel (ed.) *Global Trade Analysis: Modeling and Applications*, Cambridge University Press.

IEA (1997) 'CO_2 emissions from fuel combustion: a new basis for comparing emissions of a major greenhouse gas 1972–1995'.

—— (1997) *Energy prices and Taxes*, International Energy Agency.

APPENDIX

Table A11.1   Impact on outputs: carbon tax levied in OECD and former USSR

	ANZ	JPN	ASA	CHN	NIE	USA	ONA	SAM	WEU	FSU	MEA	ROW
AGR	0.09	0.03	0	-0.01	-0.01	0.05	0.12	-0.1	0	0.72	0.16	-0.04
COL	-0.8	-0.9	0.92	0.36	0.43	-1.97	-0.87	0.96	-2.83	-0.78	0.88	0.75
OIL	-1.85	-1.8	-0.58	-0.35	-0.99	-2.58	-2.46	-0.6	-2.91	-1.65	-0.42	-0.77
GAS	-1.47	-1.03	-0.34	-0.14	-0.5	-3.45	-2.54	-0.11	-2.15	-1.2	-0.13	-0.46
MNP	0.08	0.02	0.21	0.04	0.1	-0.14	0.51	-0.06	-0.2	0.26	1.21	0.12
FDP	0.07	0.01	-0.04	-0.03	-0.01	0.03	0.12	-0.09	0.01	0.63	0.02	-0.07
PCP	-4	-0.36	0.96	0.27	1.61	-5.23	-4.29	3.75	-3.72	-0.05	1.48	2.19
CHM	0.38	-0.37	0.53	0.3	0.46	-0.27	-1	0.14	0.17	-3.67	1.01	0.32
MTL	-0.42	-0.09	0.24	-0.03	0.11	-0.07	0.55	-0.15	-0.06	1.1	0.85	-0.01
OMF	0.31	0.01	-0.09	-0.16	-0.15	0.03	0.51	-0.16	0.07	0.87	0.45	-0.22
MEQ	0.28	-0.03	-0.19	-0.18	-0.33	0.09	0.72	-0.23	0.08	0.17	0.82	-0.22
EGD	-0.79	-0.23	0.02	0.03	0.06	-1.52	-0.22	0.01	-0.99	-0.53	0.06	0.07
TTR	0.02	0.04	-0.03	-0.01	-0.09	0.05	0.07	-0.06	0.01	0.34	0.08	-0.07
SRV	0.06	0.04	0.07	0.07	0.06	0.12	0.02	0.09	0.07	0.03	-0.2	0.1

Table A11.2   Impact on market prices: carbon tax levied in OECD and former USSR

	ANZ	JPN	ASA	CHN	NIE	USA	ONA	SAM	WEU	FSU	MEA	ROW
Land	0.24	0.33	0.38	0.33	0.34	0.34	0.38	0.08	0.14	2.4	0.72	0.3
UnSk	-0.25	0.18	0.41	0.41	0.43	0.1	-0.21	0.63	0.15	-1.82	-0.04	0.52
SkLab	-0.24	0.18	0.44	0.43	0.44	0.13	-0.23	0.68	0.15	-1.92	-0.2	0.57
Capit	-0.33	0.16	0.41	0.4	0.46	0.02	-0.36	0.64	0.1	-2.1	-0.15	0.55
NatRe	-7.26	0.06	-1.24	1.32	0.5	-16.9	-14.4	-2.46	-13.3	-10.3	-2.98	-2.29
AGR	0.36	0.33	0.4	0.41	0.4	0.37	0.38	0.52	0.41	-0.03	0	0.45
COL	23.31	23.35	2.28	1.24	1.44	24.7	23.63	2.6	24.7	23.53	1.79	2.07
OIL	14.93	15.56	-0.73	-0.28	-0.79	13.78	13.76	-0.74	14.52	14.8	-1.04	-1.13
GAS	11.52	11.87	-0.31	0.1	-0.3	8.85	8.62	0.28	10.61	9.69	-0.45	-0.5
MNP	0.43	0.45	0.4	0.47	0.42	0.67	0.31	0.59	0.64	0.42	-0.02	0.48
FDP	0.31	0.34	0.39	0.43	0.41	0.33	0.19	0.57	0.37	-0.35	0	0.47
PCP	11.2	1.34	-0.32	-0.08	-0.16	9.79	11.11	-0.11	7.45	2.33	-0.65	-0.33
CHM	0.48	1.29	0.44	0.48	0.49	0.99	1.39	0.56	0.59	3.64	0.05	0.44
MTL	0.72	0.62	0.43	0.49	0.43	0.64	0.41	0.63	0.51	0.1	0.08	0.49
OMF	0.19	0.38	0.41	0.44	0.44	0.4	0.22	0.59	0.36	-0.35	0.04	0.49
MEQ	0.2	0.38	0.4	0.44	0.43	0.32	0.2	0.58	0.32	-0.54	0.07	0.48
EGD	3.4	1.04	0.27	0.56	0.5	4.22	1.34	0.6	3.33	3.63	-0.22	0.45
TTR	0.18	0.27	0.39	0.4	0.43	0.33	0.17	0.61	0.35	-0.79	-0.08	0.49
SRV	-0.02	0.29	0.4	0.43	0.42	0.23	-0.03	0.62	0.26	-1.15	-0.05	0.5

Table A11.3 Impact on outputs: carbon tax levied in OECD, former USSR and APEC

	ANZ	JPN	ASA	CHN	NIE	USA	ONA	SAM	WEU	FSU	MEA	ROW
AGR	−0.14	−0.02	0.1	0.55	0.07	−0.04	0.04	−0.15	−0.06	0.6	0.07	−0.06
COL	−0.46	−0.57	−0.48	−1.22	−4.22	−1.77	−0.51	1.22	−2.65	−0.6	1.02	0.97
OIL	−2	−1.93	−2.02	−1.17	−4.98	−2.57	−2.45	−0.62	−2.94	−1.7	−0.54	−0.79
GAS	−1.37	−0.95	−1.12	−0.59	−3.45	−3.37	−2.46	−0.03	−2.1	−1.18	−0.09	−0.37
MNP	0.41	0.1	−0.5	−1.05	−0.91	−0.04	0.75	0.06	−0.07	0.29	1.28	0.3
FDP	−0.07	0	0.1	0.53	0.04	0.01	0.12	−0.12	−0.01	0.55	−0.03	−0.09
PCP	−3.28	0.46	−3.37	−0.74	−2.7	−5.09	−4.2	3.88	−3.6	0.02	2.51	2.57
CHM	0.36	−0.35	0.7	0.15	0.18	−0.25	−0.94	0.14	0.2	−3.69	1.01	0.35
MTL	−0.22	−0.02	−0.18	−1.45	0.12	−0.02	0.74	−0.06	0.05	1.22	0.93	0.11
OMF	0.01	−0.11	0.32	2.12	−0.01	−0.1	0.24	−0.28	−0.08	0.68	0.17	−0.39
MEQ	0.11	−0.15	0.88	0.42	0.22	0.04	0.68	−0.25	0.02	0.12	0.66	−0.25
EGD	−0.77	−0.23	−0.33	−0.68	−0.14	−1.53	−0.21	0.02	−0.99	−0.52	0.08	0.08
TTR	0	0.04	0.01	0.22	0.12	0.04	0.07	−0.07	0	0.32	0.05	−0.08
SRV	0.1	0.07	−0.12	−0.87	−0.03	0.14	0.06	0.12	0.09	0.05	−0.13	0.13

Table A11.4 Impact on market prices: carbon tax levied in OECD, former USSR and APEC

	ANZ	JPN	ASA	CHN	NIE	USA	ONA	SAM	WEU	FSU	MEA	ROW
Land	−1.21	−0.16	0.12	0.04	−0.05	−0.4	−0.29	−0.4	−0.39	1.53	0.14	−0.09
UnSk	−0.43	−0.02	−0.61	−3.14	−0.58	−0.12	−0.47	0.42	−0.07	−1.98	−0.14	0.29
SkLab	−0.4	−0.02	−0.7	−3.75	−0.59	−0.09	−0.48	0.5	−0.06	−2.06	−0.26	0.37
Capit	−0.5	−0.03	−0.6	−3.47	−0.62	−0.21	−0.61	0.43	−0.12	−2.25	−0.25	0.33
NatRe	−6.62	−0.33	−6.88	−9.96	−2.85	−16.7	−14.4	−2.7	−13.3	−10.3	−3.81	−2.25
AGR	0.04	0.09	−0.07	−1.49	−0.11	0.07	0.06	0.27	0.16	−0.3	−0.17	0.19
COL	23.9	23.85	24	25.23	20.05	24.9	24.15	2.95	24.84	23.78	1.96	2.33
OIL	14.43	15.08	14.47	15.2	15.59	13.53	13.49	−0.98	14.23	14.53	−1.4	−1.39
GAS	11.56	11.81	11.65	12	12.2	8.76	8.5	0.15	10.47	9.58	−0.48	−0.55
MNP	0.27	0.26	0.66	1.34	1.22	0.45	0.07	0.39	0.42	0.27	−0.16	0.29
FDP	0.08	0.11	−0.08	−1	−0.05	0.09	−0.08	0.34	0.14	−0.56	−0.16	0.23
PCP	11.03	1.14	8.96	9.23	7.73	9.57	10.85	−0.34	7.21	2.18	−0.91	−0.54
CHM	0.31	1.09	0.22	0.72	0.55	0.77	1.15	0.35	0.38	3.5	−0.11	0.24
MTL	0.56	0.44	0.51	1.56	0.45	0.42	0.18	0.43	0.3	−0.04	−0.06	0.3
OMF	−0.03	0.16	−0.06	−0.59	0	0.16	−0.04	0.38	0.13	−0.52	−0.14	0.26
MEQ	0.01	0.18	−0.1	−0.32	0.02	0.09	−0.04	0.37	0.1	−0.7	−0.08	0.27
EGD	3.27	0.84	3.36	6.25	2.05	4.03	1.1	0.4	3.14	3.53	−0.36	0.26
TTR	0.01	0.07	−0.02	−1.14	−0.12	0.1	−0.09	0.4	0.13	−0.95	−0.22	0.28
SRV	−0.19	0.09	−0.03	−0.9	−0.09	0.01	−0.28	0.42	0.04	−1.3	−0.18	0.29

Table A11.5   Impact on outputs: carbon tax levied in the entire world

	ANZ	JPN	ASA	CHN	NIE	USA	ONA	SAM	WEU	FSU	MEA	ROW
AGR	−0.39	−0.11	0.04	0.51	0.04	−0.21	−0.13	0.04	−0.32	0.4	1.26	0.18
COL	−0.44	−0.61	−0.45	−1.2	−4.21	−1.77	−0.5	−0.35	−2.59	−0.59	0.29	−1.04
OIL	−1.97	−2	−1.93	−1.13	−5.04	−2.4	−2.22	−2.87	−2.77	−1.67	−1.12	−2.73
GAS	−1.29	−0.93	−0.99	−0.51	−3.16	−3.04	−2.08	−5.1	−2.02	−1.27	−1.29	−1.77
MNP	0.26	0.04	−0.56	−1.06	−0.95	−0.16	0.58	0.32	−0.18	0.17	4.36	−0.05
FDP	−0.22	−0.02	0	0.5	0.03	−0.05	0.07	0.06	−0.14	0.46	0.96	0.22
PCP	−3.04	1.23	−2.33	−0.59	−1	−4.48	−3.28	−1.39	−2.68	0.24	−2.71	−1.32
CHM	0.35	−0.39	0.83	0.17	0.19	−0.27	−1.05	−0.35	0.25	−3.63	2.59	−0.13
MTL	−0.19	−0.11	−0.04	−1.4	0.2	−0.04	0.72	0.22	0.18	1.15	3.9	−0.56
OMF	−0.06	−0.19	0.14	1.97	−0.22	−0.21	0	0.06	−0.26	0.46	3.55	0.62
MEQ	0.18	−0.28	1.09	0.49	0.27	0.02	0.72	0.33	−0.02	0.13	4.43	0.64
EGD	−0.78	−0.25	−0.34	−0.66	−0.12	−1.57	−0.23	−0.09	−0.98	−0.52	−0.05	−0.36
TTR	−0.02	0.01	−0.04	0.21	0.04	0.02	0.04	−0.03	−0.05	0.28	0.81	0.24
SRV	0.14	0.14	−0.1	−0.82	−0.01	0.17	0.13	0.12	0.14	0.09	−1.09	−0.1

Table A11.6   Impact on market prices: carbon tax levied in the entire world

	ANZ	JPN	ASA	CHN	NIE	USA	ONA	SAM	WEU	FSU	MEA	ROW
Land	−2.71	−0.68	−0.57	−0.44	−0.55	−1.58	−1.43	−0.53	−1.9	0.16	1.72	−0.42
UnSk	−0.63	−0.09	−0.9	−3.4	−0.83	−0.31	−0.68	−0.74	−0.31	−2.13	−4.15	−1.48
SkLab	−0.57	−0.08	−0.95	−3.96	−0.83	−0.27	−0.66	−0.7	−0.29	−2.17	−5.01	−1.58
Capit	−0.68	−0.09	−0.86	−3.69	−0.84	−0.39	−0.79	−0.79	−0.34	−2.38	−4.61	−1.63
NatRe	−6.75	−0.79	−6.9	−10.1	−3.24	−15.9	−13.3	−15.5	−13.3	−10.7	−12	−14.4
AGR	−0.31	−0.05	−0.48	−1.79	−0.43	−0.24	−0.27	−0.42	−0.19	−0.67	−2.3	−0.76
COL	23.7	23.67	23.8	24.99	19.8	24.69	23.98	24	24.69	23.59	22.66	22.72
OIL	14.28	14.83	14.36	15.04	15.26	13.67	13.72	14.86	14.31	14.41	13.96	14.58
GAS	11.51	11.77	11.64	11.92	12.25	9.25	8.96	17.13	10.39	9.24	11.59	10.88
MNP	0.07	0.18	0.41	1.11	0.99	0.27	−0.11	−0.12	0.19	0.1	−1.82	0.07
FDP	−0.18	−0.02	−0.4	−1.27	−0.34	−0.14	−0.32	−0.41	−0.14	−0.82	−2.37	−0.65
PCP	10.87	1.07	8.76	9.04	7.49	9.7	11	8.35	7.07	2.02	8.09	7.8
CHM	0.11	1.03	−0.04	0.49	0.34	0.6	1.04	0.75	0.15	3.27	−1.24	0.34
MTL	0.37	0.35	0.28	1.33	0.23	0.24	−0.01	0.08	0.06	−0.2	−1.93	0.36
OMF	−0.25	0.07	−0.33	−0.84	−0.23	−0.03	−0.23	−0.31	−0.12	−0.71	−2.45	−0.6
MEQ	−0.18	0.1	−0.32	−0.55	−0.19	−0.09	−0.23	−0.29	−0.14	−0.87	−2.25	−0.54
EGD	3.09	0.78	3.18	6.03	1.87	3.92	0.97	0.04	2.94	3.36	−0.79	1.95
TTR	−0.19	−0.02	−0.27	−1.37	−0.35	−0.08	−0.26	−0.27	−0.11	−1.11	−2.72	−0.81
SRV	−0.38	0.01	−0.27	−1.13	−0.32	−0.18	−0.46	−0.52	−0.19	−1.45	−3.18	−0.85

Table A11.7   Impact on outputs: technological innovation in APEC Asia

	ANZ	JPN	ASA	CHN	NIE	USA	ONA	SAM	WEU	FSU	MEA	ROW
AGR	0.36	0.02	-0.02	-0.1	-0.03	0.07	0.1	0.04	0.03	0.16	0.67	0.01
COL	-1.94	-1.75	-2.96	-6.14	-1.34	-0.88	-1.89	-1.28	-0.7	-0.84	-0.01	-1.11
OIL	-1.28	-1.49	-2.15	-4.52	-1.77	-0.64	-0.74	-0.69	-0.86	-0.85	-0.45	-0.87
GAS	-1.04	-1.29	-1.96	-5.3	-2.61	0.01	0	-0.35	-0.21	-0.15	-0.48	-0.45
MNP	-0.05	-0.13	0.59	1.02	0.53	-0.16	-0.24	-0.13	-0.22	0.1	2.76	-0.07
FDP	0.25	0.02	-0.02	-0.04	0.08	0.01	0.01	0.01	0	0.11	0.31	0.01
PCP	0.15	-0.81	3.9	1.08	2.68	0.21	0.27	0.05	0.22	-0.09	0.18	-0.08
CHM	0.17	0.02	-0.07	0.56	-0.03	-0.04	0.09	0.06	-0.09	0.26	1.78	0.06
MTL	0.27	-0.14	0.41	1.43	-0.41	-0.05	-0.03	-0.01	-0.1	0.27	1.97	0.13
OMF	0.38	0.07	-0.16	-1.4	-0.3	0.09	0.29	0.12	0.1	0.27	1.83	0.18
MEQ	0.48	-0.03	-0.52	-0.08	-0.69	0.05	0.27	0.11	0.1	0.18	2.8	0.21
EGD	0.12	0.03	0.45	0.28	0.06	0.13	0.03	0	0.07	0.04	0.08	0.02
TTR	0.06	0	0.15	0.13	-0.13	0	0	0.01	-0.01	0.04	0.39	0.01
SRV	-0.06	0.02	0.28	0.99	0.25	-0.01	-0.04	-0.02	0	-0.04	-0.82	0.01
CGDS	-0.17	0.04	0.45	1.99	0.57	-0.03	-0.07	-0.03	-0.03	-0.08	-3.04	0.07

Table A11.8   Impact on market prices: technological innovation in APEC Asia

	ANZ	JPN	ASA	CHN	NIE	USA	ONA	SAM	WEU	FSU	MEA	ROW
Land	1.83	0.22	0.36	2.03	0.52	0.41	0.53	0.19	0.12	0.83	1.55	0.08
UnSk	-0.1	0.12	0.53	2.62	0.71	0.02	0.01	-0.02	-0.02	-0.12	-1.67	0.03
SkLab	-0.15	0.12	0.62	3.13	0.78	0.02	-0.01	-0.04	-0.02	-0.16	-2.25	0.03
Capit	-0.17	0.12	0.53	2.68	0.76	0.01	-0.03	-0.04	-0.02	-0.18	-1.83	0
NatRe	-8.5	-0.16	-8.15	-26.3	-0.4	-2.96	-3.91	-3.94	-3.31	-3.18	-4.93	-5.26
AGR	0.01	0.1	0.24	1.65	0.4	0.04	0.03	-0.02	-0.04	-0.03	-1.34	-0.02
COL	-3.76	-3.09	-5.2	-10.8	-3.76	-1.94	-3.52	-2.5	-1.63	-1.86	-1.57	-2.21
OIL	-2.65	-2.7	-3.77	-6.86	-3.25	-1.25	-1.44	-1.57	-1.76	-1.85	-2.7	-1.9
GAS	-2.32	-2.36	-3.87	-8.9	-4.66	0.02	-0.05	-0.66	-0.52	-0.51	-2.94	-1.05
MNP	-0.24	0.05	-0.46	-1.06	-0.62	-0.05	-0.07	-0.09	-0.07	-0.26	-1.46	-0.17
FDP	-0.12	0.08	0.16	1.04	0.29	0.01	-0.02	-0.04	-0.04	-0.12	-1.35	-0.06
PCP	-2.07	-0.15	-7.56	-9.2	-5.97	-0.81	-1.14	-0.94	-0.91	-0.45	-2.3	-1.12
CHM	-0.22	-0.15	-0.08	-0.63	-0.18	-0.07	-0.15	-0.17	-0.07	-0.35	-1.31	-0.2
MTL	-0.28	0.01	-0.3	-1.2	-0.13	-0.04	-0.07	-0.11	-0.06	-0.24	-1.22	-0.19
OMF	-0.13	0.07	0.13	0.56	0.22	-0.01	-0.03	-0.06	-0.04	-0.18	-1.26	-0.07
MEQ	-0.14	0.06	0.17	0.28	0.19	0	-0.03	-0.06	-0.03	-0.19	-1.14	-0.08
EGD	-0.77	-0.07	-2.76	-4.97	-1.12	-0.33	-0.19	-0.1	-0.27	-0.47	-1.93	-0.37
TTR	-0.19	0.09	0.05	0.84	0.34	-0.01	-0.05	-0.07	-0.04	-0.19	-1.62	-0.07
SRV	-0.16	0.09	0.07	0.73	0.32	0	-0.03	-0.05	-0.03	-0.18	-1.58	-0.06

12 APEC as an international institution

Vinod K. Aggarwal and Charles E. Morrison[1]

INTRODUCTION

The creation of the Asia Pacific Economic Cooperation forum (APEC) in 1989 was greeted with a combination of hope and scepticism. Unlike many regions of the world, regional institutions in Asia, and particularly the Asia Pacific, have been scarce. With East Asian economic success, the end of the Cold War, and shifts in power among Asian states, many saw APEC as a much-needed institution that would both facilitate economic cooperation in the region and provide for a continuing special post-Cold War association between East Asia and North America. From the beginning there were competing visions of what APEC should become, from the minimalist vision of a consultative forum to a maximalist position of an eventual trade bloc, perhaps even undertaking security functions (Morrison 1997a and 1997b). For some, APEC would be the mechanism to increase economic liberalisation in the region and bolster the stalled Uruguay Round negotiations in the General Agreement on Tariffs and Trade (GATT), a vision that was later pushed by an Eminent Persons' Group and adopted by the leaders of the APEC economies.

Over the decade, however, optimism over APEC's contributions have waxed and waned with its impact on policy making and trade liberalisation. An important high point was the 1993 meeting in Seattle, attended by leaders of the APEC economies, elevating APEC from a sleepy forum for foreign and trade ministers to a much more visible summit-level activity. Some viewed this development as a sign of APEC's coming of age as well as an effective means of putting pressure on the Europeans to come to an agreement in the Uruguay Round. The 1994 meeting in Bogor, Indonesia, led to a call for free trade and investment in the area by 2010 for the developed APEC member economies, and 2020 for the entire group. A framework of guiding principles was agreed to the following year in Osaka, and in 1996 APEC adopted an Action Plan involving unilateral concerted liberalisation as well as collective actions. The group also agreed to push for a WTO breakthrough on information technology. Its political success in pushing the Information Technology Agreement (for which much of the work had already been done in other contexts) encouraged APEC to move ahead with other 'early voluntary sectoral liberalisation' (EVSL) schema. The 1997 Vancouver meeting agreed to push ESVL in nine sectors, thus holding out hope for a major role for APEC as a key adjunct to the WTO for promoting trade liberalisation.

By 1998, however, APEC's role and promise came into sharp question. By the time of the Kuala Lumpur meetings (some would say even by the time of Vancouver) it was clear that APEC had failed to play a significant role in ameliorating the Asian financial crisis. The EVSL effort faltered as Japan and several other countries objected to the liberalisation of some sectors in the context of the economic crisis.

These negative developments and concerns about APEC's ability to foster liberalisation have been accompanied by more sceptical criticism from some analysts who view APEC as positively harmful. They note that the Asia Pacific region had become the most dynamic region in the world economy without a formalised institution, and argue that by encouraging further regionalisation of the world economy, APEC may undermine global economic institutions, leading to regional competition and conflict.

These polar views reveal the fundamental ambiguity and inadequacy in our understanding of the nature of regional institutions and their relationships with existing trade governance structures. In particular, APEC has posed a puzzle to analysts due to its novel organisational principles and norms and its informal decision-making and implementation processes. To better understand APEC as an international institution, we apply a multilevel governance framework to provide a more precise understanding of its basic characteristics and the potential and limitations of APEC as an institutional framework for effecting policy change. We argue that, to be realistic, APEC activities already adopted and policy proposals developed in other chapters in this book must be compatible with the organisational form that APEC has or is likely to take. Accordingly, we shall assess whether APEC's current and likely structural development is capable of meeting the difficult challenges and supporting the ambitious action plans that APEC has adopted in the past few years – especially in the aftermath of the Asian crisis.

This chapter is divided into six sections. Following a discussion of the theoretical framework, we turn to an analysis of the principles and norms underlying APEC and focus on the ambiguity of the commitment of members to the purposes and goals of APEC. We then turn to a discussion of how the existing principles and norms have been implemented through a relatively weak set of *de facto* rules and procedures. The next section provides an evaluation of the formal organisational elements that make up APEC's authority structures, focusing on the Secretariat, Committees and Working Groups, and other decentralised mechanisms of policy discussion and implementation. The fifth section considers the impact that APEC has had on national policies and examines its contribution to liberalisation, including its impact on the WTO and the IMF. We conclude by summarising our overall findings and suggesting possible avenues for APEC's institutional development.

ANALYSING REGIONAL GOVERNANCE STRUCTURES

We can use a comprehensive framework that allows us to examine APEC's elements and furnishes us with a means of comparing it to other regional cooperative institutions such as NAFTA and the EU.[2]

Analytical framework: governance structures and interactions

For discussion purposes, Figure 12.1 depicts APEC's elements and relationship to other institutions.

Before examining the types of factors that will influence actors' bargaining choices, we first review the elements in this figure. Starting with the centre of the chart, we can distinguish between two aspects of institutions: meta-regimes and regimes. Meta-regimes represent the principles and norms underlying international arrangements. In contrast, regimes refer specifically to the international rules and procedures that have been developed. Regimes can be examined in terms of their strength, nature and scope. Strength refers to the stringency or tightness of the multilateral rules that regulate national behaviour, while nature (in an economic context) refers to their degree of openness. Scope can be divided into two parts: issue scope refers to the number of issues incorporated into the regime; member scope refers to the number of actors (member economies) involved.

Prior to APEC's formation, the GATT was the major institution that regulated trade activities and promoted trade liberalisation. Its underlying meta-regime principle has been an encouragement of freer trade, and its norms include most-favoured nation, reciprocity, safeguards against disruptive or unfair trade, compensation, and special treatment to promote the economic development for the developing countries. The GATT regime has included rules on tariffication, subsidies and anti-dumping, the use of quotas, and free trade areas. The GATT also includes a set of procedures for handling both trade negotiations and trade disputes.

With respect to strength, nature and scope, these regime characteristics have varied over time. By and large, the GATT regime has been quite strong and specific in its rules and procedures, although countries have often breached these directives. With respect to its nature, GATT and its successor organisation, the WTO, have continued to encourage liberalisation, with provisions for trade restraint actions under specific conditions. Finally, with respect to scope, the GATT/WTO have expanded their coverage of issues. For example, in recent years, new codes have covered services, and intellectual property. In the next section, we shall examine APEC's specific meta-regime characteristics.

Other international institutions, such as the Association of Southeast Asian Nations (ASEAN) and the Australia–New Zealand Closer Economic Relations Trade Agreement (ANZCERTA), have also existed among a subset of members in the Asia Pacific region. Each organisation has its own meta-regime and regime, with varying characteristics. In pushing for an APEC agenda on trade,

Figure 12.1 Creating and reconciling APEC with existing institutions

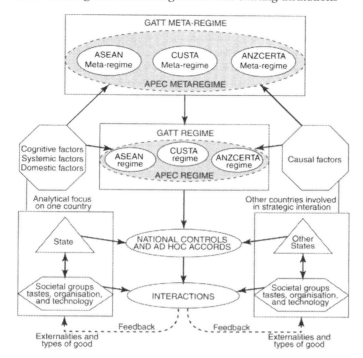

the member states had to concern themselves with two types of institutional reconciliation: (1) reconciling APEC with the broader institution of GATT/WTO; and (2) reconciling APEC with narrower institutions such as ASEAN and ANZCERTA. To date, the avenue to achieve institutional reconciliation has been through 'nested' rather than 'parallel' connections. The development of the North American Free Trade Agreement (NAFTA) as another subregional institution within APEC, and the movement toward a free trade agreement among ASEAN members (AFTA), has further complicated this nesting problem.

International regimes, whether multilateral or bilateral, are developed to regulate the actions of states. National actions can include unilateral actions or *ad hoc* bilateral or multilateral accords. Examples of these include the use of Super 301 by the United States, or bilateral discussions on specific issues between the United States and its trading partners, such as Japan and China. These measures in turn affect the types and levels of interactions that we observe in particular issue areas. Examples of such interactions, which primarily result from non-governmental activities by private actors, include trade, investment or short-term capital flows.

Causal factors in institutional development

Figure 12.2 provides a characterisation of the causal factors that explain the development and evolution of APEC (or any institutions, for that matter).

Focusing on the left-hand side of Figure 12.2, the framework specifies the theoretical elements that account for governance structures and interactions. The cognitive approach, which focuses on the supply of consensual knowledge and political demands by policy makers, has a direct impact on the development of the meta-regime. According to this view, actors are more likely to come to agreement on a set of principles and norms if a consensus exists among experts on the costs and benefits, as well as the implications of activities in a particular issue area. When demands on politicians from various interest groups can be met through international collaboration, and politicians perceive the need for new institutions, they will be motivated to draw on a cognitive consensus among experts to promote a meta-regime, and possibly a regime.

The next element is the causal factors that are likely to influence regime development at the level of rules and procedures. Traditionally, the supply-side focus has been on the presence of a hegemon or at least a dominant or leading actor, that is, a single major power in the international system. But when making their calculations on whether to 'supply' regimes, actors will be particularly concerned with maintaining compatibility with existing security and economic systems, and not solely with economic hegemony. Hence, the nature of power distribution within various nested systems will affect the formation of regimes.

On the demand side, Robert Keohane (1984) has focused on the benefits of regimes in reducing transactions costs, particularly in providing information to participants and lowering the costs associated with negotiating and implementing individual accords. These functions of regimes are clearly important, but transaction costs provide a partial explanation at best and must be considered in conjunction with other factors. Actors might also desire regimes for two other reasons. First, decision makers may try to bring lower level arrangements, that is, more specific arrangements into conformity with broader institutions. This constraint, or 'institutional nesting', discourages actors from participating in arrangements that might undermine broader accords because of their more significant concerns with these higher level systems. Second, actors may wish to control the behaviour of others, both internationally and domestically, through rule-based systems rather than through use of power capabilities. Actors, in this instance, can be either governments or private actors, and both types of actors may try to control other private or governmental actors. These factors of institutional nesting and control provide a more complete account of cooperation 'after hegemony' than does a simple focus on information diffusion or reduced costs of multilateral as compared to bilateral accords.

Figure 12.2 Causal factors in the formation of international institutions

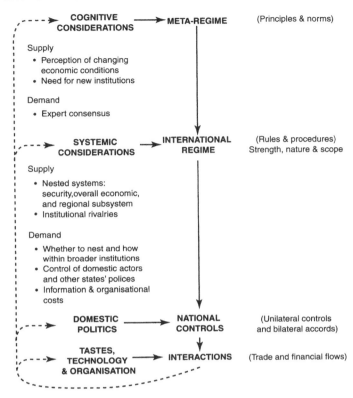

The next level concerns domestic political factors that help explain why states decide whether to comply with regime injunctions. Choices in this respect will depend on the degree to which state decision makers are insulated from interest group pressure, as well as on the dominant ideology motivating the policy makers themselves. Thus, it is not hard to imagine that for their own reasons and even in the absence of protectionist pressures from domestic interest groups, some states may attempt to evade regime restrictions or 'free-ride', thus reaping the public goods benefits of liberal international accords without complying with these arrangements themselves.

Interactions are obviously not simply affected by governance structures but by changing types of technology, organisation and taste (among other significant factors), which influence the supply and demand for goods and services. For example, as new forms of technology encourage a movement towards trade in services or, as changing corporate organisation strategies affect location decisions, interactions may change accordingly. Finally, as indicated by the feedback loop in Figure 12.2, these interactions may then drive changes in the basic causal factors that influence both governance structures and interactions.

APEC'S META-REGIME: DISPUTE OVER PRINCIPLES AND NORMS

APEC members have not been in full accord on the underlying principles and norms of this institution. Although there is a high degree of consensus with respect to some norms, even the general principles of open regionalism and voluntarism have been open to contention, helping to account for the difficulties in implementing liberalisation.

Principles in APEC: open regionalism and voluntarism

Open Regionalism. The central principle endorsed by APEC has been the idea of open regionalism, a notion originally and actively promoted by PECC. One of the key original concerns of APEC members was to reconcile this group's formation with the broader world trade organisation of the GATT.[3] Member states have continued to maintain this as a key objective, with the conclusion of the Uruguay Round and the creation of the WTO to replace GATT. This specific reconciliation effort, or 'nesting', could be accomplished in several ways. One option would be for member states to simply nest APEC in the WTO, based on Article 24 of the GATT that permits the formation of free trade areas and customs unions. This approach has failed to garner much support since APEC member economies agreed from the beginning that APEC is neither a negotiating forum nor a trade bloc.[4]

Instead, members have chosen a different route, nesting APEC by pursuing 'open regionalism'. Still, the basic thrust and interpretation of 'open regionalism' continues to be contested. Some member economies appeared to find the concept useful, principally as a device to oppose what they saw as American efforts to establish an APEC trading bloc. Indeed, 'open regionalism' was often used precisely as a defence against 'Western-style' rule-making or regime-building that some in APEC member economies feared would make them permanent dependencies on the West or overly expose their domestic economies to competition from powerful global corporations primarily with headquarters in the developed countries. However, since APEC was to engage in trade liberalisation and facilitation, open regionalism in this context also conveyed the notion that as APEC members sought to reduce barriers to goods and services among themselves, they would do so in a GATT-consistent manner.

This avenue thus raises the possibility of pursuing nesting in three additional ways. First, APEC could simply pursue unilateral liberalisation measures that would be open to all GATT signatories – whether or not they are members of APEC.[5] Second, APEC members might simply liberalise in areas that are not currently covered by the WTO, thus 'conforming' to the strictures of the

WTO. Third, some type of conditional liberalisation could be pursued, as suggested by the Eminent Persons' Group. It remains unclear if this latter strategy would actually be consistent with efforts to pursue 'open regionalism' because of the real possibility of discrimination against non-members.

The 'conditional liberalisation' notions of the EPG in particular have run into severe difficulties. Asian states and others do not like this potentially confrontational approach that might lead to problems with the EU. Many smaller Asian economies feared it would also result in their economic domination by the United States. At the same time, the United States, while endorsing the notion of unilateral liberalisation, was sceptical as to how far this would take the members of APEC on the road to their commitment of free trade and investment in the area by 2020.[6] The strategy of using APEC as a stepping stone to pursue liberalisation in the WTO in specific sectors appeared to be a compromise that would meet the objectives of many participants. Yet this EVSL notion has run into problems, as noted in the introduction and elaborated on in more detail below.

Voluntarism. A second important principle in APEC is that all actions should be taken on a voluntary basis. APEC operates on the basis of consensus. There is no voting, no power to force any member-economy to take an action against that economy's will, no sanctions or retaliation, and, indeed, officially no negotiations. In theory, the members share the same goal and each has pledged to work towards that goal. The commitment to the goal is not a legal one, but a political one (Soesastro 1994).

The principle of voluntary action is not easily reconciled with the institutional goals of free trade and investment in the region by 2020. APEC has gone to great lengths to try to preserve its basic principles while devising a process of consulting and 'concerting' under which individual members have agreed to discuss together their individual action plans and to concert as much as possible their efforts.

APEC's norms

Owing to the principle of open regionalism, APEC members have continued to express their strong concern for maintaining consistency with GATT and now WTO norms. Hence, we can usefully examine the underlying norms being promoted by its members by examining their relationship to GATT/WTO norms.[7] Turning first to substantive norms, the APEC view on most-favoured nation is clearly a central tenet of open regionalism. Although APEC restricts membership,[8] in principle all countries are considered eligible for APEC 'most-favoured nation' status – or what we might call the norm of 'inclusive MFN'.[9] Also, in line with APEC's open regional focus, the members have advocated a policy of diffuse rather than specific reciprocity.[10] In GATT negotiations, members exchange concessions on directly reciprocal terms. As we shall argue, APEC's diffuse reciprocity approach to negotiations may undermine the efficacy of a more institutionalised APEC regime.

Two important norms that have taken a lesser role in Asia-Pacific discussions, but which have been integral to the GATT/WTO, are those of safeguards and economic development. Safeguards involve restrictions under specific cases of actual or perceived damage to one's market. This norm may not have found its way into APEC at this point simply because of the nascent character of the APEC regime. However, given the high degree of government intervention that has often affected trading patterns in the region, we might expect this norm to gain prominence as attempts are made to further institutionalise APEC. Also conspicuously lacking in the current APEC accords is a sharp North–South dividing line in assigning liberalisation obligations. Although it does feature in the Seoul declaration as a call for 'due consideration to the needs of developing countries' as well as the commitment to accelerated liberalisation for developed members by 2010 as opposed to the 2020 goal for all members, actual preferences for poorer nations, as advocated in Part IV of the GATT, have failed to garner support. Still, the Seattle summit Joint Statement called for liberalisation 'with full recognition of members' differences in levels of economic development', and the Ecotech framework devised by the Osaka Action Agendas took as its central tenet the concept of economic cooperation among members with disparate developmental needs (Yamazawa 1997: 138–9).

In particular, in the non-trade issue areas of environmental protection (Vision Statement 1993) and social policy (Jakarta Declaration for a Human Resources Development Framework 1994), the developing countries' positions of sustainable development and human resource development voiced in the GATT Uruguay Round have been adopted (Dua and Esty 1997). This has the practical result of hierarchically nesting environmental and labour issues under the trade and investment liberalisation regime, allowing overall concerns for economic efficiency and competitiveness to trump any movement to afford greater protection.

We can consider two procedural norms: the notion of 'principal supplier' (that major exporters of a good should initiate negotiations) and multilateralism. As a practical matter, the United States has been very active in promoting specific sectoral liberalisation efforts, although the actual package of nine sectors in the EVSL agreement reflected compromise among the members on issues of concern to them. Multilateralism is an important element of APEC, with the members, while regionally focused, rejecting unilateral restrictive approaches. On the other hand, the meta-regime allows for bilateral negotiations as long as they can be eventually integrated into the arrangement, and strongly promotes the notion of 'concerted liberalisation' that we shall discuss below. This ambiguity was seen in APEC's provisions for integrating the Australian–New Zealand Closer Economic Relationship.

Ironically, considering all of the norms together, although APEC is a regional accord, in its present embryonic state it is more oriented toward openness than the GATT itself. In particular, the emphasis on diffuse reciprocity and inclusive MFN has served to underpin the liberal character of open regionalism.

As we shall see below, however, the tension between APEC's appearance of having a highly liberal nature and the political reality of possible free-riding by non-members may prove to be a significant obstacle in efforts to develop a strong regime.

Explaining the evolution of APEC's meta-regime

What factors account for the development of APEC's meta-regime? We argue that within the broad category of cognitive considerations, we need to focus on changes in both demand and supply factors over time. On the demand side, policy makers call for some type of arrangement in the Asia Pacific region in a manner directly related to the success or difficulties encountered in the GATT, based on the fear that regional blocs might develop if GATT collapses. On the supply side, the PECC grouping has attempted to provide the intellectual rationale for developing an inter-governmental agreement on APEC lines. Noting the success stories of most members' export-oriented policies, some Australian analysts in PECC argued that these Western Pacific countries see trade liberalisation as a 'Prisoner's delight', with unilateral liberalisation being a dominant strategy having the highest pay-offs (Drysdale and Garnaut 1992b: 4–5).

On the demand side, concern for consistency with the GATT/WTO, or better, economists' vision of what the WTO should be, has been the dominant theme in the Asia Pacific region. In view of the high dependence of Asian countries on non-Asia Pacific markets, and the WTO's role in fostering an open world trading system, we would expect policy makers to be concerned about securing an APEC that is supportive of the GATT/WTO. As problems in concluding the Uruguay Round became more apparent in the late 1980s, however, regional arrangements in the Pacific (and elsewhere) were given new impetus, both to push the global process and as a possible fallback should it fail.

On the supply side, we can identify at least four schools of thought with respect to institutions in the Asia Pacific area: (1) pure GATT/WTO-ists; (2) the PECC-led GATT/WTO-consistent school of open regionalism; (3) sceptics of open regionalism; and (4) advocates of an Asian bloc.

The pure GATT/WTO-ists argue that the WTO could be undermined by APEC, and that such arrangements will only foster a break-up of the world economy into competing economic blocs. From their perspective, such a movement will be deleterious, not only to non-Asia Pacific states, but to countries in the region as well. In addition, they point out that the Asia Pacific region has done quite well without having formal institutional arrangements. Thus, from this perspective, institutionalisation is a dangerous recipe for impeding the dynamic growth of the region.[11]

The second group, led primarily by academics and business groups in PECC, has advanced several mutually compatible arguments in promoting open regionalism. First, some argue that APEC-type arrangements will help the WTO's cause by providing impetus from a committed group of countries to advance liberalisation. This 'building block' or 'ratcheting' approach to the WTO can be seen as encouraging like-minded liberally oriented states in different regions to use their political pull to come together into a larger pro-WTO coalition.[12] As noted above, a second perspective suggests that WTO inconsistency can be avoided by simply dealing with issues that are *not* on its agenda, thus preventing conflict with other non-participating GATT members. Thus, issues such as investment, environmental concerns, technology transfer, and standards in communications would be fair game in a forum such as APEC. A third perspective, also noted above, calls for liberalising on a non-discriminatory basis, rather than seeking concessions from trading partners who are not party to an agreement. The economic logic underlying this approach is that APEC members can tolerate free riding because of their dynamic growth and proximity. According to this view, the benefits of trade barrier reductions will most probably accrue to the participants in the region (see Elek 1992: 9). Finally, support for an Asian Pacific regime also draws on the currently popular notion of 'natural' blocs, which argues that arrangements based on regional trading patterns do little to harm the multilateral economic system (see Lawrence 1991 and Krugman 1991).

The proponents of the open regional concept have not been without their critics. In this group, several scholars have argued that permitting diffuse instead of specific reciprocity allows potential free-riders to benefit from APEC liberalisation, and reflects a politically naive perspective.[13] For example, Kahler warns that 'the deeply engrained norm of reciprocity makes it unlikely that the states of the region would extend any liberalisation on a most-favoured national basis to others outside' (Kahler 1988: 343). Even the most ardent proponents of open regionalism, Peter Drysdale and Ross Garnaut, admit that 'The building of support for non-discriminatory APEC-based liberalisation may make it necessary to limit European free riding on multilateral liberalisation in some commodities — perhaps agriculture' (1992a: 18).[14]

Finally, a fourth view has found expression in Malaysia's 1990 proposal to create an East Asian Economic Group that would include ASEAN, Hong Kong, China, Taiwan, South Korea and Japan, and exclude Australia, New Zealand and the North American countries. In essence, this view reflects the concern that the world is splitting up into regional blocs as the United States presses ahead with NAFTA and the European Community admits new members. Thus, proponents of this approach argue that the time has come for Asians to develop their own grouping. In practice, however, this approach has failed to garner much support from Asian states, and has been sharply criticised by the United States. Although Malaysia did not attend the Seattle summit, as a demonstration of its displeasure with lack of support for some type of Asian caucus group, it was not joined in this boycott by other states. More recently, EAEC has found some reality in a benign form, as the proposed EAEC countries comprise the Asian end of the Asia–Europe Meeting (ASEM).

REGIME FORMATION IN APEC

We now turn to an examination of APEC's regime characteristics. To preview our discussion, compared with other regional institutions, APEC is markedly weaker, owing in part to disagreement on norms, but mainly by design. With respect to nature, APEC maintains a highly liberal stance in trade and investment, and with respect to scope, is has continued to expand the issues under its purview, and has also expanded its membership from twelve to twenty-one over its decade of existence.

Strength

As we might anticipate from the discussion of principles and norms, the absence of a strong and stable commitment to the institutionalisation of cooperation in the Asia Pacific area has contributed to the extreme weakness of the APEC 'regime'. The 1994 Bogor Declaration announced as APEC's paramount goal the complete removal of trade barriers in developed economies by the year 2010 and in developing economies by 2020. This will be achieved mainly through Individual Action Programs undertaken by member governments following the guidelines set by the Osaka Action Agenda and formalised by the Manila Action Plan (Bergsten 1997: 62). The IAP commitments to tariff reduction are non-binding and voluntary. In many cases, developed members of APEC have proposed little exceeding their Uruguay Round obligations, and ASEAN countries have pursued often-discussed initiatives started in the subregional context. Ongoing political negotiations and institutional efforts have focused on resolving the ambiguities left by the Osaka Agenda, including the issues of endpoints, benchmarks, time path, and extension of reduced tariffs to non-members.

In the environmental area, bureaucratic coordination and intervention to produce harmonisation are explicitly eschewed, and few concrete initiatives have seen implementation on a region-wide basis (see Zarsky and Hunter 1997). Moreover, since discussions of sustainable development have been handled via a separate track from trade diplomacy, environmental analysis does not inform the Individual Action Programs for trade and investment liberalisation. Furthermore, the weakness of the environmental regime is a result of controversies over the *control* effects of environmental policies on trade. Less-developed countries remain wary of ostensible environmental standards serving as non-trade barriers, while developed countries fear that environmental debates may slow liberalisation and that developing competitors may engage in a 'race-to-the-bottom' eco-dumping strategy (Brook 1997: 232).

Thus, at least in terms of strength of formal rules and procedures, APEC remains weak. As we will discuss in the section below, this does not mean that countries have not felt constrained by APEC; the pressure comes from an overall commitment to its norms, rather than formal strictures.

Issue scope

The issue scope of APEC has expanded from trade and investment liberalisation to include the environment, social issues, infrastructure and women's issues and, most recently, touched on financial coordination in the aftermath of the Asian crisis. The most significant area has been the creation by the 1996 Osaka Action Plan of Economic and Technical Cooperation (Ecotech), one of the main pillars of APEC's structure. The group was created to foster developments in technology and infrastructure in the hope of equalising disparities and promoting sustained economic growth for all member economies. On paper, Ecotech's scope covers developing human capital to safeguarding the quality of life through environmentally sound growth (Bergsten 1997: 141). In an attempt to remedy the problems of bilateral cooperation, a new model was implemented in which all interested members would participate in economic cooperation through the gathering of relevant information and policy promotion. Further, official development for infrastructure was expanded to include private assistance in the effort of relieving the financial burden from the more developed economies. The outcome of these reforms to Ecotech has led to a somewhat more responsive and effective model for economic development in which goals are better defined, implementation is regularly discussed, and performance measures are more easily monitored.

In the area of environmental protection, the emerging framework from seven years of APEC activities consists of the following components: 1) Agenda-setting by Regional Environmental Cooperation Forum, producing a series of Action Programs and Strategies; 2) Working Groups and Committees mainly comprised of engineers who operationalise objectives and develop plans for public–private cooperation; and 3) 'Capacity-building' seminars and workshops to enhance awareness, disseminate norms and develop analytical abilities.

APEC has also incorporated women's issues into the APEC committees and meetings. In the recent 1998 Senior Officers' Meetings, there was a call for a 'Framework for the Integration of Women in APEC', which would include guidelines for gender analysis, improvements to the collection and utilisation of sex-disaggregated data and approaches to the involvement of women (*Business World*, 9 March 1999).

Lastly, APEC has recently indicated a willingness to take on a greater role in addressing social problems arising from cross-border labour mobility and the East Asian crisis. The APEC focus in this area has been confined to medium- and long-term preparation of the labour force for global changes in labour needs; the regime's issue scope remains focused on quality basic education, analysis of the regional labour market, increasing the supply and quality of managers and entrepreneurs, and training geared toward liberalisation and facilitation of trade and investments in the region. On the demand side, the United States stands to benefit from harmonisation of labour standards and protection, yet it encounters resistance from the Asian members. Furthermore, workers' issues in APEC are currently nested in the trade and investment liberalisation regime, and thus concerns for economic efficiency are likely to trump any movement to afford greater protection for labour.

Another emerging issue discussed in the APEC forum has been financial coordination. SOM meetings in Manila in 1996 and then in 1997 in Vancouver had been dominated by financial issues arising from the Asian crisis. Many of the institutions in the Asia Pacific have attempted to play an active role in salvaging crisis-ridden economies, but the IMF, backed by the United States, continues to assert its dominance. In the November 1997 Vancouver APEC summit meeting, leaders endorsed the so-called Manila framework which called for the International Monetary Fund to take the lead in providing emergency loans to Thailand, Indonesia and South Korea, with APEC member nations taking only a secondary role to supplement IMF resources on a standby basis without any formal commitment of funds. Thus, with the APEC action providing the seal of the US–IMF-backed plan, alternative institutional solutions were put on hold. In particular, Japan's proposal for an Asian Monetary Fund (AMF) was vehemently criticised by the United States as potentially undercutting the conditionality imposed by the IMF. (The United States later endorsed a modified version known as the New Miyazawa Plan). And an earlier Taiwanese proposal to create a private fund amassed by healthy nations to provide loans to major companies in ailing economies facing credit squeezes and implement an ambitious plan for government-backed Asian assistance has also received a decidedly chilly response from the United States.

Membership scope

With respect to membership scope, APEC has expanded from twelve members in 1989, to eighteen in 1994 to twenty-one in 1998, including Russia. APEC has placed a moratorium on further expansion for ten years. The history of European integration advises deepening before widening to keep the momentum of cooperation and convergence from flagging, but APEC has admitted new members without deliberately following a sequencing scheme. This expansion has widened the membership to economies of vastly different size and interests with some, like Papua New Guinea and Russia, admitted almost entirely for political reasons. Some may argue that APEC widening is necessary for supporting the principle of open regionalism, while others might maintain that the open regionalism principle should make membership unnecessary. The EPG has argued for a more gradual strategy of creating a set of APEC generalised tariff preferences to extend the benefits of APEC liberalisation to developing non-members, similar to the treatment of associated non-members of the European Free Trade Association in its early years (Bergsten 1997: 15).

Nature

The proposed nature of the regime, as driven by meta-regime concerns, focuses on arrangements in existing areas covered by the WTO as well as new ones, with an emphasis on regional liberalisation. In all cases, the emphasis has been on ensuring consistency with the WTO to avoid any direct challenges to its authority. However, APEC's institutional nature differs from that of the WTO in four ways: 1) a broader agenda that includes issues of investment and services within liberalisation, and other areas of trade facilitation and economic and technical cooperation; 2) strategic interactions from repeated games where smaller gains are sought in continuous 'non-negotiations'; 3) non-legally binding, voluntary compliance with no retaliatory features ; and 4) a consensual, congenial environment (Bergsten 1997: 43). In the aftermath of the Asia crisis, several members' commitment to APEC's liberalisation goals has wavered or at least been tempered by harsh economic realities at home. Protectionism is on the rise, as evidenced by the disputes between the United States and Japan/Korea over steel, and Malaysia's and Thailand's resistance to ITA-II and the WTO Millennium Round on grounds of domestic imperatives of economic recovery.

In sum, the weak institutionalisation of APEC is increasingly heavily taxed by the expansion of issue and membership scopes, emerging reservations for its liberal nature, and diluted strength as implementation and enforcement are put on hold for countries coping with domestic trauma of the Asia crisis.

Explaining regime characteristics

Aside from the absence of an established meta-regime, the most obvious candidate to explain the weakness of the APEC regime is hegemonic stability theory. The absence of a hegemon in the region in the post-Cold War era, and the regional economic bipolarity of the United States and Japan, provide a ready explanation for the lack of a strong regime. With respect to demand factors, we discuss control and transaction costs in the following paragraphs, and the institutional aspects of the demand factors in the analysis below of APEC's contribution to liberalisation in the WTO arena.

There are a host of 'control' related issues that apply to both state and non-state actors. For example, many smaller states wished to draw their key markets, the United States and Japan, into a larger organisation that would prevent the smaller states' isolation if the trend turned toward discriminatory trading blocs. For example, this consideration appears to be an important driving force behind Australia's promotion of APEC: it was highly concerned about both an Asian and a North American bloc that could exclude it. In Australia's case, both the government and internationally competitive firms also had an interest in binding Australian foreign policy to an open market system that helps bolster its domestic liberalisation policies (Ravenhill 1992: 2). Here, then, the interests of smaller states in this case coincide with the interests of the two larger powers in the region, the United States and Japan, since both are interested in APEC for mutual control purposes as well. But we should keep in mind that a desire for mutual control is not sufficient to produce an agreement: obviously, as long as parties sharply disagree as to who will control what, regime formation is not a simple matter. For example, the United States wished to use APEC to help further liberalisation of the Japanese economy, while Japan hoped APEC would help Japan contain and control US unilateralism.

More broadly, control questions shed some light on the issue of GATT consistency. It is unlikely that APEC members will be able to secure a strong liberal-oriented regime in APEC dealing with issues currently covered under the WTO.[15] Both APEC and non-APEC states had encountered major difficulties in the Uruguay Round in convincing member states to lower trade barriers in several sectors. Thus, we can hardly expect APEC members to conclude agreements among themselves that would permit free riding by non-APEC members. In sum, with respect to scope, a control-based argument would suggest that due to APEC's open regional focus, member states are more likely to agree on non-WTO issues than on issues currently being addressed in the WTO.[16]

With respect to information sharing, and other means of reducing transaction costs, these have been an important factor driving regime evolution in the region, mostly however through the improved understanding and enforcement of global rules rather than the evolution of region-specific rules (see Higgot 1992 on this issue). In the case of intellectual property regimes, APEC has contributed through exchanges of information on the implications and respective actions to enforce the global Trade-Related Aspects of Intellectual Property Rights (TRIPS) Agreement, workshops and training projects (see La Croix 1998). In addition, driven by transaction cost calculations in increasingly competitive regional and global markets for telecom products, APEC ministers reached agreement on mutual recognition arrangements (MRAs) to speed the introduction of telecommunications equipment into one another's markets. In two stages, member states will recognise the results of equipment conformance tests carried out in exporting countries, and importing countries will recognise the certification of equipment carried out in other APEC economies (*Communications Week International*, 26 June 1998: 43).

INSTITUTIONAL DECISION-MAKING STRUCTURES

From the beginning, a substantial portion of APEC members was reluctant to support the 'institutionalisation' of APEC, resulting in its incomplete name ('four adjectives in search of a noun', in the words of Australian former Foreign Affairs Minister Gareth Evans) as well as its limited organisational machinery. Over the past decade, however, APEC has become an institution, and institutional machinery has developed accordingly.

Initially, APEC had no secretariat. Its ten working groups (established in 1990 and 1991) were led by individual member economies, and initiative and records were kept with the responsible national ministries. In ASEAN fashion, senior officials at the individual economy level became the most important decision-making structure in the organisation. They typically met four or even more times a year, and ratified all important decisions made at a lower level, or bucked up deadlocks to the ministerial level.

Two events of significance to APEC's institutional development occurred in 1993: the establishment of a small secretariat in Singapore and the initiation of a leaders' meeting. The secretariat is managed by an Executive Director, chosen annually by the incoming host economy, and is responsible to APEC Senior Officials. Although the Secretariat has increased in size, the bulk of institutional work is still in the various ministries at the national level, particularly that of the incoming host economy. Reflecting the consensual nature of the APEC process, decision making is done through committees, while the Secretariat is basically a service organ to keep records, provide logistics, and serve as a central clearinghouse in a still highly decentralised institution.

The establishment of the Leaders' Meetings was not the result of a planned or negotiated process but rather a White House initiative intended to exploit the political and institutional leadership opportunities provided by the United States' year to host APEC in 1993.[17] The Leaders' Meetings became an established part of the APEC process when President Suharto invited the leaders to meet again in 1994 during the Indonesian year to host APEC.

The Leaders' Meetings had a significant impact on the APEC process because the organisation now engaged the prestige of those at the top level of government. APEC now needed a discussion of issues and a record of accomplishment that would justify the leaders' time. Moreover, decisions and compromises could be made at the leaders' level that would have taken years or never occurred had the organisation remained a ministerial one. For example, it is virtually impossible to imagine that the vision of free trade and investment in the region would have been agreed to at the ministerial level. Indeed, a prevailing sentiment in the Indonesian bureaucracy had been against such a vision in 1994, and the Indonesian government became an advocate only because then President Suharto decided to make this vision the legacy of Indonesia's (and his) hosting of the 1994 APEC activity.

APEC's three major committees were also established in 1993–5: (1) the Committee on Trade and Investment seeks to develop an APEC perspective on trade and investment issues and pursue specific initiatives. It is responsible for overseeing the implementation of trade and investment liberalisation and facilitation measures, including the ESVL scheme. (2) The Economic Committee was created to analyse economic trends and support the trade and investment liberalisation and facilitation agenda. (3) The Budget and Management Committee advises the senior officials on budgetary, administrative and managerial issues.

Assessing the formal structures of APEC, a number of features become apparent. First, the engagement of the leaders is a prominent feature in comparison to other organisations mainly involved in trade matters. The WTO and NAFTA, for example, do not have leaders' meetings. At the same time, the Leaders' Meetings themselves are symbolic of the organisational under-development of APEC – that is, based as it is on encounters among individuals or individual governments and not rule-based.

Second, APEC's centralised formal structure remains primitive. The Secretariat is severely restricted in size and function. The constant rotation of officials makes the development of a sense of organisational identity, institutional *modus operandi* or institutional memory difficult. APEC has no official with primary loyalty to the organisation as opposed to the government from which she or he was seconded. The Secretariat has no power to take initiative as an independent actor within the APEC process. It is entirely a creature of the member economy governments. Without a stronger central institution, APEC is unlikely to develop significantly beyond a shoptalk, like the Group of Eight (Morrison 1995).

Third, the premium on consensus and the weakness of the Secretariat have encouraged the development of other features that work against institutional development. There appears to be a distressing tendency towards micro-management by committee, and the paperwork and procedures associated with the organisation suggest that it has inherited some of the worst features of the bureaucratic practices of the member economies. This problem has become all the more complicated as membership has expanded.[18]

Fourth, closely related to the structure is the shift in venue of leadership from one member economy to another. This has the positive feature of giving successive economies and their leaders a stake in the APEC process. Prior to 1998, each lead economy had a strong incentive to develop a distinctive accomplishment for its year of APEC. The weakness of this approach, however, is that APEC's economies are vastly different in size and also have different degrees of interest in and commitment to the APEC process.[19] Since some of the APEC economies are undergoing significant political change or even systemic change, a rotating APEC meeting also may coincide with internal political upheavals in the host country, reducing capacity to carry through its leadership role.

Finally, of course, there is no significant analytical capacity within APEC itself. The success of the APEC process requires considerable feedback, monitoring, and comparison – such as the relative progress of each of the member economies in achieving the APEC vision. This work has to be commissioned to other institutions, such as the Pacific Economic Cooperation Council's Trade Policy Forum (TPF). While this may be advantageous for some purposes, it may also make it difficult to respond quickly when APEC committees need analysis on a time-sensitive basis.

APEC has a plan of action, but institutionally it is not well structured as an action-oriented body. Rather the institutional machinery seems primarily designed to facilitate consultation and build consensus. The one significant advantage is the involvement of leaders, as this allows leaders to appeal directly to one another or to 'group' a recalcitrant leader. However, as the delay in reaching an ESVL package illustrated in 1998, this does not guarantee results.

ASSESSING APEC'S IMPACT ON NATIONAL POLICIES AND THE WTO

The key measure of APEC's institutional effectiveness is the grouping's ability to affect national actions to achieve common objectives. Have APEC economies taken actions as the consequence of their membership in and commitments to APEC that they would not otherwise have taken? Have they not taken other protectionist actions that they might have otherwise had there been no APEC?

APEC as a constraint on national policies

The evidence that APEC has had a constraining and shaping influence on national policy action is slight. This is not surprising in light of APEC's institutional weaknesses, and it reinforces the belief that substantial rules-building at the broad Asia Pacific regional level, separate from and in advance of the global level, is unlikely. While governments respond to pressures from the economic forces of interdependence, the rules that may appeal to the dominant interests in one economy may be anathema in another. Few national policy decisions have been directly affected by the proto-regime. On the other hand, the meta-regime may have had some influence on state policies. Studies indicate some similarity at the meta-regime level in the most engaged bureaucracies (basically foreign and trade ministries) of the key APEC member economies. Economies that once pursued strong import-substitution policies in the manufacturing sector, including China, most of the ASEAN group and Australia, have been unilaterally dismantling them. Moreover, the APEC economies, from different starting points and at different speeds, have all been moving toward increased deregulation and privatisation. Ironically, Japan, in the 1980s a strong model of government-promoting industrialisation, has become in the 1990s the region's leading example of what can happen when the economy is over-regulated.

These liberalising trends, of course, were not the result of the establishment of APEC but rather part of a worldwide phenomenon. However, APEC's association with these trends gave them additional political strength within the national context. In fact, the national bureaucracies often look to APEC and each other for reinforcement of a liberal economic policy line against domestic interests that do not share the liberalising ideology. Zhang Yunling reports that it would have been impossible for China to make the across-the-board tariff cuts it offered at the 1995 Osaka APEC meeting without the justification of needing an impressive down-payment for APEC (Aggarwal and Morrison 1998: 223–4).

Participation in the APEC process may have helped to moderate United States trade unilateralism and to provide impetus for Japan to carry out long-delayed deregulation. It has also increased the level of attention given to

GATT/WTO rules and codes in some of the APEC developing member economies. The similarity at the meta-regime level and the complementarity of national policy interest were sufficient in the initial bargaining stage to launch APEC and the ongoing process of engaging national economic interests and seeking consensus on the bargaining.

But the ongoing process of engaging national economic interests and seeking consensus on the bargaining and issue linkages has been difficult due to the domestic political dynamics of trade liberalisation in some of the most important APEC economies. The United States has demanded explicit reciprocity since the 'Reciprocal Trade Act' was first adopted in the 1930s as a means of mutually reducing trade barriers. The United States' situation is complicated by the recent withholding by Congress of fast-track authorisation from President Clinton. Congress requires reciprocity in its advance grant of authority to the President to engage in trade negotiations and, on non-tariff issues, it has a second shot to ensure its standards of reciprocity after the negotiations, through the need for its approval of the necessary implementing legislation.

Japan's situation is both very different and somewhat similar. The legislative process does not require a prior grant of authority, but political interest groups in Japan, including elements in the bureaucracy itself, have been quite effective in slowing or blocking liberalisation in many sectors. The tried and true formula for moving ahead has usually been heavy-handed *gaiatsu*, or foreign pressure. While APEC might seem to make such pressures more acceptable by 'multilateralising' and 'Asianising' them, the limits of this became apparent in 1998 with the failure of APEC to complete an ESVL package because of resistance in the Japanese Ministry of Agriculture, Forestry and Fisheries to a comprehensive package including forestry and fishery products. We turn next to this example.

EVSL and the WTO

One of the key concerns of APEC members, where the free trade and investment in the region goal was concerned, was to reconcile the group's trade agenda with the broader world trade organisation of the GATT. Member states have continued to maintain this as a key objective with the conclusion of the Uruguay Round and creation of the World Trade Organisation (WTO) to replace GATT. As noted, this nesting could be accomplished in several ways.

One avenue that appeared promising but that has run into trouble is the notion of sectoral liberalisation. At the APEC Manila/Subic meetings, the participants agreed to commit to zero tariffs in information technology. This APEC-based endorsement was then broadened at the December 1996 Singapore WTO ministerial meeting, providing for WTO-based liberalisation on six major categories of equipment: computers, some telecommunications equipment, semiconductors, semiconductor manufacturing equipment, software and scientific instruments. APEC enthusiasts have sometimes exaggerated the importance of the APEC role and minimised the already substantial groundwork in developing the IT Agreement undertaken elsewhere. Nevertheless, nesting seemed to work perfectly in this instance – the consensus developed within APEC removed some potential blocks to a broader agreement and gave momentum to the IT Agreement going into the WTO ministerial.

Following Manila, it seemed to the APEC senior officials that the sectoral approach might be the best way to pursue the APEC vision, in the hope the agreements in easier sectors might have a demonstration impact and learning effect in the more difficult areas. In particular, the United States government, which required demonstrable reciprocity to ensure Congressional approval of tariff reductions and had lost 'fast track' authority for broad agreements, championed the sectoral–regional strategy with enthusiasm, holding up the ITA as a model to promote liberalisation in a variety of other sectors.

In Vancouver in 1997, Ministers agreed to consider nine additional sectors for fast-track trade barrier reduction: chemicals, energy-related equipment and services, environmental goods and services, forest products, medical equipment, telecommunications equipment, fish and fish products, toys, and gems and jewellery. This followed a process through which each member economy had suggested sectors for early liberalisation. The sectors ultimately agreed to were intended to reflect a broad grouping of product areas, of interest to developed and developing countries alike. The Ministers also agreed to create detailed market-opening plans in the nine areas by the first half of 1998, aimed at beginning implementation in 1999. The United States led a movement to make the nine-sector liberalisation a package (Early Voluntary Sectoral Liberalisation) in order to discourage countries from picking and choosing sectors based on domestic concerns and meeting the Osaka principle of 'comprehensiveness'.

However, the early multi-sectoral liberalisation had been put on hold due to disagreements over product coverage, target tariff rates, and time frame – issues that collectively fall under the APEC principle of 'flexibility'. These debates mainly reflect the desires of Asian states, already under stress of the Asian crisis, to maintain control over the domestic effects of liberalisation and to resist arm-twisting by the United States. Again, the APEC framework failed to generate the centripetal force necessary to overcome resistance from individual interests for the benefit of the common good. At Kuala Lumpur at the 6th Leaders' Summit in November 1998, Japan, supported by other Asian countries, refused to liberalise fishing and forestry products. This development threw the US strategy of using APEC as the vanguard for sectoral liberalisation into disarray and forced the participants to send the whole package to the WTO for negotiation.

This change in approach can be viewed in either of two ways: first and optimistically, that APEC wishes to become the springboard for new WTO initiatives, thereby making the decision to transfer EVSL to the WTO a predetermined plan. This would in fact conform to the principle that APEC is not a negotiating forum and that international negotiation of trade liberalisation (as opposed to concerted national packages) should be done in a formal, global negotiating setting. Or, second, the Kuala Lumpur result could be seen as an act of desperation after APEC failed to make any progress in terms of trade liberalisation. Given Japanese opposition to the tariff reductions, the evidence would support the latter conclusion. Indeed, in June 1999, APEC forwarded six additional sectors for consideration by the WTO, without any pretence that APEC itself would serve as a negotiating forum. This development would confirm a stall in efforts to promote voluntary trade liberalisation by the year 2020, and perhaps even suggests that APEC may have to remove trade liberalisation as a priority altogether.

In parallel, the effort to extend the ITA to include additional products has run into repeated delays. Developed countries fear an influx of Asian exports and Asian countries fear the effect of liberalisation on their crisis-affected industries. Thus, for the moment, as a result in large part of the Asian crisis, APEC's role in trade liberalisation has stalled.

Even before the economic crisis, APEC had been criticised for putting 'too many eggs in the trade basket' (Morrison (1997a). The fact is, however, that APEC mushroomed into many other arenas with ministerial meetings on finance, environment, transportation, energy, ocean policy and other areas. Because the Bogor vision privileged trade and the structure of APEC failed to provide representation for other than Trade and Foreign Ministers at the leaders' level, these other arenas are generally sidelined. The most glaring example has been finance. APEC Finance Ministers met at almost the opposite end of the year from the Leaders' Meetings, meaning that their recommendations did not feed into the higher level in a timely manner. Nor were they present. The result was that prior to APEC's November 1997 Vancouver Ministerial and Leader's meetings, APEC was in danger of having done nothing relevant about the major financial crisis sweeping the region. Almost at the last moment, a hastily called Deputy Finance Ministers' meeting in Manila provided guidance for the summit, nesting any regional financial relief into the global IMF framework. However, APEC is still wrestling with its role in finance. Once again the issue of subsidiarity or nesting is at stake. What can be done better at the regional rather than the global level, and how can it be done so that regional and global arrangements are not incompatible?

CONCLUSION AND RECOMMENDATIONS

We have argued that APEC is institutionally under-developed and thus has had difficulty in supporting an ambitious trade and investment liberalisation agenda. Our assessment is based on three elements. First, at the broad 'meta-regime' level (norms and principles), APEC's principles of open regionalism and voluntarism gloss over significant differences about the institution's purpose and procedures. As a result, an ongoing debate about the meaning of open regionalism as well as the proper scope for APEC's activities hinders the effectiveness of the institution.

Second, with respect to formal regime characteristics (rules and procedures), APEC is weak, partly due to disagreements on norms but mainly by design. Lacking a consensus on rules, the member economies have pursued concerted unilateral liberalisation in the hope that peer pressure by more liberal economies will push along the more reluctant ones. APEC's institutional structure is designed to be a decentralised institution, without much formal regulatory power. Indeed, there is only moderate evidence that APEC has constrained or shaped national policy directions in significant ways. Secondment and rapid turnover of staff in the Secretariat means that there is little institutional memory or commitment apart from the commitment to member economies. APEC's scope has also expanded, both in terms of membership and in terms of the numbers of issues to be addressed. While this expansion on both accounts underscores the essentially political character of APEC and could be a positive force, given the weakness and lack of a clear mandate, such expansion comes at the expense of member like-mindedness and institutional focus.

Third, APEC's uncertain mandate as a 'non-negotiating' forum has at times been hurt by more clear-cut negotiating objectives for trade and investment liberalisation both above (GATT/WTO) and below (NAFTA, ASEAN, CER). The referral of sectors for early voluntary sectoral liberalisation (EVSL) to the WTO is a case in point. Because APEC failed to develop an internal consensus prior to its 1998 Kuala Lumpur Leaders' Meeting, the WTO had to take over.

Despite the current weak state of institutionalisation, APEC plays a valuable role in promoting regional awareness of global issues and regimes, facilitating compliance with global regimes, and adding leverage in the domestic political arena to trade liberalisation forces. In operational rules making, implementation, enforcement and adjudication, APEC thus facilitates regime building, but mainly by strengthening the operation of global regimes rather than being a locus of negotiations.

Although the building of a 'community' is an APEC objective, there is not now a strong sense of shared values, interests and vulnerabilities. But like the OECD, APEC has a socialising function – helping to develop a consensus on the basic norms and values that should govern international behaviour and underlay rules and to defend the meta-regime from threats within the APEC societies. This function of building of a 'community' is particularly relevant in the Asia Pacific context where societies are at diverse levels of economic development.

The growing breadth of APEC activities (which includes trade, investment, the environment, labour, finance, transport, tourism, fisheries, and the promotion of small and medium-sized business), has involved the creation of consultative mechanisms at both the technical and ministerial levels that did not previously exist. At a minimum, this has facilitated the development of a common vocabulary and, more ambitiously, common understandings of the basic challenges and objectives in the issue areas. At the same time, an excessively broad agenda can be hazardous, as too many issues compete for a limited amount of decision makers' attention.

It can be argued that APEC is also relevant to regime building because it increases awareness of and compliance with global regimes among the member economies. As noted above, open regionalism has often been used as a defence against foreign rule making. However, it also directs the attention of the APEC countries to the GATT/WTO regime in trade, and similar global conventions covering such areas as intellectual property protection, customs classification, value-added network services, and transportation. In these areas, there are considerable deficiencies in some APEC member economies' compliance with the global regimes, sometimes because of political or technical problems in implementation. Through information exchange and training, APEC may apply pressure for improved enforcement or help overcome technical deficiencies or simply ignorance. Moreover, the normative APEC vocabulary is full of other more operationally meaningful principles – transparency, non-discrimination, comprehensiveness, WTO-consistency, mutual benefit. These serve both as guiding principles influencing national, bilateral and subregional rules making and as a basis for other governments to challenge actions inconsistent with them.

Thus in the operational rule making, implementation, enforcement and adjudication arenas, APEC also facilitates the development of regimes, but more by acting to strengthen the operation of global regimes at the regional level than by either creating new regional regimes or by pushing for major extensions of global regimes. Rather than breaking new ground, the early efforts of APEC's working groups have been focused on understanding existing national regimes and global obligations. It remains to be seen if APEC can accomplish its objectives of promoting trade and financial liberalisation, greater environmental cooperation, and the promotion of social issues in the absence of more institutionalised mechanisms. At a minimum, considerably more effort must be focused on the design of appropriate governance mechanisms if APEC is to continue to play a pro-active role – rather than simply being a facilitator for existing international arrangements to promote cooperation.

These findings suggest several policy conclusions:

1   Although APEC's vision of free trade and investment in the region by 2010/2020 may not be realised, this vision provides a stimulus for action that has been quite useful. The organisation needs to grapple directly with how this vision can be realistically modified so that the trade ambitions do not exceed the institutional capacity of the organisation. It also needs to address how new governance mechanisms may help to strengthen APEC's ability to deliver on its objectives. These challenges require some extended and serious collective thinking – more than can be expected by the national bureaucratic mechanisms that are typically too caught up in day-to-day policy making to engage in longer-term thinking. It may be

time for a new Eminent Persons' Group to help APEC sort through these tasks at a time of some institutional disarray.

2 APEC needs to have a clearer agenda of non-trade goals while limiting the scope of its activities to fewer priority areas. At a minimum, finance needs to be addressed more consistently and in a manner that more directly connects the Finance Ministries with the Leaders' Meetings.

3 The Leaders' Meetings are a significant feature of APEC, but reflect the more personalistic rather than institutionalised nature of the APEC process. It is important that such meetings continue, both for the sake of international relations of the region and also to drive forward the APEC cooperation processes. Attention must be paid to ensuring that such meetings be perceived as valuable within national governments and taken seriously by heads of states.

4 While APEC should continue to avoid bureaucracy, the Secretariat needs strengthening along two lines. First, some attention should be given to creating longer-term positions in APEC for the head of the secretariat, and possibly some additional positions. Second, in-house analytical capabilities need to be strengthened to help APEC leaders set priorities and realistic targets.

5 Closer ties need to be developed between APEC and other regional and global organisations to facilitate wider and deeper cooperation.

6 The organisational activities should be expanded to increase the participation of NGOs and other citizen organisations to give APEC greater outreach and legitimacy. Creative ways of involving parliaments also need to be considered.

7 APEC should continue its efforts to make NTBs and other cross-border rules and regulations more transparent. Non-governmental organisations and APEC Study Centres can contribute to this process.

NOTES

1 We would like to thank Kun-Chin Lin and Rishi Chandra for their research assistance and comments on this chapter.

2 This framework is based on Aggarwal (1985) and has been applied to compare APEC and NAFTA in Aggarwal (1994).

3 The Chair summarised the first APEC ministerial meeting in 1989 as follows: '[what] has run through all our deliberations in the last two days is that the continuing economic success of the region, with all its implications for improved living standards for our people, depends on preserving and improving the multilateral trading system through progressive enhancement of, and adherence to the GATT framework'. APEC Secretariat, Selected APEC Documents: 1989–94, Singapore (1995: 37).

4 The Chair's 1989 summary, cited in the footnote above, also noted 'None of us support the creation of a trading bloc'.

5 These options are discussed in Aggarwal (1994).

6 The US had a constitutional problem since it could not unilaterally liberalise without the approval of Congress, and Congressional support was unlikely in the absence of specific gains from trading partners.

7   For an excellent discussion of GATT norms, see Finlayson and Zacher (1981). They consider five so-called substantive norms (most-favoured nation, liberalism, reciprocity, safeguards, and development) and two procedural norms (multilateralism and major supplier) in examining the evolution of the GATT.

8   In addition to the minimum criterion for membership – a border on the Pacific Ocean – the members have restricted entry without a clear explicit rationale. At the Seattle meeting in November 1993, the members decided to freeze membership for three years and develop explicit criteria for states wishing to join APEC in the meantime.

9   Note that this is an adaptation of the MFN norm. Under the GATT, MFN is required only for its members, as opposed to APEC where non-members can obtain the same benefits. GATT MFN, in this respect, should properly be referred to as 'exclusive MFN'.

10   Specific reciprocity involves the direct balancing of benefits; diffuse reciprocity entails more general give and take. See Keohane (1986) on this issue.

11   Kahler (1988) reviews the arguments that others have made in this respect.

12   This perspective views smaller coalitions of states as a potential replacement for the lack of a hegemonic power in the international system to drive negotiations in the GATT forward. For a discussion of this idea, see Snidal (1985).

13   Ravenhill (1992) makes this point. He also attacks the notion of unilateral liberalisation in the Australian context in a co-authored work (Matthews and Ravenhill 1991).

14   They do, however, go on to note that only measures aimed at export subsidies in the form of some anti-dumping tools would be appropriate as a response.

15   See the suggestions of possible issues that APEC might address in Elek (1992).

16   Collective action arguments might suggest that the relatively smaller numbers of actors in APEC might facilitate agreement. Yet, given the great political and economic disparity among countries in this grouping, the benefits of smaller numbers appears to be limited in this respect.

17   Even Australian Prime Minister Paul Keating, who had earlier proposed leader meetings, was given only the briefest forewarning of the Clinton invitations.

18   This observation is based on interviews with APEC and member economy officials.

19   From 1993 to 1997, APEC was led by fairly large and committed economies – the United States, Indonesia, Japan, the Philippines and Canada, and these countries were capable of pressing an APEC agenda of their own. This is more questionable in the case of the 1999 leader, New Zealand, or the year 2000's Brunei.

REFERENCES

Aggarwal, V.K. (1985) *Liberal Protectionism: The international politics of organized textile trade,* Berkeley and London: University of California Press.

—— (1994) 'Comparing regional cooperation efforts in Asia–Pacific and North America', in A. Mack and J. Ravenhill, *Pacific Cooperation: Building economic and security regimes in the Asia Pacific region,* Sydney: Allen and Unwin.

—— and Morrison, C.E. (eds) (1998) *Asia Pacific Crossroads: Regime Creation and the Future of APEC,* New York: St. Martins.

APEC Secretariat (1995) *Selected APEC Documents: 1989–1994,* Singapore.

Bergsten C.F. (1997) *Whither APEC? The Progress to Date and Agenda for the Future,* Washington, DC: Institute for International Economics.

Brook, Douglas, H. (1997) 'International trade and the Asian environment' in Arvind Panagariya, M.G. Quibria, and Narhiri Rao (eds) *The Global Trading System and Developing Asia,* Oxford: Oxford University Press for the Asian Development Bank.

Drysdale, P. and Garnaut R. (1992a) 'Responses and strategies', Twentieth Pacific Trade and Development Conference, Institute of International Economics.

—— (1992b) 'The Pacific: An application of a general theory of economic integration'.

Dua, A. and Esty D.C. (1997) 'APEC and Sustainable Development', in Bergsten (1997).

Elek A. (1992) 'Pacific economic cooperation: policy choices for the 1990s', *Asian–Pacific Economic Literature* 6: 1.

Finlayson, J.A. and Zacher M.W. (1981) 'The GATT and the regulation of trade barriers: regime dynamics and functions', *International Organization* 35(4): 561–602.

Higgott R. (1992) 'Pacific economic co-operation and learning: some questions about the role of knowledge and learning', *Australian Journal of International Affairs*, 46(2) (November), pp. 182–97.

Kahler, M. (1988) 'Organizing the Pacific', in Scalapino. R., Saro S., Wanandi J. and Han S. (eds) *Pacific–Asian Economic Policies and Regional Interdependence*, Berkely: IEAS.

Keohane, R.O. (1984) *After Hegemony: Cooperation and Discord in the World Political Economy*, Princeton: Princeton University Press.

—— (1986) 'Reciprocity in International Relations', *International Organization* 40(1): 1–28.

Krugman, P. (1991) 'Regional trade blocs: the good, the bad and the ugly', *The International Economy*, November/December, pp. 54–6.

Lawrence, R.Z. (1991) 'Emerging regional arrangements: Building blocks or stumbling blocks?', in O'Brien R. (ed.) *Finance and the International Economy*, Vol. 5, Oxford: Oxford University Press.

La Croix, S. (1998) 'Intellectual property and APEC', in Aggarwall and Morrison (1998).

Matthews, T. and Ravenhill J. (1991) 'The economic challenge: Is unilateral free trade the correct response?', in Richardson J.L. (ed.) *Northeast Asian Challenge: Debating the Garnaut Report* Canberra: Canberra Studies in World Affairs, No. 27, Department of International Relations, Australian National University: 68–94.

Morrison, C.E. (1995) 'The future of APEC: Institutional and structural issues', in National Center for APEC *et al.*, *APEC at the Crossroads*, Seattle, pp. 82–3.

—— (1997a) 'Development cooperation in the 21st century: Implications for APEC?', *Asian Perspective*, 21(2), Fall 1997: 37–56.

—— (1997b) 'Interdependence policy networks and security in Asia–Pacific', in Harris S. and Mack A. (eds) *Asia–Pacific Security: The Economics–Politics Nexus* Sydney: Allen and Unwin, 121–36.

—— (1998) 'Asia–Pacific regionalism and US policy toward regulatory regime-building in the region', in Jens van Scherpenberg and Elke Thiel (eds), *Towards Rival Regionalism? US and EU Regional Regulatory Regime Building*, Nomos Verlagsgesellschaft, Baden-Baden: 123–45.

Ravenhill, J. (1992) 'Discussion paper for workshop on Pacific economic cooperation', paper presented at a conference entitled, 'The Politics of Regional Trade Agreements', East–West Center, Honolulu, October 29–30.

Snidal, D. (1985) 'The limits of Hegemonic Stability Theory', *International Organization* 39.

Soesastro, H. (1994) 'Pacific economic cooperation: the history of an idea', in R. Garnaut and P. Drysdale (eds) *Asia Pacific Regionalism: Readings in international economic relations*, Pymble, NSW: HarperEducational.

Yamazawa, I. (1997) 'APEC's economic and technical cooperation: Evolution and tasks ahead', in Bergsten (1997).

Zarsky, L. and Hunter, J. (1997) 'Environmental cooperation at APEC: the first five years', *Journal of Environment & Development* 6(3).

13 Summary and recommendations[1]

Ippei Yamazawa, Peter Drysdale and Hadi Soesastro

Ten years have now passed since APEC was initiated as an annual meeting of foreign and trade ministers to sustain the momentum of market opening and economic cooperation which are of such vital importance to the growth and prosperity of the Asia Pacific region.

In these ten years APEC has undergone remarkable development, deepening and broadening its agenda and membership.

There are now twenty-one member economies within APEC and APEC's achievements in the past decade have far exceeded the expectations that were held for it at its beginnings.

In 1993 the annual meeting of leaders was inaugurated; 1994 saw the ambitious declaration in Bogor for achieving free and open trade and investment in the region by 2010 and 2020; in 1995 the Osaka Action Agenda was set out to guide the achievement of these liberalisation goals; and in 1996 the Manila Action Plan was adopted as the way forward.

The East Asian financial crisis of 1997 challenged the achievements of APEC, demonstrating both the success and limitations of the APEC process of voluntary cooperation.

The crisis was a shock to the region and to APEC's ambitions.

Although APEC was unprepared to deal with the financial crisis, it has remained an effective bulwark in sustaining commitment to the strategy of promoting outward-looking economic development. The experience of the crisis has confirmed the need to broaden the base of cooperation, beyond trade and investment issues. APEC also catalysed the development of new regional infrastructure for financial cooperation in the Manila Framework Group – to make the region more prepared for dealing with such crises in the future.

The experience of negotiating Early Voluntary Sectoral Liberalisation (EVSL) has brought home the reality that the structure of APEC is not suited to promoting traditional trade negotiations, which are best concluded through the World Trade Organisation (WTO).

But above all, the experience of the crisis demonstrates that cooperation through APEC is indispensable for recovery, for sustaining a favourable environment for expansion of trade and investment, and for strengthening the basis of financial interaction in the region.

With its diverse membership of developing and developed economies, APEC cannot function like the European Union or other legally and institutional binding arrangements. APEC's achievements are built upon its flexible modalities and is uniquely designed to suit the realities of closer economic relations among the economies of the Asia Pacific region.

From these perspectives, PAFTAD 25 sought to provide an assessment of APEC's achievements and the challenges that face it in the years ahead.

There are eight issue areas important to APEC's future achievements.

1   APEC's immediate priority is to assume leadership in promoting a new WTO round, pressing for the adoption of the Bogor vision by all members of the WTO.
*   The stumble over EVSL confirmed that APEC should press the negotiation of sensitive sectors such as agriculture, automobiles and telecommunications through the WTO, consistently with meeting its liberalisation targets. APEC should also press for the accession of China and Chinese Taipei, two important member economies, to the WTO through the Ministerial meetings in November.
2   APEC governments have undertaken significant unilateral trade liberalisation since the 1980s. APEC is on track to achieve its Bogor target for tariff reduction.
*   It does not matter whether present commitments to trade liberalisation are embedded in Uruguay Round commitments, are a direct result of commitments under APEC, or come within IMF programs – APEC provides a reference point for trade liberalisation efforts and APEC members will certainly expect to gain credit for commitments made to liberalisation in a new WTO round.
*   APEC's Individual Action Plans (IAPs) are a major channel through which liberalisation commitments are induced. The strengthening and revision of the Osaka Action Agenda and common format for IAPs will reinforce liberalisation by APEC economies alongside negotiated liberalisation through a new round.
*   APEC has huge value to members as a flag carrier for reform and trade liberalisation.
3   Facilitation measures, such as standards and conformance, customs procedures and business visa arrangements are important complements to liberalisation of border barriers to trade and commerce – and may be even more important in reducing the costs of doing business across borders within the region.
*   APEC's Collective Action Plans can encourage the achievement of targets on facilitation measures ahead of Bogor deadlines.
*   While it may be difficult to appreciate the importance of facilitation measures, the multiplication of tangible and visible signs of progress in

immigration and customs halls around the region under the APEC banner is an exciting achievement.

4 For various reasons, there are new moves to activate sub-regional arrangements and explore bilateral free trade areas (FTAs) among some member economies. They are motivated by the desire to promote economic links with particular partners and, where they are consistent with the commitment to open regionalism in APEC, should be applauded.

- It is important that sub-regional arrangements be scrutinised so that they do not discriminate against outside partners. This can be achieved so long as APEC governments meet their trade liberalisation commitments under Bogor to 2010 and 2020, unilaterally or in the course of WTO negotiations.

5 Ecotech has been a key element in APEC programs since the beginning, with the aim of building development capacity in member economies. There are few visible achievements thus far, but there is growing realisation that the 'software' element in Ecotech is essential to promotion of liberalisation, facilitation, and the strengthening of financial and other markets in member economies.

- Ecotech is not expected to make significant contributions to 'hardware' capacity, such as harbours, dams or roads.

- However, the mobilisation of resources for cooperative policy development and sharing expertise, among member economies and international organisations, is a core part of the APEC agenda.

- In addition to the areas already mentioned, environmental issues should be an area of increasing cooperation in the future.

6 APEC's objective of progressively deeper integration of Asia Pacific economies requires attention to all markets; domestic as well as international. Genuinely free trade and investment can only be achieved as part of a broader strategy to promote better policies for better markets. This will involve adopting policies to facilitate competition.

- The PECC Competition Policies based on the core principles of comprehensiveness, transparency, accountability and non-discrimination provide a reference point for policy development to strengthen all markets. It is hoped that APEC leaders will endorse non-binding principles along these lines. This will need to be followed by a long-term Ecotech effort to create the expertise and institutional capacity to encourage and enable Asia Pacific economies to adopt policies increasingly in line with such principles.

7 The need for cooperation in financial and macro-economic policies is now widely acknowledged among APEC members as an important additional aspect of APEC activities.

- The integration of Finance Ministers' meetings into the APEC leaders' and other Ministerial meetings schedule will be a valuable step in assigning these issues their proper priority.

- Programs of information exchange and technical cooperation are a special priority in this area.
- The East Asian financial crisis has made it clear that fixing exchange rates to a single major currency is likely to be an unviable strategy for most economies in the region, given the nature of financial and commodity trade interdependence in the region.
- The initiative to establish the Manila Framework Group (MFG) was an important APEC achievement and financial market cooperation and monitoring of macro-economic policies and capital market development is an important task of the MFG for member economies in the future.
- APEC should underline this achievement in response to the East Asian crisis.

8 The membership of APEC is such that there is no interest or advantage in ceding powers over regulation or enforcement to a supra-national authority in the region.

- The objective of APEC should remain the promotion of cooperation through adherence to common principles for guiding the policies of APEC governments and building confidence in mutually beneficial, deeper economic integration.
- Much has already been achieved through this process.
- While it may not be appropriate to enlarge the APEC Secretariat greatly, strengthening the organisational structure of APEC's working groups and task force activities will enhance APEC's potential.
- Active participation by the United States, Japan and China is indispensable to APEC's functioning as an effective international organisation, a fact which underlines the urgency of China's accession to the WTO.
- APEC is of immense economic and political value to all its members in mobilising the political will and energies of its members so that they may fully realise the potential for regional economic cooperation.

NOTE

1   These recommendations were conveyed to the Rt Hon Jenny Shipley, Chair of the Auckland APEC Summit, in a letter from Professor Hugh Patrick on 22 June 1999 to provide timely input to the deliberations of APEC Ministers and Leaders in September that year.

Index

For Product Safety Concerns and Information please contact our EU
representative GPSR@taylorandfrancis.com Taylor & Francis Verlag GmbH,
Kaufingerstraße 24, 80331 München, Germany

Printed and bound by CPI Group (UK) Ltd, Croydon, CR0 4YY

01/05/2025

01858365-0002